EDUCATION IN A COMPETITIVE AND GLOBALIZING WORLD

HIGHER EDUCATION

FINANCIAL CONCERNS AND MINORITY-SERVING INSTITUTIONS

EDUCATION IN A COMPETITIVE AND GLOBALIZING WORLD

Additional books and e-books in this series can be found
on Nova's website under the Series tab.

EDUCATION IN A COMPETITIVE AND GLOBALIZING WORLD

HIGHER EDUCATION

FINANCIAL CONCERNS AND MINORITY-SERVING INSTITUTIONS

LILIAN WIECK
EDITOR

Copyright © 2019 by Nova Science Publishers, Inc.

All rights reserved. No part of this book may be reproduced, stored in a retrieval system or transmitted in any form or by any means: electronic, electrostatic, magnetic, tape, mechanical photocopying, recording or otherwise without the written permission of the Publisher.

We have partnered with Copyright Clearance Center to make it easy for you to obtain permissions to reuse content from this publication. Simply navigate to this publication's page on Nova's website and locate the "Get Permission" button below the title description. This button is linked directly to the title's permission page on copyright.com. Alternatively, you can visit copyright.com and search by title, ISBN, or ISSN.

For further questions about using the service on copyright.com, please contact:
Copyright Clearance Center
Phone: +1-(978) 750-8400   Fax: +1-(978) 750-4470   E-mail: info@copyright.com.

NOTICE TO THE READER

The Publisher has taken reasonable care in the preparation of this book, but makes no expressed or implied warranty of any kind and assumes no responsibility for any errors or omissions. No liability is assumed for incidental or consequential damages in connection with or arising out of information contained in this book. The Publisher shall not be liable for any special, consequential, or exemplary damages resulting, in whole or in part, from the readers' use of, or reliance upon, this material. Any parts of this book based on government reports are so indicated and copyright is claimed for those parts to the extent applicable to compilations of such works.

Independent verification should be sought for any data, advice or recommendations contained in this book. In addition, no responsibility is assumed by the Publisher for any injury and/or damage to persons or property arising from any methods, products, instructions, ideas or otherwise contained in this publication.

This publication is designed to provide accurate and authoritative information with regard to the subject matter covered herein. It is sold with the clear understanding that the Publisher is not engaged in rendering legal or any other professional services. If legal or any other expert assistance is required, the services of a competent person should be sought. FROM A DECLARATION OF PARTICIPANTS JOINTLY ADOPTED BY A COMMITTEE OF THE AMERICAN BAR ASSOCIATION AND A COMMITTEE OF PUBLISHERS.

Additional color graphics may be available in the e-book version of this book.

Library of Congress Cataloging-in-Publication Data

ISBN: 978-1-53616-026-0

Published by Nova Science Publishers, Inc. † New York

CONTENTS

Preface		**vii**
Chapter 1	Higher Education: Opportunities to Strengthen Federal Accountability *Melissa Emrey-Arras*	**1**
Chapter 2	Higher Education: Education Should Address Oversight and Communication Gaps in Its Monitoring of the Financial Condition of Schools[*] *United States Government Accountability Office*	**15**
Chapter 3	Examining Access and Supports for Service Members and Veterans in Higher Education *Committee on Health, Education, Labor, and Pensions*	**47**
Chapter 4	Higher Education: Characteristics of Graduate PLUS Borrowers *United States Government Accountability Office*	**97**
Chapter 5	Strengthening Minority Serving Institutions: Best Practices and Innovations for Student Success *Committee on Health, Education, Labor, and Pensions*	**111**
Chapter 6	Programs for Minority-Serving Institutions Under the Higher Education Act *Alexandra Hegji*	**195**
Chapter 7	Preliminary Observations on Efforts to Foster Entrepreneurship with Historically Black Colleges and Universities *Anna Maria Ortiz*	**251**
Index		**265**
Related Nova Publications		**273**

PREFACE

Chapter 1 examines Education's role in: (1) recognizing accrediting agencies, (2) overseeing the financial condition of schools, and (3) overseeing schools' student loan default rates. Chapter 2 discusses (1) how Education oversees the financial condition of schools; (2) the extent to which Education's oversight has been effective at identifying schools at risk of closure; and (3) the extent to which Education informs schools and the public about its financial oversight. For many service members, getting an education is a critical component of transition to civilian life. Chapter 3 determines ways that the Higher Education Act is helping achieve those goals, and find areas where there are problems, and where we can make improvements. To help students and their families pay for higher education, the Department of Education provides billions of dollars in federal student loans each year through programs authorized under Title IV of the Higher Education Act as discussed in chapter 4.

Chapter 5 discusses the unique challenges facing minority serving institutions and to learn about programs and support to help facilitate student success. Chapter 6 describes the several programs devoted to financially assisting minority-serving institutions (MSIs) under the Higher Education Act. Historically Black Colleges and Universities play an important and unique role in the higher education system and in their local and regional economies. As reported in chapter 7, SBA works with many colleges and universities to provide entrepreneurial training and counseling on campuses.

Chapter 1 - In fiscal year 2018, nearly 13 million students and their families received over $122 billion in federal assistance to help them pursue higher education through programs authorized under Title IV of the Higher Education Act of 1965, as amended. Education administers these programs, and is responsible, along with accreditors and states, for maintaining accountability and protecting the federal investment in student aid for higher education. This testimony summarizes the findings and recommendations from GAO's prior reports, issued between 2014 and 2018, examining Education's role in: (1) recognizing accrediting agencies, (2) overseeing the financial condition of schools, and (3) overseeing schools' student loan default rates. This statement also updates the status of selected recommendations and a matter for congressional consideration.

Chapter 2 - Education oversees the financial condition of about 6,000 postsecondary schools whose students received $125 billion in federal student aid in fiscal year 2016. With the recent closures of several large schools, GAO was asked to review Education's financial oversight of schools. This report examines (1) how Education oversees the financial condition of schools; (2) the extent to which Education's oversight has been effective at identifying schools at risk of closure; and (3) the extent to which Education informs schools and the public about its financial oversight. GAO analyzed the most recent Education data on school closures and finances since school year 2010-11 (through 2015-16 for closures, 2014-15 for composite scores, and 2013-14 for letters of credit); examined federal laws, regulations, and guidance; reviewed accounting standards and industry practices; and interviewed Education officials, experts in school finance, and administrators at 10 schools in a nongeneralizable sample selected for variation in financial condition, enrollment, and ownership.

Chapter 3 - Determines ways that the Higher Education Act is helping achieve those goals, and find areas where there are problems, and where we can make improvements.

Chapter 4 - This is an edited, reformatted and augmented version of United States Government Accountability Office; Briefing to Congressional Requesters, Publication No. GAO-18-392R, dated March 20, 2018.

Chapter 5 - This is an edited, reformatted and augmented version of Hearing of the Committee on Health, Education, Labor, And Pensions United States Senate, One Hundred Thirteenth Congress, Second Session, Publication No. S. HRG. 113–835, dated May 13, 2014.

Chapter 6 - Minority-serving institutions (MSIs) are institutions of higher education that serve high concentrations of minority students who, historically, have been underrepresented in higher education. Many MSIs have faced challenges in securing adequate financial support, thus affecting their ability to develop and enhance their academic offerings and ultimately serve their students. Federal higher education policy recognizes the importance of such institutions and targets financial resources to them. Funding for MSIs is channeled through numerous federal agencies, and several of these funding sources are available to MSIs through grant programs authorized under the Higher Education Act of 1965, as amended (HEA; P.L. 89-329). Over the years, HEA programs that support MSIs have expanded and now include programs for institutions serving a wide variety of student populations. In FY2016, MSI programs under the HEA were appropriated approximately $817 million, which helped fund more than 929 grants to institutions. Currently, the HEA authorizes several programs that benefit MSIs:

- Title III-A authorizes the Strengthening Institutions Program, which provides grants to institutions with financial limitations and a high percentage of needy students. Title III-A also authorizes separate similar programs for American Indian tribally controlled colleges and universities; Alaska Native and Native Hawaiian-serving institutions; predominantly Black institutions (PBIs); Native American-serving, nontribal institutions; and Asian American and Native American Pacific Islander-serving institutions. Grants awarded under these programs assist eligible institutions in strengthening their academic, administrative, and fiscal capabilities. These programs are typically funded through annual discretionary appropriations, but additional annual mandatory appropriations are provided through FY2019 under Title III-F.

- Title III-B authorizes the Strengthening Historically Black Colleges and Universities (HBCUs) program and the Historically Black Graduate Institutions program, both of which award grants to eligible institutions to assist them in strengthening their academic, administrative, and fiscal capabilities. These programs are typically funded through annual discretionary appropriations; however, additional annual mandatory appropriations are provided for HBCUs through FY2019.
- Title III-C authorizes the Endowment Challenge Grant program, which has not been funded since FY1995.
- Title III-D authorizes the HBCU Capital Financing Program, which assists HBCUs in obtaining low-cost capital financing for campus maintenance and construction projects and is generally funded through annual discretionary appropriations.
- Title III-E authorizes the Minority Science and Engineering Improvement Program, which provides grants to MSIs and other entities to effect long-term improvements in science and engineering education and is funded through annual discretionary appropriations.
- Title III-F provides additional annual mandatory appropriations through FY2019 for many of the Title III-A and Title III-B MSI programs. It also provides mandatory appropriations through FY2019 for the Hispanic-serving institutions (HSIs) Science, Technology, Engineering, and Mathematics (STEM) Articulation Program, which provides grants to HSIs to increase the number of Hispanic students in STEM fields and to develop model transfer and articulation agreements.
- Title V authorizes the HSI program and the Promoting Postbaccalaureate Opportunities for Hispanic Americans (PPOHA), both of which award grants to eligible institutions to assist them in strengthening their academic, administrative, and fiscal capabilities. Typically, both programs are funded through annual discretionary appropriations, but additional annual mandatory appropriations were provided for the PPOHA program from FY2009 through FY2014.

- Title VII-A-4 authorizes Masters Degree Programs at HBCUs and PBIs, which provide grants to select HBCUs and PBIs to improve graduate educational opportunities. Typically, both programs are funded through annual discretionary appropriations, but additional annual mandatory appropriations were provided for both programs from FY2009 through FY2014.

Chapter 7 - Historically Black Colleges and Universities play an important and unique role in the higher education system and in their local and regional economies. SBA works with many colleges and universities to provide entrepreneurial training and counseling on campuses. SBA is also part of a long-standing White House Initiative to expand the capacity of HBCUs, including their ability to participate in federal programs. However, little is known about the extent to which SBA has worked with the 101 HBCUs to foster entrepreneurship among students and others. This statement is based on (1) GAO's March 2019 report (GAO-19-328R) on SBA's plans and programs for working with HBCUs and (2) preliminary observations from GAO's ongoing review of any HBCU-specific information SBA collects and reports and collaboration of selected HBCUs and SBA. GAO reviewed recent executive orders related to enhancing HBCU capacities; agency documents, including SBA's 2018 agency plan for supporting HBCUs; and statutes and regulations for key programs and activities. GAO also interviewed SBA headquarters and selected district officials based on criteria including (1) the number of HBCUs in the state, and (2) agreements, if any, between HBCUs and SBA. GAO also interviewed six HBCUs based on their relationship with SBA.

In: Higher Education
Editor: Lilian Wieck

ISBN: 978-1-53616-026-0
© 2019 Nova Science Publishers, Inc.

Chapter 1

HIGHER EDUCATION: OPPORTUNITIES TO STRENGTHEN FEDERAL ACCOUNTABILITY[*]

Melissa Emrey-Arras

WHY GAO DID THIS STUDY

In fiscal year 2018, nearly 13 million students and their families received over $122 billion in federal assistance to help them pursue higher education through programs authorized under Title IV of the Higher Education Act of 1965, as amended. Education administers these programs, and is responsible, along with accreditors and states, for maintaining accountability and protecting the federal investment in student aid for higher education.

This testimony summarizes the findings and recommendations from GAO's prior reports, issued between 2014 and 2018, examining Education's role in: (1) recognizing accrediting agencies, (2) overseeing the financial condition of schools, and (3) overseeing schools' student loan default rates. This statement also updates the status of selected recommendations and a matter for congressional consideration.

WHAT GAO FOUND

GAO has identified opportunities to strengthen federal higher education accountability in three areas: educational quality, financial stability, and federal student loan defaults.

---

[*] This is an edited, reformatted and augmented accessible version of the United States Government Accountability Office Testimony Before the Subcommittee on Higher Education and Workforce Investment, Committee on Education and Labor, House of Representatives, Publication No. GAO-19-484T, dated April 3, 2019.

Educational Quality

Accreditors—independent agencies responsible for ensuring that schools provide a quality education—must be recognized by the Department of Education (Education) as reliable authorities on educational quality. The accreditors can issue sanctions, including terminations and probations, to schools that do not meet accreditor standards. However, GAO previously found that schools with weaker student outcomes were, on average, no more likely to be sanctioned by accreditors than schools with stronger student outcomes, and Education does not make consistent use of sanction data that could help it identify insufficient accreditor oversight. In 2014, GAO recommended that Education use accreditor data in its recognition review process to determine whether accreditors are consistently applying and enforcing their standards to ensure schools provide a quality education. Education agreed with the recommendation, but has yet to use this data in this manner.

Financial Stability

Education uses a financial composite score to measure the financial health of schools participating in federal student aid programs, and increases its oversight of schools when it identifies concerns to protect against the risk of school closures. School closures, although rare, can result in hundreds of millions of dollars in unrepaid federal student loans and displacement of thousands of students. However, the composite score has been an imprecise risk measure, predicting only half of closures from school years 2010-11 through 2015-16. This is due in part to the fact that the composite score does not reflect changes in accounting practices and standards, relies on outdated financial measures, and is vulnerable to manipulation. Despite these limitations, Education has not updated the composite score since it was first established more than 20 years ago. In 2017, GAO recommended that Education update its financial composite score. Education has proposed some revisions, but changes have not yet been implemented to protect students and taxpayers against financial risks.

Student Loan Defaults

According to federal law, schools may lose their ability to participate in federal student aid programs if a significant percentage of their borrowers default on their student loans within the first 3 years of repayment. However, GAO previously found that some schools managed these default rates by hiring consultants that encouraged borrowers with past-due payments to put their loans in forbearance, an option that allows borrowers to temporarily postpone payments and bring past due loans current. Although Education officials and student loan experts said forbearance is intended to be a short-term option, GAO's analysis of Education data found that 20 percent of borrowers who began repaying their loans in 2013 had loans in forbearance for 18 months or more. These borrowers defaulted more often in the fourth year of repayment, when schools are not accountable for defaults, suggesting long term forbearance may have delayed— not prevented—default. In 2018, GAO suggested that Congress consider statutory changes to strengthen schools' accountability for student loan defaults. Legislation has not yet been enacted.

Chairwoman Davis, Ranking Member Smucker, and Members of the Subcommittee:

I am pleased to be here today to discuss the federal government's role in ensuring accountability in higher education. In fiscal year 2018, nearly 13 million students and their families received over $122 billion in federal assistance to help them pursue higher education through programs authorized under Title IV of the Higher Education Act of 1965, as amended (Higher Education Act).[1] The Department of Education (Education) administers these programs, and is responsible with the rest of the "triad"—school accreditors and states—for maintaining accountability and protecting the federal investment in higher education. Among Education's responsibilities, which are specified in the Higher Education Act and related regulations, are recognizing accreditors determined to be reliable authorities on educational quality, determining which schools are financially responsible and can participate in federal student aid programs, and ensuring that participating schools comply with related laws, regulations, and policies. However, recent news reports about students attending low quality schools, an increasing number of schools closing due in part to financial difficulties, and the substantial amount of student loans in default have raised questions as to whether this existing accountability system is sufficient for protecting students and taxpayers.

Drawing on our prior work on ensuring accountability in the higher education system, my remarks today address Education's role in (1) recognizing accrediting agencies, (2) overseeing the financial condition of schools, and (3) overseeing schools' student loan default rates. My testimony is based on our prior reports on these topics issued between 2014 and 2018 and cited throughout this statement. We used multiple methodologies to develop the findings, conclusions, and recommendations for these reports. A more detailed discussion of the objectives, scope, and methodologies, including our assessment of data reliability, is available in each report.

The work upon which this statement is based was conducted in accordance with generally accepted government auditing standards. Those standards require that we plan and perform the audit to obtain sufficient, appropriate evidence to provide a reasonable basis for our findings and conclusions based on our audit objectives. We believe that the

---

[1] Pub. L. No. 89-329, 79 Stat. 1219, 1232, codified as amended at 20 U.S.C. §§ 1070- 1099d.

evidence obtained provides a reasonable basis for our findings and conclusions based on our audit objectives.

BACKGROUND

Education's Oversight of Accreditation

The primary purpose of accreditation is to help ensure that schools provide a quality education to students. Accrediting agencies, also known as accreditors, are generally nongovernmental, nonprofit entities that work with Education and states as part of the "triad" that oversees postsecondary schools participating in federal student aid programs. The Higher Education Act and Education's regulations require accreditors to meet certain criteria and have certain operating procedures in place to be "recognized" by Education as reliable authorities on assessing academic quality (see fig. 1).[2] Accreditors must have their recognition renewed by Education at least every 5 years.[3] To recognize an accrediting agency, Education officials and the National Advisory Committee on Institutional Quality and Integrity (NACIQI), which advises the Secretary of Education on accreditation issues, review among other things whether the accreditor applies its own standards, policies, and procedures when they accredit schools.[4]

While Education is required to determine whether accrediting agencies have standards for schools in certain areas, such as student achievement and curricula, before recognizing them, the accrediting agencies are responsible for evaluating member schools to determine if they meet the accreditors' standards. The specific standards that accreditors develop in these areas can differ, and accreditors may also establish additional standards in areas not required by law.[5] When schools do not meet accreditor standards, accrediting agencies may impose sanctions, such as placing a school on probation or terminating the school's accreditation.

---

[2] 20 U.S.C. § 1099b(a), (c); 34 C.F.R. pt. 602. Education is required to publish a list of accrediting agencies that the Secretary recognizes as reliable authorities on the quality of education or training provided by the schools they accredit. 20 U.S.C. § 1001(c).

[3] See 20 U.S.C. § 1099b(d).

[4] NACIQI advises the Secretary of Education on matters related to postsecondary accreditation and the eligibility and certification process for postsecondary schools to participate in federal student aid programs. NACIQI is comprised of 18 members. The Secretary of Education appoints six members, and the leaders of both the House of Representatives and the Senate each appoint six members. NACIQI members are appointed on the basis of, among other things, their technical qualifications, professional standing, and demonstrated knowledge in the fields of accreditation and administration in higher education. 20 U.S.C. § 1011c.

[5] 20 U.S.C. § 1099b(g).

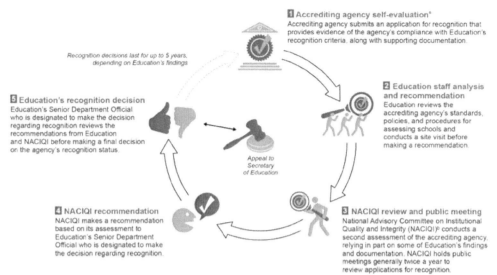

Source: GAO analysis of information from the Department of Education and relevant federal law and regulations
[a] Recognition Process: 34 C.F.R. Part 602, Subpart C.
[b] NACIQI advises the Secretary of Education on matters related to postsecondary accreditation and the eligibility and certification process for postsecondary schools to participate in federal student aid programs. The House of Representatives, the Senate, and Education each appoint six of NACIQI's 18 members. NACIQI members are appointed on the basis of, among other things, their technical qualifications, professional standing, and demonstrated knowledge in the fields of accreditation and administration in higher education. 20 U.S.C. § 1011c

Figure 1. Education's Process for Recognizing Higher Education Accrediting Agencies.

Education's Oversight of College Finances

Education conducts annual reviews of the financial condition of all schools participating in federal student aid programs to determine if they are financially responsible, based on criteria and processes established in federal law and regulations.[6] The specific financial responsibility standards that apply to each school depend on the school's ownership type, and the bulk of Education's financial oversight efforts focus on private nonprofit and for-profit schools.[7]

One key financial responsibility standard that Education uses to assess nonprofit and for-profit schools is a financial composite score that is calculated for each school based on items drawn from the school's audited financial statements. The composite score—a metric

---

[6] See 20 U.S.C. § 1099c(c); 34 C.F.R. §§ 668.15, 668.171 – 668.175, and apps. A-B.
[7] We previously reported that public schools are not required to meet some of the financial responsibility standards that apply to nonprofit and for-profit schools if they demonstrate that their liabilities are backed by the full faith and credit of a state or other government entity, but that public schools must still submit financial statements to Education and meet other standards.

for evaluating a school's financial condition—uses a formula based on three financial ratios.[8] A passing score is 1.5 to 3.0; a "zone" score is from 1.0 to 1.4, and a failing score is from -1.0 to 0.9. (See fig. 2)

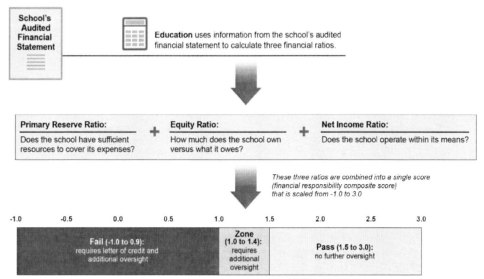

Source: GAO analysis of Department of Education information.|GAO-19-484T.

Notes: Education uses slightly different formulas when calculating these ratios for nonprofit and for-profit schools. See 34 C.F.R. § 668.172 and appendices A - B. Education does not typically calculate a composite score for public schools.

Figure 2. Summary of Education's Annual Calculation of a Financial Responsibility Composite Score for Schools Participating in Federal Student Aid Programs.

Schools that receive a zone or failing composite score, or do not meet one or more of the other financial responsibility standards, may continue to participate in federal student aid programs if they agree to additional oversight. Education may place these schools under heightened cash monitoring (increasing schools' reporting requirements and postponing the timing for receiving federal student aid payments), or require schools to post a letter of credit (a financial commitment from a bank to protect Education against potential liabilities should the school close), or a combination of the two.

Education's Oversight of School Default Rates

Education may rescind a school's ability to participate in federal student aid programs if a significant percentage of its borrowers—generally, 30 percent or more of borrowers for 3 consecutive years or more than 40 percent in 1 year—default on their federal student

---

[8] Education uses slightly different formulas when calculating these ratios for nonprofit and for-profit schools. See 34 C.F.R. § 668.172 and appendices A - B.

loans within the first 3 years of repayment. This calculation is called the cohort default rate. To compute a school's cohort default rate, Education divides the number of student loan borrowers in a cohort—those entering repayment in the same fiscal year—who have defaulted on their loans in the initial 3 years of repayment by the total number of a school's student loan borrowers in that cohort (see fig. 3).[9] The cohort default rate does not hold schools accountable for borrowers who default after the initial 3 years. Borrowers in deferment and forbearance—options that allow borrowers to temporarily postpone monthly payments— are considered to be "in repayment" and current on their loans for the purpose of calculating a school's cohort default rate, even though borrowers in these loan statuses are not expected to make any monthly payments.[10]

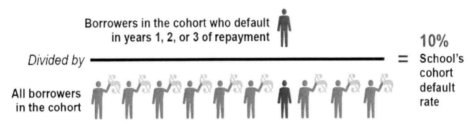

Source: GAO analysis of Department of Education information. | GAO-19-484T.

Note: For the cohort default rate calculation, a cohort includes borrowers who enter repayment in the same fiscal year. For example, the 2015 cohort includes borrowers who enter repayment in fiscal year 2015 (October 1, 2014 to September 30, 2015).

Figure 3. Example of Calculation of School Cohort Default Rate for Federal Student Loans.

EDUCATION DOES NOT USE AVAILABLE DATA TO IDENTIFY WEAKNESSES IN ACCREDITOR OVERSIGHT OF SCHOOLS' ACADEMIC QUALITY

We have previously reported on a number of challenges with the accreditation system's oversight of academic quality. Although Education is prohibited from specifying the specific content of accreditor standards, the agency is responsible for assessing whether accreditors are effectively overseeing schools' academic quality as part of their criteria for

---

[9] Repayment generally refers to the period in which borrowers are responsible for repaying their loan(s). Repayment typically begins after a 6-month grace period after a student graduates, drops below half-time enrollment, or leaves school. Cohort default rates are based on the number of borrowers who enter repayment in a given fiscal year; a borrower with multiple loans entering repayment in the same fiscal year from the same school will be included in the formula only once.

[10] Under deferment, the interest generally does not accrue on subsidized loans, but it continues to accrue on unsubsidized loans. Eligible borrowers can also postpone or reduce loan payments through either a general or mandatory forbearance; however, interest on the loan continues to accrue in each type. Most borrowers choose general forbearance, which, unlike most types of mandatory forbearance and deferment, can be issued by their loan servicer over the phone with no supporting documentation.

recognizing accreditors. Our 2014 analysis found that schools with weaker student outcomes were, on average, no more likely to be sanctioned by accreditors than schools with stronger student outcomes, and that the proportion of their member schools that accreditors sanctioned varied.[11] For example, our analysis of Education's sanction data from October 2009 through March 2014 found that two accreditors sanctioned less than 2 percent of their member schools during this time frame, compared to 41 percent sanctioned by another accreditor. Our 2017 report also discussed challenges with the accreditation system's oversight of academic quality.[12] For example, some experts and literature stated that accreditors may be hesitant to terminate schools' accreditation when they identify issues because such action would adversely affect schools' eligibility for federal student aid programs.

Despite inconsistencies in accreditors' use of sanctions, our 2014 report found that Education did not systematically examine data on accreditor sanctions that could have helped it identify insufficient accreditor oversight and thereby reduce potential risk to students and federal funds. Accreditors provide Education with records of terminations and probations.[13] However, Education officials told us that they had not used this sanction information for oversight of accreditors because Education's regulations did not have specific criteria that require them to do so. While Education is not required to use sanction data or analyze accreditor sanctions as part of the accreditor recognition process, we found that it could be useful for Education to consider these data when evaluating whether accreditors meet prescribed criteria, such as whether they consistently apply and enforce standards. Federal internal control standards call for federal agencies to track data to help them make decisions, as well as conduct ongoing, consistent monitoring to identify weaknesses.[14] Since accreditors are gatekeepers for tens of billions of dollars in federal student aid from Education, as well as the key oversight bodies for ensuring academic quality at schools, we found that failure on the part of Education to spot weaknesses in accreditors' processes could result in poor quality schools gaining access to federal funds.

To strengthen Education's oversight of accreditors, we recommended in 2014 that Education draw upon accreditor data to determine whether accreditors are consistently applying and enforcing their standards to ensure that the education offered by schools is of sufficient quality.[15] For example, Education could systematically use available information related to the frequency of accreditor sanctions or could do additional analyses, such as comparing accreditor sanction data with Education's information on student outcomes, to inform its recognition reviews. Education agreed with this recommendation and initially

---

[11] GAO, *Higher Education: Education Should Strengthen Oversight of Schools and Accreditors*, GAO-15-59 (Washington, D.C.: Dec. 22, 2014).

[12] GAO, *Higher Education: Expert Views of U.S. Accreditation*, GAO-18-5 (Washington, D.C.: Dec. 22, 2017).

[13] Accreditors are required to notify Education of all terminations and probations that they issue. 20 U.S.C. § 1099b(a)(7).

[14] GAO, *Standards for Internal Control in the Federal Government*, GAO-14-704G (Washington, D.C.: Sep. 10, 2014).

[15] GAO-15-59.

started to track the number of accreditor sanctions issued by each accrediting agency. However, Education has since questioned the usefulness of this information and has not yet used this sanction data to inform its discussions of accreditor recognition and oversight. We continue to believe that implementing the recommendation could help inform Education's reviews of accreditors and ultimately reduce potential risk to students and federal funds. For example, analyses of accreditor sanction data could help reveal patterns in individual accreditor behavior and the extent to which they are consistently enforcing standards. This recommendation remains open and we will continue to monitor Education's efforts in this area.

LIMITATIONS IN EDUCATION'S FINANCIAL OVERSIGHT METRIC HINDER ITS ABILITY TO IDENTIFY AT-RISK SCHOOLS

Holding schools accountable for their financial condition can help protect taxpayers and students against the risk of school closure, but the limitations of Education's financial composite score hamper its effectiveness at identifying at-risk schools. Although a relatively small number of schools close each year, these closures can affect tens of thousands of students and result in hundreds of millions of dollars in financial losses for the federal government and taxpayers from unrepaid student loans. However, we reported in 2017 that Education's composite score has been an imprecise predictor of school closures.[16] Half the colleges that closed in school years 2010-11 through 2015-16 received passing financial composite scores on their last assessment before they closed.[17] For example, 58 of the 96 schools that closed in school year 2015-16 had recently received passing scores. Closures can be difficult to predict in part because each school faces its own unique challenges, both financial and nonfinancial, that can eventually push it into financial trouble. Education's composite score is not designed to account for nonfinancial risks; however, it is a primary means of securing financial protections in the form of a letter of credit from schools at risk of closure.

The composite score's inconsistent performance in identifying at-risk schools is due in part to limitations of the underlying formula and the fact that it has remained unchanged for more than 20 years. The composite score is based on common financial ratios that Education selected in 1997 after consulting with an accounting firm, school officials, and other experts. However, the composite score formula has not been updated since then and several experts and school officials we interviewed identified three key weaknesses:

---

[16] GAO, *Higher Education: Education Should Address Oversight and Communication Gaps in Its Monitoring of the Financial Condition of Schools*, GAO-17-555 (Washington D.C.: Aug. 21, 2017).

[17] In addition, some schools with failing composite scores may not be at immediate risk of closure. For example, almost 80 percent of the schools that failed the composite score in school year 2010-11 were still operating more than five years later (as of June 2016).

- *Accounting changes*: The composite score has not kept pace with changes since 1997 in accounting practices and standards, creating ambiguity and making it more difficult to apply the formula in a uniform manner. Accounting practices and standards are periodically updated, for example, to improve the comparability and usefulness of financial reporting. When these updates diverge from the components and definitions in Education's composite score, certain components of the composite score are no longer directly linked to items on schools' audited financial statements. These accounting changes can also cause large shifts in schools' composite scores. For example, administrators at one school we talked to said changes to state laws have affected how some schools categorize their endowment holdings in financial audits, and that this had the effect of reducing the school's composite score from passing to not passing. However, Education has not updated the composite score formula to ensure the score is a reliable measure of financial health.
- *Outdated financial measures*: The composite score does not incorporate new financial metrics that would provide a broader indication of schools' financial health. For more than 20 years, the composite score formula has remained unchanged as the field of financial analysis has continued to evolve with new measures becoming important as economic conditions change. For example, liquidity (i.e., access to cash) has become an important financial measure since the 2007-09 economic downturn, when some schools had trouble meeting payroll and fulfilling contractual obligations. More sophisticated methodologies used by credit rating agencies have sometimes resulted in assessments of a school's financial condition that are strikingly different from the school's composite score. For example, in 2016, two credit rating agencies assigned non-investment grade (i.e., junk bond) ratings to 30 schools that received passing composite scores from Education.
- *Vulnerability to manipulation*: We previously reported that the composite score can be manipulated by some schools that take on long-term debt (e.g., loans with terms in excess of 12 months) because these debts can increase a school's composite score and help it avoid requirements to post a letter of credit. Long-term debt usually represents a long-term investment in a school's campus and buildings, and the composite score formula treats this type of debt in a positive manner.[18] An accountant for multiple schools told us that some schools have taken advantage of this provision and taken on a million dollars in debt in order to obtain a passing composite score. Corinthian Colleges, which closed in 2015, also exploited this

---

[18] Education included long-term debt in the formula for the primary reserve ratio (which measures whether a school has sufficient resources to cover its expenses) to address concerns that schools would be discouraged from making investments in capital improvements if these funds were not counted in the ratio, according to Education guidance. See Dear Colleague Letter GEN-01-02.

vulnerability to boost its composite score and avoid having to post a letter of credit that could have been used by Education to cover some of the hundreds of millions in student loan discharges resulting from the school's closure, according to company documents and Education documents and officials.

These three weaknesses with the financial composite score hamper Education's ability to effectively fulfill its statutory responsibility to determine whether schools participating in federal student aid programs are financially responsible. Identifying and responding to risks is a key component of federal internal control standards, but Education's financial composite score formula has remained unchanged for over 20 years despite significant changes in the financial landscape of higher education.[19] To address these limitations, we recommended in our 2017 report that Education update the composite score formula to better measure schools' financial conditions and capture financial risks. Education generally disagreed with this recommendation and stated that the issues identified in our report did not necessarily mean that the composite score was an unreliable measure of schools' financial strength. Since our report was issued, new regulations have gone into effect specifying that certain financially risky events, such as those related to litigation and certain accreditor actions, will generally trigger a recalculation of a school's composite score.[20] In addition, Education has also published proposed regulations that would update some of the definitions of terms used to calculate a school's composite score to conform with changes in accounting standards and also make an adjustment to how the formula treats long-term debt, which according to Education would be intended to make the formula less susceptible to manipulation.[21] However, Education has not finalized these regulations and has not released a timeline for when it plans to do so, nor has it indicated that it has any broader plans to update the composite score, as we recommended. Since the existing composite score calculation remains unchanged, we are leaving this recommendation open and will continue to monitor Education's efforts in this area.

EDUCATION'S ABILITY TO HOLD SCHOOLS ACCOUNTABLE FOR LOAN DEFAULT IS LIMITED BY SCHOOLS' ABILITY TO DISTORT THEIR COHORT DEFAULT RATES

The cohort default rate, which is specified in federal law,[22] is a key measure for holding schools accountable for borrower outcomes and for protecting borrowers and the federal

---

[19] GAO-14-704G.

[20] This recalculation is generally based on the existing composite score formula. See 34 C.F.R. § 668.171.

[21] Student Assistance General Provisions, Federal Perkins Loan Program, Federal Family Education Loan Program, and William D. Ford Federal Direct Loan Program, 83 Fed. Reg. 37,242 (July 31, 2018).

[22] See 20 U.S.C. § 1085(m)(1)(A).

government from the costs associated with default. However, in 2018 we reported that this rate has limitations as an accountability tool.[23] Some schools managed their 3-year cohort default rate by hiring consultants that encouraged borrowers with past-due payments to put their loans in forbearance, an option that allows borrowers to temporarily postpone payments and bring past-due loans current. At five of the nine default management consultants we selected (that served about 800 schools), we identified examples when forbearance was encouraged over other potentially more beneficial options for helping borrowers avoid default, such as repayment plans that base monthly payment amounts on income. Four of these consultants also provided inaccurate or incomplete information to borrowers about their repayment options in some instances.

Although Education officials and student loan experts said that forbearance is intended to be a short-term option, our analysis of Education data found that 20 percent of borrowers who began repaying their loans in 2013 had loans in forbearance for 18 months or more during the 3-year cohort default rate period. Spending this much time in forbearance reduces the potential for borrowers to default within the 3- year period, thus helping improve a school's cohort default rate. However, postponing loan payments through forbearance can increase borrowers' loan costs in the long term. For example, a typical borrower with $30,000 in loans who spends the first 3 years of repayment in forbearance would pay an additional $6,742 in interest, a 17 percent increase, over the life of the loan. In addition, borrowers in forbearance for 18 months or longer defaulted more often in the fourth year of repayment, when schools are not accountable for defaults, than they did during the 3-year period. While forbearance can help borrowers avoid default in the short term, this finding suggests that forbearance may have delayed—not prevented— default, potentially resulting in increased costs to the federal government. Reducing the number of borrowers in long-term forbearance and directing them toward other options for avoiding default, such as repayment plans that base monthly payment amounts on income, could help reduce the number of borrowers that later default and may eventually save the federal government money. Specifically, for William D. Ford Federal Direct Loans issued in fiscal year 2018, Education estimates that it will not recover over 20 percent of defaulted loans. These unrecovered defaulted loan amounts total an estimated $4 billion, according to our analysis of Education's budget data.[24]

Schools are seldom held accountable for their students' defaults, in part because of the high rate of borrowers in long-term forbearance. To examine the impact of long-term forbearance on schools' 3-year default rates, we recalculated schools' cohort default rates by excluding borrowers who were in forbearance for 18 months or more and who did not

---

[23] GAO, *Federal Student Loans: Actions Needed to Improve Oversight of Schools' Default Rates*, GAO-18-163 (Washington D.C.: April 26, 2018).

[24] The estimate accounts for collection costs and uses a net present value basis to account for the effect of time on the dollar value of missed payments due to default and subsequent default collections. The total estimate of defaulted dollars not recovered does not include Direct PLUS or Consolidation loans, which are other types of federal student loans offered by Education.

default during the 3-year period. We found that over 260 additional schools—receiving a combined \$2.7 billion in Direct Loans and Pell Grants in academic year 2016-2017—would potentially have had a default rate high enough to put them at risk of losing access to federal student aid programs.[25]

The reduced effectiveness of cohort default rates as a tool for holding schools accountable creates risks to the federal government and taxpayers, who are responsible for the costs associated with high rates of default. Since the way the cohort default rate is calculated is specified in federal law, any changes to its calculation would require legislation to be enacted amending the law. Our 2018 report suggested that Congress consider strengthening schools' accountability for student loan defaults, for example, by revising the cohort default rate calculation or using other accountability measures to complement or replace the cohort default rate. In the 115th Congress, proposals were introduced to revise, supplement, or replace the cohort default rate, though none of the legislation was enacted. This matter for congressional consideration remains open. We continue to believe that strengthening the accountability measure for loan defaults could further protect borrowers and the billions of dollars of federal student aid the government distributes each year.

In conclusion, the large federal investment in higher education makes it essential that the federal government maintain a robust system of accountability to protect students and taxpayers. My statement has highlighted three actions Education and Congress could take to strengthen the existing accountability tools for educational quality, financial sustainability, and student loan defaults. Students deserve to go to schools that provide a quality education and are financially stable. Taxpayers deserve an accountability system that protects federal student aid funds from going to schools that are financially irresponsible or push borrowers into forbearance for long periods in order to reduce the school's cohort default rate. We believe that fully implementing the two recommendations and matter for congressional consideration discussed in this testimony would improve federal accountability, help students, and potentially lead to financial savings for taxpayers.

Chairwoman Davis, Ranking Member Smucker, and Members of the Subcommittee, this completes my prepared statement. I would be pleased to respond to any questions that you may have at this time.

---

[25] Pell Grants are awarded to undergraduate students with financial need to help finance their postsecondary education.

In: Higher Education
Editor: Lilian Wieck

ISBN: 978-1-53616-026-0
© 2019 Nova Science Publishers, Inc.

Chapter 2

HIGHER EDUCATION: EDUCATION SHOULD ADDRESS OVERSIGHT AND COMMUNICATION GAPS IN ITS MONITORING OF THE FINANCIAL CONDITION OF SCHOOLS[*]

United States Government Accountability Office

ABBREVIATIONS

Corinthian	Corinthian Colleges Inc.
Education	Department of Education
ITTITT	Educational Services Inc.
FASB	Financial Accounting Standards Board
Multi-regional Division	Multi-regional and Foreign Schools Participation Division
SEC	Securities and Exchange Commission

WHY GAO DID THIS STUDY

Education oversees the financial condition of about 6,000 postsecondary schools whose students received $125 billion in federal student aid in fiscal year 2016. With the

---

[*] This is an edited, reformatted and augmented version of United States Government Accountability Office; Report to Congressional Requesters, Publication No. GAO-17-555, dated August 2017.

recent closures of several large schools, GAO was asked to review Education's financial oversight of schools.

This chapter examines (1) how Education oversees the financial condition of schools; (2) the extent to which Education's oversight has been effective at identifying schools at risk of closure; and (3) the extent to which Education informs schools and the public about its financial oversight. GAO analyzed the most recent Education data on school closures and finances since school year 2010-11 (through 2015-16 for closures, 2014-15 for composite scores, and 2013-14 for letters of credit); examined federal laws, regulations, and guidance; reviewed accounting standards and industry practices; and interviewed Education officials, experts in school finance, and administrators at 10 schools in a nongeneralizable sample selected for variation in financial condition, enrollment, and ownership.

WHAT GAO RECOMMENDS

GAO recommends that Education (1) update the financial composite score to better measure schools' financial conditions, (2) improve its guidance to schools on how it calculates the composite score, and (3) provide public data on final composite scores for all schools. Education disagreed with the first recommendation, agreed with the second, and will further evaluate the third. GAO continues to believe these recommendations are valid, as discussed in the report.

WHAT GAO FOUND

The Department of Education (Education) reviews the annual audits of postsecondary schools to assess compliance with financial responsibility standards for schools that participate in federal student aid programs and increases its oversight of schools that do not meet these standards. In school year 2014-15, Education reviews found that about 450 of approximately 6,000 schools that participate in federal student aid programs did not receive a passing financial composite score (a measure of schools' financial health). Education may secure financial assurances from schools that do not meet the standards, in the form of a letter of credit, to help cover federal costs if a school closes and students become eligible to have their federal student loans forgiven. Education has also taken steps to expand its oversight of certain large schools and companies that own multiple schools through more frequent monitoring and additional reporting requirements.

School closures are relatively rare, but limitations of Education's composite score hamper its effectiveness at identifying at-risk schools. About 95 schools closed in school year 2015-16, according to Education data. The vast majority of closures in the past 5 years were small schools (less than 500 students), but recent closures of several large schools affected thousands of students and resulted in over half a billion dollars in federal losses from unrepaid student loans. The composite score has been an imprecise risk measure, predicting only half of closures since school year 2010-11, although schools can close for nonfinancial reasons as well. GAO identified three key limitations of the composite score:

- Accounting changes: It does not reflect updates in accounting practices.
- Outdated financial measures: It does not incorporate new financial metrics that would provide a broader indication of schools' financial health, such as liquidity, historical trend analysis, or future projections.
- Vulnerability to manipulation: It allows some schools to take advantage of a feature of the composite score calculation to inflate their scores by taking out loans, thereby avoiding requirements to post letters of credit.

Despite these limitations, Education has not updated the composite score since it was first established 20 years ago. Identifying and responding to risks is a key component of federal internal control standards, and Education's failure to update its key financial measure makes it harder for Education to identify and manage schools at risk of closure.

Education does not fully explain to schools key aspects of its financial oversight nor does it disclose complete results to the public. Effective communication is a key principle of federal internal control standards. However, Education's guidance to schools does not sufficiently detail how it calculates the composite score; administrators GAO interviewed at 7 of 10 selected schools expressed confusion about their scores' calculations. Schools that are unable to accurately estimate their scores may not be able to effectively plan for the costs of obtaining a letter of credit. Further, the most recent composite scores publicly released by Education left out 17 percent of schools, whose students received over $8 billion in federal student aid. As a result, students do not have access to available information on whether their schools are financially sound so they may confidently invest their time and money.

August 21, 2017

The Honorable Rosa DeLauro
Ranking Member
Subcommittee on Labor, Health and Human Services,
Education, and Related Agencies
Committee on Appropriations
House of Representatives

The Honorable Richard Durbin
United States Senate

The Honorable Brian Schatz
United States Senate

Approximately 13 million students and their families in the United States rely on federal student aid programs to help them achieve their higher education goals.[1] The Department of Education (Education) administers these federal student aid programs, which provided $125 billion in assistance to eligible students in fiscal year 2016. However, the recent closures of several large postsecondary schools have interrupted the education of tens of thousands of students, leaving them unsure of how to complete their education and placing the federal government at risk for millions of dollars in unrepaid student loans. To help guard against these events, Education monitors the financial condition of about 6,000 schools that participate in federal student aid programs.[2] Education monitors the financial health of these schools on an annual basis to determine if they are financially responsible and able to fulfill their obligations. When it identifies financial concerns, it can implement additional oversight to protect against potential losses to the federal government that could result if the school were to close, since students affected by a school closure may be eligible to have their federal student loans forgiven. For example, Education reported that the 2015 closure of Corinthian Colleges has already resulted in over $550 million in loan relief, with that amount expected to climb. In light of these issues, you asked us to review Education's financial oversight of schools that participate in federal student aid programs.

This chapter examines (1) how Education oversees the financial condition of schools; (2) the extent to which Education's oversight has been effective at identifying schools at risk of closure; and (3) the extent to which Education informs schools and the public about its oversight of the financial condition of schools.

To address these questions, we conducted our review of Education's financial oversight of schools using the following approaches:

- To determine how Education oversees the financial condition of schools, we analyzed Education's data on schools' financial responsibility composite scores (a measure of schools' financial health) and Education's additional oversight of schools not meeting federal financial responsibility standards for participating in

---

[1] For this report, we define federal student aid programs as financial aid programs authorized under Title IV of the Higher Education Act of 1965, as amended (Higher Education Act) (codified at 20 U.S.C. §§ 1070-1099d).

[2] In order to participate in federal student aid programs, schools must meet the Higher Education Act's definition of an institution of higher education and comply with other requirements, including those related to financial responsibility. In this we report we use the term "school" to refer to a domestic institution of higher education that has participated or is currently participating in federal student aid programs.

federal student aid programs from school years 2010-11 through 2014-15, the most recent year of data available.[3] We also analyzed Education data on schools that were required to provide a letter of credit to the department due to financial concerns for school years 2010-11 through 2013-14, the most recent year of data available. We assessed the reliability of these data by reviewing Education's data systems and documentation, tracing 40 randomly drawn records back to the source documents, and interviewing Education officials, and we determined that the data were sufficiently reliable for our reporting purposes. To examine Education's oversight processes, we reviewed relevant federal laws, regulations, and policy guidance on the financial responsibility standards for schools that participate in federal student aid programs. We also interviewed Education officials in a nongeneralizable selection of three regional offices with responsibility for monitoring schools' finances.[4]

- To assess the effectiveness of Education's oversight, we analyzed 10 years of Education's data on school closures from school year 2006- 07 to 2015-16, with more detailed analysis of closures since school year 2010-2011. We assessed the reliability of these data by reviewing Education's data system and checking the data for completeness against news reports of school closures, and we determined that the data were sufficiently reliable for our reporting purposes. To assess the composite score and identify any potential limitations, we reviewed the composite score formula and compared it to Financial Accounting Standards Board standards, industry practices, and practices identified in previous GAO reports on financial risk assessments.[5] Additionally, we assessed Education's composite score against government standards for internal controls for identifying and responding to risks. We also interviewed experts in higher education finance and accounting, officials from the two largest credit rating agencies, and representatives from four higher education associations.[6] While they provided their perspectives, the views from these experts and representatives are not generalizable.

- To determine the extent to which Education communicates with schools and the public about its financial oversight, we examined Education's guidance to schools and its annual public disclosure of schools' financial composite scores for school year 2014-15. We also interviewed officials at 10 schools about their experiences

---

[3] In this report we use school year to refer to the "award year" as defined in the Higher Education Act; the 12-month period that begins on July 1 of one year and ends on June 30 of the following year.

[4] We selected these regional offices to reflect a range in office caseloads, the types of schools they oversee, and geographic diversity.

[5] The Financial Accounting Standards Board is an independent, private nonprofit organization that establishes financial accounting and reporting standards for public and private companies and nonprofit organizations that follow generally accepted accounting principles.

[6] We selected these four higher education associations because of their expertise and knowledge of school finances and the federal financial responsibility standards for schools participating in federal student aid programs. We also included associations representing both nonprofit and for-profit schools.

with Education's financial oversight and calculation of the financial composite score. We selected this nongeneralizable sample based on a range of criteria, including school financial responsibility composite score, enrollment size, and ownership type (nonprofit and for-profit).[7] While these interviews cannot be generalized to the larger school population, they reflect the types of experiences schools may have with Education's financial oversight. We also interviewed Education officials about their policies and procedures and asked Education officials we interviewed from the regional offices about the guidance they provide to schools. We assessed Education's actions against federal internal control standards for communicating with external parties.

We conducted this performance audit from December 2015 to August 2017 in accordance with generally accepted government auditing standards. Those standards require that we plan and perform the audit to obtain sufficient, appropriate evidence to provide a reasonable basis for our findings and conclusions based on our audit objectives. We believe that the evidence obtained provides a reasonable basis for our findings and conclusions based on our audit objectives.

BACKGROUND

In order to participate in federal student aid programs (which provide federal loans, grants, and other aid to eligible students) authorized under Title IV of the Higher Education Act, schools must demonstrate that they are financially responsible, based on criteria and processes established in federal law and regulations.[8]

---

[7] We also included schools owned by publicly traded companies and private equity firms. We did not interview officials at public schools because Education generally does not calculate a composite score for these schools. Instead, public schools are required to demonstrate that their liabilities are backed by the full faith and credit of a state or other government entity, among other requirements.

[8] See 20 U.S.C. § 1099c(c); 34 C.F.R. §§ 668.15, 668.171 – 668.175, and apps. A-B. In November 2016, Education issued a final rule revising its financial responsibility regulations, among other things. These revisions were scheduled to take effect July 1, 2017. See Student Assistance General Provisions, Federal Perkins Loan Program, Federal Family Education Loan Program, William D. Ford Federal Direct Loan Program, and Teacher Education Assistance for College and Higher Education Grant Program, 81 Fed. Reg. 75,926 (Nov. 1, 2016). In May 2017, a lawsuit was filed challenging the final rule in federal district court. California Ass'n of Private Postsecondary Schools v. DeVos, No. 1:17-cv-00999 (D.D.C. May 24, 2017)). In light of the pending litigation, Education delayed key provisions of the final rule, including those related to the financial responsibility standards for schools participating in federal student aid programs. The agency also stated that it plans to review and revise the final rule through the negotiated rulemaking process. See Student Assistance General Provisions, Federal Perkins Loan Program, Federal Family Education Loan Program, William D. Ford Federal Direct Loan Program, and Teacher Education Assistance for College And Higher Education Grant Program, 82 Fed. Reg. 27,621 (June 16, 2017). Since then, two additional lawsuits have been filed in federal district court, challenging the Secretary's delay of the final rule. See Bauer v. DeVos, No. 1:17-cv-01330 (D.D.C. June 6, 2017) and Massachusetts v. Dep't of Educ., No. 1:17-cv-01331 (D.D.C. July 6, 2017). Unless otherwise clear from context, any citations to Education's regulations pertain to the regulations in effect at the time we did our work. Participating schools

Education's Office of Federal Student Aid conducts annual reviews of schools' financial conditions as part of the department's commitment to ensuring institutional accountability and protecting federal interests.[9] Education assesses schools against the financial responsibility standards and requires schools that do not meet the standards to receive additional oversight.[10] In some cases, Education requires schools to provide financial guarantees to protect against federal financial losses if the school closes and its students become eligible to have their student loans forgiven.[11]

Financial Responsibility Standards

The specific financial responsibility standards that apply to each school depend on the school's ownership type, i.e., public, nonprofit, and for- profit (see Table 1). The bulk of Education's financial oversight efforts focus on private nonprofit and for-profit schools. Public schools are not required to meet some of the financial responsibility standards that apply to nonprofit and for-profit schools if they demonstrate that their liabilities are backed by the full faith and credit of a state or other government entity. However, public schools must still submit financial statements to Education and meet other standards.

Loan Discharges for School Closures

Students who attended a school that closed may be eligible to have the full balance of their outstanding federal student loans discharged if they are unable to complete their program of study due to the closure of the school. A loan discharge relieves the borrower from having to repay his or her loan. These students are also eligible to be reimbursed for any amounts previously paid on those loans. To be eligible, students generally must (1) have been enrolled when the school closed or withdrew no more than 120 days before the school's closing date, and (2) not have completed the program of study at another school (e.g., by transferring credits earned at the closed school to another school).

Source: GAO analysis of Department of Education documents. | GAO-17-555

---

may also be required to comply with other requirements in the Higher Education Act and Education's regulations related to their financial condition, but in this report we focus on the financial responsibility standards.

[9] See Student Assistance General Provisions, 62 Fed. Reg. 62,830 (Nov. 25, 1997).

[10] If Education determines that a school is not financially responsible, it may also fine the school, or limit, suspend, or terminate the school's participation in federal student aid programs.

[11] The Higher Education Act authorizes student loans to be discharged in a number of circumstances, including school closure. See generally 20 U.S.C. § 1087 and 34 C.F.R. § 685.212.

Table 1. Key Financial Responsibility Standards for Schools Participating in Federal Student Aid Programs

Nonprofit and For-Profit Schools	Public Schools
Financial composite score: The school must receive a passing score on Education's composite measure of three financial ratios designed to gauge a school's financial health. **Refund reserve and timeliness:** The school must have sufficient cash reserves to return unearned federal student aid funds to Education as required when a student withdraws from school and make these returns in a timely manner, as applicable. **Meeting all financial obligations:** The school must be meeting all of its financial obligations, including making required refunds to students under its refund policy and repaying any federal student aid debts to Education. **Debt payment status:** The school must be current in paying its debts.	**Full faith and credit:** Public schools are not subject to certain financial responsibility standards if the school demonstrates to Education that its debts and liabilities are backed by the full faith and credit of the state or another government entity.
Nonprofit and For-Profit Schools	**Public Schools**
Past performance and affiliation: A school is not considered financially responsible if the school has violated certain federal student aid program requirements, or if a person who exercises substantial control over the school owes a debt for such a violation. For example, a school is not considered financially responsible if it has been cited during the last 5 years for failing to submit an audit as required. **Auditor opinion of financial statements:** The school is generally not considered financially responsible if the opinion expressed by the auditor in the school's audited financial statements is adverse, qualified, or disclaimed, or the auditor expressed doubt about the continued existence of the school as a going concern (i.e., doubt about a school's ability to continue operating for the next 12 months).	

Source: GAO analysis of selected federal regulations in effect as of June 2017 and the Federal Student Aid Handbook for school year 2016-17. | GAO-17-555

Note: For more information on these financial responsibility standards, see 34 C.F.R. pt. 668, subpart L.

Financial Oversight of Schools by Accreditors

Accreditors also play a role in assessing the financial condition of schools that participate in federal student aid programs. These independent organizations are responsible for applying and enforcing standards that help ensure that the programs offered by schools are of sufficient quality to achieve their stated objectives.[12] Accreditors must have standards related to a school's financial capability.[13] Financial assessments by an accreditor may include regular reviews of schools' annual financial statements and an accreditor may request additional reporting from schools with problematic financial conditions. When a school does not meet its accreditor's standards, the accreditor may

---

[12] Under the Higher Education Act, in order to be eligible to participate in federal financial aid programs, a school must be accredited by a nationally recognized accrediting agency that has been determined by Education to be a reliable authority as to the quality of the education or training offered. 20 U.S.C. §§ 1001(a)(5), 1099b.

[13] See 20 U.S.C. § 1099b(a)(5). Among other things, accreditors' standards are required to assess schools' fiscal capacity as appropriate to the specified scale of operations.

impose sanctions or take other actions. We previously found that accreditors most frequently sanctioned schools for failure to meet standards on financial capability, rather than standards on academic quality or administrative capability.[14]

EDUCATION FOCUSES OVERSIGHT ON SCHOOLS NOT MEETING FINANCIAL RESPONSIBILITY STANDARDS AND HAS INCREASED OVERSIGHT OF CERTAIN TYPES OF SCHOOLS

Education Reviews Schools' Annual Audits and Places Additional Requirements on the Small Percentage of Schools Not Meeting Financial Responsibility Standards for Schools that Participate in Federal Student Aid Programs

To assess a school's compliance with the financial responsibility standards for participating in federal student aid programs, Education reviews the school's annual financial statements and compliance audits.[15] These audits must be prepared for the school by an independent auditor, and in general, for-profit schools have 6 months and nonprofit and public schools have 9 months after the school's fiscal year ends to submit the audits to Education. Either the auditor or a school official transmits the documents to Education's eZ-Audit website and enters specific financial information needed for Education's oversight.[16] Education officials told us that an Education contractor initially screens the financial audits for completeness and flags any audits that indicate a school may not have met the financial responsibility standards required to participate in federal student aid programs. The contractor sends any audits that warrant further review to the appropriate Education division responsible for the school, where Education staff then conduct a full assessment to determine if the school is in compliance with these financial responsibility standards, according to Education officials. For example, an Education analyst assesses whether the school followed requirements to return any federal student aid funds owed to Education in a timely manner.

---

[14] GAO, *Higher Education: Education Should Strengthen Oversight of Schools and Accreditors*, GAO-15-59 (Washington, D.C.: Dec. 22, 2014).

[15] See 34 C.F.R. § 668.23. In general, Education requires audits of for-profit schools to comply with the Education Inspector General's Audit Guide, and audits of nonprofit and public schools to comply with applicable Single Audit Act requirements.

[16] When a company is the sole owner of multiple schools, according to Education guidance, the agency reviews one consolidated financial audit for the parent company, and then calculates a single financial composite score for these schools based on the company's overall financial condition.

A financial composite score is also calculated for each nonprofit and for-profit school based on items drawn from the school's audited financial statements (see Figure 1).[17] The composite score—a metric for evaluating a school's financial condition—uses a formula based on three financial ratios.[18] A passing score is 1.5 to 3.0; a "zone" score is from 1.0 and 1.4, and a failing score is from -1.0 to 0.9.

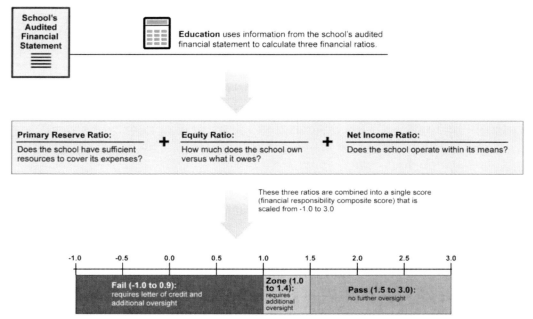

Source: GAO analysis of Department of Education information. | GAO-17-555
Notes: Education uses slightly different formulas when calculating these ratios for nonprofit and for-profit schools. See 34 C.F.R. § 668.172 and appendices A - B. Education does not typically calculate a composite score for public schools.

Figure 1. Summary of Education's Annual Financial Responsibility Composite Score Calculation for Schools Participating in Federal Student Aid Programs.

A small percentage of schools fail to meet Education's financial responsibility standards each year, primarily due to low (i.e., zone or failing) composite scores, according to our analysis of Education data. In school year 2014-15, the most recent year for which data are available, 13 percent of schools receiving composite scores had zone or failing composite scores. These 454 schools collectively enrolled over 550,000 students.[19] In prior

---

[17] Education can also use schools' other financial information entered into the eZ-Audit website or request additional information from schools to calculate composite scores.

[18] Education uses slightly different formulas when calculating these ratios for nonprofit and for-profit schools. See 34 C.F.R. § 668.172 and appendices A - B.

[19] For the purposes of our analyses, we considered a school to be an entity with a unique identification number assigned by Education (known as an OPEID) because Education reports financial responsibility information on an OPEID basis. However, depending on how schools are organized, an OPEID may correspond with one or multiple campuses.

years, only a few dozen schools at most did not meet one or more of the other financial responsibility standards.[20]

The percentage of schools not receiving passing composite scores has been relatively consistent since school year 2010-11, fluctuating by only a few percentage points over the past 5 school years, according to our analysis of Education's composite score data. A higher percentage of for- profit schools received non-passing scores than nonprofit schools. For example, 10 percent of for-profit schools had failing composite scores compared to 5 percent of nonprofit schools in 2014-15. Additionally, 5 percent of for-profit schools and 4 percent of nonprofit schools had zone composite scores (see Figure 2).

Schools that receive a zone or failing composite score, or do not meet one or more of the other financial responsibility standards, may continue to participate in federal student aid programs if they agree to additional oversight.[21] Depending on the specific circumstances (as outlined below), Education may apply one or both of the following measures:

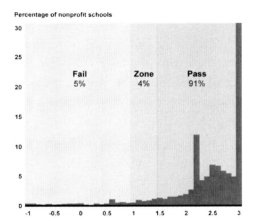 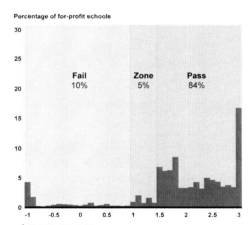

Source: GAO analysis of Department of Education data. | GAO-17-555
Note: Percentages may not add up to 100 due to rounding.

Figure 2. Distribution of Financial Composite Scores by School Type, School Year 2014-15.

---

[20] The most recent available data on noncompliance with the other financial responsibility standards were for school year 2013-14. In that year, for example, 52 schools were cited for having insufficient cash reserves for refunds or failing to make timely refunds to Education, and 3 schools had a "going concern" opinion in their financial statements, in which the auditor expressed substantial doubt about the school's ability to continue operating for the next 12 months.

[21] The type of additional oversight varies depending on the circumstances. Schools that receive a zone composite score but meet the other financial responsibility standards can continue to participate if the school agrees to operate under heightened cash monitoring and comply with other oversight requirements. If a school receives a failing composite score, receives a zone score for more than 3 consecutive years, or fails to meet any of the other financial responsibility standards, it is required to provide a letter of credit worth at least 10 percent of the school's federal student aid funds from its most recent fiscal year in addition to agreeing to heightened cash monitoring and other oversight requirements. Alternatively, schools may submit a letter of credit equal to 50 percent or more of the school's federal student aid funds from the most recent fiscal year, which allows the school to participate without being subject to heightened cash monitoring or the other oversight requirements. See 34 C.F.R. § 668.175.

- Heightened cash monitoring: When a school receives a zone or failing composite score, or fails other financial responsibility standards, Education may place it on heightened cash monitoring. This increases the reporting requirements for the school and postpones its ability to draw down federal student aid payments from Education until after funds are paid to students.[22] Schools can also be placed on heightened cash monitoring for nonfinancial reasons, such as concerns about a school's administrative capability or accreditation status.

  Education placed 456 schools on heightened cash monitoring for not meeting financial responsibility standards at some point during school year 2014-15.[23] This was by far the most common reason schools were placed on heightened cash monitoring, according to our analysis of Education's data. Collectively, these schools enrolled over 1 million students.

- Letter of credit: Education requires a school that has a failing composite score or fails other financial responsibility standards to submit a letter of credit to continue to participate in federal student aid programs. Schools obtain the letter of credit from a bank, which charges them a fee for this service—typically a percentage of the value of the letter of credit. The letter of credit protects Education against potential liabilities for student refunds, loan cancellation costs, and other costs associated with a school closure.[24] A letter of credit must be worth at least 10 percent of the school's federal student aid funds from its most recent fiscal year, although the amount may be more, depending on the circumstances. For example, Education may increase the letter of credit if a school fails more than one of the financial responsibility standards, according to agency officials.

  Education required 269 schools to post letters of credit specifically due to failing composite scores in school year 2013-14 (the most recent year for which letter of credit data were available), according to our analysis of Education data. Another 74 schools were required to post letters of credit for not meeting other financial responsibility standards, such as having an adverse audit opinion or untimely refunds. Nearly half of the letters were for the minimum of 10 percent of the

---

[22] Education has two levels of heightened cash monitoring (HCM), known as HCM1 and HCM2. Schools placed on HCM1 must disburse funds to students before they draw down federal student aid from Education. HCM2 is a higher level of oversight, for which Education requires schools to disburse funds to students and then submit documentation of their eligibility to Education for review before it releases federal student aid funds to the school. This delays a school's ability to access federal student aid for 30 to 60 days after disbursing these funds to students, according to Education officials we spoke with. Education officials explained that schools are not typically placed on HCM2 solely due to financial responsibility concerns; instead, HCM2 is used for more serious compliance issues, such as fraud. The officials said that these compliance issues are typically found by an Inspector General audit or an Education program review, which evaluates a school's compliance with federal student aid program requirements.

[23] In school year 2014-15, 427 were placed on HCM1 (132 nonprofit and 295 for-profit schools), 25 schools were on HCM2 (6 nonprofit and 19 for-profit schools), and 4 for-profit schools were moved from HCM1 to HCM2 during the year.

[24] In the case of a school closure, Education can cash the letter of credit to cover any outstanding debts owed by the school.

school's prior year federal student aid funding. These letters of credit ranged from about \$5,000 to over \$92 million in school year 2013-14.

Education Has Taken Steps to Increase Oversight of Certain Types of Schools, Including Those Owned by Publicly Traded Companies and Private Equity Firms

Education has taken steps to improve its oversight of large schools with campuses in multiple locations, including schools owned by publicly traded companies and private equity firms. Education formed the Multi- regional and Foreign Schools Participation Division (Multi-regional Division) in 2014 to centralize its monitoring of large school groups with campuses in more than one region.[25] This division currently monitors 47 companies that collectively own 330 schools with thousands of campuses including major publicly traded companies that operate schools, private equity firms, and privately held companies. Together these schools enrolled 1.7 million students who received about 26 percent of all federal student aid in school year 2014-15 (over \$15 billion), according to our analysis of Education's federal student aid data.

The Multi-regional Division provides centralized and increased oversight of these large school groups. Education had previously divided oversight responsibility among its seven regional offices based on the location of each school, regardless of school size and type of ownership. Since large school groups generally operate schools in multiple regions, Education officials we spoke with said creating the Multi-regional Division provided a more holistic review of a parent company's financial condition, and created one central contact point at the department. An Education financial analyst experienced in assessing large schools conducts a full review of each school's financial audits and independently assesses the school's compliance with the financial responsibility standards for schools participating in federal student aid programs, according to Education officials.[26] Additionally, in response to the abrupt closure in 2015 of Corinthian Colleges, a large for-profit school with over 100 campuses across the country at its peak, Education officials said the Multi-regional Division has adopted new tools that provide a more complete picture of the financial condition of these companies, including:

- Regular monitoring of financial information: The Multi-regional Division uses additional information beyond the annual financial audits to track the financial condition of schools. For example, this division actively monitors Securities and

---

[25] A school group is a group of schools with a common owner.
[26] In contrast, an Education financial analyst in the other school participation divisions generally only reviews the financial audits of other schools when compliance issues are identified during the initial audit screening by an Education contractor.

Exchange Commission (SEC) disclosures from the publicly traded companies that own schools, such as quarterly financial reports and notices of significant financial developments. This division also subscribes to an online service that provides corporate profiles and access to additional financial information and ratios.

- Additional reporting requirements: The Multi-regional Division requests additional information from its schools with zone or failing composite scores. For example, these schools are required to submit biweekly cash flow statements, monthly student enrollment numbers, and graduation projections.

Publicly Traded Companies and Private Equity Firms

A publicly traded company is a company whose stock is available for purchase by the general public and is traded on public markets, such as the New York Stock Exchange. Publicly traded companies are required to regularly disclose certain business and financial information to the public.

Private equity firms manage investments generally available only to institutions and other large investors. Private equity firms acquire ownership stakes in companies and seek to profit by improving operating results or through financial restructuring, and then selling companies to another firm or through a public stock offering.

Source: GAO analysis of Securities and Exchange Commission documents and a Congressional Research Service report. | GAO-17-555

The Multi-regional Division has also begun a new effort to expand its monitoring of schools owned by private equity firms, which have become increasingly involved in higher education. In 2015, 10 of the 50 largest for-profit schools, whose students received nearly $1.3 billion in federal student aid that year, were owned by private equity firms.[27] Education officials and other experts we spoke with said these types of schools can pose several oversight challenges, in part because the ownership structure can be complex (e.g., subsidiaries and parent companies) and split among multiple owners. As a result, while a private equity firm may not be the sole owner, it may exercise significant management control over a school. Another risk is that private equity firms are not subject to regular SEC reporting requirements, unlike publicly traded companies that own schools, limiting the financial information available to Education.

To better understand the oversight challenges posed by these types of schools, Education has recently started to identify schools that are fully or partially owned by the same private equity firms to determine if they should be treated as a single school group rather than as individual schools, according to an Education official. If these schools are

---

[27] In February 2017, a group of private equity firms purchased the publicly traded company that operated the largest for-profit school (University of Phoenix), whose students received over $2 billion in federal student aid in school year 2014-15.

treated as a single school group they would be required to submit company-wide financial statements that may reveal additional financial risks that would be missed at the individual school level.

In November 2016, Education issued a final rule revising the financial responsibility regulations, which established additional financial and nonfinancial situations for which Education would be able to require a letter of credit from schools.[28] The final rule was generally scheduled to take effect July 1, 2017; however, Education has delayed the effective date of key provisions, including those related to financial responsibility, and has also announced plans to review and revise the final rule through the negotiated rulemaking process.[29]

WHILE SCHOOL CLOSURES ARE RARE, LIMITATIONS IN EDUCATION'S OVERSIGHT HAMPER ITS ABILITY TO IDENTIFY AT-RISK SCHOOLS

Although the Number of School Closures Is Small, Abrupt Closures of Large Schools Can Result in Substantial Costs

A relatively small number of schools close each year. For example, according to our analysis of Education data, 96 schools closed during school year 2015-16, accounting for less than 2 percent of the approximately 6,000 schools that participated in federal student aid programs.[30] However, the number of school closures remains higher than in previous years, primarily due to a rise in for-profit school closures (see Figure 3).

The vast majority of schools that have closed over the past 5 years enrolled fewer than 500 students. Although these closures were disruptive to the students and communities involved, the resulting federal financial losses from such closures were limited, given the size of the school. Federal financial losses can also be limited when the school ceases operations in an orderly process over several months. A well- managed closure can give students time to complete the current school term and make arrangements to transfer and continue their education at another school.

---

[28] 81 Fed. Reg. 75,926 (Nov. 1, 2016). In addition, the final rule established a new federal standard and a process for determining whether a borrower has a defense to repayment on a loan based on an act or omission of a school.

[29] 82 Fed. Reg. 27,621 (June 16, 2017). As previously mentioned, the rule was delayed pending resolution of a federal lawsuit challenging the rule. Federal lawsuits have also been filed challenging Education's delay of the rule.

[30] Of these closures, 15 were nonprofit schools (accounting for 1 percent of nonprofit schools), 79 were for-profit schools (accounting for 4 percent of for-profit schools), and 2 were public schools (accounting for less than 1 percent of public schools).

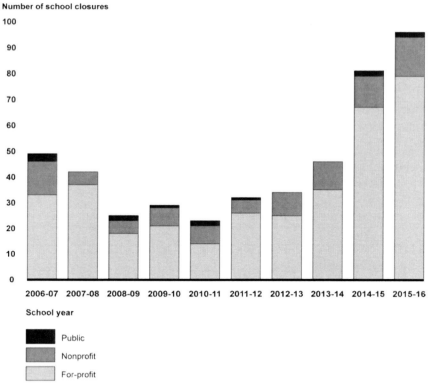

Source: GAO analysis of Education's Postsecondary Education Participants System data. | GAO-17-555

Figure 3. School Closures by School Type, School Years 2006-07 through 2015-16.

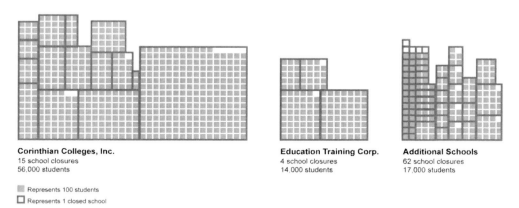

Source: GAO analysis of Education's Postsecondary Education Participants System and Integrated Postsecondary Data System. | GAO-17-555

Notes: The figure illustrates student enrollment 2 years prior to closure for the few cases in which schools had not reported prior year enrollment data to Education. Enrollment data were unavailable for five of the closed schools. Another large for-profit provider of higher education, ITT Educational Services Inc., closed in the following school year 2015-16.

Figure 4. School Closures by Enrollment Size, School Year 2014-15.

Abrupt School Closures: Corinthian Colleges and ITT Educational Services

Before its closure in April 2015, Corinthian Colleges Inc. (Corinthian) was one of the country's largest for-profit providers of higher education, enrolling more than 72,000 students who received roughly $1.4 billion dollars in federal student aid. Corinthian had been under heightened oversight from Education since June 2014 for failing to respond timely to Education's inquiries about its job placement rates. At the time of its closure, Corinthian had already sold the majority of its campuses, as part of an agreement with Education for an orderly closeout of its schools. Corinthian could not find a buyer for its remaining campuses, which it abruptly closed in April 2015. At the time of its closure, according to Education, Corinthian appeared to be in compliance with the financial responsibility standards for schools participating in federal student aid programs, but was later found by Education to have manipulated its composite score.

The following year, ITT Educational Services Inc. (ITT), another large for-profit provider of higher education, abruptly closed all of its 136 campuses in September 2016, affecting more than 35,000 students. Education had placed ITT under heightened oversight and required the school to post a letter of credit since August 2014 for failing one of the financial responsibility standards for schools participating in federal student aid programs. Specifically, ITT was late in submitting its required financial audit following a Securities and Exchange Commission investigation into allegedly undisclosed losses from the company's private student loan programs. In June and August 2016, Education placed additional restrictions on ITT and prohibited some of its schools from enrolling new students with federal student aid in response to adverse actions by the school's accreditor. By September, ITT ceased all operations.

Source: GAO analysis of Department of Education and company documents. | GAO-17-555

Abrupt closures of large schools, although infrequent, create bigger challenges for students and Education. Large school closures can affect tens of thousands of students and result in hundreds of millions of dollars in financial losses for the federal government and taxpayers. For example, 70,000 students were enrolled at schools owned by two companies that closed in school year 2014-15—almost four times the total number of students enrolled at the other 62 schools that closed that year (see Figure 4). When a large school closes, more students may be eligible for discharge of their federal student loans.[31] For example, of the more than 450 total schools that closed over the past decade, the closure of 6 large schools (or companies that owned schools) accounted for two- thirds of loan discharges during that period. Regardless of school size, the effect from school closures is often worse if the closures occur abruptly with little or no advance warning, because these schools generally do not have time to establish transfer arrangements that allow students to easily continue their education at another school. Students affected by an abrupt closure may

---

[31] See, generally, 20 U.S.C. § 1087 and 34 C.F.R. § 685.212. Borrowers may also assert, as a defense to repayment, certain acts or omissions by the school.

32 *United States Government Accountability Office*

therefore be more likely to apply to Education for a discharge of their federal loans. This was the case with Corinthian Colleges, which in 2015 abruptly closed its campuses with only a few hours' notice to students. Due to the abrupt closure as well as other factors, Education has thus far approved more than $550 million in student loan discharges for former Corinthian College students.[32]

Education's Key Financial Oversight Measure Has Limitations and Does Not Reflect Advances in Financial Analysis

Limitations of Education's composite score have made it an imprecise predictor of school closures. Half the colleges that closed from school years 2010-11 through 2015-16 received passing financial composite scores on their last assessment before they closed. For example, 58 of the 96 schools that closed in school year 2015-16 had recently received passing scores. Closures can be difficult to predict in part because each school faces its own unique challenges that can eventually push the school into financial trouble. Schools can also close for nonfinancial reasons (e.g., loss of accreditation, legal action), or a combination of both financial and nonfinancial factors.[33] For example, Dowling College faced accreditation issues, enrollment declines, and financial problems prior to its closure in 2016, according to reports from Education and school officials. Education's composite score is not designed to account for nonfinancial risks; however, the financial responsibility standards for schools participating in federal student aid programs are Education's primary means of securing financial protections through a letter of credit from schools at risk of closure. If the composite score more accurately identified schools at risk of closing, it would enable Education to obtain letters of credit prior to their closing to protect the federal government against possible financial losses.[34] In addition, some schools with failing composite scores may not be at immediate risk of closure. For example, almost 80 percent of the schools that failed the composite score in school year 2010-11 were still operating more than five years later (as of June 2016).

The composite score's inconsistent performance is due in part to limitations of the underlying formula and the fact that it has remained unchanged for 20 years. The composite score is based on common financial ratios that Education selected in 1997 after consulting

---

[32] This amount, according to Education reports, includes both closed school discharges and borrower defense discharges, which provide loan forgiveness to students when a school has misled them or engaged in other misconduct.

[33] Education's historical data on school closures do not include sufficient information on the cause of each closure to determine whether or not a school closed for financial reasons or if the closure occurred abruptly or through a managed process.

[34] Education relies on other oversight mechanisms, such as compliance and program reviews, to assess nonfinancial risks. For example, Education conducts an annual risk assessment of all schools participating in federal student aid programs and uses both financial and nonfinancial information to select schools for program reviews. However, Education does not request a letter of credit from schools for nonfinancial concerns.

with an accounting firm, school officials, and other experts.[35] However, it has not been updated since then and several experts and school officials we interviewed identified weaknesses with the composite score formula. These weaknesses include the effect of subsequent accounting changes, advancements in financial analysis, and the formula's vulnerability to manipulation.

Accounting Changes

Education's composite score formula has not kept pace with changes since 1997 in standard accounting practices, resulting in large swings in the composite scores of some schools over time and creating the potential for differing interpretations. Accounting practices and standards are periodically updated, for example, to improve the comparability and usefulness of financial reporting. Changes to state laws can also affect how schools categorize certain financial items in their annual audits and can have significant effects on their composite scores, according to school officials and experts we spoke with. For instance, they said several states have recently passed laws changing how schools manage and report on their endowments. However, when one school applied these reporting changes to its financial audit, the composite score formula no longer captured a third of the school's endowment, reducing the school's composite score from passing to not passing, according to school administrators we interviewed. Administrators at two other schools we spoke with also said that upcoming changes to accounting standards related to leases and revenue recognition will affect school financial statements that will in turn impact the composite score.[36] However, despite the significant effect that accounting changes can have on schools' scores, Education has not reexamined the composite score formula to ensure the score is a reliable measure of financial health.

As accounting practices continue to diverge from the components and definitions in Education's composite score, schools' financial audits may not contain all the necessary information to calculate their score, making it more difficult for Education to apply the formula in a uniform manner. For example, certain components of the composite score are no longer linked directly to items on schools' audited financial statements. For example, one college accountant we spoke with said that certain inputs for the formula, like construction in progress and unsecured related-party receivables (e.g., donation pledges from a member of the school's board of directors), are not always included in a schools' audited financial statements if the auditor determines the dollar amount is not significant. In these cases, Education must rely on additional unaudited information from a school to calculate its composite score. This problem will be compounded by new accounting

---

[35] The composite score was originally developed through Education's rulemaking process. For a summary of the rulemaking process used to establish the financial responsibility regulations for schools participating in federal student aid programs, including the development of the financial ratios, see 62 Fed. Reg. 62,830 (Nov. 25, 1997).

[36] See Financial Accounting Standards Board (FASB), Leases (Topic 842), Update 2016- 02, (Norwalk, CT: February 2016) and FASB, Revenue from Contracts with Customers (Topic 606), Update 2014-09, (Norwalk, CT: May 2014).

standards for nonprofit organizations that go into effect in December 2017 that will change the reporting categories for net assets on schools' financial statements.[37] As a result, key reporting items in schools' financial audits will no longer align with Education's composite score formula. These differences create ambiguity and make it more difficult to apply the formula in a uniform manner. For example, officials at two of the four higher education associations we interviewed said their member schools have raised concerns that Education staff inconsistently interpret and apply certain components of the formula, increasing the likelihood that Education's measures may not correctly and consistently identify financially troubled schools.

Financial Analysis Improvements

Education's composite score formula does not capture recent advances in financial analysis that could provide a broader indicator of a school's financial health. When the composite score formula was designed in 1997, it was based on the key measures of financial health that were available at the time. Over the last 20 years, the composite score formula has remained unchanged, but the field of financial analysis has continued to evolve with new measures becoming important as economic conditions change. For example, liquidity (i.e., access to cash) has become an important financial measure since the 2007-09 economic downturn, when some schools had trouble meeting payroll and fulfilling contractual obligations. In response, credit rating agencies and industry best practices have incorporated liquidity measures into their methodologies. The Financial Accounting Standards Board has also recognized the importance of liquidity measures and its updated standards call for nonprofit organizations, including schools, to report additional information about liquidity in their financial audits beginning in 2018.[38] However, Education's current composite score focuses on schools' overall wealth rather than on spendable cash and liquid investments. As a result, the score may overstate the assets available to a school to spend on operations.

Credit rating agencies have also adopted broader assessments of financial risk that can provide a more accurate indication of a school's financial health than Education's current composite score. For example, while Education's composite score is solely based on annual snapshots of a school's finances, the two credit rating agencies we interviewed use methodologies that include a broader assessment of a school's historical trends and future projections. For example, analysts we interviewed at one credit rating agency said they incorporate 5 to 10 years of historical trends and 2 to 3 years of future projections into their

---

[37] In 2016, FASB issued an accounting standards update for how nonprofit entities should report assets on their financial statements. This update adopted two new categories for reporting net assets (net assets with donor restrictions and net assets without donor restrictions) rather than the previous three (permanently restricted net assets, temporarily restricted net assets, and unrestricted net assets). This change will be effective for fiscal years beginning after December 15, 2017. However, Education's composite formula is based on the old asset categories that will soon be out of date. FASB, Not-for-Profit Entities (Topic 958): Presentation of Financial Statements of Not-for-Profit Entities, Update 2016-14, (Norwalk, CT: August 2016).

[38] FASB Update 2016-14.

school assessments. This allows these agencies to capture downward trends or emerging risks in a school's finances that Education's composite score could miss. The more sophisticated methodologies used by credit rating agencies have sometimes resulted in assessments of a school's financial condition that are strikingly different from the school's composite score. For example, in 2016, these rating agencies assigned non-investment grade (i.e., junk bond) ratings to 30 schools that received passing composite scores from Education.

Our previous work also provides examples of other federal agencies that use broader assessments of financial risk, and highlights the importance of reevaluating and periodically updating financial measures. For example, federal banking regulators, such as the Federal Deposit Insurance Corporation, use a composite rating system to assess the financial condition of banks in six broad areas: capital, asset quality, management, earnings, liquidity, and sensitivity to market risk. Federal banking regulators have also taken steps to incorporate a more forward- looking approach into their rating system based on lessons learned from bank failures during the 2007-09 financial crisis.[39] In a different industry, the Department of the Interior recently issued revised measures to assess the financial strength of offshore oil and gas operators in response to our recommendation.[40] These would replace the department's previous measures, which relied on a company's net worth, with nine new financial ratios that are intended to provide a broad assessment of a company's financial capacity.

Vulnerability to Manipulation

A few schools have taken advantage of a feature of the composite score formula to manipulate their scores, which enabled them to avoid having to post a letter of credit. In some ways, the formula incentivizes schools to take on long-term debt (e.g., loans with terms in excess of 12 months) because these debts increase a school's composite score. Long-term debt usually represents a long-term investment in a school's campus and buildings, and the composite score formula treats this type of debt in a positive manner.[41] However, an accountant for multiple schools told us that some schools have taken advantage of this provision and taken on a million dollars in debt in order to obtain a passing composite score. For example, administrators from one school we interviewed said they were planning to borrow at least $6 million in the coming year for facilities expansion and improvements, but also to increase the school's composite score to 1.5, which would allow the school to avoid having to post a letter of credit.

---

[39] GAO, *Bank Regulation: Lessons Learned and a Framework for Monitoring Emerging Risks and Regulatory Response*, GAO-15-365 (Washington, D.C.: June 25, 2015).

[40] GAO, *Offshore Oil and Gas Resources: Actions Needed to Better Protect Against Billions of Dollars in Federal Exposure to Decommissioning Liabilities*, GAO-16-40 (Washington, D.C.: Dec. 18, 2015).

[41] Education included long-term debt in the formula for the primary reserve ratio (which measures whether a school has sufficient resources to cover its expenses) to address concerns that schools would be discouraged from making investments in capital improvements if these funds were not counted in the ratio, according to Education guidance. See GEN-01-02.

Corinthian Colleges took out short-term loans and reported them as long- term debt to manipulate its composite score, according to Education documents. The company borrowed $43 million on the last day of its fiscal year 2011 to improve its composite score and then immediately repaid it, according to company documents and Education officials. Corinthian again took out loans toward the end of fiscal year 2012 ($58 million) and fiscal year 2013 ($86 million) and quickly repaid them, which Education concluded boosted the school's composite score and helped it avoid having to post a letter of credit. Education officials we spoke with said they were not aware of the full extent of Corinthian's composite score manipulation until it was too late, and the company had closed its schools and declared bankruptcy before Education could request a letter of credit. If Education had addressed this vulnerability earlier, it could have required Corinthian to post a letter of credit that could have covered some of the over $550 million in loan discharges resulting from the school's closure.

Education officials we spoke with said they plan to take steps to address this type of composite score manipulation, but these efforts may be too narrowly focused. Education's Office of the Inspector General in a February 2017 report raised concerns about Corinthian Colleges' manipulation of its composite score, and recommended that Education update its procedures to address this vulnerability in the future.[42] Education agreed with the recommendation and plans to instruct its staff to collect and review additional information from schools to determine if they may be manipulating composite scores. However, it is unclear how Education plans to identify these schools. Education officials have told us that they do not think this type of manipulation is prevalent since it is advantageous only to schools on the cusp of receiving a passing score. However, our analysis indicates that a significant number of schools receive composite scores near the threshold, where this type of manipulation could be beneficial. For example, about 30 percent of for- profit schools received composite scores in school year 2014-15 that were close to the passing threshold (i.e., in the 1.5-1.9 range). Given the large number of schools that might have incentives to manipulate their scores, a narrowly targeted approach may not be sufficient.

These three weaknesses with the composite score hamper Education's ability to effectively fulfill its statutory responsibility to determine whether schools participating in federal student aid programs are financially responsible. Several Education officials we spoke with, however, maintain that the composite score is still a good measure of a school's financial condition. Identifying and responding to risks is a key component of federal internal control standards, but Education's financial composite score formula has remained unchanged for 20 years despite significant changes in the financial landscape of higher education.[43] Unless the agency updates the composite score formula to better measure

---

[42] Department of Education Office of Inspector General, *Federal Student Aid's Processes for Identifying At-Risk Title IV Schools and Mitigating Potential Harm to Students and Taxpayers*, ED-OIG/A09Q0001 (Washington, D.C.: Feb. 24, 2017).

[43] GAO, *Standards for Internal Control in the Federal Government*, GAO-14-704G (Washington, D.C.: Sep. 10, 2014).

schools' financial conditions and capture financial risks, Education lacks reasonable assurance that the current composite score is a reliable indicator of financial health and is therefore constrained in its ability to protect students and taxpayers against significant financial risks.

EDUCATION DOES NOT FULLY EXPLAIN ITS KEY FINANCIAL MEASURE TO SCHOOLS OR DISCLOSE COMPLETE RESULTS TO THE PUBLIC

Education's Guidance to Schools Does Not Provide Complete Information on Some Components of the Composite Score

In its written guidance to schools about the financial responsibility standards for schools participating in federal student aid programs, Education does not fully explain how it treats certain components of the composite score formula, which has created confusion for some schools. According to a 2012 higher education association report, Education's interpretation of some composite score components is different than schools would expect, which creates confusion and uncertainty for schools.[44] However, Education's Federal Student Aid Handbook (Education's comprehensive annual guide to the statutory, regulatory, and administrative requirements for federal student aid programs) and its step-by-step guide to assist schools with submitting their annual financial and compliance audits do not explain all of Education's interpretations. The Handbook instead refers schools to the regulations, which lay out the composite score formula but do not provide detailed definitions of the various formula components or information on how Education applies this formula in practice.[45] Officials we interviewed at 7 of 10 selected schools expressed confusion about key aspects of the formula and officials at one higher education association told us such confusion has occurred at several other schools. This lack of understanding makes it difficult for schools to correctly estimate their composite scores, contrary to Education's stated intention in the 1997 rule establishing the formula that the composite score methodology would be easily understood by schools and its belief that schools could readily calculate their composite scores from their audited financial statements.[46] In some cases, the lack of understanding can result in schools incorrectly anticipating a passing score and being surprised when they do not pass. For example, officials at three of the

---

[44] National Association of Independent Colleges and Universities, *Report of the NAICU Financial Responsibility Task Force*, Washington D.C., November 2012.

[45] Education has previously published two Dear Colleague letters to explain how it treats one component of the composite score—long term debt—but has not communicated its approach on other complex issues, such as pension plan liabilities, in a systematic way.

[46] 62 Fed. Reg. 62,830 (Nov. 25, 1997).

seven schools that were confused said their schools unexpectedly received zone or failing scores because they did not understand how Education treated several components of the composite score calculation. Officials at the four other schools also said they did not fully understand how Education calculated their schools' composite scores.[47]

Education officials acknowledged schools' confusion about its composite score calculation, but the agency has not taken steps to clarify or supplement its guidance. Education officials we interviewed identified specific components of the composite score that are most often the source of discrepancies between schools' calculations and Education's final score. They included most of the same issues that school officials raised during our interviews (construction-in-progress, pension plan liabilities, endowments, and long-term debt), and two others—unsecured related party receivables (e.g., donation pledges from members of the school's board of directors) and intangible assets (e.g., trademarks or patents owned by a company). The 2012 higher education association report also identified similar areas of concern.[48] In response to previous concerns about the composite score, Education sent a detailed letter to one higher education association in 2010 explaining its rationale for, and treatment of, certain components, but has not made this potentially useful information broadly available by updating its current guidance to schools. This communication gap does not meet the federal internal control standard of effective communication, which calls for management to communicate with external parties in a way that enables them to help the organization achieve its objectives and address risks[49]. As a result, it is difficult for schools to accurately anticipate and plan for Education's oversight of their finances and for the cost to obtain a letter of credit should it be needed.

Education's Public Disclosures about Schools' Financial Scores Are Incomplete

Each year, Education publishes composite scores on its website for most nonprofit and for-profit schools, but does not include the scores for hundreds of these schools.[50] Of all nonprofit and for-profit schools that participated in federal student aid programs in 2014-15, 17 percent are missing composite scores in Education's annual public disclosures, including many large, for-profit schools. Collectively, students at these schools received

---

[47] One of these four schools received a higher composite score than it had expected, according to officials we interviewed.

[48] National Association of Independent Colleges and Universities, *Report of the NAICU Financial Responsibility Task Force*, Washington D.C., November 2012.

[49] GAO-14-704G.

[50] See the Department of Education's Federal Student Aid Data Center, School Data website, currently found at: https://studentaid.ed.gov/sa/about/data-center/school.

over $8 billion in federal student aid and these schools include 7 of the 30 largest nonprofit and for-profit recipients of federal student aid.

These omissions happen primarily because Education does not publicly disclose composite scores for all schools that are owned by the same company. Education calculates a single composite score for this group of schools based on the company's consolidated financial statements.[51] Schools with a common owner therefore receive the same composite score. However, Education publicly reports a composite score for only one school in this commonly owned school group, and does not provide the composite score for any of the other schools in the group. For example, Kendall College and Walden University are both owned by the same company. However, Education publishes a composite score for Kendall College, which enrolls about 1,000 students, but not for the substantially larger Walden University, which enrolls over 50,000 students. As a result, students and others seeking the composite scores of certain schools, such as Walden University, are not able to find them.[52]

Incomplete information on the final composite scores for all schools deprives students of information on whether a school is financially sound enough for them to confidently invest their time and money. Although it has limitations, the composite score is a key indicator of Education's assessment of schools' financial conditions and can provide some useful information to students. Federal internal control standards call for effective communication with external stakeholders, and Education has prioritized the importance of providing students increased transparency about their higher education options in its strategic plan.[53] Even if a school is not at immediate risk of closure, public information on its financial condition is important since research has indicated that a school's financial struggles can have negative effects on its operations. For example, two studies that we reviewed found that financial shortfalls can cause schools to reduce course offerings and increase class sizes.[54] Two other studies have also found that declines in schools' resources per student can result in reduced student supports and lower rates of graduation.[55] Given how a school's financial condition can affect student outcomes, the current gaps in the

---

[51] When a company is the sole owner of multiple schools, according to Education guidance, the agency reviews one consolidated financial audit for the parent company, which Education uses to calculate a single composite score for all of the schools based on the company's overall financial condition.

[52] Education also omits from its public disclosures the small number of schools that are in the process of appealing their composite score because they are not yet final. Schools can appeal their composite score to Education and the agency does not publish any composite scores that are under appeal. From 2007 to 2015, only 10 schools appealed their scores.

[53] GAO-14-704G and U.S. Department of Education, *Strategic Plan for Fiscal Years 2014 -2018*, (Washington, D.C.: Mar. 10, 2014).

[54] For example, see Phil Oliff, Vincent Palacios, Ingrid Johnson, and Michael Leachman, *Recent Deep State Higher Education Cuts May Harm Students and the Economy for Years to Come* (Washington, D.C.: Center on Budget and Policy Priorities, Mar. 19, 2013); and Sarah Bohn, Belinda Reyes, and Hans Johnson, *The Impact of Budget Cuts on California's Community Colleges* (San Francisco, CA: Public Policy Institute of California, March 2013).

[55] For example, see John Bound, Michael F. Lovenheim, and Sarah Turner, *Why Have College Completion Rates Declined? An Analysis of Changing Student Preparation and Collegiate Resources*, American Economic Journal: Applied Economics, Vol. 2, No. 3 (July 2010); and Douglas A. Webber and Ronald G. Ehrenberg, *Do Expenditures Other Than Instructional Expenditures Affect Graduation and Persistence Rates in American Higher Education*, National Bureau of Economic Research, NBER Working Paper No. 15216 (August 2009).

public information on schools' composite scores make it difficult for prospective students to make informed decisions about their investment in higher education.

CONCLUSIONS

When financially struggling schools abruptly shut their doors, it can leave students without education options and force taxpayers to cover the cost of discharged student loans. Effective financial oversight of postsecondary schools is therefore essential to help ensure that schools fulfill their obligations to students and for protecting taxpayer investments in federal student aid. Education relies on the composite score as one of its primary tools for assessing the financial condition of schools. However, Education has not addressed multiple limitations of the composite score that have emerged over the last 20 years. Unless Education takes action to update the composite score formula, students and taxpayers will continue to be exposed to significant financial risks.

Although it has limitations, the composite score can still be a source of information for schools and students. However, the lack of clear guidance for schools on the composite score formula and its components creates confusion and uncertainty among school administrators. When schools do not understand how Education calculates composite scores, it is difficult for schools to anticipate whether they will receive a passing score or to plan for additional oversight should they fail. This can result in unwelcome surprises for schools, such as unexpectedly having to obtain a letter of credit. Improving Education's guidance to schools would allow them to more accurately estimate their composite scores and understand how they are being evaluated. In addition, a school's financial condition can have an impact on students' educational prospects, but gaps in the public information on schools' composite scores limit their usefulness as a resource for students. Without complete and transparent data on schools' financial conditions, it may be difficult for students to make informed decisions as to whether a school is a safe investment of their time and money.

RECOMMENDATIONS FOR EXECUTIVE ACTION

To improve oversight of school finances and provide better information to schools and the public about its monitoring efforts, the Chief Operating Officer of the Office of Federal Student Aid should take the following actions:

- Update the composite score formula to better measure schools' financial conditions and capture financial risks.

- Improve guidance to schools about how the financial composite score is calculated, for example, by updating current guidance to include explanations about common areas of confusion and misinterpretation for schools.
- Increase the transparency of public data on schools' financial health by publicly listing the final composite score for each school.

AGENCY COMMENTS AND OUR EVALUATION

We provided a draft of this chapter to Education for review and comment. Education provided written comments, which are summarized below and reproduced in appendix I. In its written comments, Education generally disagreed with the first recommendation, agreed with the second, and stated it would further evaluate the third.

In its written comments, Education also said that while our report recognized some of its efforts to improve its oversight of certain schools, the report did not provide a complete picture of the department's efforts. For example, Education noted that it had created a new office to oversee large school groups, required at-risk schools to provide more frequent financial and enrollment information, and enhanced information sharing. However, our report does describe the specific tools and processes Education highlighted in its comments that are relevant to the financial oversight of schools. For example, we described the creation of the Multi- regional Division to oversee large school groups, additional financial and enrollment reporting requirements for at-risk schools, and monitoring additional financial information sources.

With respect to the first recommendation to update the financial composite score formula, Education stated that our report does not show that any changes in accounting standards have made the composite score calculations less reliable. As discussed in our report, the components and definitions in Education's composite score do not reflect changes in accounting practices. As a result, some aspects of Education's formula are no longer directly linked to information in schools' audited financial statements. This makes the composite score difficult to apply in a consistent, uniform manner. This problem will be compounded by new accounting standards that go into effect later this year that change how nonprofit schools will report net assets on their financial statements. Education stated that it will work with the Financial Accounting Standards Board on future changes to the accounting standards that may affect a school's composite score calculation; however, revisions to the underlying composite score formula are necessary to ensure consistency with accounting practices and to realign the formula with the information schools report in their audited financial statements.

Education also stated that the observed differences between the composite scores and credit rating agencies' assessments of 30 schools does not support that the composite score is an unreliable measure of the relative financial strength of those schools. As we stated in the report, the composite score formula has remained unchanged for 20 years, in contrast to the practices of other federal agencies and credit rating agencies that have reevaluated and adjusted their metrics to take advantage of new financial measures and to respond to evolving risks. For example, the two credit rating agencies we interviewed have adopted more sophisticated methodologies that include financial assessments of schools' historical trends and future projections. The discrepancies between Education's composite score and the credit ratings of these agencies for some schools indicates that Education's measure could be missing some indictors of financial risk. Given the increasing number of school closures in recent years and the multiple weaknesses we identified with the composite score, we continue to believe that Education should update its composite score formula to better measure schools' financial conditions and manage financial risks.

Further, Education stated that the composite score's vulnerability to manipulation is a factor to consider and address, but does not in itself undermine its usefulness because any financial measure could be manipulated once the elements of the measure are known. However, the cases discussed in our report illustrate how the formula can incentivize schools to take on additional debt. While intentional manipulation of any formula is always a possibility, changes are needed to address this known weakness with the composite score formula that schools have actively exploited to manipulate their scores and avoid additional oversight. These three key weaknesses collectively raise significant concerns about the effectiveness of the composite score as a measure of schools' financial conditions. We identified a number of schools with passing composite scores that subsequently closed, affecting thousands of students and resulting in over half a billion dollars in federal losses from unrepaid student loans. We continue to believe that Education should address these weaknesses by updating the composite score formula to better protect students and taxpayers going forward.

With respect to the second recommendation to improve its guidance to schools about how the financial composite score is calculated, Education stated that it agrees that additional general guidance to schools would be helpful. The department also stated that it will update the guidance in its Federal Student Aid Handbook and may provide answers and related guidance to some frequently asked questions on its website.

With respect to the third recommendation to publicly list the final composite score for each school, Education stated that it agrees that transparency in providing financial responsibility outcomes for schools is important. Education also stated that it will further evaluate the recommendation to ensure that any action it takes will provide information to the public that is precise, fair, and accurate. As we noted in the report, Education does not publicly disclose composite scores for all schools that are owned by the same company or schools that are appealing their scores. Our recommendation calls for Education to list the final composite score for all schools, including schools owned by the same company, not scores that are still under review. Since Education already discloses composite scores for the vast majority of schools, it is unclear why information on the financial condition of schools that are owned by the same company should not be available to the public. We continue to believe that Education should take action to address this recommendation to increase the transparency of public data on schools' financial health.

As agreed with your offices, unless you publicly announce the contents of this chapter earlier, we plan no further distribution until 30 days from the report date. At that time, we will send copies to the appropriate congressional committees, the Secretary of the Department of Education, and other interested parties.

Melissa Emrey-Arras
Director, Education, Workforce, and Income Security Issues

APPENDIX I: COMMENTS FROM THE DEPARTMENT OF EDUCATION

July 19, 2017

Ms. Melissa Emrey-Arras
Director, Education, Workforce
  and Income Security Issues
United States Government Accountability Office
Washington, D.C. 20548

Dear Ms. Emrey-Arras:

Thank you for providing the Department of Education with a draft copy of the Government Accountability Office's (GAO's) report, "Higher Education: Education Should Address Oversight and Communication Gaps in Its Monitoring of the Financial Condition of Schools" (GAO-17-555; Job Code 100488). We appreciate the hard work that went into the audit and the opportunity to comment on the draft report.

As noted by GAO, Education has taken steps to increase its oversight of certain schools. In December 2014, Federal Student Aid (FSA) created an office that is responsible for monitoring large school groups and currently monitors 47 companies, including major publicly traded companies, private equity firms, and privately held companies, which collectively own 330 schools. FSA has implemented significant new tools and processes to identify at-risk schools and mitigate potential student and taxpayer harm, including more frequent financial and enrollment reporting requirements for at-risk schools, enhanced information sharing, subscriptions to industry analyses for fiscal information about publicly traded schools, and enhancements to the annual risk model used to select schools for program reviews. While the draft GAO report recognized some of this, we do not believe that the draft provides a complete picture of the Department's work in this area; we discuss this further in our response to Recommendation 1.

In the report, GAO recommended the Secretary of Education take the following actions, which are followed by the Department's responses:

Recommendation 1: Update the composite score formula to better measure schools' financial conditions and capture financial risks.

Response: The Department regulations require that audited financial statements be prepared in accordance with generally accepted accounting principles, and audited in accordance with generally accepted government auditing standards. (34 CFR 668.23(d)) The Financial Accounting Standards Board (FASB) updates the accounting standards to improve the information reported about an entity in an audited financial statement. Changes made to the accounting standards become an integral part of the audited financial statements that are submitted annually to the Department by institutions. The Department monitors changes to the accounting standards to ensure the financial analysis staff is consistently determining the composite scores for institutions. The goal of the composite score, established through direct and open dialogue with the community when the regulations were developed, was to create a relative financial health measure for all institutions using a common standard, while still taking into consideration the key differences that exist between different sectors of postsecondary educational institutions. This blended approach also takes into consideration the total financial circumstances and resources available to an institution in a uniform manner.

In its report, GAO interviewed community members who, in their opinion, identified a number of perceived weaknesses in the composite score formula. The Department has considered similar concerns raised by some community members about the questioned treatment of certain items in the composite score calculation. The Department has also acknowledged that it will work with FASB on future changes to the accounting standards that may impact an institution's composite score calculation.

GAO states that the Department does not have reasonable assurance that the composite score is a reliable indicator of financial health, but has not shown how any changes in the accounting standards have made the Department's composite score calculations less reliable. The fact that GAO identified 30 schools that would have been rated differently by credit rating agencies does not support that the composite score was an unreliable measure of the relative financial strength of those schools. GAO acknowledges that there is a potential for the components used in the composite score to be manipulated. Any financial measure that the Department would use for evaluating financial health could be manipulated once the elements of the financial measure are known. The potential for a component of the financial measure to be manipulated is a factor to consider and address, but does not in itself undermine the benefits of using the composite score analysis.

The Department hopes that the benefits of providing more guidance as discussed in Recommendation 2 mitigate the disagreements with the community that are related to Recommendation 1, and we will continue to work with individual schools to take into consideration additional information that may have an impact on a school's composite score calculation.

Recommendation 2: Improve its guidance to schools about how the agency calculates the financial composite score, for example by updating its current guidance to include explanations about common areas of confusion and misinterpretation for schools.

Response: As indicated by GAO, in the past, the Department has provided a detailed explanation of its rationale, and treatment of certain components of the composite score

calculation. The Department agrees that additional general guidance on how it calculates the composite score would be useful to schools. The Department will update its current guidance to schools in the Federal Student Aid Handbook and may post online the answers and related guidance for frequently asked questions.

Recommendation 3: Increase the transparency of its public data on schools' financial health by publicly listing the final composite score for each school.

Recommendation 3: Increase the transparency of its public data on schools' financial health by publicly listing the final composite score for each school.

Response: The Department agrees transparency in providing the financial responsibility outcomes for schools is important. The Department makes available each year a list of institutions and their composite scores, but that list does not include every school within a school group nor institutions where a composite score is still under review. The Department will further evaluate this recommendation to ensure that any action it takes ensures that the information provided to the public is precise, fair, and accurate.

I appreciate your examination of this important issue.

Sincerely,

Matthew D. Sessa
Deputy Chief Operating Officer

In: Higher Education
Editor: Lilian Wieck

ISBN: 978-1-53616-026-0
© 2019 Nova Science Publishers, Inc.

Chapter 3

EXAMINING ACCESS AND SUPPORTS FOR SERVICE MEMBERS AND VETERANS IN HIGHER EDUCATION[*]

Committee on Health, Education, Labor, and Pensions

Thursday, May 22, 2014
U.S. Senate,
Committee On Health, Education, Labor, And Pensions,
Washington, DC.

The committee met, pursuant to notice, at 10:03 a.m. in room SD–430, Dirksen Senate Office Building, Hon. Bernie Sanders, presiding.

Present: Senators Sanders, Harkin, Casey, Franken, Baldwin, Murphy, Warren, and Burr.

OPENING STATEMENT OF SENATOR SANDERS

Senator SANDERS. Good morning.

Thank you all for coming, and I want to extend a special thanks to our panelists who have a whole lot to say on a very important issue.

I want to thank, for a moment, Chairman Harkin, for inviting me to chair this Health, Education, Labor, and Pensions committee roundtable today, and I am pleased to be joined by Senator Burr, Senator Baldwin, and others, I suspect will be coming.

---

[*] This is an edited, reformatted and augmented version of Examine Access and Supports for Service Members and Veterans in Higher Education, Publication No. S. HRG. 113-838, dated May 22, 2014.

The Department of Defense estimates that approximately 250,000 to 300,000 service members will separate annually over the next 4 years. That is more than 1 million brave men and women transitioning back to civilian life.

As Chairman of the Senate Veterans' Affairs committee, and Senator Burr is the ranking member of that committee, I think we can tell you how important it is that these service members get the tools they need for successful transition. I think we can all agree that for many service members, getting an education is a critical component of that transition.

Today's discussion will help us determine ways that the Higher Education Act is helping us achieve those goals, and find areas where there are problems, and where we can make improvements.

Today, the unemployment rate for veterans who served after 9/11 is higher than the unemployment rate for nonveterans. The Bureau of Labor Statistics reports that as of April 2014, the unemployment rate for post–9/11 veterans was 6.8 percent. In reality, if you factor in people who are working part-time when they want to work full-time, that number is probably higher.

We are making progress in lowering those numbers and a major contributing factor has been the post–9/11 G.I. bill, which has gone further to support student veterans than any of its predecessors. And I consider it to be a landmark piece of legislation in helping something like 1 million veterans and their families.

Since 2009, the V.A. has paid more than 1 million post–9/11 beneficiaries more than $40 billion. This is a significant piece of legislation. In 2013, it was one of the largest of the Federal Government's education programs. The V.A. estimates the number of beneficiaries will continue to grow.

To support those veterans using this benefit, and to ensure that they get the most out of it, V.A. has expanded its VetSuccess on Campus programs to 94 locations around the country. VetSuccess counselors are V.A. employees who work on college campuses and provide a range of services that holistically address the needs of student veterans as they integrate into college life from adjustment counseling, to vocational testing, to career counseling. These counselors also assist veterans with disability accommodations and pro-vide referrals for health services through V.A. medical centers, community-based outpatient clinics or vet centers.

Despite its success, there are still aspects of the post–9/11 G.I. bill that can be improved. In fact, to help keep costs manageable for student veterans, I introduced legislation, along with Senator Burr, that would require public colleges and universities to provide certain recently discharged service members the in-State tuition rates. This legislation is included as a provision of the pending bill S. 1982, the Comprehensive Veterans Health and Benefits Military Retirement Pay Restoration Act.

Veterans often choose to begin their education immediately following separation from the military, making the university campus a primary entry point into civilian society. This can be a mixed blessing, as veterans are often nontraditional students whose attention is divided between having a family, maintaining a home, and working a full-time job.

Fortunately in addition to V.A., there are also things that schools can and are doing to assist veterans during this stressful time. However, the traditional higher education system has only just begun to accommodate the needs of nontraditional students. Institutions must learn how to best accommodate unique issues facing our military and veteran students including students who can unexpectedly be called to active duty and must interrupt their coursework for unknown lengths of time.

In addition to these unique challenges, I am concerned that active duty service members and student veterans are suffering the consequences of a continued failure by some corporations to comply with the protections guaranteed to them in Federal law.

I, along with many other members of this committee, was deeply troubled last week when it was revealed that the Department of Justice had filed a lawsuit and proposed settlement alleging Sallie Mae violated the rights of approximately 60,000 service members by failing to comply with provisions of the Servicemembers Civil Relief Act.

The Veterans' Affairs committee held a hearing on this issue last year, and I will echo my comments. We must continue to improve education and outreach on the protections of the SCRA. Industry must redouble its efforts to improve the compliance with the Act.

And finally, aggressive enforcement of these protections must continue when violations occur.

I firmly believe that the brave men and women serving our country should not be subjected to the types of behavior we have seen from some in the private sector. These continuing violations are completely unacceptable and that behavior must cease.

Let me conclude by saying that what I hope we can accomplish today is to foster a productive conversation about how schools are meeting the needs of veterans and service members, what more can be done to ensure veterans are not putting themselves into financial trouble in order to get an education and, ultimately identify what this committee, and the Veterans committee by extension, can do to assist with these efforts.

I believe we have the right people here to answer these questions. I want to thank all of you for being here, and I look forward to a productive discussion.

Senator Burr.

STATEMENT OF SENATOR BURR

Senator BURR. Thank you, Senator Sanders, and thanks to Chairman Harkin and Ranking Member Alexander for giving us the opportunity to preside over this hearing.

The series of Higher Education Act reauthorization hearings have been bipartisan in nature and extremely informative for the committee as we undertake a rewrite of our

Nation's higher education laws. I applaud Senator Harkin and Senator Alexander for their commitment to these hearings and to the comedy with which they have both handled this.

North Carolina is home to almost 800,000 veterans making my State one of the largest homes for veterans in the country. We take pride in that status, but also in the fact that a large percentage of those veterans choose to stay for our high quality colleges and universities.

Today, we will hear from Kimrey Rhinehardt, vice president of Federal Relations at the University of North Carolina Chapel Hill or the University of North Carolina. The UNC System, through its UNC SERVES initiative, has become a model for the country for how a large university system can integrate veterans returning from service into the college setting in a way that caters to their individual needs, but also provides an environment that enhances their opportunity for completion.

It is important to keep in mind how unique today's veteran and service member students actually are. Recent data indicates 62 percent are first in their family to attend college compared to 43 percent for nonveteran civilian students. They also tend to be much older and an average age of 33 compared to their civilian peers 22.

These students tend to commute to school, carry a full-time job, have dependents, which all makes the circumstances different and worth a college or a university's consideration when providing on- campus services.

Additionally, as troops return from Iraq and Afghanistan, postsecondary institutions are facing the largest influx of veterans on their campus in generations. Higher education has a role to play in ensuring these heroes have an opportunity to succeed on their campus. I am proud of UNC's success in this regard. And I urge my colleagues to listen carefully to the good things happening in my State that can inform best practices for all States.

With that, I hope that today's roundtable provides a robust conversation about these issues and I look forward to hearing from a great panel of witnesses. I welcome them all.

Thank you.

Senator SANDERS. Thank you, Senator Burr.

Senator Baldwin.

STATEMENT OF SENATOR BALDWIN

Senator BALDWIN. Thank you, Mr. Chairman.

I am delighted that you have held this hearing today and I very much look forward to having a conversation with our witnesses.

It is of the utmost importance that our warriors are able to work toward their education goals while actively serving and once they return from the battlefield. Leaving school with significant student loan debt is a reality for too many Americans, but it is a particularly acute problem for our veterans, and this is unacceptable. We have to do everything in our power to ensure that our service members and veterans have the financial, social, and emotional support needed to succeed.

Again, thank you for convening us. Thank you to our Ranking Member, and I look forward to the discussion that will ensue. Senator SANDERS. Thank you.

Senator Franken.

STATEMENT OF SENATOR FRANKEN

Senator FRANKEN. I want to thank the witnesses for being here and I want to thank, you, Senator Sanders for all your work on veterans issues; thank you, Senator Burr.

There are a lot of issues here that we will get into today, one of which is the skills that are—and I know Dr. Langdon, you speak this in your testimony—the skills that our veterans come to their college careers already having, and many have worked in communications and very high tech communications in a war zone, and then do not get any kind of credit for that. And I think that is among the issues that I discuss with veterans who are in colleges in Minnesota.

There are a lot of other issues that we will get to today, and I want to thank you, Mr. Chairman, for holding this hearing, and look forward to your testimony, and our discussion. Thank you.

Senator SANDERS. Thank you very much, Senator Franken.

OK. We have a great panel. Let me begin by introducing Lauren Thompson Starks, who serves as Senior Policy Advisor at the U.S. Department of Education in the Office of the Under Secretary.

While at the Department, she has worked on a range of issues in higher education including interagency efforts to support career readiness for veterans and service members, and has worked with the V.A. to help redesign the Transition Assistance Program.

Ms. Starks, welcome, and thanks for being here.

STATEMENT OF LAUREN THOMPSON STARKS, SENIOR POLICY ADVISOR, OFFICE OF THE UNDER SECRETARY, DEPARTMENT OF EDUCATION, WASHINGTON, DC

Ms. THOMPSON STARKS. Senator Sanders, Burr, and members of the committee.

Thank you for the opportunity to participate in this roundtable. I am pleased to share how the U.S. Department of Education, working together with our partner agencies, is contributing to efforts that support the postsecondary success of service members, veterans, and their families.

I would like to focus my remarks on the Department of Education's initiatives designed to increase access to quality and affordable educational institutions, remove barriers to degree completion, and foster practices that strengthen campus cultures for student, veteran, and service members' success.

Following the President's August 2011 call to action for a comprehensive Federal approach to supporting a career-ready military, we have collaborated with the Departments of Defense, Veterans Affairs, Labor and other agencies on a redesign of the Transition Goals Plans Success program.

Transition GPS is strengthening and expanding the information, counseling, and support available to transitioning service members. The Department of Education is providing expertise in areas such as postsecondary access, affordability, Federal financial aid, and adult learning strategies. We have contributed to the development and evaluation of modules on accessing higher education, and the career and technical training modules, and we have also continued to advise on program direction and assessments.

Our core efforts also include providing our agency partners with transparency tools and resources to help students and families garner information about postsecondary access and costs, identify programs that meet their individual needs, and select among quality institutions and available Federal student aid options.

Interagency coordination is not only helping to bridge the gap between military service and educational opportunities, but it is also helping to remove barriers to degree completion once students are enrolled.

In August 2013, the Departments of Defense, Education, and Veterans Affairs formed the Academic Credentialing Task Force. The Task Force is dedicated to increasing awareness of promising practices and policies that promote awarding academic credit at postsecondary institutions for prior military training and experience.

It is also facilitating the ability of these institutions to understand how military training and experience is relevant to their programs of study. And through these efforts, is supporting degree completion and career readiness among our Nation's veterans.

The Department is also collaborating with our agency partners to support the implementation of the Principles of Excellence Executive Order No. 13607. These Principles are designed to ensure that service members, veterans, and their families are offered quality educational opportunities, and have the educational and financial information needed to make informed choices.

The Principles ask educational institutions to do more to ensure support services for service members and veterans, which ultimately help foster learning communities where all students can thrive.

The Principles also signal the Administration's commitment to strengthening accountability, and enforcement, and oversight within Federal education benefit programs. They are enhancing transparency to facilitate educational comparisons through tools like the Financial Aid Shopping Sheet and are also enabling mechanisms that empower students and families to get the support they need and deserve such as the new centralized student complaint system.

As part of efforts to build on the Executive order, the Departments of Education and Veterans Affairs in conjunction with more than 100 education experts convened to review approaches that could be scaled and replicated to foster veterans' success on campus. The result was the 8 Keys to Success, a voluntary effort to promote best practices with the goal of fostering postsecondary environments that are committed to veterans' success, and to also ensure that veterans have access to the information they need to make decisions concerning their benefits.

The 8 Key offer concrete steps postsecondary institutions can take to assist veterans and service members who are transitioning and assist them in completing their college degrees and obtaining career-ready skills.

The strategies include a variety of steps including creating a culture of connectedness on campus, using uniform sets of data tools to collect and track information relating to veterans, and also collaborating with local communities and organizations.

In closing, the Department of Education will continue working with our agency partners as we strengthen the ladders of opportunity for our veterans and service members to reach their educational and career goals.

Thank you very much for this opportunity to highlight this information, and I look forward to today's discussion with you and fellow roundtable participants.

[The prepared statement of Ms. Starks follows:]

Prepared Statement of Lauren Thompson Starks

Chairman Sanders, Ranking Member Burr, and members of the committee, thank you for the opportunity to participate in this roundtable. I am pleased to share how the U.S. Department of Education (ED), working together with our partner agencies, is contributing to efforts that support the postsecondary success of service members, veterans, and their families.

I would like to focus my remarks on ED's initiatives designed to increase access to quality and affordable educational institutions, remove barriers to degree completion, and foster practices that strengthen campus cultures for student veteran and service member success.

Federal Interagency Collaboration and Technical Assistance to Improve Access to Quality and Affordable Educational Institutions, and Streamline Degree Completion

Following the President's August 2011 call to action for a comprehensive Federal approach to supporting a career-ready military, we have collaborated with the Departments of Defense, Veterans Affairs, Labor, and other agencies on a redesign of the "Transition Goals, Plans, Success" (Transition GPS) program, which strengthens and expands information, counseling, and support available to transitioning service members.

ED is providing expertise in areas such as postsecondary access, affordability, Federal financial aid, and adult learning strategies. We have contributed to the development and evaluation of modules on accessing higher education and career and technical training, and have continued to advise on program direction and assessments.

Our core efforts also include providing our agency partners with transparency tools and resources to help students and families garner information about postsecondary access and costs, identify programs that meet their individual needs, and select among quality institutions and available Federal student aid options.

Interagency coordination is not only helping to bridge the gap between military service and educational opportunities, but it is also helping to remove barriers to degree completion once students are enrolled.

In August 2013, the Departments of Defense, Education, and Veterans Affairs formed the Academic Credentialing Task Force. The Task Force is dedicated to increasing awareness of promising practices and policies that promote awarding academic credit at postsecondary institutions for prior military training and experience, facilitating the ability of these institutions to understand how prior military training and experience is relevant to their programs of study, and supporting degree completion and career-readiness among our Nation's veterans.

Supporting the Implementation of the "Principles of Excellence" Executive Order

Executive Order 13607, "Establishing Principles of Excellence for Educational Institutions Serving Service Members, Veterans, Spouses, and Other Family Members," (Principles) offers principles designed to ensure that service members, veterans, and their families are offered quality educational opportunities and have the educational and financial information needed to make informed decisions. The Principles ask educational institutions to do more to ensure support services for service members and veterans, which ultimately helps foster learning communities where all students can thrive.

The Principles signal the importance, to student consumers, families, and institutions, of the Administration's commitment to strengthening accountability, enforcement, and oversight within Federal education benefit programs. They are enhancing transparency to facilitate educational comparisons, through tools like the Financial Aid Shopping Sheet, and are enabling mechanisms that empower students and families to get the support they need and deserve in accessing education benefits through the new centralized student complaint system.

Promoting Best Practices for Veteran Student Success

As part of efforts to build on E.O. 13607, the Departments of Education and Veterans Affairs, in conjunction with more than 100 education experts, convened to review approaches that could be scaled and replicated to foster veterans' success on campus. The result was the '8 Keys to Success"—a voluntary effort to promote best practices with the goal of fostering postsecondary environments that are committed to veterans' success and to ensure that veterans have access to the information they need to make informed decisions concerning their Federal educational benefits.

The "8 Keys" offer concrete steps postsecondary institutions can take in order to assist veterans and service members in transitioning to postsecondary education, completing their college degrees, and obtaining career-ready skills. The strategies include creating a culture of connectedness on campus, coordinating and centralizing campus efforts for all veterans, collaborating with local communities and organizations to align services and supports for veterans, implementing an early alert system, utilizing a uniform set of data tools to collect and track information relating to veteran students (i.e., retention and degree completion), and developing systems to ensure sustainability of effective practices.

ED will continue working with our agency partners as we strengthen ladders of opportunity for our veterans and service members to reach their educational and career goals. Thank you for the opportunity to highlight this information about key Department initiatives, and I look forward to today's conversation with you and fellow roundtable participants.

Senator SANDERS. Thank you very much, Ms. Starks.

Dr. Thomas Langdon serves as director of State Liaison and Educational Opportunity in the Office of the Under Secretary of Defense for Personnel Readiness. In this role, he oversees the Department of Defense's Tuition Assistance Program, the TAP program, which allows nearly 280,000 service members to attend college courses at little or no cost.

Dr. Langdon, thanks for being here.

STATEMENT OF THOMAS L. LANGDON, DIRECTOR, STATE LIAISON AND EDUCATIONAL OPPORTUNITY, UNDER SECRETARY OF DEFENSE, PERSONNEL, AND READINESS, OFFICE OF THE DEPUTY UNDER SECRETARY OF DEFENSE FOR MILITARY, COMMUNITY, AND FAMILY POLICY, ALEXANDRIA, VA

Mr. LANGDON. Chairman Sanders, Senator Burr, and distinguished members of the HELP committee.

It is an honor to be able to contribute to today's discussion on the Department of Defense's voluntary education program. My remarks will highlight several ways the DOD provides oversight to facilitate service member education success. First, just a little about me so you may better understand my perspective.

I enlisted in the Air Force in March 1977 as a military police officer. I spent nearly 29 years on active duty and I was heavily involved with education, mine and others. Without military tuition assistance and caring and competent counsel, meeting my educational goals would have been difficult at best. It is no exaggeration to say without the DOD voluntary education program I would not be sitting before you today.

Over the past year, DOD has enhanced its programs and services to ensure that service members have access to education opportunities throughout their military careers. Education helps grow leaders who will sustain our force readiness and continue to make valuable contributions in the support of our Nation.

For many, the decision to go to school is a complex one and proper oversight by DOD and the services, education counseling, and access to important information allows the service member to make informed choices. DOD's programs attract a large percentage of the eligible military population because they are designed to meet the unique needs of the off-duty service member.

Each year, approximately one-third of our service members enroll in postsecondary coursework. Colleges and universities, through an extensive network, deliver classroom instruction at hundreds of military installations around the world and online to an ever-increasing percentage of our service members. During 2013, over 277,000 service members took more than 827,000 courses and earned over 55,000 degrees and certificates.

Participation in DOD-supported voluntary education requires a service member to visit an education center, either in-person or online, through their services education portal. There are approximately 200 DOD education sites worldwide.

At these centers, professional education counselors brief service members on their education options, provide assistance and develop an education plan, recommend tailored courses of study to meet their education goals, and provide information on financing to include DOD tuition assistance, grants, loans, or other available funding options.

Over the past year, the Department's priority has been implementing the requirements of the Executive Order 13607, establishing principles of excellence. These efforts are part of a robust interagency collaboration between the Consumer Financial Protection Bureau, the Federal Trade Commission, the Departments of Defense, Education, Veterans Affairs, and Justice.

The initiatives include enhancements to the DOD Voluntary Education Partnership Memorandum of Understanding that just was issued on the 15th of May; the postsecondary education complaint system and the development of the postsecondary education outcome measures. In addition, DOD has participated in interagency Military Credentialing and Licensing Task Force which is dedicated to identifying, supporting, and sharing strategies for institutions of higher education. One of the major efforts is for a better understanding of the Joint Services Transcript process.

Service members rely on DOD voluntary education programs to help them attain their personal and professional goals, and it is made possible because DOD and the entire Federal Government recognize the high value of education programs supporting military advancement and the successful transition of service members to civilian workforce.

The Department remains committed to effectively delivering voluntary education programs that meet the changing needs of our service members.

I thank you for the opportunity to be here today, and I look forward to your questions.

[The prepared statement of Mr. Langdon follows:]

Prepared Statement of Thomas L. Langdon

Chairman Sanders, Ranking Member Burr, and distinguished members of the HELP committee, it is an honor to be able to contribute to today's discussion on the Department of Defense's (DoD) Voluntary Education Program. I will highlight the Memorandum of Understanding (MOU) between DoD and individual institutions of higher learning and the new interagency Postsecondary Education Complaint system.

The Department's Voluntary Education Program provides valuable learning opportunities for servicemembers, contributing to enhanced readiness of our forces. Education helps our servicemembers be better Soldiers, Sailors, Airmen, and Marines. Through education and experience, using tuition assistance (TA), we grow leaders, who will sustain our force readiness and continue to make valuable contributions in support of our Nation. Allow me to share the profile of typical TA users.

- They work full-time and are part-time students;
- They take an average of three courses per year and less than 1 percent ever reach the $4,500 annual ceiling;
- The majority complete their education after leaving the military;
- They attend multiple institutions and take about 7 years to earn an Associates Degree;
- They do not usually graduate from the school where they took their first course;
- They blend how they attend school between traditional classroom and online (79 percent take some online courses);
- They do not immediately seek employment upon earning their degree; and
- They have breaks in their education due to circumstances such as deployments and transfer of duty station.

For many, the decision to go to school is a complicated one and proper oversight by DoD and the Services, education counseling, and access to important information allows servicemembers to make informed choices. DoD programs are designed to meet the unique needs of the military off-duty student and, therefore, attract a large percentage of the eligible military population.

Approximately one-third of our servicemembers enroll in post-secondary courses leading to undergraduate and graduate degrees or certificates each year. Colleges and universities, through an extensive network, deliver classroom instruction at hundreds of military installations around the world and on-line, to an ever-increasing percentage of our servicemember students. Additionally, servicemembers can also earn college credits for learning that takes place outside the traditional classroom through College Level Examination Program (CLEP) testing and assessment of their military training.

DoD has increased its assistance over the last year through its Voluntary Education programs and services, ensuring that opportunities for learning continue to exist for servicemembers throughout their military careers and preparing them for lifelong learning after they leave the military.

Oversight of Military TA—Facilitating Service Member Success

Participation in DoD-supported Voluntary Education requires servicemembers to visit an education center, either in person or on-line through their Service education portal. There are approximately 200 DoD education sites worldwide, including contingency areas in Afghanistan. At these centers, professional education counselors present servicemembers with an extensive menu of options, provide details about specific programs, recommend tailored courses of study that meet servicemembers' goals, and provide information on education financing, including information on the TA program, grants, loans and other available funding options. Prior to using military TA, servicemembers must establish an education goal and an education plan. Servicemembers, through their Service's education portal, request TA for a course(s) outlined in their approved education plan, and an education counselor reviews the servicemembers' education record and education plan prior to granting approval.

Even with the financial support DoD provides, nearly all servicemembers, and especially those taking graduate level courses, incur out-of-pocket expenses. This gives each student a financial stake in their success. Also, servicemembers failing to complete or receiving an 'F' in a course must reimburse DoD for the TA received for the course, and servicemembers' failing to maintain a 2.0 undergraduate or 3.0 graduate grade point average (GPA), must pay for all courses until they raise their GPA sufficiently.

Oversight of Military TA—Ensuring Quality Education Programs

Over the last year, the Department's priority was to finalize implementation of our efforts consistent with Executive Order 13607: Establishing Principles of Excellence for Educational Institutions Serving Service Members, Veterans, Spouses and other Family Members. This includes multiple initiatives, such as the launch of a centralized online reporting system, enhancements to the DoD Voluntary Education Partnership Memorandum of Understanding (MOU), and development of postsecondary education outcome measures. All of these efforts are part of a robust interagency collaboration among DoD and the Departments of Education, Veterans Affairs, and Justice, along with the Consumer Financial Protection Bureau and the Federal Trade Commission. These agencies are working together to enable military students and their families to make good educational choices using comprehensive information about the available programs and institutions that offer them.

The quality of education provided to our servicemembers is essential to the Department, and underpinning this effort is DoD's requirement that all post-secondary institutions participating in the TA program, whether they are physically located on our installations or elsewhere, be accredited by an accrediting body recognized by the U.S. Department of Education. Currently, over 3,200 institutions with more than 4,400 sub-campuses, have signed the DoD MOU. The new MOU was published in the Federal Register on May 15, 2014, as part of Change 2 to Department of Defense Instruction (DoDI) 1322.25, and it requires all participating institutions to adhere to the Principles of Excellence as listed in Executive Order 13607:

- Provides students with an education plan;
- Informs students of the availability and eligibility of Federal financial aid before arranging private student loans;
- Ensures new course or program offerings are approved by the institution's accrediting agency before student enrollment;
- Allows servicemembers to be re-admitted to a program if they are temporarily unable to attend class or have to suspend their studies due to military requirements;
- Provides a refund policy for military students consistent with the refund policy for students using Department of Education Federal student aid (Title IV); and
- Designates a point of contact for academic and financial advising.

DoD is also working on other education initiatives. The interagency effort to identify postsecondary education outcome measures will provide information on available educational programs to support informed decisionmaking about educational choices, especially as they relate to veterans and servicemembers. The Departments of Defense, Education, and Veterans Affairs have worked together to propose a set of outcome measures to capture important information on students' experiences during school, upon completion of a degree or certificate, and post-graduation, using existing administrative data.

DoD also participates in the interagency Military Credentialing and Licensing Task Force. The President established this forum to identify opportunities for servicemembers to earn civilian occupational credentials and licenses without the need for additional training. The Interagency Academic Credentialing Workgroup is dedicated to identifying, supporting, and sharing strategies for institutions of higher education to use when evaluating military training and experience in order to award appropriate amounts of academic credit for the skills and knowledge servicemembers gain through their service. For example, we have developed multiple webinars for the education community to help them better understand the Joint Service Transcript (JST) and the American Education Council (ACE) evaluation process.

The JST provides documentary evidence to colleges and universities of the professional military education, training, and occupation experiences of servicemembers and veterans. JST is an official transcript tool that validates and documents those courses and occupations for servicemembers and veterans. From November 1, 2014 through April 7, 2014, 4,873 transcripts were requested and sent to colleges and universities.

ACE's Military Evaluations program has reviewed and made college credit recommendations for thousands of military courses since the early 1940s and, in 1974, began the evaluation of military occupational specialties. More than 2,200 higher education institutions recognize the ACE course credit recommendations for granting credit to their military students. The webinar sessions clarify the review process and the quality measures that are used in determining credit recommendations and increase the awareness, use, and benefit of the JST.

The explanation of both the ACE evaluations and JST will be included in the updated Transition GPS Accessing Higher Education curriculum, which will communicate the transfer of academic credit and military training to transitioning servicemembers. The goal was to update portions of the Education part of the Transition Assistance Program to better educate transitioning servicemembers on the proper award of academic credit. While some postsecondary institutions have active policies in place to award credit, the ultimate goal of the workgroup is expanding the number of institutions with effective military credit policies.

Finally, the Defense State Liaison activities have been integral to facilitating change at the State level. As of May 15, 2014, 45 States have passed legislation or an Executive order requiring their educational institutions to evaluate military training and experience toward the award of academic credit. In addition, 31 States have enacted legislation regarding in-State tuition impacting newly separating servicemembers.

DoD Oversight of Military TA—Preventing Predatory Practices

DoD has strengthened its policies regarding on-installation access to our servicemembers. Institutions' access to military installations is allowed only in order to provide education, guidance, and training opportunities, and to participate in education fairs. Marketing firms or companies that own and operate higher learning institutions do not have access. Institutions must meet the following requirements:

- Have a signed MOU with DoD;
- Be chartered or licensed by the State government in which the services will be rendered;
- Be State-approved for the use of veteran's education benefits;
- Participate in title IV programs (eligible and participating under Department of Education rules, students are eligible for Federal support);
- Be accredited by an accrediting body recognized by the U.S. Department of Education; and
- Have an on-base student population of at least 20 military students.

On January 30, 2014, DoD along with agency partners—Veterans Affairs, Education, Justice, the Consumer Financial Protection Bureau, and the Federal Trade Commission—launched the new Postsecondary Education Complaint System (PECS). The online reporting system, part of the Executive order on Principles of Excellence, is intended to help ensure that students are equipped with comprehensive information to make school and program choices that meet their educational goals. It is designed to empower military students and their families to report negative experiences with educational institutions and provide the Federal Government the information it needs to identify and address unfair, deceptive and misleading practices.

The initial reaction to the PECS has been overwhelmingly positive. Within 24 hours of launch, the PECS received over 1,740 unique web page views and 37 complaints. As of May 15, 2014, DoD has processed 146 complaints. DoD is committed to working with each educational institution and student to reach a resolution that satisfies both parties. Over 60 percent of the complaints are regarding DoD or institutional processes or policies as opposed to substantiated complaints against a school such as deceptive recruiting and marketing practices. The complaint records and their resolutions are contained within a centralized repository, the Consumer Sentinel Network, making the information accessible by the Departments of Veterans Affairs, Defense, and Education, all of whom review schools for compliance and program eligibility, as well as the law enforcement agencies that would prosecute any illegal practices. The inter-agency team is also engaged in establishing servicemember and veteran outcome measures directed by Executive Order 13607 that will assist in ensuring continued quality at both the program and institution level. These measures will attempt to determine performance through metrics such as retention rates, persistence rates, and time-to-degree (or credential) completion.

Conclusion

Servicemembers rely on the DoD Voluntary Education Program to help them become better Soldiers, Sailors, Airmen, Marines, and citizens. During fiscal year (FY) 2013, approximately $540,400,000 taxpayer dollars supported 277,800 servicemembers who took 827,100 courses and were awarded 55,700 degrees/certificates. This was possible because DoD and the entire Federal Government are unified when it comes to placing a high value on educational programs that support the professional and personal development and the successful transition of servicemembers to the civilian workforce. It is an honor and a privilege to work among a team of professionals dedicated to providing our servicemembers and their families with high-quality educational opportunities in pursuit of their personal and professional goals. The Department of Defense remains committed to effectively delivering voluntary education programs that meet the changing needs of the military. Mr. Chairman, this concludes my statement.

Senator SANDERS. Dr. Langdon, thanks very much.

William Hubbard is the vice president of External Affairs for the Student Veterans of America. Mr. Hubbard joined the Marine Corps at age 17 and continues to serve with the 4th Marine Logistics Group as a drilling reservist out of Joint Base Anacostia-Bolling. He is a graduate of American University where he studied international relations.

Mr. Hubbard, thanks very much for being here.

STATEMENT OF WILLIAM HUBBARD, VICE PRESIDENT OF EXTERNAL AFFAIRS, STUDENT VETERANS OF AMERICA, WASHINGTON, DC

Mr. HUBBARD. Senator Sanders, Senator Burr, and esteemed colleagues.

Thank you for having Student Veterans of America here today to share our thoughts on examining access and supports for service members and veterans in higher education. As the premiere advocate for student veterans in higher education, it is our privilege to share our on-the-ground perspective with you today.

In 2008, veterans in colleges and universities across the Nation came together to form SVA, using a network of peer to peer relationships and determined to achieve beyond expectations, these veterans applied years of hard learned lessons in the service to the classroom, and they succeeded.

To begin, we believe it is important to outline how we define success for student veterans. Success is when a student veteran makes a well-informed educational decision, achieves personal academic goals without incurring student loan debt, and secures gainful employment that propels them forward in their career aspirations.

First, consolidation of information on how to make the most of the G.I. bill benefit is critical. This information could potentially help veterans avoid wasting months of G.I. bill benefits which may lead to veterans taking out unnecessary loans. The V.A.'s G.I. bill Comparison Tool is a good example of the kind of work we see as necessary.

Second, as veterans graduate across the country, we believe that their debt burden will ultimately be the single largest inhibiting factor to long-term success. As a contributing factor to this debt, we remain concerned that some technical and career colleges claim to offer credentials and certifications, but students are not able to complete specific exams due to a lack of proper accreditation leading to the loss of valuable benefits and years of study.

There are different pieces to the puzzle that we must identify for the student veteran to fully achieve their goals; institutions, individuals, and communities. We refer to these as the three pillars. When these are strong, student veteran achievement is high. These pillars set veterans up for success in the academic setting and after graduation.

With programs like the Department of Veterans Affairs, that success on campus and support from postsecondary institutions, veterans are operating in environments where they are prone to excel. With the right tools and resources, SVA sees no limit to what student veterans can achieve in higher education and beyond.

When empowered with environmental factors for success, the investment that America has made in the G.I. bill and its veterans becomes an even clearer asset to the economy. By increasing access to higher education and removing barriers to degree attainment, we can set up our veterans for long-term success.

We thank Senator Sanders, Senator Burr, and our present colleagues for your time, attention, and devotion to the cause of veterans in higher education.

As always, we welcome your feedback and questions on this important topic.

[The prepared statement of Mr. Hubbard follows:]

Prepared Statement of William Hubbard

Senator Sanders, Senator Burr and esteemed members of the HELP Committee: Thank you for inviting Student Veterans of America (SVA) to submit our thoughts on "Examining Access and Supports for Servicemembers and Veterans in Higher Education." As the premier advocate for student veterans in higher education, it is our privilege to share our on-the-ground perspective with you today.

In 2008, veterans in colleges and universities across the Nation came together to form SVA. Using a network of peer-to-peer relationships, and determined to achieve beyond expectations, these veterans applied years of hard-learned lessons in the service to the classroom, and they succeeded.

SVA's top priorities include improving access to higher education and scaling effective services that empower student veterans to graduate on time, with little-to- no student debt, while preparing student veterans for fulfilling futures. We look forward to this important conversation and hope to share the perspective of student veterans in higher education with you today.

A Look at the Current Landscape

Setting the Definition of "Success"

To begin, we believe it is important to outline how we define "success" for student veterans. Success is when a student veteran makes well-informed educational decisions, achieves personal academic goals without incurring student loan debt, and secures gainful employment that propels them forward in their career aspirations.

The Importance of Higher Education for Veterans

As quintessential nontraditional students, student veterans face a myriad of challenges that most of their peers in the classroom do not; they are generally older, more likely to have families, and often have significant financial responsibilities not shared by most 18- to 22-year-olds. However, unlike other nontraditional students, many veterans deal with the added challenge of juggling academics with their transition to higher education. In some cases, temporary withdrawals from school to deploy or train are the norm for many National Guardsmen or Reservists, which often elongates their path to completion or it can put it on hold altogether.

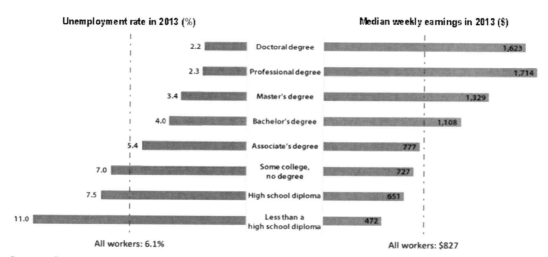

Source: Current Population Survey, U.S. Bureau of Labor Statistics, U.S. Department of Labor
Note: Data are for persons age 25 and over. Earnings are for full-time wage and salary workers.

Figure 1. Earnings and unemployment rates by educational attainments.

Regardless of the challenges, it is clear that a postsecondary degree or credential is critical for success in today's global economy. Using data from the last fiscal year, the Bureau of Labor Statistics illustrated the importance of higher education, as seen in Figure

1. For those who achieved an associate's degree, unemployment dropped to 5.4 percent and for those with a bachelor's or greater, that drops even further to 4 percent and below.[1]

Increasing Access to Higher Education

The Key Components of Consumer Awareness

The decision to pursue a degree in higher education can be daunting for some, but recent developments like the Department of Veterans Affairs' (VA) GI Bill Comparison Tool have made that process more approachable. We continue to work with the VA to refine this tool so future generations can access critical information to support their decisionmaking process. We believe this is a good first step, but this tool is not the complete solution. Further consolidation of information on how to make the most of the GI bill benefit is necessary. This information could potentially help veterans avoid wasting months of GI bill benefits, which may lead to veterans taking out unnecessary loans.

As veterans graduate across the country, we believe that their debt burden will ultimately be the single largest inhibiting factor to long-term success. There is a common misconception that veterans who go to school on the GI bill have a "free ticket", but we know this is simply not true.

As an earned benefit, not only is it not free, it may not always cover the full cost of an education. Some student veterans take longer to complete their degree, due to being nontraditional students. In such scenarios, student veterans likely take on additional loans to complete or risk withdrawing short of graduation. While many veterans may not have a clear understanding of how much their education benefits will impact their overall cost of attendance, others face abusive and misleading practices across sectors of education that can result in undue and unnecessary debt burdens.

We remain concerned that some technical and career colleges claim to offer credentials and certifications, but students are not able to complete specific exams due to a lack of proper accreditation, leading to the loss of valuable benefits and years of study. We applaud the bipartisan efforts of the dozens of State Attorneys General working to curb this practice among the worst offenders, and would like to work with this committee and the Congress to improve the laws preventing this despicable practice.

We also find that being able to access a full range of financial data is critical for institutions to be able to effectively counsel their students on their financial status, as well as for the individual to have the highest level of consumer awareness. Greater awareness allows student veterans to make informed choices that are aligned with their personal career aspirations.

---

[1] U.S. Bureau of Labor Statistics, U.S. Department of Labor, "Earnings and unemployment rates by educational attainment", *http://www.bls.gov/emp/ep_chart_001.htm* (Access May 2, 2014).

A Continued Fight for In-State Tuition

Many student veterans continue to be forced to pay out-of-State tuition costs, despite being "state-less" as a direct result of their military service. It is for this reason that the Veterans of Foreign Wars, the American Legion, and SVA continue to ardently fight for in-State tuition for all veterans at the State and Federal levels. Less than half of all States offer in-State tuition for veterans and we continue to press the importance of this issue as a top contributor to education debt.[2] We call on this group of leaders to continue to work toward ending this unnecessary and unjust punishment for the transient lifestyle in which our military is called to serve.

Supporting Student Veteran Achievement

There are different pieces to the puzzle that must be identified for the student veteran to fully achieve their goals. We refer to these as the "Three Pillars" that contribute to student veteran success, and we encourage this group of leaders and other researchers to focus on them individually as well as collectively.

- Pillar 1—*Institutions:* Institutional support for student veterans is an important aspect of maintaining a strong pipeline of successful veteran graduates. The ability of the college or university to efficiently process student veteran benefits, transfer credits, or assist in job placement, is of crucial importance to the success of veterans. Flaws at this level, as well as unwelcoming or distrustful academic or professional environments, continue to act as major barriers to the success of some student veterans.
- Pillar 2—*Individuals:* Establishing an environment for the student veteran to fluidly interact with the institution and the community is a determining factor in whether or not they will achieve their goals. Those who do not feel welcome may not persist in their studies.
- Pillar 3—*Communities:* An established network across various university offices, academic networks, and career services enables the student veteran to make the transition from the campus to a fulfilling career. This may start with the institution's outreach to potential employers, but is ultimately the responsibility of all of us to ensure that employers understand the strengths of veterans in the workplace.

When the Three Pillars—institutions, individuals, and communities—are strong, student veteran achievement is high. These pillars set veterans up to succeed in an academic setting and after graduation. With programs like the Department of Veterans Affairs'

---

[2] Student Veterans of America, ''The Fight for In-State Tuition for Veterans'', *http://www.studentveterans.org/what-we-do/in-state-tuition.html* (Access May 2, 2014).

"VetSuccess On Campus" (VSOC), and support from postsecondary institutions, veterans are operating in environments where they are prone to excel.

Our Final Thoughts

With the right tools and resources, SVA sees no limit to what student veterans can achieve in higher education and beyond. When empowered with environmental factors for success, the investment America has made in the GI bill and its veterans becomes an even clearer asset to our economy. By increasing access to higher education and removing barriers to degree-attainment, we can set our veterans up for long-term success.

We thank Senator Sanders, Senator Burr, and our present colleagues for your time, attention, and devotion to the cause of veterans in higher education. As always, we welcome your feedback and questions on this important topic.

Senator SANDERS. Mr. Hubbard, thank you very much for your testimony.

David Carlson is the coordinator of Student Veteran Services at the University of Vermont. Originally from Burlington, VT, David served for 4 years in the U.S. Marine Corps as an infantry assaultman from 2004 to 2008. He deployed twice in support of operation Iraqi Freedom fighting in Fallujah, Iraq in 2005 and Ramadi, Iraq in 2006 where he was commended for his actions while under direct enemy fire.

After completing his military service, David enrolled at the University of Vermont using the post–9/11 G.I. bill. David was a cofounder of the Student Veterans organization on UVM's campus and later served as the Vermont state director for Student Veterans of America.

Mr. Carlson, thanks very much for being with us.

STATEMENT OF DAVID CARLSON, COORDINATOR OF STUDENT VETERAN SERVICES, UNIVERSITY OF VERMONT, BURLINGTON, VT

Mr. CARLSON. Good morning, Mr. Chairman, Senator Burr, members.

Respectfully, the University of Vermont is a public research land grant university located in Burlington, VT. I am the coordinator of Student Veteran Services for UVM and as Senator Sanders said, I served in the United States Marine Corps where I deployed three times in 4 years, and then attended UVM on the post–9/11 G.I. bill.

For me, UVM was a great place to transition from being an active duty Marine back into the civilian world. I learned to leverage and articulate the skills, leadership, and attitude that I gained in the Marines, and apply them in the workforce.

My current position has two main roles, which allow me to be successful supporting veteran transitions. The first role is very basic. It is helping students understand the admission process at the University and how to access V.A. education benefits. That involves assisting with the application process, submitting accurate enrollment information, monitoring V.A. payments, and making sure that students understand their V.A. education benefits.

To accomplish that, we have to understand V.A. and DoD systems, have associated norms and rules for accessing information and accomplishing tasks, and likewise, so do institutions of higher learning.

Students navigating both V.A. and higher education systems must understand the differences between those disparate bureaucracies in order to be successful.

This is the basic level and no further levels of support can be successful without that process taking place accurately and in a timely fashion. I am still learning and will continue working hard to learn how to quickly, accurately, and correctly certify student enrollment. V.A. technical support, liaison availability, and partnership are critical to the success of schools administering V.A. education benefits.

My second role at UVM is implanting an all-inclusive student veteran support system, which focuses on educating students about what is available to them on campus and in the community.

UVM is creating a system of support and encouragement for veterans throughout the entire higher education process from engagement with student veterans through the higher education process. From first contact with a prospective student all the way through successful academics, to graduation, and engagement with the career center. That support includes academic; financial aid; social, that is peer support through student veteran organization, a student-run club and member of Student Veterans of America; mentorship, for example, faculty, staff, and senior students; and personal wellness.

When describing what I do, I think of Maslow's hierarchy of needs. We need to make sure that students understand their benefits and that they are working before we can proceed to providing higher levels of support. It is important for me to note that I see both student and system barriers to accessing higher education for military veterans at UVM. Many veterans might be reticent to receive help, but as a veteran coordinator we have personal domain expertise, I use my experience to breakdown some of those barriers with knowledge, social management, and awareness.

I work hard to build trust-based relationships with students, which gives me the ability to become a trusted advisor and build bridges through previous layers of distrust or misunderstanding with V.A. or UVM.

The fact is that this is high stakes. This is an important issue which has the ability to influence people's lives, student success or failure in their future are somewhat dependent on being successful in college. That is important to me. Student veteran success matters to me in a huge, personal way and I am so thankful and humble to have had access to a fantastic education benefit.

Thank you for the opportunity to be here today and I look forward to your questions.

[The prepared statement of Mr. Carlson follows:]

Prepared Statement of David Carlson

Good morning, the University of Vermont is a public research land-grant university located in Burlington, VT. My name is David Carlson and I am the coordinator of Student Veteran Services for UVM. I served in the U.S. Marine Corps, where I deployed three times in 4 years, and then attended UVM using the Post-9/11 GI bill. For me, UVM was a great place to transition from being an active duty marine back to the civilian world. I learned to leverage and articulate the skills, leadership, and attitude I gained in the marines, and apply them in the workforce. My current position has two main roles which allow me to be successful supporting veterans' transitions.

- *The first role is basic; it is helping students understand the admission process at the University and how to access to VA education benefits.* That involves assisting with the application process, submitting accurate enrollment information, monitoring VA payments, and making sure that students understand their VA education benefits. To accomplish that, we have to understand that VA and DoD systems have associated norms and rules for accessing information and accomplishing tasks and, likewise, so do institutions of higher learning. Students' navigating both VA and higher education systems must understand the differences between those two disparate bureaucracies in order to be successful. That is the basic level, and no further levels of support can be successful without that process taking place accurately and in a timely fashion. I am still learning, and will continue working hard to learn how to quickly, accurately and correctly certify student enrollment. VA technical support, liaison availability and partnership are critical to the success of schools administering VA education benefits.
- *My second role at UVM is implementing an all-inclusive student veteran support system which focuses on educating students about what is available to them on campus and in the community.* UVM is creating a system of support and encouragement for veterans through the entire higher education process, from first contact with a prospective student all the way through successful academics, to graduation and engagement with the Career Center. That support includes academic, financial aid, social (i.e., peer support through the Student Veteran Organization, a student-run club and member of Student Veterans of America), mentorship (e.g., faculty, staff, senior students), and personal wellness. When describing what I do, I think of Maslow's Hierarchy of Needs. We need to make sure students understand their benefits, and that they are working, before we can proceed to providing higher levels of support.

- *It is important for me to note, that I see both student and system barriers to accessing higher education for military veterans.* Many veterans might be reticent to receive help but as a veteran coordinator with personal domain expertise, I use my experience to break down some of those barriers with knowledge, social management and awareness. I work hard to build trust-based relationships with students which gives me the ability to become a trusted advisor and build bridges through previous layers of distrust or misunderstanding with VA or UVM.
- *The fact is that this is high stakes.* This is an important issue which has the ability to influence people's lives; students' success or failure, and their future, are somewhat dependent on being successful in college. That's important to me. Student veteran success matters to me in a huge personal way and I'm so thankful, and humble to have had access to a fantastic education benefit.

Thank you for the opportunity to be here today and I look forward to your questions.

Senator SANDERS. Thank you, very much, Mr. Carlson.

Senator Burr, did you want to introduce Ms. Rhinehardt?

Senator BURR. Mr. Chairman, I will never pass on the opportunity to introduce not only a person who I think is intricately involved in the issue that we are here to discuss, and that is veterans' education and her role at the University of North Carolina System. She was somebody whom I had the opportunity to have on my staff for a period of time, who understands the side of the dais that we are on, and who understands what it is like to sit behind those of us who get all the accolades for what we do, and never get recognized for the tremendous work that our staff does at the committee and at the personal level.

Kimrey Rhinehardt, one, is passionate about the job she does. She understands in great depth the people that are impacted by the legislation that we write. And she is passionate about making sure that, at the end of the day, her influence is for us to do the right thing.

She has been instrumental in the academic outreach by the University of North Carolina to active duty DoD, to our bases in North Carolina, to the continuing education of our active duty forces. She is also instrumental in trying to understand and continuing to refine the difficulties of integration of a veteran into today's college life. And, someone whom I think has a unique perspective on what those individuals go through and what institutions need to do to accommodate a host of different needs that present themselves with the decisions that veterans come with.

Let me also say, Mr. Chairman, as you know, she has been an outspoken advocate for yours and my effort to require States to offer in-State tuition which, I personally believe, is the right thing for us to do as a Nation, both from a policy standpoint and from a fiduciary standpoint.

Kimrey, welcome back.

STATEMENT OF KIMREY RHINEHARDT, VICE PRESIDENT OF FEDERAL RELATIONS, UNIVERSITY OF NORTH CAROLINA, CHAPEL HILL, NC

Ms. RHINEHARDT. Thank you, Senator Burr, Mr. Chairman, I certainly hope that my mother and husband are watching right now.

Thank you for inviting me to this important conversation. I would like to point out that my colleague from Vermont was a Marine assigned to Camp Lejeune in North Carolina. And I believe my fellow panelists have done an outstanding job of articulating all of the same challenges that UNC students face. So I am going to get right to the point, and maybe take a different approach.

I work for the people of North Carolina. My employer, the University of North Carolina System is a large, 16-campus university system with 220,000 students, 55,000 faculty and staff. Approximately 8,000 of our students use some form of V.A. benefit to pay for their education. As Senator Burr has already articulated, North Carolina is a big military State and we are very proud of this.

While 99.5 percent of us sleep quite comfortably in our beds at night, our friends and neighbors in North Carolina in uniform are protecting and promoting our freedom in places where we do not vacation.

These men and women and their families have endured an unprecedented operational tempo and I am sure that we can all agree, they have more than earned the right to pursue a high quality and affordable higher education.

I have worked with North Carolina's military since 2009 and here is what I have learned from them. They are smart. They are motivated. They find the university to be overwhelming. They want us to tell them how to navigate campus, preferably on one piece of paper without footnotes, caveats, and unnecessary runarounds. They do not want to ask for help. They have experience that cannot be replicated in the classroom setting. They do not want anything handed to them; they want to earn it.

They do not understand why they have to take four semesters of Spanish when they are fluent in Dari and have used their language skill to negotiate a real outcome in Afghanistan. They like having other military affiliated students in their classes. They will not hesitate to challenge a professor's theory.

Many do not want to talk about their military life. They want to find other people like them on campus. They do not have time to waste on climbing walls. They already did that. They pursue their degree efficiently.

Here is what professors and other students tell me they have learned from military students.

"Wow. They are really smart. They do their homework, turn it in on time, and do not make excuses. They add a valuable dimension to classroom discussion. They make everyone around them smarter just by being there. They want to learn. We do not know what we do not know about them. I should not have asked them what it was like over there. We assume they all have PTSD, but they do not. They want more military- affiliated students in their classes and veterans that look just like you and me."

Administrators ask the UNC System office, "Tell us how to do this right. We want to get it right." So how does a university become a place of transition for veterans? Intentionally. We have come together as a university community to recalibrate normal. This new normal may take work, but it is worth it.

The education that the service member needs is mission-critical because the most important weapon that he or she has is not an assault rifle, but their mind. And when the service member makes the transition to veteran in civilian society, we want that veteran to remain in North Carolina for the long term. We want veterans to receive in-State tuition in the State of North Carolina. We want Medal of Honor awardees like Kyle White to receive in-State tuition in the State of North Carolina. The University can, and should be a natural place of transition for the veteran. They have earned their benefit.

The University of North Carolina System commits itself to partnering with the military because national security should be a priority for all of us, not just the less than $\frac{1}{2}$ of 1 percent of us that put the uniform on. We could all do something to contribute. The faculty, staff, and students of the University of North Carolina stand ready to do our part.

Thank you, Mr. Chairman. This concludes my testimony.

[The prepared statement of Ms. Rhinehardt follows:]

Prepared Statement of Kimrey Rhinehardt

Mr. Chairman and members of the committee, thank you for inviting me to join you today. Thank you for your leadership.

The University of North Carolina system is comprised of 16 university campuses. We have 220,000 students and approximately 55,000 faculty and staff across the State of North Carolina. Nearly 8,000[3] of our students use VA educational benefits to pay for some or all of their post-secondary education.

North Carolina is a big military State with 800,000 veterans, six major military installations with the third largest active military force in the country. This active- duty force is comprised of 120,000 personnel, 12,000 members of the National Guard and their nearly 145,000 spouses and children.

---

[3] UNC: Fall 2013 data.

As the State's public university, we are working hard to enroll, educate and graduate as many academically prepared service members, veterans and family members as possible. Our motivation is simple and our actions are intentional: the success of student veterans and their families at UNC institutions is linked to the success of the University and our State's future.

In October 2010, the University of North Carolina system convened a working group known as "UNC SERVES (UNC Systemwide Evaluation and Recommendation for Veterans Education and Services), to evaluate and recommend specific action steps for improving how the University system and its individual institutions serve veterans and their families. The UNC SERVES working group issued its report in April 2011.

The University is making steady progress toward implementing UNC SERVES recommendations. Annually, we issue the 'UNC SERVES Resource Guide" to highlight systemwide and campus progress with each of the action items. The UNC SERVES working group report and Resource Guides may be reviewed online at: http://www.north carolina.edu/frc/uncserves/serves.html.

Centralized Information Sharing and One-Stop Shopping for Veterans

Veterans are not typical students. Student veterans come to us from a highly structured, bureaucratic environment of the military and are often uneasy with the loosely structured, bureaucratic environment of the University. University admissions and enrollment processes can be complex. This is especially true for veterans. One of our top priorities is to centralize information sharing using a technology-based platform to provide a virtual "one-stop-shop" for veterans. To access the University's virtual one-stop-shop: http://www.uncserves.northcarolina.edu.

Another technology-based resource in development is the North Carolina Military Educational Positioning System or 'NCMEPS." This Web site provides military-affiliated students with important resources to explore North Carolina's higher education options: both public and private. To access NCMEPS: http://www.ncmileps .northcarolina.edu.

Data Collection and Reporting

The University has established systemwide, uniform data collection procedures to ensure that we can identify and track the academic progress of service members, veterans, spouses, and dependent family members.

UNC Institutions Align Academic Programs to Student Needs

UNC campuses have a legacy of working with military-affiliated students and the military installations in North Carolina. Representing all UNC institutions, the UNC system office has academic advisors at Fort Bragg, aboard Camp Lejeune and at Coast Guard Air Station Elizabeth City.

The University has specialized programs of interest to veterans and active duty military service members. Veterans are attracted to these programs because their military learning and experiences align with the academic program and prepare them for their desired career. And, many courses are structured to complement an adult student's life. Many student veterans have family responsibilities, part-time or full-time employment and other obligations.

Closing

The education that the service member needs is mission critical because the most important weapon that he or she has is not an assault rifle—but their *mind*. And, when the service member makes the transition to veteran in civilian society we want that veteran to remain in North Carolina for the long term.

The University can and should be a natural place of transition for the veteran. They have earned their educational benefit.

The University of North Carolina system commits itself to partnering with the military because national security should be a priority for all of us—not just for the *less than half of 1 percent of us* that serve in the armed forces. We can all do something to contribute. The faculty, staff and students of the University of North Carolina stand ready to do our part.

Thank you, Mister Chairman. This concludes my testimony.

Senator SANDERS. Thank you all very much for your important testimony on a very important issue.

We are all, as Ms. Rhinehardt indicated, deeply appreciative and knowledgeable about the sacrifices made by so many. And our job, and what this hearing is about, is to make sure that when people come back, they get the best education that they possibly can. And what we are here to discuss is what is going right and what is not going right, how do we improve it?

Let me just start off with a very general question to Mr. Carlson, who is from my hometown. In a broad statement, Mr. Carlson, how is the G.I. bill working at the University of Vermont? What is positive about it, and what are some of the impediments and negatives that you see that veteran students are facing?

Mr. CARLSON. Thank you, Senator Sanders.

The post–9/11 G.I. bill at the University of Vermont overall is working well and it worked well for me.

Many of the positives are that according to lot pays for a student's in-State tuition and fees, it provides them with a very decent housing allowance to survive on while they are pursuing their education.

However, some of the negatives are that it does cover that in- State tuition as we have discussed. The University of Vermont has recently increased from 35 to 45 undergraduate

Yellow Ribbon Scholarships, which represents a tremendous amount of matched dollars from UVM and from the V.A. to allow out-of-State students to choose to attend the University of Vermont, to make that good transition, to come to a place where the campus climate is very accepting of diversity, whether that diversity is military or any other culture.

Some of the real challenges that are experienced are accurately and quickly reporting enrollment information from the University of Vermont, which is its own large bureaucracy to V.A., which is its own bureaucracy. The two do not speak the same language and so, I find myself in the middle translating and ultimately de-conflicting when something goes awry. That is what I have to say.

Senator SANDERS. Let me ask Ms. Rhinehardt the same question. What is working well about the G.I. bill, and what are some of the impediments and problems that you see?

Ms. RHINEHARDT. What is working well is that we have 8,000 students using a form of V.A. benefit on our campuses. And so for that, we thank the Federal Government and this Congress for extending that benefit.

What is not working well is when the change was made to find savings associated with the G.I. bill a couple of years ago. Because of North Carolina's unique circumstances in which we have a pretty significant differential between out-of-State tuition and in-State tuition, we were actually able to cover many out-of-State students using the highest in-State tuition under the old rules. When the rules changed, we had a lot of students who were admitted under one set of rules and then enrolled thinking, "This is my tuition," and were handed a great big surprise.

Since that time, we have been fighting, really with anyone that will listen, to try to get in-State tuition for these students in North Carolina. That is our biggest challenge.

Senator SANDERS. These students are faced with a gap of several thousand dollars.

Ms. RHINEHARDT. Oh, many more thousands.

Senator SANDERS. What?

Ms. RHINEHARDT. I mean, probably close to $13,000–$14,000. Senator SANDERS. Over a period of years?

Ms. RHINEHARDT. A year.

Senator SANDERS. A year? The gap is that high?

Ms. RHINEHARDT. Yes, sir. And you know, our friends in the private institutions— I do not want them to lose anything—but they have a much more generous benefit. They receive up to $18,500 or something along those lines. And when you are in a State like North Carolina, where your tuition is extraordinarily low, it would be great if we could have the $18,500 cap.

Senator SANDERS. OK. Other people.

Mr. Hubbard, what is working well? What do you see?

Mr. HUBBARD. Thank you, Senator.

I would say more broadly, the positive side of things: access. Student veterans are able to access an education whereas previously, they would not have had that opportunity.

Many individuals have commented to me repeatedly,

"I am the first generation student in my family. Had I not had the G.I. bill, I would not have been able to have gotten an education. This has brought me to a different level of education. I have gotten a higher degree than I had before."

Which I think goes against the theory that individuals are using the G.I. bill to specifically get an Associate's Degree or a lower certification. They are going on to pursue higher levels of education with their G.I. bill.

On the side of things that could be improved, I think individuals are often left to make a decision between a 4-year degree and perhaps a degree that would take longer, something in a STEM field, for example, engineering, math, science, technology. Those degrees may take a longer period of study, and as a result, they are forced to make that decision, in many cases, when they are balancing their family and trying to figure out how to pay for that fifth year, they often pursue a different field.

I think also my colleague, Mr. Carlson, pointed out a great example of processes. The processes need to be improved so that they are streamlined to allow for a student veteran to take their benefit and make the most of it.

Senator SANDERS. OK. Thank you very much.

Senator Burr.

Senator BURR. Senator Sanders, let me share with my colleagues just a couple of things that Kimrey did not say.

North Carolina's subsidy to higher education is extremely high for in-State students. I think that is obvious. We consider one to be an in-State student after they have a 1-year residency in North Carolina.

So to Kyle White, who is a Medal of Honor winner as of last week, who chose to go to school in North Carolina after he separated from the active duty, his first year was as an out-of-State student where he accumulated debt matched with his G.I. bill, but his second, third, and fourth year became an in-State student under today's reimbursement.

Our active duty forces that are stationed within North Carolina, their children receive in-State tuition on Day One. And we are going to do the right thing in North Carolina, but I think it is important for us to recognize the inequity that we created between public and private and it is magnified when you take a State like North Carolina that has a significant subsidy.

Let me ask you, Mr. Carlson. What is the in-State/out-of-State tuition at your institution?

Mr. CARLSON. Thank you, Senator.

The in-State/out-of-State tuition gap, in-State tuition is generally about 40 percent of the out-of-State tuition.

Senator BURR. OK. Another high subsidy.

Mr. CARLSON. It is significant. Yes, sir.

Senator BURR. Mr. Hubbard, the Veterans Affairs committee, which Senator Sanders ranks, and I am the ranking member, has jurisdiction over many veterans education programs which, specifically under the Higher Education Act, we can change. It might be easy for the college going process for veterans and service members.

What changes should we make, in your estimation, that would make it easier?

Mr. HUBBARD. Thank you for the question, sir.

I believe often that there needs to be more communication, or needs to be more transparency. As student veterans come in, they need to have the right information to make the right decisions about their education benefits.

If you are going to a university, for example, that is not accredited or might not allow you to have the certification at the end— that information in the end—you basically lose benefits. You lose a period of study. So that consumer information is very important.

And then, having the communication with the school and the school have communication with the V.A. or DoD, as it were. I think that is very important. That entire process, that lifecycle, that education for veterans is very important.

Senator BURR. Kimrey, what prompted the UNC System to embark on UNC SERVES and that initiative?

Ms. RHINEHARDT. The president at the time, Erskine Bowles, looked at me and said, "Ms. Rhinehardt, you are getting down to Fort Bragg and you are going to find out what is going on with them down there." So I went down and I learned a whole lot about what I did not know, and immediately saw this incredible opportunity for our State. When you have special operations community as large as it is in this State.

I spent 3 days this week embedded in a negotiation exercise with Green Berets, and there were students from other UNC campuses there. And I was like, "What better opportunity is there?"

We began to understand what the opportunity was and then we brought together people from across the UNC System, faculty, staff, and students. We all got in a room and said, "What do we want to do about this? What do we want to change about the way we do business and the way we serve these students?"

In very short order, which is not like a university, we issued a report that said, "These are the things we want to do." That report did not sit on a shelf. We were very active. We monitor. We look at each of the best practices that, I will say, many of which came from the ACE Tool Kit, which is a very helpful tool for us. We learned what we did not know and now that we know, we can go do it.

So I would say that is the thing that defines a university campus from being very active and aggressive in a campus that appears to not be doing something. It is not that they do not want to; they just do not know what to do.

Senator BURR. What metrics does UNC use to gauge success?

Kimrey Rhinehardt. We look at whether or not campuses have established central points of contact in key offices like financial aid office, the registrar's office, making sure that all of that information is published in a one-stop shop format. It is virtual. It is online. And our office makes sure that it is up to date so the veterans do not have to hunt and peck all over campus to figure out, "Where do I go?" That is the first thing.

The second thing is that, you know, "Is your campus developing programs that align with service member training and needs?" We have many programs that offer courses on Saturdays and Sundays, and then we will have follow on study throughout the semester.

An adult student cannot go to class on Monday, Wednesday, and Friday at 11 a.m. generally. I mean, I certainly cannot. I have a 9-year-old who goes to school. I work full-time and it is not different than someone like me.

So to me, this military community is a microcosm of the much larger challenge, which is, how do we serve all nontraditional students?

Senator BURR. Thank you.

Thank you, Mr. Chairman.

Senator SANDERS. Thank you very much.

Senator Baldwin.

Senator BALDWIN. Thank you, Mr. Chairman.

As the entire panel has experienced, veterans often need financial aid beyond their G.I. benefits. And the Student Veterans of America's research has shown that many veterans continue their education beyond earning a certificate or undergraduate degree and need the support of aid provided under Title IV of the Higher Education Act.

We know that as nontraditional students, veterans often must work, as well as attend to family and other obligations, as we just heard.

However, working while in school can result in these veterans reducing or even eliminating their title IV aid because their income may exceed the Higher Education Act's Income Protection Allowance.

I have been working toward the introduction of legislation that will address this issue head-on by raising the Income Protection Allowance for all students, including veterans, whether they are working to support themselves or supporting a family.

I am hoping that the panel can help articulate the need for financial support beyond the G.I. bill and address the unique financial needs of the working student veteran. And I am hoping that you can also speak to how legislation to raise the Income Protection Allowance would help veterans come out of school with less debt.

Mr. Carlson and Mr. Hubbard, I wonder if you can kick off the discussion of this topic?

Mr. HUBBARD. Thanks for the question, Senator.

I believe you actually raise a very important point and that is nontraditional students in higher education. What we are finding is with our research, as you pointed out, over half veterans are doing well in higher education and we are seeing to raise that number.

I think this points out something important, and that is, we have found a system, a process, a unique approach to supporting the nontraditional student in higher education. If we can apply that to other nontraditional students along with legislation like you point out, to raise the Income Protection Allowance, I think we can come onto a process that will enable nontraditional students to succeed.

Research on nontraditional students is very old. At best estimates, 20 to 30 percent says that nontraditional students are graduating. Obviously, with student veterans in the upwards of 50-plus percent, that is much higher.

If we can bring that gap together, I think we will have found a very significant breakthrough.

Mr. CARLSON. Thank you for the question, Senator.

I believe that when we think about nontraditional students, especially military veterans, rolling out essentially what is concierge service, a single point of contact, so that they can have all of the information that they need directly, up front and they do not have to go from office to office within the university and within the Department of Veterans Affairs to understand what their benefits are. And if and when they are going to have an outstanding balance that would not be paid by those V.A. benefits, it is important for them to have that information up front and have it be complete so that they can make an informed decision.

Senator BALDWIN. Ms. Rhinehardt.

Ms. RHINEHARDT. I would like to point out, and laud the Student Veterans of America because of their work with the Million Records Project. What they did is they started to go deeper into understanding the analyses of who is doing what, how well are they doing. But what they did is they used data that actually reflects a much more accurate picture of who these students are. They worked with the Clearinghouse, the National Student Clearinghouse.

I know that this Congress and the Department of Education are working closely to try to get IPEDS up to better reflecting transfer student needs and nontraditional students. But really, what SVA has done has really been the opening salvo for understanding who these students are, but using the most accurate date.

Senator BALDWIN. Mr. Chairman.

Senator SANDERS. Please.

Senator BALDWIN. I trust we will have a second round of questioning, so I will let my colleagues go, but I will followup with the program you were talking about because I think there is some interesting discussion that we can have about that too.

Senator SANDERS. Thank you, Senator Baldwin.

Senator Franken.

Senator FRANKEN. Thank you, Mr. Chairman.

Last year, I visited Inver Hills Community College in Minnesota and I met with a group of veteran and military students who talked about how the training and skills that they had learned in the military do not easily transfer to college credits.

One veteran told me that he did top secret communications work when he was deployed and yet, when he returned home, he could not transfer that training or knowledge into college credits in communications.

This is for anyone: what can be done to support the veteran military students who have existing skills from military service or training, and are not able to turn those skills into college credits? Anyone. Just jump in.

Mr. HUBBARD. Thank you, Senator.

I think that is actually a critical point the Student Veterans of America is working very hard toward. The idea of credits and credentialing is something that has come up time and time again, as I am sure you are aware of as well.

I think there is a double approach here. From the student veteran perspective, it is a matter of translating those skills so that the universities can understand where they do apply; so coming from that side. And then from the other side, for the actual institution of higher learning, for them to accept those credits is often a difficult fight as well. If both of them can meet in the middle, I think that will be an opportunity for these student veterans in all States, to benefit from.

A great example is if you, as you point out, have a communications background. You have done communications work for the military. Maybe you have done it for several years and you have proven that you have those skills. If the universities then point you to a Communications 101 class, that is a waste of your time.

If you can go to a higher, or at least test out of some of those more basic courses, that will shorten your time to degree, which will then allow you to save those benefits for later education purposes.

Mr. CARLSON. Senator, thank you for the question.

I think a big step forward that was made in that regard is the Joint Services Transcripts. Previously, as a Marine, I went to the University of Vermont with a SMART Transcript, which was Navy and Marine Corps, and some of those courses that I had completed while I was in the military may or may not have transferred to UVM, depending on their content and length.

But as I see students coming in now with a Joint Services Transcript, many more of those credits are able to come into the university.

Senator FRANKEN. Ms. Rhinehardt.

Ms. RHINEHARDT. I am so glad you asked that question because the University of North Carolina is actually just beginning its intentional effort to divide the Military Articulation Agreement among all of our campuses, and we are turning, actually, to Minnesota's model for how to do that.

Minnesota is leading the way nationally in articulating military learning into academic credit. Thank you to the State of Minnesota for helping UNC figure out the way forward on this.

Senator FRANKEN. We are getting there. How often are those kinds of skills that are learned during deployment and military service and military training are aligned with the skills gap that we have. We have higher unemployment among our veterans coming back and our young veterans especially.

To what extent are those unbelievable skills that they have acquired while serving, do the higher education schools go and I am talking about 2-year community and technical colleges as well as the 4-year and say, "Wow. This aligns so well with these jobs that exist that people cannot fill."

Ms. RHINEHARDT. Sir, I have a great answer for you.

Senator FRANKEN. Good.

Ms. RHINEHARDT. Sorry, I get excited. He told you I got excited. Senator FRANKEN. I know. That is good.

Ms. RHINEHARDT. UNC Chapel Hill School of Medicine, the chief of emergency medicine and the chair of the Jaycee Burn Center happen to have a military background, and they started working with the 18 Delta Combat Medics and their instructors down at Fort Bragg. And over the course of time, developed such a strong relationship that the combat medic instructors are actually coming up to Chapel Hill campus doing rotations embedded with all of the medical school faculty. It is actually going a step beyond that now, because they now understand each other and understand the skills that they have.

UNC Chapel Hill—they do not currently have a physician assistant program—but we have a high need for rural emergency medicine professionals. And many of these men and women would love to live in North Carolina.

And so, UNC Chapel Hill is actually in the process of developing a P.A. program that factors in the combat medic experience so that they do not have to go all the way as another P.A. candidate would. That experience is factored in. They do not have to learn how to take a pulse on Day One.

Senator FRANKEN. You are kind of suggesting that people who deployed in the military in the last 13 years somehow may be more expert on emergency medical service than they are given credit for.

Ms. RHINEHARDT. Well, the chief of emergency medicine, if he were here, would tell you that he does probably three or four tracheotomies every couple of years. And the guys, the 18 Delta's probably do over 400 or 500.

Senator FRANKEN. OK. Thank you. I am out of time, but I would love to, Madam Chair, have a second round if I can.

Senator BALDWIN. I think we will be able to accommodate that.

Before I call on Senator Murphy, one of the distinctions between a roundtable and a formal hearing is that you, as witnesses, can react to one another's answers, et cetera. And I do not think we went over how you should seek that recognition, if you are interested. But because of Ms. Rhinehardt's deep background with the Senate, she already knew just where to put your nameplate and we will make sure to call on you.

Senator Murphy.

STATEMENT OF SENATOR MURPHY

Senator MURPHY. Thank you very much, Madam Chair.

We spend a lot of great time here talking about what happens when you are there at the college and how to best accommodate veterans. I wanted to spend my few minutes talking about how we help service members pick the right college.

We are really proud of what we have done in Connecticut as all my colleagues are. We have tuition waivers for veterans to attend our public universities. We have private, nonprofit universities like the University of New Haven which goes so far as to actually raise private dollars in an emergency fund to cover the gap that sometimes exists before the G.I. benefits kick-in.

But the reality is that 37 percent of post–9/11 G.I. bill benefits are not going to State universities or to private nonprofit universities; they are going to for-profit universities. And 50 percent of DoD tuition assistance—50 percent—is going to for-profit universities. Many of these universities do not have, as their primary motivating factor the education of veterans, but they have profit as their motivation. And we actually have an Executive order that the President released, No. 13607, in 2012 that would try to get our hands around this problem of often very troublesome targeting and marketing of these for-profit universities to veterans.

Dr. Langdon, your statistics are cautionary in the sense that we are proud of how many veterans are getting to school, but the fact that it is taking, on average, 7 years to get an Associate's Degree. Some of that, clearly, is for legitimate reasons and nontraditional students take longer, but part of that is probably because there are a lot of veterans that are not getting the right information about what the best school is for them.

So I wanted to ask this question, a broad one, to the panel and maybe start with Dr. Langdon and Ms. Thompson Starks. What could we be doing better to try to give veterans the information they need to pick the right choice, and should we not be worried about this huge transfer of benefits going to for-profit; which, as the committee's own report shows, are not delivering the same outputs for students that UVM, and the UNC's System, and the University of Connecticut System are?

Mr. LANGDON. Sir, very good question, and on behalf of DoD, as we approach it when we look at military tuition assistance, the thing that I must bring forward is, of course, the presidential Executive order that you have mentioned. From that, the Department of Defense has updated, just released on the 15th of May the new Department of Defense Education Partnership Memorandum of Understanding, MOU. In that, we addressed a lot of the issues that you are referring to.

For example, institutions providing education programs through DoD will provide meaningful information on financial attendance; will not use unfair and deceptive practices; implementation of rules to strengthen exiting procedures and access to installations, along those lines.

What we also realize is that we now have a robust interagency information sharing. At the installation level, as it is fed down through the services, the service members are counseled and they are talked about what their goals are and what they want to try to achieve.

And I submit to you this, a profile of a TA user, Tuition Assistance on active duty. They are a full-time worker, part-time student. As you say, they take an average of three courses per year and less than 1 percent ever reach their cap of that $4,500. The majority complete their education after leaving, and there are seven or eight more that go that way, to your point about 7 years.

Within this new construct, they now must have an education plan. It must be through a university or school that signs an MOU that has to meet specific accreditation requirements, which is national and regional accreditation. They must adhere to all the principles of excellence that has been outlined in order to receive, first receive, the tuition assistance dollars.

As we work through that now, the biggest changes are making sure that that service member has a vetted, approved plan, they stay on-plan, and it is something that they can translate.

One final point, sir. An active duty member may go to a lot of universities. The online venue is very attractive because a lot of the flagship or larger schools—UNC, whomever—is a campus-based program. And as you know, a lot of our service members, if they spend any time, they are going to move several times.

And so, they are taking coursework at universities that fit that schedule or that work life. But we have made huge strides in that matter.

Thank you, sir.

Senator MURPHY. Ms. Thompson Starks.

Ms. THOMPSON SPARKS. Thank you for an opportunity to respond.

The Department of Education starts from a philosophy that in order to help students make good choices, we have to give them information and tools that enable them to make quality decisions. We are doing a number of things to provide important information with respect to cost comparisons across colleges, financial aid strategies that students can use to reduce their debt, and also to select quality institutions.

A number of these efforts have been implemented through the Principles of Excellence Executive Order and our role working with our agency partners. We were working very closely with DoD and V.A. on the G.I. bill comparison tool which draws upon data from Education's IPEDS system, and we have also been involved, as you know, as I mentioned in my opening remarks, in the implementation of the financial aid shopping sheet, which is now being used by more than 2,000 institutions.

Through those efforts, we do hope that this is enabling students to make well-informed decisions about college options.

Senator MURPHY. Thanks.

Mr. Hubbard.

Mr. HUBBARD. Thank you, Senator. I would like to applaud the DoD and their Tuition Assistance Program for taking those steps. I think that is an active measure that is absolutely necessary.

I would also point to the comparison tool, which my colleague brought up. That comparison tool allows student veterans to make decisions on information, not guesses. That is very important. With the Million Records Project that Student Veterans of America published, which allowed a similar approach to make decisions for policymakers at the higher education level on veterans on data, not guesses. Anecdote is great, and that can point you in the right direction, but it is not something you can base a sound decision on.

I would also note that for an individual to go to the comparison tool to find the school that they are interested in, and then to take it a step further by actually contacting a Student Veterans of America chapter or veterans on that campus. That allows them a very clear, on the ground perspective that, I think, is absolutely critical. If you are not talking to veterans who are actually experiencing what is going on, on the ground, you might have a flawed assessment. I mean, you can have a lot of pretty pictures on a lot of nice-looking Web sites, but at the end of the day, if you are not talking to people who are in the actual experience themselves, you probably are not going to get a clear picture of what is going on.

I would applaud Senator Warren for her efforts on student debt. I think as individuals make better informed decisions, the student debt will come down. However, for the time being, this is still an important issue. People are going to schools that have false marketing practices and aggressively pursue veterans for their G.I. bill.

This results in them losing benefits because they are not getting a degree with that G.I. bill benefit that they are spending. As a result, they end up losing time with that G.I. bill and have to take out further debt.

Senator MURPHY. Mr. Carlson.

Mr. CARLSON. Thank you, Senator.

One of the things that I do as a part of my role at the University of Vermont is work very closely with perspective students who are incoming to the University and who are in that search process. And when I am speaking with a perspective student veteran who is deciding which school to attend, if the most important part of his or her decision-making process is, "How easy is it to use V.A. benefits here?" I think that is a problem.

I think that students should be choosing schools based on academic programs, support systems, proximity to family, or other personal reasons and not just based on how easily they perceive to be able to use V.A. benefits at that institution.

Senator BALDWIN. Senator Warren.

STATEMENT OF SENATOR WARREN

Senator WARREN. Thank you, Madam Chairman.

I am glad to hear about the work to help prospective students get critical information when they are making decisions about where to go to school. But we still have many who are in programs that are happy to take the military member's Federal benefits, but do not deliver on their promise of providing a good education.

And as we know, this is a serious problem for any student, but even worse for those who are using G.I. benefits. Once a veteran entrusts a college with those hard-earned benefits, there is no second chance if the school turns out to be of very poor quality.

Prior to this year, veterans and active duty military had few places to turn to share their stories and get help when they were mistreated by colleges.

In January, the Federal Government launched a system for veterans and members of the military to file complaints about bad experiences they had with colleges. The Complaint Portal is a collaboration among several Federal agencies, including the Department of Veterans Affairs, the Department of Defense, the Department of Education, and the Consumer Financial Protection Bureau.

My question is, Dr. Langdon, how does the DoD plan to use the data that you are collecting from complaints to improve the Tuition Assistance program?

Mr. LANGDON. Madam, it is a very good question. To caveat to my prior statement, not only must the schools be regionally and nationally accredited, but they also must be V.A. approved, and they also must be title IV approved.

There are many levels that we wanted to make sure that the service member, when they were going to school, that they were going to protect.

Senator WARREN. I understand about the front end. My question is you are collecting now a lot of complaint data.

Mr. LANGDON. Yes.

Senator WARREN. What I want to know is how do you plan to use the complaint data?

Mr. LANGDON. As we brought it into date, ma'am, we have had 146 complaints since January, complaints field since January when it was brought on. That is not a huge number, considering as the number that I have given you of 285,000.

What we are finding of that data, of those complaints, they are not actually complaints against a school per se. It is unknown policies or, "I did not know what a policy was." It was a process or policy procedure.

What we have realized, ma'am, is that we need to now start touching back with the universities, the ones that our students are going to and trying to help them understand what we are hearing and what we are finding about where the policies need to be, how the explanations need to go, just as to my colleague to the left here mentioned that before. It is easily accessible UNC on their policy. That is what we are using.

Senator WARREN. Just so I understand, sir.

Mr. LANGDON. Right.

Senator WARREN. At this point, your plan is to investigate each one of these complaints.

Mr. LANGDON. As they come in, yes.

Senator WARREN. As they come in. And let me just ask while we have this out here, Ms. Thompson Sparks, why does the Federal Government not collect complaints from all students?

Ms. THOMPSON SPARKS. I am not sure I have the specifics to answer that question. However, I will say that the collection of data is of utmost importance to us.

Senator WARREN. But how about complaint data?

Ms. THOMPSON SPARKS. The Department of Education is participating as part of the centralized complaint system. And to date, I do not have the exact number of complaints we have received, but I know it is feeding back into our understanding of how our title IV borrowers are utilizing their aid.

Senator WARREN. Mr. Hubbard.

Mr. HUBBARD. That is actually an excellent point, I think, Senator. And that is veterans are highlighting issues that have been occurring for individuals in higher education across the board. I think only until recently as these veterans have spoken out that these issues have surfaced.

For veterans, they have no problem, necessarily saying, "Hey, I have earned these benefits and they are being used poorly." I think to that end, we could encourage more veterans and more individuals in higher education to take similar steps.

Collecting data across the board for individuals in higher education? Extremely important. If we are not doing that, we are letting all individuals down. Veterans that go to school will be let down because their peers are being let down. The educational environment as a result is hurt, and that hurts everyone across the board.

Senator WARREN. Thank you.

Mr. Carlson.

Mr. CARLSON. Thank you, Senator.

One of the main complaints that I hear about the post–9/11 G.I. bill specifically is the ability for a veteran to separate from the military and then enter into a program that is V.A.-approved and is degree-seeking as a matriculated student at a school.

The post–9/11 G.I. bill will pay up to two terms while they are seeking continuing education courses to become matriculated, degree-seeking students. However, one of the real problems that I have run into is that at many schools, and University of Vermont is one of them, over the summer term there are many different meeting sessions with different beginning and end dates. And from the V.A. perspective, well for the University of Vermont, it is one semester. From V.A.'s perspective those are each separate terms.

I have students, when we think about nontraditional students and student veterans being some of the most nontraditional, we have individuals who entered UVM in the spring semester who are trying to be degree-seeking, matriculated students in the fall who can only get a portion of their summer course paid. And that is something that I have seen that is a real problem. It is a barrier to them becoming degree seeking students.

Senator WARREN. Ms. Rhinehardt.

Ms. RHINEHARDT. Yes, ma'am. We all sit here, with complaints about rising tuition and the cost of going to college. And as I listen to my fellow panelists—I heard, I do not know, on the fourth iteration of a DoD MOU or third. I lost track. The Department of Education is doing something, CFPB is doing something, the V.A. is doing something.

Back home in North Carolina, we have a lot of State legislators asking us, "Why do you have so much middle management?" Well, because we have to keep up with all of these processes and make sure we are inputting all these things to comply. Every minute that we are working to comply with multiple agencies that may or may not be coordinating, that is a minute that is taken away from serving the veteran.

Senator WARREN. I am sorry, Ms. Rhinehardt. I want to make sure I understand you. What we are talking about here is an established complaint system that has only been established since January, and it is there to take complaints directly from veterans or active duty service members who are having a problem with a college.

Are you saying that when we get a followup from the Department of Defense that they should not be following on those complaints to find out what the veteran's problem is with the college and whether or not the college is appropriately addressing it because it takes your time?

Ms. RHINEHARDT. No, ma'am. Actually, I did not address the complaint system at all.

Senator WARREN. That was what my question was about—the complaint system and whether we should have a complaint system. Not just for veterans and active duty military, but we should also have a complaint system for all students.

I want to make the point that having a complaint system in place is a powerful tool for accountability. In a little over 2 years the Consumer Financial Protection Bureau has handled nearly a quarter of a million complaints about financial products. Service members, veterans, and their families are only a small portion of those who have complained, but they have already recovered more than $1 million from financial institutions through this complaint system.

Every complaint, however, has been valuable because it tells an agency what kind of problems exist and where they exist and permits that agency to examine the institutions that are failing those they are supposed to serve.

Most recently, the CFPB complaint data formed the basis of a $97 million settlement against Sallie Mae for overcharging veterans on their student loans. We should take seriously the importance of developing robust complaint systems and using the data that come from those systems.

Thank you, Madam Chairman.

Senator BURR. Madam Chair, could I say to my colleague, there has been a complaint system that has been available to every student, not just to veterans. It is the accreditation agency. Any student, since I can remember, could file a complaint with the accrediting agency of that institution. And I am not saying that is prefect for veterans, but we have not been without a mechanism for students to complain to people who can affect whether the accreditation of that institution is intact or not.

Senator WARREN. I appreciate the Senator's comments about a complaint system that is in place. But when we have had the accreditors in here to talk about the process under which they consider accreditation and whether or not they actually take steps, I think we can conclude that it has not been a very effective process for making sure that students' complaints are heard or acted upon.

Senator BURR. My good friend raises a good question.

Senator BALDWIN. The Chair is here to call upon Senator Casey.

Senator BURR. My good friend raises a question that is the subject of debate for higher education reauthorization and I take it that way. But let me just be on the record, it does not take the Federal Government stepping in to create something. We should make sure that what we have got in place works and I support what DoD is doing. I think it is important for the veteran's program. But if we have got something that is broken, then let us make it work.

Senator BALDWIN. Senator Casey.

STATEMENT OF SENATOR CASEY

Senator CASEY. Thanks very much, and I appreciate the testimony of the panelists. I know I missed a lot of your testimony here today, but appreciate the work you have done to provide written testimony that we will benefit from. And I also appreciate the commitment that you have made on these issues.

When I consider what our obligations are to veterans, I think it starts with that basic understanding that I have often said is not good enough for us at the time of a military engagement to pray for veterans. It is also our obligation to make sure that we are worthy of their valor. And being worthy of their valor means getting the policy right, and that is what you are helping us with when it comes to helping veterans get their higher education and job readiness opportunities when they come back.

I need to do a little bragging for just a moment about my State, if you do not mind. We all do that at some point. We are all allowed to do this, but a couple of institutions that were ranked by "U.S. News & World Report" in November 2013 for their efforts on behalf of veterans and student veterans. Penn State was ranked No. 1 and Drexel University came in 12th. Temple and Duquesne were tied for 24th. I am pretty happy about that and I want to make sure they heard that I bragged about them. Maybe no one else has done that today.

There are some good models out there and we want to draw upon them and use them as templates.

One question I had, and I will start with Mr. Hubbard and then broaden it from there. You and your organization helped us put together legislation, the Veterans Education Counseling Act, which as its purpose to empower veterans seeking an education by making sure that they know they are entitled to basic education counseling.

A lot of this revolves around so-called Chapter 36 Education Counseling. Our bill asks the V.A. to make it clear the differentiation between the Chapter 36 education counseling and the so-called Chapter 31 Vocational Rehabilitation program.

We want to make sure that they are aware of what they are entitled to. That sounds almost elementary or self-evident, but as we know, often in Government sometimes even if you have a good policy in place, folks do not know about it because we do not often do a good job of telling them.

I want to start with you, Mr. Hubbard, about that concept in the bill, but also anything else that you hope we would do as it relates to not just policy on veterans education, but making sure that we can make sure that folks are aware of what benefits are there for them.

Mr. HUBBARD. Thank you, Senator.

I appreciate that. I will point out that Drexel was a recent Chapter of the Month for Student Veterans of America, so they are doing excellent things.

Senator CASEY. Thank you for helping me do my job. I appreciate that.

Mr. HUBBARD. That is what we are here for.

I believe that the 1-year out counseling is something that is critical. Counseling, in general, is obviously very important, but catching them 1 year out before they are end of active service, they are EAS, is critical.

We are not doing that as well as we should, and it does sound elementary that individuals would be informed about what they are entitled to. That does not always happen. It simply just does not happen in a lot of cases. I think that is just a product of the system. Not a lot of individuals, by the time it gets down to the unit level or even below to the individual level, it is just not happening.

That information is important for individuals to be able to actually make a clear, informed decision. If they do not have that information, who knows what is going to happen. They might say, "Well, I am not entitled to go to school." "Well, you just did 4 years in the Marine Corps. Of course you are."

A second point I would like to make is that of access. If you have the information to make the right decisions, that is obviously a precursor. But if you cannot access your benefits, if the system is too difficult to process it, if your claim gets lost, if an individual finally gets to the university but finds out they cannot afford it because they do not have in-State tuition, for example. You do not have that access and that is going to be a critical barrier.

A side note to that, that issue is something that we are critically looking at. If an individual racks up a lot of debt, they go through school. Maybe they did not get their degree, but they come out, now they cannot pursue a career. They have a difficult time paying off their bills, and this is something that we are very concerned about.

Senator CASEY. I may come back to that, but I know, Mr. Carlson, Ms. Rhinehardt.

Mr. CARLSON. Thank you, Senator.

Some of the work that I do with prospective students when I am sitting with a military veteran, and often their family, across the desk from me and I say, "Hey, it is great. You got Chapter 33 post– 9/11 G.I. bill. Do you know how that works and do you know how it works at the University of Vermont," because each institution of higher learning has some different policies and procedures in place. And a lot of times I hear, "Oh, yes. Absolutely. I know exactly what it pays."

Then I go through exactly what it will do, and sometimes there can be a little bit of a shock. There can be, ''Oh, I did not know that it did not cover out-of-State tuition." And more often it is very positive saying, "Wow, I did not know that it paid really that much and that I got this amazing housing allowance while I am engaged."

Whenever I have a student, a prospective student or a current student who does not understand their benefit entirely, I think it is very important that we begin that education process early in their separation period.

Senator CASEY. Just ask before moving on, what is the best delivery mechanism to do that? In other words, obviously, the V.A. But I want to get a better understanding of what is the problem here if that information is not transmitted to the veteran?

Mr. CARLSON. Yes, sir. I believe that a lot of information in the military is passed through peer experience and through peer engagement. There is a lot less of the texting, email, kind of things for the chain of command that comes down from the platoon commander to the squad leader to the individual Marine or soldier or airmen.

I think that implementing peer engagement along that point would be something that is very helpful.

Senator CASEY. OK. Yes.

Ms. RHINEHARDT. To brag on our Marines at Camp Lejeune a little bit. Their process, which I think is now a Marine Corps wide process, is that all new Marines on their very first day of coming in after they stand in the yellow footprints, and get their haircut, and figure out where they are is that they start their education pathway that day.

Senator CASEY. OK.

Ms. RHINEHARDT. They start to determine how their military career is going to factor into an eventual civilian career. And I know that my colleagues at Camp Lejeune were very instrumental in developing that pathway. So it is happening within the service branches and it is not perfect. Nothing is, but it is a really good start.

At the University of North Carolina, I would like to agree that with all of their points that transparency and information sharing is critical. That is why we have developed an online portal called the North Carolina Military Educational Positioning System. We want it to be a one-stop shop place for any student, veteran, spouse, or dependent to go in and use decision tree models to figure out, based on their own personal circumstances, here are your options to consider. We do not ever inform them of what the right option is. We just lead them to their ultimate choices. And they can save that under a personalized account. And we intentionally decided that we did not want this to be limited to just public institutions in the State. We understand that we cannot educate every citizen in the State of North Carolina. We need our private institutions to help us do that.

We want to make sure that the veteran or the service member has access to the institution that is right for them.

Senator CASEY. Thank you.

Ms. Starks. I will not ask anymore because we are getting close on time. We have two minutes.

Ms. THOMPSON STARKS. Thank you. We know how important counseling and early information is for all students to make important decisions about pursuing higher education. And I want to mention three action areas, in particular, that have been significant in the Department's contributions to support service members and veterans.

The first is working with our agency partners on the redesign of Transition GPS. The emphasis has really been on a military lifecycle model, which enables service members to get access to critical information before they are separating. This is really important. It is meeting service members at the point at which they are making important choices about the path to pursue after military service.

The second, I would like to mention that we have pursued, through our Office of Federal Student Aid, is a financial aid tool kit that includes information and resources, from fact sheets to how-to videos that are really targeted toward counselors and those that are working with students. We have also customized a guide for military service members and veterans to provide key information about their Federal benefits.

And third, I would like to mention that we are doing training and direct outreach to DoD's Transition GPS accessing higher education facilitators, which is really helping to build capacity on the ground, and provide the important information to their team.

Senator CASEY. Great. Thank you. Mr. Hubbard, you are on borrowed time.

Mr. HUBBARD. I know. Thank you, Senator. I appreciate that.

If I can actually just quickly emphasize a quick point that my colleague and fellow Devil Dog made and that is the peer experience. I think this touches on an absolutely critical point. While I do appreciate the institutional support and think that is a necessary precursor, without that, I think anything else is a moot point.

I will say that peer-to-peer access to information is probably the most important point in this conversation. That is how individuals, Marines, sailors, soldiers, and airmen, get their information from each other.

Senator CASEY. Yes.

Mr. HUBBARD. And so that is truly probably the most critical point.

Senator CASEY. Thank you very much.

Thank you, Senator Baldwin.

Ms. RHINEHARDT. Just to quickly respond. You can have all the advanced information in the world, so long as you know what your plan, what your outcome looks like. We have a lot of folks within the military who are receiving involuntary discharge orders. They do not realize they are not going to be in the military next year. They are not contemplating going to school at this moment. So we need to remember that there are a lot of folks out there that their lives have just changed and it is beyond their control.

Senator CASEY. Thank you.

Senator BALDWIN. I think we are going to do a quick second round and I will start with my own questions.

I would like to return to the Million Records Project. I understand SBA has been working in collaboration with the Department of Veterans Affairs and the National Student Clearinghouse on that project to help us, as policymakers and veterans and citizens, better understand the education and career outcomes of veterans.

And I also believe that, in order to help veterans and service members meet their goals, they have to have clear, outcome-driven information on which to base educational decisions.

Two years ago, when I was a member of the House of Representatives, I was proud to support both the Camp Lejeune Families Act and the Improving Transparency of Educational Opportunities for Veterans Act, both of which require reporting on educational outcomes for veterans by the Department of Defense and the Department of Veterans Affairs.

The Camp Lejeune Families Act required reporting on student outcomes such as certificate degree attainment, credit hours, and other qualifications earned. The Improving Transparency of Education Opportunities for Veterans Act of 2012 also required the V.A. to report on important metrics such as graduation rates, cohort default rates, median amount of debt, and many other metrics.

I have a twofold question. First, are there additional metrics that you think that policymakers and the Federal Government ought to be collecting in order to get a better idea of how our veterans and service members are progressing through higher education?

And second, how can we make this information on student outcomes, such as degree or certificate attainment or the financial metrics such as cohort default rates, readily available and much more easily digestible for students seeking that data?

I will start with you, Mr. Hubbard and then Ms. Rhinehardt.

Mr. HUBBARD. Thank you, Senator.

I think the Million Records Project was groundbreaking research. It was the first time in over 70 years that we actually had a clear picture of how veterans were doing in higher education.

This kind of research has not been done since World War II. Why it was not done previously? Hard to say, but it was a very difficult process to do. But we were happy and excited to be able to offer that to policymakers, such as those in the Senate.

This data-driven approach is something that we take very seriously at Student Veterans of America. We do not base decisions on whim or anecdote. We base decisions on the data. We look at the data for our thoughts.

I think that schools could do a lot to compare themselves to this data. We did not necessarily look at institutional level data. We looked at a broad understanding to get a baseline across the 10 years of G.I. bill use.

I think institutions, if they were to compare themselves and make sure that they are tracking that data, tracking their own outcomes of veterans, they could look inward and figure out, are they doing better, worse, what is working, what is not.

That is something that we are also looking at in phase 2 of the Million Records Project to understand the qualitative reason for the outcomes that we are seeing. Figure out what we can do to perhaps improve those numbers.

To your point about additional metrics, I think in our phase 2, we are looking at several different features like Vet Success on Campus. Is that working? What are the outcomes of that, the impact of that on student education?

And then also in terms of loans, I think that is something that we are also very interested in. There is currently no way for an individual to have an aggregated view of their current debt or loans that they have. You have the Department of Education's loans and Federal loans that are out there. You also have private loans and those two do not necessarily talk.

If we can come up with an approach that would aggregate this information, it would allow universities to have a better understanding of how their students are doing, and it would also allow individuals to have a better understanding of how they are doing.

Currently, the only system we know out there that does this is the National Student Clearinghouse's Meteor Program. This is something that we are very interested in and think could benefit students widely.

Senator BALDWIN. Senator Burr.

Senator BURR. Thanks, Senator Baldwin.

Ms. Starks, since Senator Warren brought up the Sallie Mae settlement, may I ask you some questions?

Pamela Moran was employed by the Department of Education's Office of Postsecondary Education here in the summer of 2011. Are you familiar with her June 9, 2011 letter, in her capacity as a Department official to the Consumer Bankers Association Education Finance Council, the National Council of Higher Education, and the Student Loan Servicing Alliance responding to their request for clarification regarding SCRA compliance and proper treatment of veterans? Where she said,

"We agree that when a member of the military does not clearly specify an end date for their service, that is a reasonable approach to interpreting the service dates on military orders to identify the start and end dates for the interest relief rate relief."

Are you familiar with that letter?

Ms. THOMPSON STARKS. No, sir. I do not have that letter. Senator BURR. Are you familiar with the letter?

Ms. THOMPSON STARKS. No, I am not.

Senator BURR. Do you consider a letter from Ms. Moran to be as an authority within the Department of Education providing guidance to the student loan industry representatives to say that there is a start and an end date must be present in a service member's request in order for a lender to grant the request?

Ms. THOMPSON STARKS. Sir, thank you for the question.

Since I am not familiar with that letter, and do not have the letter with me, I will just say that I know that this is an issue that we are taking very seriously.

Senator BURR. But that was the Department's policy. That was the guidance that they gave to lenders. Do you agree with that?

Ms. THOMPSON STARKS. I am sorry. I cannot comment on that.

Senator BURR. Is this an issue that the Department has said that, as a matter of fact, they announced it would issue guidance for student loan servicers clarifying this contradictory guidance that have been issuing to the field from what the Department of Justice and FDIC have been putting out in the field.

Is this a guidance that is being reconsidered currently at the Department of Education?

Ms. THOMPSON STARKS. I will say that we are taking steps working closely with the Department of Justice to ensure accountability and that our service members are getting the 6 percent interest rate cap to which they are entitled.

I do know that we are directing all of our servicers to match borrow portfolios to the DoD–SCRA data base, which should ensure that eligibility is determined more quickly and that paperwork burdens are reduced.

I will also say that as we are conducting these reviews, we are preparing additional guidance to try to streamline borrower processes and provide additional clarifications as to what our expectations are. We take this very, very seriously and know that serving our borrowers is of our utmost and highest priority.

Senator BURR. Ms. Starks, I think the Department has said publicly, ''We are going to clarify our guidance because of this decision,'' which means that their interpretation was it was not clear.

It seems the Department could provide more guidance to servicers by clearing up the differences between active duty personnel as defined under the Higher Education Act whereas the SCRA provides benefits for members during periods of military service creating a distinction between reservists and active duty personnel overall.

So which statute is accurate in your determination, the Higher Education Act or the SCRA? And to whom does the 6 percent interest rate benefit accrue to?

Ms. THOMPSON STARKS. Sir, I very much appreciate your questions and I would be very glad to take those questions back and provide a response for the record.

Senator BURR. I appreciate that and I think I have made the point that this is why it is difficult for servicers to provide these products because we cannot get clarity on whether you fall this way or that way.

And I would just say to my colleague who, since we are the last Indians here, it is important that not only Congress be specific in the legislation we write. It is absolutely crucial that the agencies in their guidance provide accurate, thoughtful guidance. This is not something we should let the Department of Justice determine in the end and penalize somebody because of the guidance that they got from an agency of the Federal Government.

I thank the Chair.

Senator BALDWIN. I thank Senator Burr for co-chairing this roundtable with me. I want to thank the participants for, first of all, those of you who have served, thank you for your service. Thank you for your participation today. Your testimony is very helpful to us.

I request that the record remain open for 10 business days for members to submit statements and additional questions for the record.

I appreciate the participation of my colleagues.

And with that, the committee will stand adjourned.

[Whereupon, at 11:43 a.m., the hearing was adjourned.]

In: Higher Education
Editor: Lilian Wieck

ISBN: 978-1-53616-026-0
© 2019 Nova Science Publishers, Inc.

Chapter 4

HIGHER EDUCATION: CHARACTERISTICS OF GRADUATE PLUS BORROWERS*

United States Government Accountability Office

April 17, 2018

The Honorable Mike Lee Vice
Chairman

Joint Economic Committee
United States Senate

The Honorable Bill Cassidy
United States Senate

The Honorable Tom Cotton
United States Senate

To help students and their families pay for higher education, the Department of Education (Education) provides billions of dollars in federal student loans each year through programs authorized under Title IV of the Higher Education Act of 1965, as amended.[1] As of September 2017, over 42 million borrowers held nearly $1.4 trillion in

---

* This is an edited, reformatted and augmented version of United States Government Accountability Office; Briefing to Congressional Requesters, Publication No. GAO-18-392R, dated March 20, 2018.
[1] Pub. L. No. 89-329, §§ 401-467, 79 Stat. 1219, 1232-1254 (codified as amended at 20 U.S.C. §§ 1070-1099d).

federal student loans. Graduate students have been eligible for Graduate PLUS (Grad PLUS) loans to help finance their education since July 1, 2006.[2] Grad PLUS loans are not need-based and students can borrow up to the cost of attendance, such as tuition, fees, and room and board, minus any other estimated financial assistance.[3] Grad PLUS loans are also different than many other federal student loans because they do not have fixed annual or aggregate—referred to in this chapter as "lifetime"—limits.

Education currently offers a variety of repayment plans for federal student loan borrowers, including, among others, the Standard plan and several Income-Driven Repayment plans. Income-Driven Repayment is an umbrella term that describes a number of repayment plans available to eligible borrowers that primarily base payment amounts on a borrower's income, and extend repayment periods from the typical 10 years under the Standard plan to 20 or 25 years, with any remaining balance forgiven at the end of the loan repayment period. Since 2009, several Income-Driven Repayment plans have been made available to borrowers, and these plans may help reduce some of the challenges borrowers face in repaying their loans.[4] Grad PLUS borrowers may choose to participate in Income-Driven Repayment plans if the borrower and the loans meet the applicable criteria.

Education also offers the Public Service Loan Forgiveness program, which allows borrowers, including those with eligible Grad PLUS loans, to have their loans forgiven after 10 years of qualifying payments if they meet certain requirements. To receive loan forgiveness, borrowers must participate in a qualifying repayment plan and make 120 on-time monthly payments while employed full-time in a public service job.[5] Borrowers were first eligible to start making qualifying payments under the Public Service Loan Forgiveness program in 2007. The first potentially eligible borrowers began applying for forgiveness in 2017.

You asked us to review issues related to Grad PLUS loans and borrowers. This chapter examines (1) what is known about Grad PLUS borrowers and the loan repayment plans they use to manage their debt, and (2) how the addition of loan limits might affect the number and type of borrowers, and the amount of money awarded for Grad PLUS loans.

To address both objectives, we analyzed data from Education's National Student Loan Data System, a database with information on federal student loan borrowers. We used National Student Loan Data System data on Grad PLUS borrowers from award years 2007

---

[2] 20 U.S.C. § 1078-2. The Graduate PLUS loan program was created by the Higher Education Reconciliation Act of 2005, which modified a pre-existing program—the Parent PLUS loan—to include graduate students. See Pub. L. No. 109-171, § 8005(c), 120 Stat. 4, 158-59 (2006).

[3] Cost of attendance is an estimate of a student's educational expenses for one period of enrollment (such as an academic year). Cost of attendance includes, among other things, tuition and fees, books and supplies, room and board, transportation, and other miscellaneous personal expenses (e.g., the cost of purchasing a personal computer). See 20 U.S.C. § 1087ll.

[4] GAO, Federal Student Loans: Education Needs to Improve Its Income-Driven Repayment Plan Budget Estimates, GAO-17-22 (Washington, D.C.: November 15, 2016).

[5] 20 U.S.C. § 1087e(m); 34 C.F.R. § 685.219. Qualifying repayment plans include the Income-Driven Repayment plans and the Standard plan. Public service jobs include, among others, full-time jobs in government or at a tax-exempt nonprofit organization.

(July 1, 2006- June 30, 2007) through 2017 (July 1, 2016-June 30, 2017).[6] We also analyzed data from Education's 2012 Baccalaureate and Beyond survey, a nationally representative longitudinal survey of students' education and work experiences following completion of a bachelor's degree. The 2012 data set includes students who completed bachelor's degree requirements in the 2007-2008 academic year. We selected this data set because it was the most recent Baccalaureate and Beyond data available and the only Baccalaureate and Beyond data that captured students with Grad PLUS loans. The survey sample includes 1,239 Grad PLUS borrowers, and results are weighted estimates.[7] To assess the reliability of the National Student Loan Data System and the Baccalaureate and Beyond data sets we reviewed data documentation, and, for the National Student Loan Data System data set, interviewed agency officials knowledgeable about these data. Because the Baccalaureate and Beyond data are of a sample (rather than the entire population) of Grad PLUS borrowers, we express precision of the results produced from the analysis of these data at the 95 percent confidence level. We found that both of the data sets were sufficiently reliable for our purposes in describing the characteristics of Grad PLUS borrowers, the repayment plans they use to manage their debt, and how the addition of loan limits might affect Grad PLUS borrowers.

We also modeled three scenarios with varying graduate borrowing and income amounts. The three scenarios were based on the 2012 data set of Education's Baccalaureate and Beyond survey data to portray a range of hypothetical borrowers. These simulations are intended for illustrative purposes.[8] Additionally, we analyzed National Student Loan Data System data to describe the effect of hypothetical Grad PLUS loan limits. These loan limits were selected to illustrate a range of alternatives for our analysis. To identify the effect of loan limits, we tested annual loan limits—or limits on the amount that individuals can borrow in 1 year—of $10,000, $20,000, and $25,000, and lifetime loan limits—or

---

[6] For borrowers who consolidated their Grad PLUS loans with one or more other federal loans into a single, new "consolidation" loan, we did not analyze actions—such as defaults or changes to repayment plans—that occurred after the consolidation took place. Fewer than 25 percent of Grad PLUS borrowers consolidated their Grad PLUS loans, which represented less than 25 percent of overall Grad PLUS disbursements. The figures we present from the National Student Loan Data System data set have been rounded.

[7] All percentage estimates presented are plus or minus 5 percentage points unless otherwise noted.

[8] We calculated total repayment for each scenario under the Standard plan and three Income-Driven Repayment plans– Income-Based Repayment, New Income-Based Repayment, and Pay As You Earn–to focus on plans with income-eligibility requirements. For the applicable requirements for these three Income-Driven Repayment plans, see 34 C.F.R. § 685.209(a) (Pay As You Earn) and 34 C.F.R. §§ 682.215, 685.221 (Income-Based Repayment and New Income-Based Repayment). Due to similar requirements, New Income-Based Repayment and Pay As You Earn produced identical results in our models, so we grouped those plans together. For these models, we utilized interest rates from award year 2018, assumed that borrowers were unmarried and had no dependents, and matched other assumptions to those used by Education's online student loan repayment calculator. These assumptions include that federal poverty guidelines would follow the Congressional Budget Office's inflation projections, and that borrowers would experience 5 percent annual income growth. We also assumed that all of the borrowers' student loan debt was eligible for the relevant repayment program and that borrowers were eligible for the Public Service Loan Forgiveness program. Finally, the available survey data we used to inform our assumptions about borrower income after attaining a degree only included data on earned income rather than adjusted gross income (which is used to calculate payment amounts for our three selected Income-Driven Repayment plans). This may cause our income assumptions to be slightly higher than the income information Education uses in determining income-based repayment amounts for certain borrowers.

limits on the amount that individuals can borrow in a lifetime—of $50,000, $100,000, and $125,000. For both types of limits, we calculated the number of borrowers who would be affected and summed the amount of Grad PLUS funding they collectively would not have been able to borrow given those respective limits.[9] For this analysis, we assumed that borrowers over a hypothetical limit would have instead borrowed up to the limit, and we counted any amount above that limit as funds that would not have been awarded.

We conducted this performance audit from January 2017 to April 2018 in accordance with generally accepted government auditing standards. Those standards require that we plan and perform the audit to obtain sufficient, appropriate evidence to provide a reasonable basis for our findings and conclusions based on our audit objectives. We believe that the evidence obtained provides a reasonable basis for our findings and conclusions based on our audit objectives.

On March 20, 2018, we briefed your staff on the preliminary results of this study. This chapter formally conveys the information provided during this briefing, as summarized below (see enclosure I for the briefing slides).

- Grad PLUS borrowers: As of June 30, 2017, the median Grad PLUS borrower had taken out over $140,000 in federal student loans (including Grad PLUS, undergraduate, and other graduate loans).[10] Nearly $27,000 of that amount was Grad PLUS loans. From award years 2007 through 2017, Education disbursed $71 billion in Grad PLUS loans to 1.7 million unique borrowers, with borrowing amounts per borrower of $5,000 (10th percentile of borrowers) to $98,554 (90th percentile of borrowers). To manage their debt, the majority of Grad PLUS borrowers in repayment status as of June 2017 used the Standard 10-year repayment plan. As of June 2017, 36 percent of Grad PLUS borrowers in repayment status had ever participated in an Income-Driven Repayment plan. As of June 2017, 11 percent of Grad PLUS borrowers in repayment status had been certified as eligible for Public Service Loan Forgiveness. As of March 2017, 2 percent of borrowers had defaulted on at least one Grad PLUS loan.[11] The most common degree types pursued by Grad PLUS borrowers are master's degrees and doctoral professional practice degrees.[12] In each of the three hypothetical scenarios

---

[9] For annual loan limits, we calculated the number of borrowers who had borrowed more than each of the respective limits in any given award year.

[10] On average, Grad PLUS borrowers had taken out $178,418 in federal student loans (including Grad PLUS, undergraduate, and other graduate loans) as of June 30, 2017. In comparison, during the same time period (award years 2007-2017), borrowers who took out one or more federal loans for undergraduate studies but did not take out loans for graduate studies had borrowed an average of approximately $16,300 in federal student loans, according to Education.

[11] In comparison, the default rate was 22 percent among borrowers who had taken out one or more federal undergraduate loans but no graduate loans during the same time period (July 2006-March 2017), according to Education data.

[12] Doctoral professional practice degrees include, for example, chiropractic, dentistry, law, medicine, optometry, osteopathic medicine, pharmacy, podiatry, and veterinary medicine.

we reviewed, Grad PLUS borrowers who were in Income-Driven Repayment plans would pay back less with Public Service Loan Forgiveness than otherwise. If borrowers were not enrolled in Public Service Loan Forgiveness, in some cases they would pay back more under Income-Driven Repayment plans than under the Standard plan.

- Loan limits: The lowest annual Grad PLUS loan limit we modeled—$10,000— would have reduced awards to over 1.2 million borrowers and decreased overall disbursements by $41.6 billion. The highest annual limit we modeled—$25,000— would have reduced awards to more than 600,000 borrowers and decreased disbursements by $16.5 billion. Based on available survey data, the largest groups of borrowers who would be affected by our hypothetical lifetime limits would be those in doctoral professional practice programs and those in law and health-related fields of study.

AGENCY COMMENTS

We provided a draft of this chapter to the Department of Education (Education) for its review and comment. In an e-mail dated March 28, 2018, an Education official indicated that Education had no comments.

Melissa Emrey-Arras,
Director, Education, Workforce, and Income Security Issues

BRIEFING TO CONGRESSIONAL REQUESTERS, MARCH 20, 2018

Agenda

- Objective
- Background
- Scope and Methodology
- Findings

Objectives

- What is known about Graduate PLUS borrowers and the loan repayment plans they use to manage their debt?
- How might the addition of loan limits affect the number and type of borrowers, and the amount of money awarded for Graduate PLUS loans?

Background

- Graduate PLUS (Grad PLUS) loans have been available to borrowers since July 1, 2006. These loans are not need-based and students can borrow up to the cost of attendance (such as tuition and room and board) minus any other estimated financial assistance.
- Grad PLUS loans have higher interest rates and loan origination fees than other federal student loans.[13]
- In addition to Grad PLUS loans, a borrower may receive up to $20,500 annually in unsubsidized Stafford loans, or up to $138,500 total in subsidized and unsubsidized Stafford loans, including loans received for undergraduate study. Subsidized loans are loans for which borrowers are generally not responsible for paying interest while in school or during certain grace and deferment periods; on unsubsidized loans, borrowers must ultimately pay all interest.
- The Department of Education (Education) offers a variety of repayment plans for Grad PLUS borrowers, including the Standard plan and several Income-Driven Repayment plans. The Standard plan generally has a repayment period of 10 years. Unlike the Standard plan, Income-Driven Repayment plans set repayment amounts based on borrower income and offer loan forgiveness after 20 or 25 years, depending on the plan.
- Borrowers in Income-Driven Repayment plans who work in public service may be eligible to participate in the Public Service Loan Forgiveness program. These borrowers may have their outstanding loan balances forgiven after 120 monthly payments in eligible plans.

Scope and Methodology

To address our objectives, we analyzed:

---

[13] Interest rates for loans first disbursed from July 1, 2017 to June 30. 2018 are 4.45 percent (undergraduate Stafford), 6 percent (graduate Stafford), and 7 percent (Grad PLUS). Origination fees for loans first disbursed from Oct. 1, 2017 to Sept. 30, 2018 are 1.066 percent (Stafford) and 4.264 percent (Grad PLUS).

National Student Loan Data System Data

- The National Student Loan Data System is an Education database with information about federal student loan borrowers.
- We used the portion of the National Student Loan Data System that encompasses all Grad PLUS borrowers, and includes Grad PLUS borrowing data from award years 2007 (July 1, 2006-June 30, 2007) through 2017 (July 1, 2016-June 30, 2017). The figures we present from this data set have been rounded.
- For borrowers who consolidated their Grad PLUS loans with one or more other federal loans into a single new "consolidation" loan, we did not analyze actions, such as defaults or changes to repayment plans, that occurred after the consolidation took place. As of March 2017, fewer than 25 percent of Grad PLUS borrowers consolidated their Grad PLUS loans, and those who did represented less than 25 percent of overall Grad PLUS disbursements.

Baccalaureate and Beyond Survey Data

- Baccalaureate and Beyond is a nationally representative longitudinal survey of students' education and work experiences post-bachelor's degree undertaken by Education; the 2012 data set includes students who completed bachelor's degree requirements in the 2007-2008 academic year.[14]
- A 2012 survey sample includes 1,239 Grad PLUS borrowers. Results are estimates. All percentage estimates presented are +/- 5 percentage points, unless otherwise indicated.[15]

Hypothetical Borrower Scenarios

- To estimate repayment outcomes under certain student loan repayment plans, we modeled three scenarios with differing graduate borrowing and income amounts based on Education's survey data to portray a range of hypothetical borrowers from the beginning of repayment until the loans are paid off or forgiven.[16]
- We calculated total repayment amounts for each scenario under the Standard plan and three Income-Driven Repayment plans—Income-Based Repayment, New Income-Based Repayment, and Pay As You Earn—to focus on Income-Driven Repayment plans with income-eligibility requirements.[17]

---

[14] We selected this data set because it was the most recent Baccalaureate and Beyond data available and the only Baccalaureate and Beyond data that captured students with Grad PLUS loans.

[15] We express precision of the results at the 95 percent confidence level.

[16] These data came from the 2012 data set of Education's Baccalaureate and Beyond survey.

[17] Due to similar requirements, New Income-Based Repayment and Pay As You Earn produced identical results in our models, so we grouped those plans together.

- For these models, we utilized interest rates from award year 2018, assumed that borrowers were unmarried and had no dependents, and matched other assumptions to those used by Education's online student loan repayment calculator. These assumptions, which we built into our models, include that federal poverty guidelines would follow the Congressional Budget Office's inflation projections and that borrowers would experience 5 percent annual income growth. We also assumed borrowers were eligible for the Public Service Loan Forgiveness program.

We conducted this performance audit from January 2017 to April 2018 in accordance with generally accepted government auditing standards. Those standards require that we plan and perform the audit to obtain sufficient, appropriate evidence to provide a reasonable basis for our findings and conclusions based on our audit objectives. We believe that the evidence obtained provides a reasonable basis for our findings and conclusions based on our audit objectives.

Summary of Findings

- As of June 2017, the median Grad PLUS borrower had taken out over $140,000 in federal student loans overall—including nearly $27,000 in Grad PLUS loans.[18]
  - Of Grad PLUS borrowers in repayment status, less than 40 percent had ever participated in Income-Driven Repayment plans, and a smaller proportion have been certified as eligible for Public Service Loan Forgiveness.
- Over award years 2007-2017, the lowest Grad PLUS annual loan limits we modeled—$10,000—would have reduced awards to 1.2 million unique borrowers and decreased overall federal student loan disbursements by $41.6 billion.
  - Based on available survey data, the largest groups of borrowers who would be affected by certain lifetime limits would be those in doctoral professional practice programs and those in law and health-related fields of study.[19]

Sources: GAO analysis of data from the National Student Loan Data System and Baccalaureate and Beyond survey.

Overview of Grad PLUS Borrowing

- According to our data analysis, $71 billion was disbursed to 1.7 million unique borrowers from award years 2007 through 2017.

---

[18] The $140,000 figure is for all federal student loans, including those from both undergraduate and graduate studies.
[19] Doctoral professional practice degrees include, for example, chiropractic, dentistry, law, medicine, optometry, osteopathic medicine, and pharmacy.

Table 1. Grad PLUS Loan Amounts per Borrower (as of June 2017)

	Average	10th percentile	Median	90th Percentile
Disbursed	$41,530	$5,000	$26,863	$98,554
Outstanding	$32,670	$0	$10,857	$97,229

- *Income-Driven Repayment:* As of June 2017 36 percent of Grad PLUS borrowers in repayment status had ever been in an Income-Driven Repayment plan.
- *Public Service Loan Forgiveness*: As of June 2017 11 percent of Grad PLUS borrowers in repayment status had been certified as eligible for Public Service Loan Forgiveness.
- *Default:* As of March 2017 2 percent of borrowers had defaulted on at least one Grad PLUS loan. In comparison the default rate was 22 percent among borrowers who had taken out one or more federal undergraduate loans but no graduate loans during the same time period (July 2006-March 2017) according to Education data.

Source: GAO analysis of data from the National Student Loan Data System. Notes: "Disbursed" amounts include only the funds that students received. In contrast, "outstanding"amounts include principal (disbursed funds) and interest minus loan payments borrowers had made as of June 30, 2017. This is why outstanding amounts may be less than disbursed amounts. Default rates exclude defaults that occurred after loans were consolidated.

Total Federal Borrowing by Grad PLUS Borrowers

- Virtually all Grad PLUS borrowers (99.9 percent) have other federal student loans.
- From award years 2007-2017, disbursements from all federal student loans totaled $306 billion, with an outstanding balance of $229 billion as of June 2017 (see figure).
- Disbursements per borrower:
  - o Average: $178,418
  - o 10th percentile: $56,865
  - o Median: $140,950
  - o 90th percentile: $347,887
- Outstanding balance per borrower:
  - o 10th percentile: $0 (loans repaid)
  - o Median: $110,830
  - o 90th percentile: $281,944

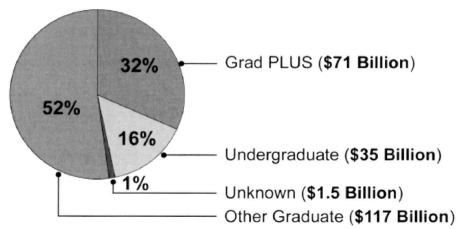

Source. GAO analysis of U.S. Department of Education's National Student Loan Data System. I GAO-18-392R Notes: Excludes $79 billion in loans that have been consolidated, which can include loans from undergraduate and/or graduate studies. All figures have been rounded to the nearest billion. Percentages may not sum to 100% due to rounding.

Total Federal Student Loan Disbursements to Graduate PLUS Borrowers, Award Years 2007-2017.

Academic Characteristics of Grad PLUS Borrowers

Table 2. Selected Degree Programs in which Grad PLUS Borrowers Enrolled

Degree Program	Percent Enrolled
Master's Degree	49%
Doctoral Degree - Professional Practice (e.g., Medicine, Law, Dentistry)	43%
Doctoral Degree - Research/Scholarship	4%

Table 3. Selected Fields of Study in which Grad PLUS Borrowers Enrolled

Field of Study	Percent Enrolled
Legal professions and studies	29%
Health professions and related sciences	26%
Business, management, and marketing	9%
Education	8%

Source: GAO analysis of data from Baccalaureate and Beyond survey.

Note: The data in these tables represent the highest degree program that borrowers had enrolled in, as of 2012, after completing their bachelor's degrees.

- In comparison, during the same time period (award years 2007-2017), borrowers who took out one or more federal loans for undergraduate studies but did not take out loans for graduate studies had borrowed an average of approximately $16,300 in federal student loans, according to Education.

Impact of Income-Driven Repayment Plans on Hypothetical Borrowers

Key Takeaways

Table 4. Impact of Income-Driven Repayment Plans and Public Service Loan Forgiveness (PSLF) on Hypothetical Borrowers

Borrower 1: Total Graduate Borrowing - $24,800 (Grad PLUS - $4,800), Initial Adjusted Gross Income - $21,000		
Repayment plan	Estimated Repayment	Estimated Repayment with PSLF
10-Year Standard	$33,329	$33,329
Income-Based Repayment	$51,849	$9,405 -1
New Income-Based Repayment/Pay As You Earn	$23,771	$6,270
Borrower 2: Total Graduate Borrowing - $82,000 (Grad PLUS - $25,000), Initial Adjusted Gross Income - $45,000		
Repayment plan	Estimated Repayment	Estimated Repayment with PSLF
10-Year Standard	$110,751	$110,751
Income-Based Repayment	$168,669	$54,685
New Income-Based Repayment/ Pay As You Earn	$103,129	$36,457
Borrower 3: Total Graduate Borrowing - $195,000 (Grad PLUS - $89,000), Initial Adjusted Gross Income - $95,000		
Repayment plan	Estimated Repayment	Estimated Repayment with PSLF
10-Year Standard	$265,168	$265,168
Income-Based Repayment	$377,953	$149,019
New Income-Based Repayment/ Pay As You Earn	$268,459	$99,346

Source: GAO analysis of data from Baccalaureate and Beyond survey. Note: Income-Based Repayment resulted in higher payments for the scenarios because borrowers pay 15 percent of discretionary income for up to 25 years, while under New Income-Based Repayment and Pay As You Earn borrowers pay 10 percent of discretionary income for up to 20 years.

- In each of the hypothetical scenarios we modeled, borrowers who were in Income-Driven Repayment plans would pay back less if they participated in Public Service Loan Forgiveness.[20]
- If borrowers were not enrolled in Public Service Loan Forgiveness, in some cases, they would pay back more under the Income-Driven Repayment plans than under the Standard plan.

Effect of Hypothetical Grad PLUS Loan Limits

Table 5. Effect of Hypothetical Grad PLUS Loan Limits on Borrowers, Award Years 2007-2017

Hypothetical Loan Limits	Number of Borrowers with Grad PLUS Loans Above Limit	Amount Not Awarded
$125,000 Lifetime	90,449 (5% of all Grad PLUS borrowers)	$4,028,534,070
$100,000 Lifetime	164,592 (10%)	$7,129,139,076
$50,000 Lifetime	502,597 (29%)	$22,387,424,998
Hypothetical Loan Limits	Number of Borrowers with Grad PLUS Loans Above Limit in at Least One Academic Year	Amount Not Awarded
$25,000 Annual	635,733 (37%)	$16,539,786,840
$20,000 Annual	801,298 (47%)	$22,894,630,371
$10,000 Annual	1,223,354 (71%)	$41,647,546,107

Source: GAO analysis of data from the National Student Loan Data System. Notes: Lifetime loan limits would restrict the cumulative amount of student borrowing (referred to by Education as "aggregate limits"). Annual loan limits would restrict the academic year amount of student borrowing.

- The lowest hypothetical annual loan limit on Grad PLUS that we modeled ($10,000) would have reduced the amount 1.2 million borrowers received and decreased overall federal disbursements by $41.6 billion. To determine the amount not awarded, we assumed that borrowers over a hypothetical limit would instead have borrowed up to the limit; we counted any amount over that limit as funds that would not have been awarded.

Key Characteristics of Borrowers Above Hypothetical Grad PLUS Loan Limits

Below we provide data on the *degree types* and *fields of study* for Grad PLUS borrowers above certain borrowing amounts. Because some borrowers had not completed

---

[20] We estimated what borrowers would pay with and without Public Service Loan Forgiveness.

their programs at the time of the 2012 survey, we examined borrowers who had attained a degree, as well as borrowers who were still enrolled in graduate school.

Borrowers with more than $100,000 in Grad PLUS loans

- Of those who had *attained* a degree
  - o 96 percent received a doctoral professional practice degree [CI: 87% to 100%]
  - o 77 percent studied Legal Professions and Studies [CI.49% to 94%]
- Among those still *enrolled* at the time of survey follow-up, at least one-third studied Health Professions and Related Sciences [CI: 34% to 85%]

Borrowers with more than $50,000 in Grad PLUS loans (including borrowers with over $100,000 in Grad PLUS loans)

- Of those who had *attained* a degree
  - o 71 percent received a doctoral professional practice degree [CI: 59% to 81%]
  - o 59 percent studied Legal Professions and Studies [CI: 46% to 71%]
- Among those still *enrolled* at the time of survey follow-up, 47 percent studied Legal Professions and Studies [CI: 32% to 62%] and 37 percent studied Health Professions and Related Sciences [CI: 25% to 51%].

Source: GAO analysis of data from Baccalaureate and Beyond survey. Notes: All percentages are estimates. Figures in brackets are 95 percent confidence intervals. Some confidence intervals are particularly wide due to the small sample of respondents who had borrowed above these limits.

In: Higher Education
Editor: Lilian Wieck

ISBN: 978-1-53616-026-0
© 2019 Nova Science Publishers, Inc.

Chapter 5

STRENGTHENING MINORITY SERVING INSTITUTIONS: BEST PRACTICES AND INNOVATIONS FOR STUDENT SUCCESS[*]

Committee on Health, Education, Labor, and Pensions

Tuesday, May 13, 2014
U.S. Senate,
Committee on Health, Education, Labor, and Pensions,
Washington, DC.

The committee met, pursuant to notice, at 10 a.m., in room SD– 430, Dirksen Senate Office Building, Hon. Kay Hagan presiding.

Present: Senators Hagan, Murray, Casey, Warren, Alexander, Paul, Burr, and Scott.

OPENING STATEMENT OF SENATOR HAGAN

Senator HAGAN. The Senate Committee on Health, Education, Labor, and Pensions will now come to order. Today's hearing is titled Strengthening Minority Serving Institutions: Best Practices and Innovations for Student Success. I want to thank all of our witnesses for coming today from all over the country. It's truly a pleasure having you here, and I look forward to hearing your testimony.

---

[*] This is an edited, reformatted and augmented version of Hearing of the Committee on Health, Education, Labor, And Pensions United States Senate, One Hundred Thirteenth Congress, Second Session, Publication No. S. HRG. 113–835, dated May 13, 2014.

I want to thank Senator Paul, who will be here soon, for serving as the Ranking Member today and for all of the work he and his staff have done for this hearing.

Senator Alexander, thank you for being here.

Senator ALEXANDER. Thank you.

Senator HAGAN. This marks the ninth hearing that the HELP Committee has convened in advance of the Higher Education Act reauthorization. This morning, we are here to discuss the unique challenges facing our minority serving institutions and to learn about programs and support to help facilitate student success. I'm very excited to be able to hold a hearing on this topic, as I have been a strong supporter of minority serving institutions since before I came to the U.S. Senate.

My State of North Carolina is home to 10 historically black colleges and universities, or HBCUs. I have visited many of these campuses across the State, and I have seen first-hand the great work that they are doing to prepare students for the world ahead.

Last year, I hosted a summit with chancellors and presidents from North Carolina's HBCUs to discuss their unique challenges and ways we could strengthen the schools. It was an informative and productive conversation, and I'll discuss some of the ideas that came as a result of that meeting a little later.

While I'm very familiar with HBCUs because of their strong presence in North Carolina, I'm excited to be discussing all minority serving institutions. Today's conversation on the role these institutions play in our higher education system could not have come at a better time.

According to the 2012 U.S. census, it's estimated that by 2050, the United States will have no clear racial or ethnic majority. All of our institutions will soon be looking toward these institutions that we have here today to learn how to best serve their increasingly diverse populations. Minority serving institutions vary in mission, diversity, and history, but they are all connected to the complex racial and ethnic histories of the United States.

These institutions have a long history of helping students succeed who may not have otherwise gone to college. We must be committed to providing the best educational opportunities for all students, and we must ensure that they have the support they need to access and to graduate from college.

To accomplish this goal, it is essential that we invest in, and support the work of, our minority serving institutions. Together, the MSIs enroll 2.3 million students, including black, Hispanic, Native American, Asian American, and Pacific Islander American students.

Collectively, MSIs represent a rich cohort of schools, including our HBCUs, our predominantly black institutions, our Hispanic serving institutions, American Indian tribal controlled colleges and universities, Native American serving non-tribal institutions, Alaska Native, and Native Hawaiian serving institutions, and Asian American and Native American Pacific Islander serving institutions.

The MSIs serve a disproportionate amount of first-generation, low-income students. The greatest strength of these institutions lies in their extensive experience working with and serving under- represented students and the communities in which they are located.

As we work to increase college completion rates and close the educational achievement gaps in this country, we must be focused on better meeting the needs of underserved populations of students. To help us understand the importance of MSIs and the students they serve, we're going to hear today from a group of distinguished panelists.

You will share with us your stories and insights about the challenges facing your institutions and discuss the innovative strategies that your schools are employing to meet the needs of this diverse student population. I ask that you keep your oral statements to less than 5 minutes. I thank you for your written statements which I have read and which have been submitted for the record.

Senator Paul, I'm sure, will be joining us.

Senator Alexander, do you have any comments that you would like to make?

STATEMENT OF SENATOR ALEXANDER

Senator ALEXANDER. Let me just thank you for holding the hearing. Senator Paul is expected before long, and I'm looking forward to the testimony.

Tennessee has a rich history of historically black institutions. One of them is Lane College, and one of my favorite stories is one that Alex Haley used to tell about his father, Simon P. Haley, who, in his parents' words, was wasted. In other words, he wasn't required to be a sharecropper. They let him go on to North Carolina AT&T, and he met a man in the summer who paid for this scholarship. He was in the first class of African Americans to graduate from Cornell University.

He went back to Lane College to teach and raised four children, one a teacher; one an architect; one George Haley, who was required to sit by himself at the University of Arkansas in law school because he was black and later became an ambassador; and then the fourth child, who Simon P. Haley thought wasn't going to amount to anything. So he took him down and put him in the Coast Guard, and that was Alex Haley. So the historically black colleges have had a great role here, and I'm delighted to be here.

Senator Paul is our ranking Republican member, and if it's all right, Madam Chairman, if he could make his opening statement, and I would reserve any other comment until later.

Senator HAGAN. Senator Alexander, I appreciate your comment on North Carolina A&T. That's one of our HBCUs in North Carolina, and it happens to be in the city where I live, in Greensboro. It's a great university.

Senator Paul.

OPENING STATEMENT OF SENATOR PAUL

Senator PAUL. Thank you, Senator Hagan and Senator Alexander, for allowing me to be the Ranking Member today. I get an unusual promotion to do this, but I appreciate the opportunity.

Kentucky is famous for a lot of both good things and bad things that happened in education over time. We're proud of our historically black colleges, Kentucky State. We're proud of the fact that Berea College was one of the first integrated colleges in the South. We're not so proud of the fact that after about 50 years of being integrated, they passed a law in the Kentucky State Legislature banning integration, which continued to be the law until, I believe, *Brown* v. *The Board*.

But Kentucky has essentially been a microcosm of both good and bad things happening. Kentucky State University is our main historic black college, and the president has been Dr. Sias, who has been the president for the last 10 years. She is retiring, and I'd like to take this opportunity to congratulate her on a great term and being Kentucky State's first female public university president.

Kentucky State has had several famous graduates. I'll mention a few. Marion Kelly was the first Undersecretary of the Department of Labor under President George Herbert Walker Bush. Ersa Hines Poston was the first African American to head the U.S. Civil Service Commission, and Whitney M. Young, a graduate, was a famous civil rights leader and head of the National Urban League.

Also in Kentucky in the 19th century, we had a university by the name of State University, which was one of the first universities to educate African Americans when there were no other opportunities. It has recently been resurrected and rechartered and reaccredited, thanks really to the leadership of Dr. Kevin Cosby in Louisville, and it's been a great asset to rejuvenating part of our town of Louisville.

One of its famous graduates was William Warley, who, I think, really has been underappreciated in history. But there was a case in 1917, *Buchanan* v. *Warley*, which was one of the most famous Supreme Court cases where we overturned Jim Crow housing segregation laws. This was way back in 1917. The problem still persisted for a long time. The Supreme Court actually did the right thing, though, in 1917, and William Warley was a famous Republican and founder of the NAACP and also led this court case as one of the first NAACP trial cases that they fought in the early days.

One of the things I've noticed as I've traveled around the country, meeting with African American leaders in each city that I go to, is that Morehouse grads are everywhere. Anybody a Morehouse grad today? I laughingly call them the Morehouse Mafia because they're everywhere. But a good friend of mine, Elroy Sailor, has introduced me to a lot of their grads. He graduated from Morehouse and now is a partner and co-founder and CEO of Watts Partners here in DC.

In my travels, I've met many Morehouse grads. Nate Ford has become a friend. He's a Morehouse grad and vice president of Energy Partners and former director of engineering for the city of Detroit. Ashley Bell is a Morehouse grad who is now a candidate for commissioner for Hall County, GA, and is a candidate for the State board of education in Georgia—all Morehouse grads.

So there's some great success stories out there, and I get tired sometimes of hearing all the bad stories. I'm glad and I hope some of what we'll hear today are some of the good stories and the success stories that we're having, both with education and with individual success.

I think part of the success, though, we have to—and Senator Alexander has been a leader in this—we have to think about how we educate people, not only at the college level, but getting people to college and getting them ready. I think one of the real answers is through charter schools and through school choice. I think if we're able to do that, I think there's much more potential that we can find for everyone.

I want to thank Senator Hagan for convening this hearing and for allowing me to participate, and I thank the panel for attending.

Senator HAGAN. Thank you, Senator Paul. I'm so appreciative that we continue to work on these issues on the HELP Committee on a bipartisan basis.

Now to introduce our witnesses.

Senator Murray, would you like to introduce Dr. Bassett?

STATEMENT OF SENATOR MURRAY

Senator MURRAY. Thank you very much to Senators Hagan and Paul for holding a hearing talking about how we can strengthen and support our minority serving institutions to make sure their students are able to succeed. We all know the economic returns on investing in education. College graduates tend to earn more and have lower unemployment rates than their less-educated peers.

But disadvantaged, first-generation, low-income students face significant challenges accessing and completing postsecondary education. Children from well-off families are more likely to earn a college degree than children from other economic backgrounds. And higher education is still unattainable for far too many families, especially under-represented minorities, which is why this hearing is so important.

I'm so excited to be here today to introduce my colleagues to Heritage University and its president, John Bassett. Heritage University is a very unique institution. It's located on the Yakama Indian Reservation in my home State of Washington. Heritage is the successor to Fort Wright College which was established in 1907 by Catholic nuns.

Years later, two American Indian women approached Fort Wright College, wanting to expand educational and training opportunities for their preschool teachers, and their dream eventually became a reality when Fort Wright College closed its doors and became Heritage College in 1982. Its initial enrollment was 85 students, and its first president was a Catholic nun, Sister Kathleen Ross.

The university has grown considerably over the past 30 years, and today Heritage University offers everything from certificates to master's degrees. It has an open enrollment policy and opens its doors to students from other community colleges by offering online courses. Nearly 80 percent of Heritage students are Pell eligible, 75 percent are women, and over 50 percent are over the age of 25.

Almost all of their students are first-generation college students. Heritage University also serves a very diverse population. Over 50 percent of its students are Hispanic, and 10 percent are Native American.

As chair of the Senate Budget Committee, I know an educated workforce is critical for our long-term economic and fiscal outlook. The United States once led the world in having the highest percentage of college graduates. Today we rank 12th. If we want to remain globally competitive and expand our college access and completion rates, we should support the education goals of under-represented minorities, the fastest growing U.S. demographic, and we should partner with minority serving institutions like Heritage University.

Despite its growth, a few things about Heritage University have not changed. It is still opening its doors to all students. It still serves the students, the community, and the State of Washington, and it still operates an early learning center.

Thank you, John, for making this trip to the other Washington to share your successes about Heritage University. We look forward to all of your testimony today, and I'm sorry that I have to chair a Budget Committee and won't be able to be here. But we certainly will be following and working with all of you.

Thank you very much.

Senator HAGAN. Thank you, Senator Murray. And I did learn this morning that Dr. Bassett spent 9 years at NC State University in Raleigh, NC. So we'll take claim to that, too.

Senator Casey, if you could introduce Dr. Marybeth Gasman, please.

STATEMENT OF SENATOR CASEY

Senator CASEY. Madam Chair, thank you. Ranking Member Paul, thank you, and thanks to the members of the panel who are here for your testimony and for the information and testimony you will provide regarding best practices at a lot of great institutions.

I have the privilege as a Senator representing Pennsylvania to introduce Dr. Marybeth Gasman. Dr. Gasman serves as a Professor of Higher Education at the Graduate School of Education at the University of Pennsylvania. She is also director of the Penn Center on

Minority Serving Institutions, which is focused on gathering research and data to assess best practices, innovation, and ideas related to minority serving institutions.

In 2006, Dr. Gasman received the Penn Graduate School of Education Excellence in Teaching Award, and we commend you for that. She has also been a leading voice on minority serving institutions and has published on the topic extensively, having written or edited 18 books—I wish I could say I've done that—18 books and contributed to top peer review journals in her field. Dr. Gasman serves on the Board of Trustees at Paul Quinn College, a historically black college in Dallas, TX, and on the Advisory Board of the United Negro College Fund's Frederick D. Patterson Research Center.

She received her bachelor of art's degree at Saint Norbert College and her master's of science and doctorate from Indiana University. I look forward to her testimony, and I am grateful that she is here today.

Thank you.

Senator HAGAN. Thank you, Senator Casey.

Next, we have Dr. Lomax, president and CEO of the United Negro College Fund. Under Dr. Lomax's leadership, UNCF has raised $1.5 billion and has helped more than 92,000 students earn college degrees and launch careers. Annually, the United Negro College Fund's work enables 60,000 students to go to college with UNCF scholarships and attend its 37-member historically black colleges and universities.

Dr. Lomax, thank you very much for all of the great work that you have done and are continuing to do with the UNCF.

Following Dr. Lomax, we will hear from Mr. Oakley, president of Long Beach City College. Eloy Ortiz Oakley was appointed as the superintendent-president of the Long Beach Community College district in 2007. Since he started at Long Beach Community College, he has forged innovative partnerships with schools districts, universities, and Goldman Sachs to improve student success on the campus.

Our next witness is from my home State of North Carolina. Dr. DeSousa is the assistant vice chancellor of student retention at Fayetteville State University.

Dr. DeSousa, you have the distinct pleasure today of testifying in front of the committee with two Senators from North Carolina. Senator Burr, would you like to welcome our witness?

Senator BURR. Senator Hagan, thank you.

Jason, I welcome you, as I do all the witnesses that are here today. Let me just say that North Carolina represents the largest pool of HBCUs in the country with 11.

Dr. Bassett, I'm not sure how we lost you, but we'll get you back eventually, I'm sure.

This hearing is important to our State and, more importantly, to our country and to the students that benefit from it. Let me say this, Senator Hagan, that Dr. DeSousa has quite a record every place he's been. But when we look for things to model, we look for people with quantitative data that proves that what they're doing works.

By every score, as it relates to retention, GPA, everything at Fayetteville State, the programs that he oversees, the programs that he has put in place, performance counts. And we've seen GPAs go up, we've seen retention go up, and we've seen the hiring of those graduates go up.

Congratulations. We've got something to learn, and I urge my colleagues to listen to what they've done at Fayetteville State. Thank you.

Senator HAGAN. Thank you, Senator Burr.

And thank you, Dr. DeSousa.

We're going to begin with Dr. Gasman for our testimony. And once again, please limit your remarks to approximately 5 minutes. Once you have concluded with your remarks, we will begin the question and answer portion of this hearing.

Dr. Gasman.

STATEMENT OF MARYBETH GASMAN, PHD, PROFESSOR OF HIGHER EDUCATION AND DIRECTOR OF THE CENTER FOR MINORITY-SERVING INSTITUTIONS AT THE UNIVERSITY OF PENNSYLVANIA, PHILADELPHIA, PA

Ms. GASMAN. Thank you for having me today. I appreciate it. What I'm going to do is just give a quick overview of minority serving institutions in general, and then I'm going to talk about three areas, and that will be the STEM area, men of color, and also teacher education.

Minority serving institutions emerged in response to a history of inequity, lack of minority people's access to majority institutions, and significant demographic changes which are continuing to change in our country. So as a result, they are educating a really unique niche of students in the Nation. As we've heard, they serve a disproportionate amount of low-income and students of color.

I did want to point out a few things that they are particularly good at. They boast very diverse faculties and staffs, much more diverse than the majority of institutions across the Nation. They provide environments that have a significant impact on student learning, and they cultivate future leadership.

They also offer role models of similar racial and ethnic backgrounds for students, which research has proven to be instrumental in student success. And they provide programs of study that challenge students and make up for the deficiencies that happen at the K through 12 level. An investment in these institutions moves us all forward.

There are roughly 599 minority serving institutions, depending on how you count them, in the United States, and they educate 20 percent of all undergraduates. That's a pretty significant percentage. Over 50 percent of MSI students receive Pell grants, and if you look at HBCUs, in particular, that goes up to 84 percent. If you look at tribal colleges, that goes up to 74 percent. The tuition at these institutions is 50 percent lower than at majority institutions.

I want to move to the STEM area. Research tells us that we need a million more STEM workers in order to be competitive on a global scale. Minority serving institutions can help us, because they disproportionately prepare students in STEM. If you look at the top 20 institutions that award STEM degrees, for example, to Asian and Pacific Islander students, seven of these institutions are what are called AANAPISIs, Asian American and Pacific Islander serving institutions.

Ten HSIs, Hispanic serving institutions, are among the top 20 institutions awarding STEM degrees to Latinos. If we look among HBCUs in the top 20, we find 10 HBCUs awarding the most degrees to blacks and African Americans. So they are hugely significant in the STEM area.

As of late, we've heard a lot about President Obama's My Brother's Keeper initiative. I think that we all, hopefully, care about the future of men of color. But they are disproportionately at risk in the United States. But if you look at minority serving institutions, they are doing the lion's share of work with men of color, and I don't think that people realize it.

Over 36 percent of men of color who are enrolled full-time are at minority serving institutions. Nearly 50 percent of men of color enrolled part-time are at minority serving institutions. Keep in mind that minority serving institutions only make up 7.8 percent of our colleges and universities. They are disproportionately educating men of color. They are also disproportionately graduating men of color.

The last area I want to focus on is teacher education. One of the things that we know is that our teaching force is not diverse, but our student body is, and it's becoming more and more diverse. If you look at the census projections for 2050, you see that there's a large increase with the country becoming majority-minority. So it's very, very important that we have a teaching force that reflects this growing diversity.

MSIs produce 11 percent of all teaching degrees. But if you look a little bit deeper, what you see is that they are accounting for 53.5 percent of all bachelor's degrees in teaching that are going to Latinos, that they are producing over half of the degrees for Asian Americans, that they are producing nearly a third for African Americans. They are having a significant impact, and we have some really wonderful models in that area.

The last thing that I'd like to say is that I made five recommendations, and I'm not going to go over them right now. But I would hope that you would ask questions related to my recommendations around supporting fundraising infrastructure at MSIs—I think that's incredibly important—around the collection of data that actually shows the value of MSIs—I think that Jason's work really exemplifies that—and also around an investment in teacher education. I think those are three of the most important recommendations that I made.

I look forward to the conversation. Thank you.
[The prepared statement of Ms. Gasman follows:]

Prepared Statement of Marybeth Gasman, PhD

Overview of Minority Serving Institutions (MSIg4s)

Minority Serving Institutions emerged in response to a history of inequity, lack of minority people's access to majority institutions, and significant demographic changes in the country. Now an integral part of American higher education, MSIs— specifically Historically Black Colleges and Universities (HBCUs), Tribal Colleges and Universities (TCUs), Hispanic Serving Institutions (HSIs), and Asian American and Native American Pacific Islander Serving Institutions (AANAPISIs)—have carved out a unique niche in the Nation: serving the needs of low-income and under- represented students of color. These institutions boast diverse faculties and staffs, provide environments that significantly enhance student learning and cultivate leadership skills, offer role models of various racial and ethnic backgrounds, provide programs of study that challenge students, address deficiencies resulting from inadequate preparation in primary and secondary school, and prepare students to succeed in the workforce and in graduate and professional education. Because MSIs enroll a substantial share of minority students, many of whom might not otherwise attend college, the continuous development and success of these institutions is critical for realizing our Nation's higher education and workforce goals and for the benefit of American society overall. MSIs play vital roles for the Nation's economy, especially with respect to elevating the workforce prospects of disadvantaged populations and reducing the under-representation of minorities and disadvantaged people in graduate and professional schools and the careers that require post-baccalaureate education and training. By virtue of their Federal legislation, MSIs enroll a largely disproportionate population of students of color. If the Federal Government seeks to widen educational access to this population, they should increase the Nation's investment in these institutions.[1]

Minority Serving Institutions by the Numbers[2]

599 Minority Serving Institutions

- 34 TCUs

---

[1] Clifton Conrad and Marybeth Gasman, Lessons from the Margins: What American Higher Education can Learn about Empowering All Students to be Successful in College. Cambridge, MA: Harvard University Press, forthcoming 2015.

[2] Marybeth Gasman and Clifton Conrad, Minority Serving Institutions: Educating All Students. (Philadelphia, PA: Penn Center for Minority Serving Institutions, 2013).

- 105 HBCUs
- 315 HSIs
- 145 AANAPISIs
- 3.6 million undergraduates are enrolled in MSIs—20 percent of all undergraduate students.
- Over 50 percent of all MSI students receive Pell Grants.
- Tuition at MSIs is on average 50 percent lower than majority institutions.

Individual MSI Sector Descriptions and Contributions

Tribal Colleges and Universities

The 34 colleges and universities that are regular members of the American Indian Higher Education Consortium are spread across 13 States and include 13 4-year and 21 2-year colleges. With nearly 30,000 students enrolled, TCUs have grown significantly since the first tribal college, Dine´ College in Arizona, opened its doors (under the name Navajo Community College) over four decades ago. Predominantly public institutions (over 75 percent), TCUs vary in enrollments from under 100 to nearly 3,000 students. Most TCUs are located on reservations: among the 34 TCUs are four urban or suburban campuses, three campuses located in distant or remote towns, and 27 rural campuses. With their roots in Native American movements for self-determination, TCUs were established to provide educational opportunities for a local tribe(s) and expand a network of regional higher education opportunities for Indians and non-Indians alike. TCUs serve as places where students find the support and social capital they need to get degrees that lead to careers. TCUs have also focused considerable educational resources on the survival and development of socially and economically marginalized communities, and these institutions have helped maintain and invigorate tribal languages and cultures while at the same time developing curricula that speak to the experiences and backgrounds of Native Americans.[3]

Hispanic Serving Institutions

Colleges and universities that serve large numbers of Hispanics date to the founding of the University of Puerto Rico (1903). In the 1960s and 1970s, drawing on the example of the African American civil rights movement and Historically Black Colleges and Universities (HBCUs), Latino student and community activists advocated changes in admissions policies and founded grassroots Hispanic colleges. Boricua College (1968), Hostos Community College (1969), and National Hispanic University (1981) are living legacies of community action. Leaders of *de facto* Hispanic Serving Institutions founded the Hispanic Association of Colleges and Universities (1986) and coined the phrase

---

[3] Ibid.

'Hispanic Serving Institution." This name became official Federal policy in 1992, and since the 2008 amendment of the Higher Education Act, "Hispanic Serving Institution" came to designate any accredited and degree-granting public or private nonprofit institution with an undergraduate Hispanic full-time equivalent student enrollment of 25 percent or higher coupled with substantial enrollment of low-income students. In the absence of a formal Federal list of HSIs, the name is generally applied to institutions that meet the Federal institutional and enrollment criteria. Based on these criteria, 315 institutions in the 50 States, Puerto Rico, and the District of Columbia qualified as HSIs in 2012. Scattered across 15 States and all institutional sectors, these institutions—just over 6 percent of all degree-granting institutions—enrolled almost four million undergraduates, including one quarter of all minority undergraduates in higher education in the United States, and nearly one-half of Hispanic undergraduates. Predominantly public (70 percent) and 2-year (49 percent) institutions, HSIs also count among their numbers 10 research universities and more than 50 master's degree institutions. As a group, these institutions play a critical role in making college accessible and starting Hispanic students on the path to degrees. HSIs are some of the most diverse institutions in the United States, serving as critical points of access to technology, information, and public space for communities with few such resources.[4]

Historically Black Colleges and Universities

HBCUs were officially defined in the 1965 Higher Education Act as a "college or university that was established prior to 1964, whose principal mission was, and is, the education of black Americans." Born out of segregation and spread across 20 States, the District of Columbia, and the U.S. Virgin Islands, these 105 institutions have played a critical role in providing education to Black Americans since the founding of Cheney University in 1837. In 2011 HBCUs made up 2 percent of the degree granting title IV institutions and enrolled nearly 346,338, students—including 1.6 percent of all undergraduate students in the United States, 3.7 percent of total minority undergraduates, 3 percent of White undergraduates, and 11 percent of Black undergraduates. HBCUs get students, especially Black students, to degrees, and they do this at the same rate as majority institutions but with less funding. HBCUs have long graduated a disproportionate percentage of the Black students who earn bachelor's degrees and who go on to graduate or professional schools. In 2012, HBCUs accounted for nearly 18 percent of bachelor's degrees awarded to Black students. HBCUs not only guide students in attaining the benefits of a first college degree (income, employment) but also contribute to students' momentum toward further education and the professions. But HBCUs do more than produce degrees: HBCUs contribute to their students'—especially their Black students'—psychosocial

---

[4] Ibid. See also, Marybeth Gasman, Benjamin Baez, and Caroline Sotello Turner, *Understanding Minority Serving Institutions.* (Albany, NY: State University of New York Press, 2007).

adjustments to college and career as well as to their cultural awareness, self-confidence, and social capital.[5]

Asian American and Native American Pacific Islander Serving Institutions

In 1960 the Asian American and Pacific Islander (AAPI) population was less than one million, but it has nearly doubled in size every decade since then, changing the face of America and subsequently American higher education. This rapid growth is the result of immigration patterns, and these patterns have also led to an increased presence of the AAPI population on college campuses across the Nation. As a result, a small group of institutions now identify—through a Federal designation and funding program—as Asian American and Native American Pacific Islander Serving Institutions (AANAPISIs). In 2009, the Congressional Research Service determined that 116 institutions met the requirements of the Federal designation. However, there are 145 eligible institutions in 2014; the numbers are growing quickly. Ten percent of these institutions' student populations are low-income Asian Americans or Pacific Islanders. Although the model minority myth perpetuates the false belief that all Asian Americans are academically advanced, AAPI students are in reality quite diverse and have needs that are similar to other under-represented racial and ethnic populations. There are 48 different ethnicities among the AAPI population, and these individuals speak more than 300 languages. Of note, the most poverty stricken of the AAPI groups in terms of socioeconomic status are the Hmong (38 percent live below the poverty line), Samoans, (20 percent live in poverty), and Filipinos (6 percent live below the poverty line). Still finding their identity, AANAPISIs are already unearthing the activist spirit within AAPI populations, creating pathways to graduate school for low-income AAPIs, providing them with mentors, and contributing to a Pan-Asian outlook that empowers the larger AAPI community.[6]

Areas of Disproportionate MSI Impact

MSIs and Production of Science, Technology, Engineering, & Math (STEM) Degrees[7]

Seventy-six percent of scientists and engineers with a bachelor's degree in the United States are White. If the Nation is to maintain its legacy of innovation in science and technology, we should look to MSIs to address the racial and ethnic disparities in STEM education, as diversity leads to innovation. Between 2006–10, many MSIs have been

---

[5] Ibid. See also, Marybeth Gasman, Valerie Lundy Wagner, Tafaya Ransom, and Nelson Bowman, *Unearthing Promise and Potential: Our Nation's Historically Black Colleges and Universities,* (San Francisco: Jossey-Bass, 2010).

[6] Robert Teranishi, Asian American and Native American Pacific Islander Serving Institutions: Areas of Growth, Innovation, and Collaboration. (New York, NY: National Commission on Asian American & Pacific Islander Research in Education, 2012).

[7] Marybeth Gasman and Clifton Conrad, *Minority Serving Institutions: Educating All Students.* (Philadelphia, PA: Penn Center for Minority Serving Institutions, 2013).

among the top 20 academic institutions that award science and engineering degrees to racial minority graduates.

- Of the top 20 institutions that award science and engineering degrees to Asians or Pacific Islanders, seven identify as AANAPISIs. These include large, regional universities, such as San Jose State University, which is located in the California Bay Area, and the University of Hawaii at Manoa.
- Ten HSIs are among the top 20 institutions that award science and engineering degrees to Hispanics/Latinos. Most of these institutions are located in California, Texas, and Puerto Rico.
- Ten HBCUs are among the top 20 institutions that award science and engineering degrees to Blacks/African Americans. These institutions vary in size and public and private status, and include institutions such as Alabama A&M University and Hampton University, which is located in Virginia.
- Of the top 20 institutions that award science and engineering degrees to Native Americans, only one TCU—Haskell Indian Nations University—is included. Considering that most TCUs are community colleges, with few awarding degrees beyond the associate level, this is not alarming.

Minority Serving Institutions and Men of Color[8]

According to the Department of Education, data indicate that boys and men of color are disproportionately at risk. There are large disparities in preparation for boys and young men of color at all levels. Moreover, a disproportionate number of Black and Latino men are unemployed or in the criminal justice system. These factors contribute to the undermining of families and local communities. Last, as a result of these circumstances, men of color are more likely to be the victims of violent crimes. Minority Serving Institutions can and do play a large role in countering these statistics and changing the lives of men of color. Consider these data:

- Over 36 percent of men of color with full-time college enrollment are found at Minority Serving Institutions.
- Nearly half (48.6 percent) of men of color with part-time college enrollment are found at Minority Serving Institutions.
- Of the 196,110 bachelors degrees conferred to men of color, 24 percent (n = 58,657) are awarded by MSIs.

---

[8] Data prepared for My Brother's Keeper Initiative by the Penn Center for Minority Serving Institutions (Marybeth Gasman, Andrés Castro Samayoa, & Thai- Huy Nguyen), 2014. All data culled from the National Center for Educational Statistics.

- Twenty-two percent (n = 50,829) of men of color with associate degrees earned by them at Minority Serving Institutions.
- MSIs represent less than 8 percent of all postsecondary institutions in the Nation.

Minority Serving Institutions and Teacher Education[9]

Between July 1, 2011 and June 30, 2012, there were 108,054 bachelor's degrees in education conferred in the United States. Of these 11,588 were conferred by MSIs (11 percent). Of note, MSIs account for 53.5 percent of all education bachelor's conferred to Latinos, over half of education degrees for Native Hawaiians and Pacific Islanders (54 percent), nearly a third for Blacks (32 percent) as well as over a third for Asians (35 percent). Across MSIs, the institutions within each sector that confer the most teaching degrees are Oglala Lakota College (TCU), the University of Texas, El Paso (HSI), Jackson State University (HBCU), and California State University-Fullerton (AANAPISI).

Recommendations for Empowering Minority Serving Institutions and Low-Income Students of Color

1. Colleges and universities with strong endowments and alumni giving thrive and are able to support students in more comprehensive ways (e.g., institutional aid and student support services). Investments at the Federal level in MSIs should focus on building fundraising infrastructure in order to ensure long-term stability rather than short-term fixes.[10]
2. Forty-six percent of MSIs are community colleges that enroll a largely disproportionate population of part-time students of color. Increasing investments in MSIs affects not only racial minority students, but also minorities who are also considered non-traditional—over the age of 25, working full-time and/or have family dependents for which to care.[11]
3. Evidence suggests that the interventions, funded through MSI Federal legislation, actually work in improving student outcomes. In order for more students to reap the benefits of these interventions, more funding is needed to bring them up to scale, using exemplary programs as models. Exemplary models include math

---

[9] Data prepared for a W.K. Kellogg Foundation-sponsored project titled "The Role of Minority Serving Institutions in Adopting and Implementing the New State Standards and Providing Leadership in Teacher Education" by researchers at the Penn Center for Minority Serving Institutions (Marybeth Gasman, Andre´s Castro Samayoa, Kerry Madden, Karla Silva, and Carolina Davila). All data culled from the National Center for Educational Statistics.

[10] Marybeth Gasman and Nelson Bowman III, *A Guide to Fundraising at Historically Black Colleges and Universities* (New York: Routledge Press, 2010).

[11] Data prepared for a forthcoming report on community colleges that are also MSIs by the Penn Center for Minority Serving Institutions (Thai-Huy Nguyen, Valerie Lundy Wagner, Marybeth Gasman, Melanie Wolff, Desmond Diggs, Andre´s Castro Samayoa, and Carolina Davila) All data culled from the National Center for Educational Statistics.

shame interventions at Chief Dull Knife College, peer mentoring in science at Morehouse College, computer-assisted learning at El Paso Community College, and the Full Circle Project at Sacramento State University. See *Minority Serving Institutions: Educating All Students* report for more details.[12]

4. The Federal Government should require MSIs to *collect data on student outcomes* across various stages—including retention, developmental education, attainment, and post-college employment. Likewise, the Federal Government should provide MSIs with funding to make data collection regular and manageable as most MSIs lack the infrastructure to collect good data. Having good, solid data on hand increases MSIs performance at the State level where outcomes-based funding is becoming the norm and in their interactions with private foundation and corporations looking to fund MSIs.[13]

5. As 11 percent of teacher education degrees nationwide were conferred by MSIs and a disproportionate number of teacher education degrees among students of color, it is essential to invest in teacher education programs at MSIs. Students in these programs are more likely to return to urban and rural communities to teach and can have a lasting impact on students of color in these communities. As the Nation's demographics change—as predicted by the U.S. Census—it will become even more important to have a teaching force that reflects the diversity of the Nation as research shows that having a teacher of the same racial or ethnic background increases student performance.[14]

Senator HAGAN. Thank you, Dr. Gasman.
Dr. Lomax with the United Negro College Fund.

STATEMENT OF MICHAEL L. LOMAX, PHD, PRESIDENT AND CEO, UNITED NEGRO COLLEGE FUND, WASHINGTON, DC

Mr. LOMAX. Thank you, Senator Hagan and Senator Paul, for the opportunity to testify on this important topic. Since our founding 70 years ago, UNCF's primary mission has been to increase the number of African American college graduates and especially from our 37 private member HBCUs.

---

[12] Marybeth Gasman and Clifton Conrad, *Minority Serving Institutions: Educating All Students.* (Philadelphia, PA: Penn Center for Minority Serving Institutions, 2013).

[13] Clifton Conrad, Marybeth Gasman, Todd Lundberg, et al, *Collecting and Using Data at Minority Serving Institutions*, Philadelphia, PA: Center for Minority Serving Institutions, University of Pennsylvania, October 2013.

[14] Recommendation based on data noted in reference 9.

Strengthening Minority Serving Institutions

HBCUs are a best buy in American education because of their strong record in graduating low-income minority students. The Nation's network of public and private historically black colleges enroll 10 percent of all African American undergraduates and graduate nearly 20 percent of all African Americans with college degrees and 27 percent of African Americans with STEM degrees, and at an affordable price, 30 percent less than other colleges.

Today, HBCUs face a financial crisis. The institutions themselves and the students they serve were hard hit by the Great Recession and, more recently, have suffered losses from abrupt changes in Federal student financial aid policies, such as the devastating change in underwriting rules for parent-plus loans that caused many students already in college to withdraw.

UNCF and our member institutions understand that it is our responsibility to confront these financial challenges and we are doing our part. In all, UNCF awards $100 million in scholarships each year to over 12,000 students with a significant share attending HBCUs. But the painful reality is that today, UNCF can provide scholarship assistance to only 1 of every 10 qualified applicants.

Our member institutions are working hard to assure our long- term viability through more effective practices throughout their academic enterprises. To assist them, UNCF established our Institute for Capacity Building, or ICB, to provide grants, technical assistance, and professional development. With ICB support, for example, Claflin University increased alumni giving to over 50 percent, a giving rate higher than some elite institutions.

Four institutions, Clark Atlanta University, Oakwood University, Texas College, and Voorhees College, increased their applicant pools by at least 25 percent and first-time student retention by 13 percent. And Shaw University developed an institution-wide student loan default prevention initiative that reduced its cohort default rate by nearly 40 percent over 3 years.

Our institutions recognize they must change the way they do business in order to accelerate progress in closing achievement and attainment gaps. The reauthorization of the Higher Education Act represents an opportunity to spur innovation and new solutions at our institutions. With Federal venture capital, HBCUs could experiment, pilot, evaluate, and scale up promising best practices for student success.

The HEA reauthorization also presents an opportunity to develop a holistic approach to helping more students of color go to and graduate from college. For example, the Federal student aid system must be improved so that it works better for low-income families. Reinvesting in Pell grants and summer Pell grants is essential to helping poor students finish college faster and at a lower cost.

Moreover, the complexity of Federal student aid is both a barrier to college access for low-income families and a regulatory burden on institutions. It should be streamlined. Stafford and Plus loans should be improved with lower interest rates, more effective loan counseling, and reasonable credit criteria.

Finally, Congress should establish a universal and automatic income-based student repayment system administered by the Federal Government. This could solve the student loan default problem and eliminate the need for cohort default rate measures that penalize HBCUs and smaller institutions and force them to focus on loan collection and not academic improvement.

UNCF believes that a mind is a terrible thing to waste, but a wonderful thing to invest in. This is a sentiment I believe we can all support. I look forward to answering your questions.

Thank you.

[The prepared statement of Mr. Lomax follows:]

Prepared Statement of Michael L. Lomax, PhD

Introduction

Good morning and thank you Senator Hagan, Senator Paul, Chairman Harkin, Ranking Member Alexander and the entire committee for the opportunity to testify before you on a subject of critical importance to those of us who are working every day to enable more minority students to reach their full potential.

I am Michael Lomax, president and CEO of UNCF. UNCF is the Nation's largest higher education organization serving students of color, perhaps best known by our iconic motto, "A mind is a terrible thing to waste®." UNCF was founded 70 years ago to consolidate fundraising for America's private Historically Black Colleges and Universities (HBCUs) and our primary goal is to increase the number of African American college graduates from our member institutions through fundraising to support scholarships. In addition, we both advocate for and support increasing African American graduates from other HBCUs and all U.S. colleges and universities, assuring these young people have the skills they need to excel in the 21st century economy. To underscore our philosophy that investing in young people will pay dividends for the entire nation, we have updated our motto to: "A mind is a terrible thing to waste but a wonderful thing to invest in®."

During UNCF's 70 years, we have raised over $4 billion in scholarship aid to help more than 400,000 students of color earn their degrees at HBCUs and 900 other colleges and universities across the country. We administer $100 million in scholarships annually through 400 scholarship and internship programs. UNCF's largest program is the Gates Millennium Scholarship, founded in 1999 by The Bill and Melinda Gates Foundation through a $1.6 billion grant to be used for scholarships for high-achieving, low-income African American, American Indian/Alaska Native, Asian Pacific Islander and Hispanic American students across the country.

The HBCU Value Proposition

UNCF's core mission, however, remains its partnership with the Nation's 37 private HBCUs, part of a network of 100 public and private HBCUs. Collectively, these institutions enrolled 235,000 undergraduate students in 2012, primarily first-generation, low-income and minority students.

The HBCUs that partner with UNCF play a unique role in the Nation's educational environment, preparing the next generation of professional and civic leaders needed by communities, employers and the Nation, especially as the country trends toward a population and workforce in which the combined minorities are actually in the majority. In fact, recent studies by UNCF's Frederick D. Patterson Research Institute demonstrate that HBCUs often outperform larger, better-known and better-funded institutions at enrolling and graduating low-income students.[15]

In many ways, HBCUs are a "best buy" for students and the Nation. HBCUs represent 3 percent of all 4- and 2-year colleges and universities; enroll 10 percent of all African American undergraduates; confer 19 percent of all African American bachelor's degrees; and generate 27 percent of African American undergraduate STEM degrees, even though operating costs are among the lowest in the Nation. When the National Science Foundation ranked all colleges based on the number of African American graduates who went on to earn doctoral degrees in science and engineering, HBCUs took the top 10 places, ahead of elite private universities.

HBCU accomplishments include the following:

- Since 2008, Spelman College in Atlanta, GA has averaged a 6-year graduation rate of 77 percent—the highest of the 100 HBCUs and substantially above the national average of 59 percent.
- Claflin University in South Carolina has been recognized nationally as a leader by implementing a comprehensive plan that increased its retention rate by 8 percentage points in a single year; the university's 2012 retention rate was 74 percent—one of the highest of all HBCUs and slightly above the national rate.
- Nearly 50 percent of graduates with bachelor's degrees from Xavier University in New Orleans, LA are in the science, technology, engineering and mathematics (STEM) fields.
- In March 2014, a team of investigators from five HBCUs (Prairie View A&M University, Texas Southern University, Savannah State University, Tougaloo College, and Jarvis Christian College) was the first selected team of HBCUs to send a research payload to the International Space Station.

---

[15] [1]UNCF, Frederick D. Patterson Research Institute. 2012. *Understanding HBCU Retention and Completion.*

HBCUs attain these results at an affordable price for students—30 percent less, on average, than other institutions, with fewer resources available to them—and with operating budgets that average less than 50 percent of those of other 4-year colleges. At the same time, the vast majority of HBCU students are economically disadvantaged and academically unprepared for the rigors of college. Yet, our institutions get these students across the finish line.

HBCU Challenges and Opportunities

At UNCF, we are encouraged that the Nation is focused on producing more college graduates in order to secure a bright future for our citizens and country. UNCF brings a sense of urgency to the prospect of producing more African American graduates, particularly as we face significant challenges and much remains to be accomplished to meet our goals.

Most important, HBCUs continue to face severe fiscal challenges. In fact, the money raised by UNCF for its 37 member HBCUs has become more important today than ever, as our member schools are experiencing a financial crisis as severe as any in UNCF's history. Already under-resourced, HBCUs have lost over $250 million since 2011 in reduced Parent PLUS Loans, Pell Grants and other sources of critical Federal support for student financial aid, academic programs and student support services. Over 75 percent of students at HBCUs rely on Pell Grants—a substantially greater share than the 45 percent, on average, at other institutions.

In addition to the financial crisis, college readiness remains a significant barrier to the success of students at our institutions. Research tells us that students from poor families have lower educational aspirations, inadequate secondary-level academic preparation, and are less likely to persist and complete their degrees.

The good news is that interest from African American high school students in attending HBCUs has been on the rise for over a decade. Between the 2001–2 and the 2012–13 school years, UNCF member institutions saw a 78 percent rise in applications and a 64 percent increase in admissions. These numbers are comparable to all 4-year institutions.

However, while enrollment at all 4-year institutions rose by 21 percent over the period, enrollment at UNCF's member HBCUs remained essentially flat, rising by only 5 percent. We believe the reason for this is a lack of student financial aid.

I'm often asked how colleges that serve an almost exclusively African American population can still be relevant in today's world. The answers are quite simple. First, HBCUs do a very good job at educating their students. Based on research from UNCF's Patterson Research Institute, we know that HBCUs outperform non-HBCUs by 14 percentage points when it comes to graduating demographically identical low-income student populations.[16]

---

[16] Ibid.

There are also deeper reasons for continued demand for HBCUs. I've talked to thousands of students about their interest in attending an HBCU, and they tend to raise three points to explain why they want to attend a historically Black college. First, they say the schools feel like home—they feel like family. Second, they believe HBCUs will let them explore themselves as an individual, rather than as a statistic. And finally, at an HBCU, they feel they can learn more about where they come from. This is a powerful set of motivators that echoes research from UNCF's Patterson Research Institute, and I believe will continue for many years to come.

HBCU's have played—and are poised to continue to play—an outsized role in helping greater numbers of minority youth obtain a college degree. These strengths also lay the foundation for HBCUs to innovate and lead in a rapidly evolving higher education landscape. The traditional 18- to 22-year-old student population is no longer the typical college student in America. Today, non-traditional students— working, career seeking and family supporting adults—are looking to obtain degrees or some type of postsecondary credential. And they are demanding a more personalized and convenient education that can be accessed online—anytime, anywhere, any place. The ground is literally shifting right under HBCUs and our institutions need to get out in front of the coming earthquake. HBCUs can become more adept at serving and reaching out to:

- High-achieving students from low-income families, many of whom don't even apply to college because they believe they cannot afford it;
- Older students who work full-time and need to take classes via non-traditional formats (virtually, on weekends, in blended formats, at an accelerated pace, assessing credit for prior experiences and competencies, etc.);
- The over 35 million students who have earned some college credit but have not graduated, to provide them alternatives for earning their degrees; and
- International residents who have visas and have worked in the country but have not earned a degree.

What UNCF Is Doing to Increase African American College Attainment

Addressing College Readiness

UNCF is working to address the college readiness gap by making the case that the Nation must invest in students earlier in the educational pipeline. The pre-K through college pipeline is broken for communities of color, and particularly for African Americans. According to ACT, Inc., only 5 percent of African American high school graduates meet college readiness benchmarks across four major subjects (English, reading, math, and science). Through our local community engagement efforts across the country, UNCF is actively working to build support for effective school reform, and to make students and families aware that the high school diploma is no longer a ticket to the middle class. UNCF's Patterson Research Institute is developing high-quality research so that we have the data and analysis to support this work and, indeed, all of UNCF's major streams of work.

Addressing Financial Need

UNCF is working hard to meet the strong demand by young African Americans for an education at our member schools, but donations have not kept pace with the demand, particularly in the aftermath of the Great Recession. In all, UNCF awards $100 million in college scholarships each year to over 12,000 students, with a significant share attending HBCUs. However, the ratio of applications to available scholarships is approaching 10 to 1.

In 2009, thousands of students were at risk of being forced to leave college without their degrees largely due to the recession and the inability of their families to fill in the financial gap. In response, UNCF launched a just-in-time scholarship program (Campaign for Emergency Student Aid) that has raised over $20 million and helped over 8,000 students pay outstanding tuition and dormitory bills so students could graduate and begin their careers. Indeed, a relatively small scholarship averaging $1,500 has made the difference between a college dropout and a college graduate.

In 2010, UNCF partnered with Citibank and the Knowledge is Power (KIPP) charter schools to launch the UNCF College Account Program (UCAP), with a $7.5 million gift from the Citi Foundation and Citibank. The UCAP program is a custom- designed college savings and scholarship initiative operating in Chicago, Houston, New York City, the San Francisco Bay Area and Washington, DC. KIPP elementary, middle and high school charter school students receive $50 and an equal match when they open a college savings account. Their contributions are matched up to $250 per year. In addition, high school seniors are eligible to receive scholarships for up to 5 years, further mitigating unmet financial need experienced by low-income students. KIPP regional coordinators work with Citibank branch offices to host financial literacy workshops for families and 'bank days" for students. Over 8,000 students and families have enrolled since UCAP's inception, and more than $1.1 million in student contributions and matching funds has been achieved.

UNCF has redoubled our efforts to increase donations from the private sector, and we have revamped our operations to better serve UNCF members and students. We know that investing in students through UNCF works. Our Patterson Research Institute examined the effectiveness of our scholarships and found that an African American freshman who receives a $5,000 UNCF scholarship returns for her sophomore year at a 94 percent rate, graduates in 6 years at a 70 percent rate—which is considerably higher than the 59 percent 6-year graduation rate at all 4-year institutions—and sees her likelihood of graduating increase by over 7 percentage points.[17] In contrast, the national 6-year graduation rate for

---

[17] UNCF, Frederick D. Patterson Research Institute. 2013. Building Better Futures: The Value of a UNCF Investment.

African Americans is 40 percent. If we could increase that rate by over 7 percentage points, we would graduate close to 16,000 additional African Americans with bachelor's degrees each year. That is an investment that pays dividends not only to those students, but also to the country at large.

Enhancing HBCU Institutional Capacity

Because HBCUs serve low-income students, their budgets are always tight and endowments are limited. That challenges the ability of HBCUs to operate effectively and efficiently and to evolve in response to higher education best practices—processes that better-funded institutions can afford to take for granted.

UNCF presidents understand that building internal capacity in all aspects of their academic enterprise is key to both educational excellence and the long-term viability of their institutions. In response to this need, UNCF launched the Institute for Capacity Building (ICB) with support from the Kresge Foundation—whose visionary work on HBCU institutional advancement programs provided a model for ICB. Since 2006, UNCF has raised more than $30 million for ICB, which provides grants, technical assistance, consultative services and professional development opportunities to strengthen the ability of all UNCF member institutions, as well as other minority- serving institutions, to meet 21st century challenges.

ICB's core program areas focus on:

- *Institutional Advancement*, including enhancing the capacity of UNCF institutions to raise more private, unrestricted sources of funding and, especially, to increase giving by alumni;
- *Enrollment Management*, including building communities of best practice across the UNCF network of institutions aimed at increasing student enrollment and improving retention and graduation rates;
- *Curriculum and Faculty Enhancement*, including fostering solutions to help faculty excel in HBCU academic environments;
- *Fiscal and Strategic Technical Assistance*, including doing "deep dives" around issues of fiscal management, institutional effectiveness and compliance with accreditation and Federal student aid requirements;
- *Facilities and Infrastructure Enhancement*, including building "green" at MSIs; and
- *Executive Leadership and Governance*, including providing leadership training for college presidents, senior administrators and board chairs.

The convergence of financial, technical and "on the ground" support has brought about new capacities that in some cases are unprecedented within UNCF campuses. For example, through the *Institutional Advancement Program*, 10 institutions[18] developed comprehensive strategies for annual giving that increased total private gifts by 57 percent over a 3- to 4-year period. For example, Bennett College in North Carolina increased its total number of donors by 42 percent and donations climbed by 70 percent. Claflin University in South Carolina more than doubled its first-time alumni donors, achieving an alumni participation rate of over 50 percent, which exceeds the participation rate at some elite universities and is twice the average 24 percent rate at private baccalaureate institutions according to the Council for Aid to Education's 2013 Voluntary Survey of Education.

Through the *Enrollment Management Program*, four pilot institutions (Clark Atlanta University (Georgia), Oakwood University (Alabama), Texas College (Texas) and Voorhees College (South Carolina) increased their applicant pools by at least 25 percent and first-time student retention by 13 percent. Clark Atlanta University also increased its 5-year graduation rate by 2 percentage points.

ICB's *Curriculum and Faculty Enhancement Program* helped Virginia Union University (VUU) prepare undergraduate students to become math and science teachers in the Richmond, VA public school system. The ICB grant also helped VUU to develop courses, student learning communities and co-curricular activities in math and science.

The *Fiscal and Strategic Technical Assistance Program* included the establishment of an Accreditation Registry. This registry allows UNCF to offer a central data base of experts in critical areas as institutions prepare for accreditation visits and reviews. Miles College in Alabama improved its assessment of graduates' status by using National Student Clearinghouse Student Tracker, made possible with ICB grant funds. Shaw University in North Carolina developed an institution-wide student loan default prevention and management initiative that led to a nearly 40 percent reduction in its cohort default rate in 3 years.

Through the *Facilities and Infrastructure Enhancement Program*, UNCF launched a Building Green at Minority-Serving Institutions Initiative, which serves as a coordinating collective for sustainability efforts at historically black, tribal, Hispanic- serving and Asian American/Pacific Islander-serving institutions. The initiative identifies barriers to building green and incorporates principles of sustainable design and energy efficiency into campus building projects. As a result, the number of buildings and structures on MSI campuses that are registered for LEED certification has increased 30 percent. Lane College in Tennessee upgraded lighting in its athletic center, created a sustainability committee and began energy audits. Tougaloo College in Mississippi worked with MIT CoLab, a technical assistance partner, to establish a student-led Green Team to increase recycling, expand the community garden and support curriculum updates.

[18.] Benedict College, Bennett College, Claflin University, Huston-Tillotson, Jarvis Christian College, Morehouse College, Philander Smith College, Talladega College, Virginia Union University and Wiley College.

Promoting STEM and Innovation

Recognizing the potential of HBCUs to be hubs of innovation, and the need to dramatically increase African American participation in the innovation economy, UNCF embarked on a new course to expand its reach and impact through a major STEM initiative. HBCUs already have a strong track record in launching the STEM careers of African Americans. UNCF is building on these efforts to change the face of STEM with its groundbreaking partnership with Merck. The UNCF/Merck Science Initiative (UMSI), a $44 million program now in its 18th year, has produced more than 600 world-class African American research scientists in biological, chemical and related disciplines. The UMSI capacity building program is increasing the research participation levels among undergraduates, enhancing career development and fostering a culture of inquiry on campus.

In 2013 and 2014, UNCF launched the centerpiece of its new STEM initiative— a national HBCU Innovation Summit held in Silicon Valley. The purpose of the Summit was to build bridges between HBCUs and the technology community, and to develop and enhance the innovation and entrepreneurial capacity of HBCUs— with the goal of establishing productive innovation-entrepreneurial ecosystems across the HBCU network.

Using Research, Data and Analysis for Continuous Improvement and to Drive Results

UNCF is supporting the national conversation about how to provide a quality education to all by developing and using data, research, evaluation and assessment to inform our work on minority education and to drive results. Since its founding in 1996, UNCF's Patterson Research Institute, frequently quoted in this document, has conducted research on the educational status and progress of African Americans.

The first publication in a growing body of research in K–12 education, Patterson's study, "Done to Us, Not With Us: African American Perceptions of K–12 Education" is helping to inform UNCF's work in target cities focused on increasing parental involvement for students of color and low-income backgrounds. Patterson is documenting the impact of UNCF scholarships on the students who receive them, and also analyzing the performance and progress of UNCF member institutions along key dimensions, such as access, affordability, persistence and completion.[19] One such study, just completed, examined the affordability of the 37 UNCF member institutions benchmarked against peer institutions. It concluded that our institutions offer African Americans a viable, affordable avenue toward a college degree—with average total prices that are 26 percent lower than at comparison institutions.[20] This study is one of an ongoing series exploring how African Americans pay for college, policies and regulations that influence their ability to finance

---

[19]. UNCF, Frederick D. Patterson Research Institute. 2013. *Building Better Futures: The Value of a UNCF Investment.*
[20] UNCF, Frederick D. Patterson Research Institute. 2014. *Lower Costs, Higher Returns: UNCF HBCUs in a High-Priced College Environment.*

college attendance; and various institutional and individual factors that pay a role in how money facilitates college access, retention and completion.

Recommendations for the Higher Education Act Reauthorization

The challenges and opportunities facing HBCUs come at a critical juncture in our Nation's drive to produce more African American college graduates—a time when a college education is both more essential and more expensive than ever. The reauthorization of the Higher Education Act (HEA) presents an important opportunity to develop a holistic approach to moving more students to and through college, particularly students of color. I would like to turn to UNCF's policy recommendations for renewing the HEA, particularly as they relate to HBCUs.

Re-Invest In and Modernize Pell Grants

As you know, Pell Grants are the cornerstone of our national commitment to make higher education accessible and affordable for all, but especially those students who lack the financial means to attend college but stand to gain the most from a college education.

UNCF urges the committee to re-invest in and modernize Pell Grants to meet 21st century needs. We recommend that the committee reverse the programmatic cuts made between 2011 and 2013, which drained more than $53 billion in vital college assistance from financially needy students. These reductions work against students at HBCUs who have the greatest financial need and often take longer to complete their degrees due to financial constraints. Accordingly, we support (1) restoring the 'summer" Pell Grant that enables students to earn their degrees faster and at a lower cost; (2) restoring the income threshold to $32,000 for an automatic Pell Grant and (3) repealing the 6-year limit for Pell Grant eligibility. Further, the Federal Government should make an early Pell Grant funding commitment to low-income high school students to increase college-going rates and improve K–12 academic outcomes by helping these young people to believe that college is possible. Finally, the complexity of the Federal student aid process and regulations is both a barrier to college access for low-income students and a burden on institutions. We urge the committee to explore the many ways in which financial aid experts have suggested to streamline a financial aid system that is confusing to students and parents.

Improve Parent PLUS Loans

When the Department of Education unilaterally tightened the credit requirements that determine eligibility for Parent PLUS Loans in October 2011, we learned just how critical these loans are to college access for thousands of students across the country, and especially to those students at HBCUs. Initially, 400,000 students nationwide and 28,000 students at HBCUs were impacted. Ultimately, HBCUs experienced a 45 percent drop in the number of students whose parents were able to obtain Parent PLUS Loans in the 2012–13 academic year and suffered a $155 million or 35 percent reduction in Parent PLUS Loan revenue from already tight budgets. While the situation has improved somewhat in the 2013–14 academic year, thousands of low-income students continue to be denied access to the HBCU of their choice because of Parent PLUS Loan denials.

UNCF member presidents are working in good faith in negotiated rulemaking sessions on this issue at the Department of Education. However, should the Department of Education issue regulations this fall that fail to adequately address this problem, UNCF will seek this committee's support for a legislative remedy.

Further, we recommend several statutory improvements for the Parent PLUS Loan program, including: (1) lowering interest rates and origination fees; (2) incorporating loan counseling for parents so that they borrow only what they need and understand their loan obligations; (3) extending the eligibility period to 2 award years; (4) incorporating more flexible repayment options; and (5) granting institutions flexibility to provide additional Federal aid to students in good academic standing whose parents are denied PLUS loans.

Delay Cohort Default Rate Sanctions

Cohort default rates are an emerging issue that looms large over our institutions. Beginning this year, institutions can lose title IV eligibility if they exceed a 3-year cohort default rate of 30 percent for 3 consecutive years. That is a death sentence for any college or university.

In the short term, HBCUs seek a 2-year delay in sanctions relating to cohort default rates. Cohort default rate sanctions unfairly penalize HBCUs, which are at greatest risk of losing Federal student aid eligibility because their students disproportionately rely on Federal loans to attend college, and borrow greater amounts, due to their limited financial means. Some HBCUs could exceed the 30 percent threshold if just a few students default because of their small enrollments. Moreover, when the new CDR requirements were enacted in 2008, neither Congress nor the HBCU community anticipated that graduates would be entering the worst job market since the Great Depression. The recession and sluggish recovery impacted the ability of many graduates to find employment and, thus, timely repay their loans.

Redesign the Student Loan Program by Establishing a Universal and Automatic Income-based Student Loan Repayment System

Unfortunately, the Federal Government is holding colleges accountable for student repayment of Federal education loans, when the loans are issued by the Federal Government and institutions do not have flexibility to reduce the amounts that students borrow below the statutory loan limits. Ensuring that students repay their loans is a distraction for our institutions and a drain on limited resources since schools must hire consultants to identify and track students who become delinquent on their loan repayments. UNCF member institutions want to focus on the academic needs of their students. The Federal Government should lift the burden of loan debt collection off their shoulders.

UNCF supports the establishment of a universal and automatic income-based student loan repayment administered by the Federal Government. Australia, the United Kingdom and other countries have figured this out; they have implemented successful systems for the government to collect on student loans through automatic, income-based repayment. In these countries, there is no student loan default problem. This is a solution that is simple, streamlined and a sensible way to support students who must take out loans to finance their futures, without burdening institutions with the role of debt collector.

Support and Spur Innovation at HBCUs

HBCUs could be important engines of innovation—generating and testing new ways of meeting the needs of an increasingly diverse student population; addressing the current challenges faced by higher education in providing quality education anytime, anywhere; any place; preparing students for a changing economy; and moving research ideas out of the laboratory and classroom into the marketplace. The HEA provides basic formula support to HBCUs through the title III, part B program, which supports basic operating needs. But, HBCUs could do so much more, if they only had the opportunities and resources.

New venture capital should be authorized within HEA to provide the resources and incentives for HBCUs to experiment, pilot, evaluate and scale up promising best practices for student success and to catalyze centers of innovation where the best minds can integrate education and research in exciting and new ways to drive innovation. The possibilities are almost limitless.

Modernize Title III Formula Grants

Title III, part B discretionary and mandatory grants are the bedrock of Federal financial support to our institutions, providing essential formula-based aid for academic programs, fiscal and management improvements, and technology. We support continued authorization for both the discretionary and mandatory programs, with several changes that we believe will strengthen the program. We recommend provisions expressly permitting title III funds to be used for creating or improving institutional capacity to offer distance education programs. In addition, UNCF supports expanding the authorized use of title III funds for supportive services, similar to the current authorization under the title V program.

Expand the HBCU Capital Financing Program

The HBCU Capital Financing Program provides HBCUs with access to low-interest loans not available elsewhere to support physical infrastructure and facility improvements. This program is a good news story for both HBCUs and taxpayers. As a result of previous investments, HBCUs have provided students with enhanced learning and living environments, rebuilt and restored historic buildings, and provided jobs in their communities, with little risk to the government since each borrowing institution must contribute 5 percent of loan proceeds to a pooled escrow fund to cover any potential delinquencies or defaults. UNCF supports an increase in cumulative loan authority from the current $1.1 billion set in 2008 to $3 billion to accommodate institutional infrastructure needs over the period of the next HEA reauthorization. In addition, we request that interest rates for loans for STEM-related facilities be lowered, to facilitate an expansion of the capacity of HBCUs to produce STEM graduates.

Recognize "Degree of Difficulty" in the Proposed College Rating System and Do Not Distribute Federal Student Assistance Based on College Ratings

Finally, UNCF would like to comment on the college rating system proposed by President Obama—officially named the Postsecondary Institution Ratings Systems. UNCF agrees that institutions should be held accountable for the quality of higher education they deliver. Nonetheless, we are concerned because the President's plan has the potential to punish HBCUs that are already doing the hard work that needs to be done by educating large proportions of low-income, minority students, while privileging those institutions whose metrics look good on paper but have done little to get more minority students to the finish line.

The President's plan also does not appear to take into consideration capacity and resource constraints that disadvantage HBCUs, and that can limit the ability of an institution to provide the necessary student support services so that underprepared students can succeed academically and institutional financial aid that can help students stay in school.

Dr. Walter Kimbrough, president of Dillard University, developed an apt metaphor for college performance ratings based on the scoring used in competitive diving.[21] In diving, swimmers receive a raw score from 1 to 10 based on dive execution. That score is averaged by the judges and then multiplied by the degree of difficulty for the overall score. For any college rating system to be fair and accurate, "degree of difficulty" in serving students must be calculated when judging institutional performance. Institutional raw scores must be adjusted to account for differences in the socio-economic composition of student populations, student academic preparation, institutional resources and other factors beyond an institution's control, using a valid methodology.

UNCF opposes awarding and distributing Federal student assistance funds based on college ratings, as the President has proposed. We believe that such a system would result in significant inequities in the allocation of Federal financial aid to low-income students, undermine access and choice, and turn on its head the longstanding principle that Federal student assistance is awarded based on need.

Senator HAGAN. Thank you, Dr. Lomax. Mr. Oakley.

---

[21] Walter Kimbrough. 2013. Inside Higher Education. *When Rating Colleges, Think Diving*.

STATEMENT OF ELOY ORTIZ OAKLEY, BA, MBA, PRESIDENT OF LONG BEACH CITY COLLEGE, LONG BEACH, CA

Mr. OAKLEY. Thank you, Chair Hagan, Ranking Member Paul, and distinguished members of the committee. Thank you for inviting me here today to discuss these very important topics. I have the pleasure of serving as the president of Long Beach City College in Long Beach, CA, and I'm honored to be here today in support of this committee's policy work that will shape America's future. And I'm very grateful that you have exhibited interest in what we're doing in Long Beach.

I testify before you today as a veteran of the U.S. military, as a Latino American, and as a first-generation college student who attended a California community college and had the opportunity to transfer to a University of California campus. This issue of strengthening MSIs to increase the number of under-represented students that obtain a quality college credential is something that drives my presidency and I believe is a major economic imperative for our Nation.

The members of this committee are well aware of the demographic shifts in America and of the stubborn education achievement gaps that threaten our economic prosperity. While this gap is closing, it still has major economic and policy implications that I believe should be addressed by the reauthorization of the Higher Education Act.

Long Beach City College serves a diverse student population like many other urban community colleges. More than 83 percent of our students are from minority ethnic groups. The college has held the Hispanic serving institution designation for the past 17 years. Forty-one percent of our students received Pell grants, and more than 70 percent received need-based aid from California in 2012–13. In addition, 62 percent of our students are first-generation college students.

To improve student success, my college has implemented several key programs that have significantly increased college access and success for our students. The foundation of these efforts is in the Long Beach College Promise. The Long Beach College Promise is a partnership between the Long Beach Unified School District, the third largest school district in California, Long Beach City College, and California State University Long Beach.

The College Promise guarantees students from the Long Beach Unified School District the opportunity to pursue a college education locally. Students and families know what steps are required, and, in return, they receive preferential admission to Long Beach State, and if they decide to attend Long Beach City College, they receive additional financial assistance.

Through the College Promise, we have been able to reduce financial and structural barriers which prevent students from pursuing college. California's Little Hoover

Commission cited the College Promise as a model that should be replicated throughout California.

Our partnership also provided us an opportunity to address one of the most significant barriers for under-represented students, placement into remedial courses. Until recently, more than 90 percent of Long Beach City College students were being placed into remedial courses, making them much less likely to succeed in college.

Our research staff conducted research that proved high school grades were the best predictor of success in college level courses. Prior to this research, my college, like most colleges throughout the Nation, used standardized test scores to place incoming students.

Based on this research, my college developed the Promise Pathways initiative in 2012. We use predictive analytics to assess and place students into English and math courses based on their high school achievement instead of standardized assessment tests.

As a result of these changes, successful completion rates of transfer-level English in the first year increased from 12 percent to 41 percent, and in math from 5 percent to 15 percent. Students were placed directly into college level courses, and they succeeded at the same rate as other students who had to take several semesters of remedial courses.

These findings are not unique to Long Beach City College. The potential extends well beyond California and throughout the Nation. These results have been validated by several other community colleges in California, as well as from research from the Community College Research Center.

National organizations like the American Association of Community Colleges and Complete College America are calling for community colleges to shift assessment and placement away from relying solely on placement exams. While this doesn't solve all of our problems of completion, we believe that this is an important step in the right direction. And we believe it will help more students earn more degrees in a much shorter period of time.

I believe we are on the right path. I look forward to your questions and thank you again for inviting me here today.

[The prepared statement of Mr. Oakley follows:]

Prepared Statement of Eloy Ortiz Oakley, BA, MBA

Chairman Harkin, Ranking Member Alexander, and members of the committee, thank you for inviting me here today to discuss two important topics that have significant impact on our Nation: strengthening Minority Serving Institutions (MSIs) and best practices and innovations for student success.

My name is Eloy Ortiz Oakley and I serve as the superintendent-president of Long Beach City College, in Long Beach CA. I am honored to be here today in support of the very important policy work of this committee. Your work will shape the future of America and I am grateful that you have an interest in learning more about how we serve students in Long Beach. I testify before you today as a veteran of the U.S. military, a Latino American and a first generation college student who transferred from a California community college to a University of California campus. The issue of strengthening MSIs to increase the number of under-represented and first generation students who obtain a quality college credential is an issue that drives my presidency at Long Beach City College and is a major economic imperative for our Nation.

As you are aware, community colleges and in particular MSIs are the gateway to higher education credentials for millions of Americans and are critical to meet the Nation's need to prepare a globally competitive workforce in the 21st Century and beyond.

According to the U.S. Department of Education data, Latinos represented 14 percent of the total Fall 2012 enrollment at degree-granting institutions. In Fall 2012, 57 percent of Latinos attended 2-year public institutions and 43 percent attended 4-year public institutions. According to U.S. Census Bureau data, Latinos are significantly less likely to complete their education—about 11 percent of 22–24-year- old Latinos have attained at least a bachelor's degree, half of the national average for this cohort (22 percent). This gap, which fortunately is closing, has major economic and policy implications and should be addressed in the reauthorization of the Higher Education Act (HEA).

Long Beach City College (LBCC), like many urban community colleges, serves a diverse student population in terms of ethnic and racial demographics, economic status, native language and college preparation. More than 83 percent of our students are from minority ethnic groups and LBCC has held the Department of Education's Hispanic-Serving Institution (HSI) designation for the past 17 years. As you can see, LBCC exemplifies the face of America's future.

Latino students are our largest student cohort and represent more than 52 percent of our student body. Latino enrollment at LBCC has risen substantially in the last decade, from 28 percent in 2002, and is expected to continue to increase given enrollment demographics of our largest local K–12 system, in which 84 percent of the students in the 2013–14 school year represent ethnic minority groups and 55 percent are Hispanic. LBCC also serves large numbers of African American (18 percent) and Asian/Pacific Islander (14 percent) students.

LBCC also serves a student population with significant financial need. Forty-one percent of our students received Pell grants and more than 70 percent received need-based State aid in the form of Board of Governors enrollment fee waivers in the 2012–13 academic year. In addition, 62 percent of our students are first-generation college students.

LBCC has implemented several key interventions and programs that have significantly increased student success, which I will discuss in more detail later. Even as the college has seen improvements in the number of students completing key academic milestones, stubborn achievement gaps persist. According to the California Community College Chancellor's Office (CCCCO) Student Success Scorecard data for the 2007–8 6-year cohort, Latinos demonstrated an overall completion rate of 36 percent versus 48.5 percent for Whites. Closing this and other achievement gaps and increasing the number of students receiving a community college credential or becoming transfer ready are the primary goals of LBCC and should be incentivized through the HEA.

Scalable Interventions: Long Beach College Promise and Promise Pathways

LBCC has implemented several key interventions and programs that have significantly increased college access and success for our exceptionally diverse student body. The foundation of these efforts is the Long Beach College Promise—a partnership between Long Beach Unified School District, Long Beach City College and California State University, Long Beach.

Through the College Promise, our local public education institutions forged a partnership to improve preparation, access and success for our local students and specifically to address the barriers that first-generation students face in matriculating to and succeeding in higher education.

Together, we have built a holistic system that begins in elementary school and extends through college completion. At its core, the College Promise guarantees students from the Long Beach Unified School District the opportunity to pursue a college education locally. Students and families know what steps are required and in return receive access to preferential admission consideration at Long Beach State and financial assistance if they decide to attend Long Beach City College.

Here are just a few statistics to show what this partnership has accomplished in the 6 years since the inception of the College Promise:

- More than 31,000 fourth-graders have attended day-long field trips to LBCC, and 31,000 fifth-graders have attended field trips to CSULB.
- More than 57,000 middle-school students and their parents have completed and signed Long Beach College Promise Pledges, which commits parent and student to satisfactorily completing college and career preparatory courses.
- More than 5,600 students have had a free first semester at LBCC, intended to mitigate financial barriers to attending college.
- There has been 43 percent increase in LBUSD students enrolling at California State University, Long Beach despite significant increases in overall selectivity.

California's Little Hoover Commission cited the College Promise as a model that should be replicated throughout California saying:

"Regional partnerships such as the Long Beach College Promise not only get high school students to think of themselves as college-bound, but to prepare themselves so they are in a better position to succeed once they are there."[22]

Through the College Promise, we have been able to reduce financial and structural barriers which too often prevent students from pursuing college.

Our partnership also provided an opportunity to address one of the most significant barriers to increasing college completions, especially for under-represented students: placement into remedial (developmental) courses.

Placement into remedial education is a significant barrier to completion. A recent report from the Community College Research Center at Teachers College, Columbia University (CCRC) found that only 28 percent of community college students who take a developmental education course go on to earn a degree within 8 years, and many students assigned to developmental courses drop out before completing their sequence and enrolling in college-level courses. These numbers are particularly chilling since national figures show that 68 percent of community college students enroll in at least one remedial course.[23] These numbers are significantly higher for Latino and African American students.[24]

At Long Beach City College, 90 percent of incoming students were being placed into remedial courses in English, math or reading. Despite all of our work to align curricula and to improve preparation, Long Beach Unified graduates were only doing slightly better.

Our close relationship with Long Beach Unified provided both the opportunity and the impetus to seek a new approach. Long Beach City College research staff examined 5 years of data from incoming freshmen from Long Beach Unified high schools to identify the best predictors for success in college courses. The research showed that high school grades were the best predictors of success in college-level courses and yet LBCC, like most colleges, relied primarily upon standardized test scores to place incoming students.

The impact of this disproportionate emphasis on standardized test scores has been profound: many students who would likely succeed in transfer level English and math were being diverted into remediation—often multiple semesters in each subject. This misalignment between high school preparation and college placement was causing unnecessary remedial placements, slowing and too often halting altogether, momentum toward a degree or transfer, and disproportionately affected students of color.

Based on the opportunity this research presented and other best practices, Long Beach City College developed the Promise Pathways initiative, which launched in the fall of 2012. The initial cohort of freshman consisted of 976 diverse students and the results they achieved are impressive. LBCC used predictive analytics to assess and place these students into English and math courses based on their high school achievement, instead of

---

[22] A New Plan for a New Economy: Reimagining Higher Education, Little Hoover Commission 2013; p. 35.
[23] What We Know About Developmental Education Outcomes, Community College Research Center; January 2014.
[24] Remediation: Higher Education's Bridge to Nowhere, Complete College America, 2012.

standardized assessment tests. Assessment into college-level English increased from barely 10 percent using traditional assessment in the previous cohort to almost 60 percent using multiple measures assessment. Assessment into college-level math increased from less than 10 percent to over 30 percent.

LBCC also provided these students with clear first-semester education plans and registration priority to ensure that students enrolled in these foundational courses upon entry into college. Students were also encouraged to enroll full-time and 85 percent of the cohort did.

As a result of these changes, first time students in Promise Pathways were much more likely than students in previous cohorts to successfully complete transfer-level English and math and to achieve key early milestones in their first year. Successful completion rates of transfer-level English in the first year jumped from 12 percent in the previous year to 41 percent. For transfer-level math, successful completion in the first year increased from 5 percent to 15 percent. (See graph.)

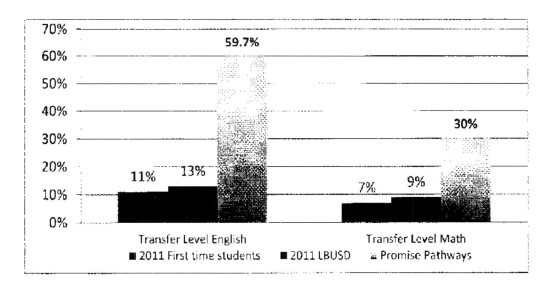

Figure 1. Percentage of students assessed into transfer-level in English and Math by cohort.

Importantly, despite dramatically expanding placement directly into college-level coursework, those students succeeded at the same rates as students who had received multiple semesters of developmental instruction and had persisted through multiple years at the college (both typically predictors of higher rates of success), and outperformed other first-time students who tested in via the assessment, providing powerful validation of the initiative.

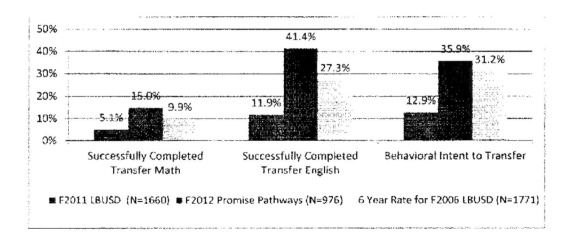

Figure 2. F2012 Promise Pathways achievement in first year vs. 6-year rates of achievement for most recent (F2006) six-year cohort from LBUSD available.

Access to, entry into and, most importantly, completion of transfer-level courses increased for all demographic groups. Rates of achievement of these milestones increased for every demographic group with some of the largest relative gains made by Latino and African American students. In fact, the rates of achievement of these milestones by students of color in the Promise Pathways in 2012 outpaced those of white students in 2011 in nearly every case.[25]

The 2013 Promise Pathways cohort of more than 1,300 students and comprised of students from three school districts showed similar gains mid-year and demonstrates that the positive effects of using multiple measure-based placement is not limited to a single school district.

The implications of our initial efforts are clear: basing assessment and course placement upon a blunt instrument like a placement test needlessly impeded many of our students who already had the tools to succeed by putting them in remedial courses that they didn't need and that often failed to improve student outcomes.

Tremendous gains were made by adjusting in how we placed students to align with evidence of their previous achievement. But what is most promising and important for this committee to know is that these findings are not unique to Long Beach City College. The potential reach of this extends throughout California and the United States.

LBCC's award-winning Predictive Placement model[26] has been tested at other community colleges in California, and according to a recent report from the RP Group, our efforts "helped catalyze . . . a growing network of colleges reproducing and refining this

---

[25] Overview and disaggregation of the impact of the Fall 2012 Promise Pathways on key educational milestones, LBCC Office of Institutional Effectiveness; 2013.
[26] President Oakley accepted the 2014 James Irvine Leadership Award in recognition of the Promise Pathways initiative. LBCC's research received the 2014 Mertes Award for Excellence in Community College Research & the 2012 RP Group Excellence in College Research Award.

approach and using its results to inform local use of multiple measures in placement.[27] The California Community College Chancellor's Office is developing a statewide multiple measures database, based on the methods developed at Long Beach City College, to enable expanded use of high school grades to place students.[28]

Several studies from the Community College Research Center at Teachers College, Columbia University strongly support the use of multiple measures using high school achievement in assessment of students' readiness for college-level work.[29] Findings from one large scale study found that 'one in four test-takers in math and one in three test-takers in English are severely mis-assigned under current test- based policies, with mis-assignments to remediation much more common . . . [and u]sing high school transcript information—either instead of or in addition to test scores—could significantly reduce the prevalence of assignment errors.'[30]

National organizations like the American Association of Community Colleges[31] and Complete College America[32] are calling for community colleges to shift assessment and placement away from primary reliance upon traditional standardized placement tests. Several States, most notably Florida and North Carolina, have recently implemented significant changes to assessment and placement practices in their community colleges.[33]

While improving assessment and placement alone will not solve our completion challenges, it clearly is one of the most effective steps that can be taken and will produce savings for taxpayers and students by not forcing students to retake coursework they had already successfully completed but also will help more students earn degrees and certificates by removing barriers and help them do so more quickly. The saved opportunity costs of 1–2 additional years of college being replaced with 1–2 additional years of adult earning potential for thousands of students at LBCC alone are tremendous. At the national level, adding 1–2 years of earning potential back to the productive adult lives of millions of citizens would be a significant boost to our Nation's economy. When combined with other efforts to improve remediation, create clear pathways for students and to target resources toward completion, evidence-based placement is an essential ingredient to meeting our goal for having 60 percent of adults earn a post-secondary credential.

We believe that LBCC is on the path to continued success. There are many ways in which the Federal Government can assist these and other efforts to increase success of under-represented students. These recommendations follow.

---

[27] Stepping Up: Progression in English and Math from High School to College, Willet & Karandjeff, RP Group; 2014.

[28] Multiple Measures Assessment Project, RP Group; 2014.

[29] Do High-Stakes Placement Exams Predict College Success?, Scoot-Clayton, CCRC; 2012 & Predicting Success in College: The Importance of Placement Tests and High School Transcripts, Belfield & Crosta, CCRC; 2012.

[30] Improving the Targeting of Treatment: Evidence from College Remediation, Scott-Clayton, Crosta & Belfield, CCRC; 2012.

[31] Empowering America's Community Colleges to Build the Future: Implementation Guide, AACC; 2014 p. 18.

[32] Core Principles for Transforming Remedial Education: A Joint Statement, Complete College America; 2012 pp.3–4.

[33] "Reimagining Remediation," Community College Week, Paul Bradley; Jan. 6, 2014.

Committee on Health, Education, Labor, and Pensions

Implications and Recommendations for Federal Policy

Expand Support for MSIs through Title III & V

- As our Nation and its colleges and universities become more diverse, the need for programs to support completions of minority students is increasing. Unfortunately, current program and funding levels are not keeping pace with the increased demand. Competition for HSI, PBI and AANAPISI is intense and many deserving institutions and students are not funded under the HEA currently. While we understand that funding remains a challenge, we do believe that increased support is a solid investment in our Nation's future productivity.
- Competitive grants are currently available to colleges designated as an AANAPISI, HSI, and PBI. Colleges are precluded from applying for more than one competitive grant even when they qualify for more than one designation. Colleges that qualify for multiple MSI designations—like LBCC in which 83 percent of our students are minority students—should be allowed to apply for title III & V competitive grants in more than one of the designations. Multiple MSI grants will enable colleges with large minority populations to scale interventions to meet all students' needs and encourage more innovation in interventions resulting in improved outcomes for more under-represented students. Because these grants are targeted to specific populations at a given college, there is no reason why the current limitation should be retained.

Support Use of Student Data for Placement

Too often, Federal policies like Family Educational Rights and Privacy Act (FERPA) inhibit efforts like LBCC's Promise Pathways program, which uses grades to help students. The sharing of student data can improve transition between K– 12 and college, lead to improved assessment and placement, create opportunities for personalized interventions, and assist colleges in preparing student plans at the time of enrollment. LEAs and higher education institutions should be further permitted to use data to help students so long as student privacy is protected. And even though promising steps are being taken in California, data sharing agreements between the California Department of Education and the Chancellor's Office continue to be cumbersome and difficult to deploy. We also believe that earnings information should be made available on all undergraduate students, assuming, again, that privacy is maintained.

Promote College Readiness

- Institutions should be given incentives, including funding, to work with their local secondary schools to engage in practices that ensure students receive adequate preparation for higher education. Enhanced counseling, dual enrollment offerings, and early college assessment (leading to better choices in high school curriculum) have been found effective in increasing student preparation. Creating incentives will encourage more K–20 partnerships such as the Long Beach College Promise. This proposal is also supported by the national community college association (American Association of Community Colleges).

Restore & Expand Pell Grant Program

- The year-round Pell Grant, which is so critical to older, working students, needs to be restored, as does eligibility for ability-to-benefit (ATB) students. Year-round Pell Grants will allow more students to take courses that lead to degrees and transfer preparation during the summer and winter intersessions, which will decrease time to degree and increase awards. Given the current lifetime limit on Pell Grants, there is no logical reason not to re-instate the year-round Pell Grant. California was disproportionately impacted by the loss of ATB eligibility and we believe that this was a short-sighted policy, particularly given that the State bears the primary cost of educating these students, and believes that they merit support by the Federal Government as well.
- Higher education should be viewed as an investment both in the U.S. economy as well as the attainment of greater equity for individuals. Adequate funding for this foundational program must be retained. In particular, the base appropriated grant of $4,860 must be sustained so that automatic inflation-adjusted increases are implemented. More than 3.3 million community college students—about 34 percent—received a Pell Grant last year.

Simplify Filing the Free Application for Federal Student Aid (FASFA)

- Currently, too many community college students fail to file the FAFSA. There are a variety of reasons for this, including cultural barriers, a reluctance to become enmeshed with the Federal Government, a lack of awareness of the true cost of the education, and the complexity (and steps involved) in the application process. Students cannot access student financial if they don't first apply for it, and further action in this area is needed. This includes continued simplification of the aid application as well as greater early awareness efforts, perhaps through the tax-filing process.

Use Financial Aid to Create Incentives for Student Success

- Community colleges always have and always will emphasize the 'open door'' that is a central part of their heritage. However, new incentives for students to come ready for higher education and to persist in it are appropriate in a changing environment. Some studies show that "aid like a paycheck" and financial incentives for completion may play a helpful role in persistence. The student aid programs may need to allow for new types of programs, particularly shorter term offerings, to be eligible for student aid. We also urge Congress to avoid negative sanctions such as creating more stringent standards of satisfactory academic progress or limiting access to aid for relatively less well-prepared students.

Promote Innovations that Accelerate Student Progress to Quality Credentials and Outcomes

- As described above in LBCC's case, much effective innovation is occurring at the local and State level. The Federal Government could leverage these developments through a number of approaches. These could include providing incentives for innovation and for the expansion of evidence-based models through FIPSE, community college innovation programs, Higher Education Race to the Top, or other initiatives that provide States and institutions with the resources and flexibility needed to test, develop, and take successful strategies to scale.

Transfer

- Substantial benefits accrue the many students who complete degree and certificate programs at community colleges. However, for many students, attainment of the baccalaureate degree is necessary for economic success and a family sustaining job. The increasing premium being placed on the baccalaureate degree merits deliberate policies focused on helping more community college students continue through to receive the Bachelor's Degree (B.A.). For this reason, more reliable and efficient pathways to the B.A. degree for community college students need to be generated while also insuring that more students achieve Associate Degrees and/or certificates on the way. Incentivizing State policies such as California's Associate Degree for Transfer (SB 1440) programs that improve the transfer process between community colleges and State universities through streamlined transfer pathways and the elimination of excess credit units will increase the number of minority students transferring to a 4-year college, improve the diversity of universities and increase the number of minority students obtaining a B.A.

Align Federal Laws and Regulations

- The committee should act to align Federal laws related to higher education and workforce preparation—HEA, ESEA, Perkins, WIA—so that requirements (e.g., eligibility, reporting requirements, performance metrics) do not add unnecessary compliance costs for institutions and allow for greater transparency in programs performance, while promoting system-level student success innovations. The current set of overlapping and conflicting requirements is a serious drag on the higher education system. We strongly support the ongoing effort by members of this committee to reduce Federal regulations on higher education institutions.

Senator HAGAN. Mr. Oakley, thank you very much for your opening statement. Dr. DeSousa from Fayetteville State University.

Statement of D. Jason Desousa, EdD, Assistant Vice Chancellor of Student Retention, Fayetteville State University, Fayetteville, NC

Mr. DESOUSA. Good morning, Chairwoman Hagan, Ranking Member Paul, Senator Burr, and distinguished members of the Senate Health, Education, Labor, and Pensions Committee. Thank you for inviting me to testify about student success and best practices that are being implemented at Fayetteville State University.

I am a proud graduate of Morgan State University in Baltimore, MD. As an undergraduate, the enriching educational experiences, effective mentoring, and supportive campus environment helped shape the person I am today. I would be remiss if I did not mention the role of my academic advisor, Ms. Margaret Barton, who set the very highest levels of academic and personal expectations for others and me. I believe that every HBCU in this country has a Margaret Barton, one who academically challenges students yet nurtures and supports them.

My career in education includes several stints in seven public and private HBCUs in the country. Fayetteville State University is comprehensive, regional, constituent institution of the University of North Carolina. At Fayetteville State University, 66 percent of the students are African American, 5 percent Hispanic, 75 percent Pell eligible, 20 percent military affiliated, the highest percentage of total enrollment in the University of North Carolina system. In addition, nearly half are adult learners, and 95 percent of our students are in-State, most of whom come from the rural regions of North Carolina.

At FSU, African American males represent the lowest performing campus subgroup. We are making strides in turning that around.

On average, during the period of 2005 to 2010, male students have accounted for 36 percent of our first-year, first-time students in contrast to females. The average rate at which males persisted to graduation during such periods and for which 4-year data were available was 10 percent, demonstrating that FSU attracted a small proportion of men and, more troubling, graduating them at lower rates.

Because most academic performance measures showed that males were underperforming, FSU was intentional about initiating a set of student success interventions for male students, starting in 2012 with a unique assistant vice chancellor for student retention and male initiative position, a coordinator for academic resources, supplemental instruction, program associate, and a cadre of peer tutors help along with the program.

FSU's major male initiative, the MILE, Male Initiative on Leadership and Excellence, takes advantage of over $400,000 in title III funds to develop targeted student success initiatives and practices. In its initial year, the initiative helped increase retention rates of males from 67 percent in 2010 to 74 percent in 2011.

In addition to its emphasis on academic success, the university's male initiative now focuses on financial literacy, a desired educational outcome for the university, through a new summer course entitled Black Men Banking on Their Future, a hybrid course which has a field component on Wall Street in New York City. FSU male initiatives helped attract a College Access Grant from the University of North Carolina General Administration. We were one of five institutions to receive the grant for the purpose of strengthening minority male mentoring.

We have a very strong relationship with Fayetteville Tech Community College through a specialized grant from The Links. Through this Links grant, we're able to partner Fayetteville Tech Community College's male initiative with the Bronco MILE, Fayetteville State University's male initiative, and have realized important gains in terms of creating expectations that will improve the rates at which transfer students from Fayetteville Tech Community College come to Fayetteville State University. Many HBCUs are improving African American male college completion rates through similar innovative programs, including the Morgan State University MILE and the North Carolina Central University Centennial program.

Fayetteville State University is working very hard to ensure Federal investments are yielding high returns. Additionally, we are doing our part to leverage resources by partnering with majority institutions and others to provide greater academic support services to our students.

I look forward to answering your questions.

[The prepared statement of Mr. DeSousa follows:]

Prepared Statement of D. Jason Desousa, EdD

Introduction

Good morning. Chairwoman Hagan, Ranking Member Paul, and distinguished members of the Senate Health, Education, Labor and Pensions Committee, my name is Dr. D. Jason DeSousa, assistant vice chancellor of Student Retention for Fayetteville State University (FSU). Thank you for inviting me to testify about student success and the best practices that are being implemented at FSU.

Additionally, please allow me to thank Fayetteville State University's Chancellor James Anderson and Provost Jon Young for the support and resources that they have provided me to implement practices that undergird student success for the University's students. I would be remiss if I did not thank Dr. George D. Kuh, Indiana University Professor Emeritus of Higher Education, for guiding and mentoring me through graduate school at Indiana University.

I am a proud graduate of Morgan State University, an HBCU in the State of Maryland. As an undergraduate, the enriching educational experiences, effective mentoring, and supportive campus environment, helped shape the person I am today. Based on my high school performance and standardized test scores, I was fortunate enough to be accepted to Morgan State University. It was Morgan's ''talent development'' philosophy that inspired my confidence and motivated me to be a resilient student with superb habits of the mind—habits that prepared me for graduate school at Bowling Green State University (Bowling Green, OH) and Indiana University Bloomington (Bloomington, IN). I would be remiss if I did not mention the role of my academic adviser, Mrs. Margaret Barton, who set the very highest levels of academic and personal expectations for others and me. Every HBCU has a Margaret Barton—one who academically challenges students yet nurtures and supports them.

My career in education includes several stints on seven public and private HBCU campuses. On those campuses, the enrollments ranged from 850 to 9,000 and I have seen first-hand what works and where resources are needed to gain more success. I hope you will leave today with a better understanding of what we are doing at Fayetteville State to create success for all students and in particular for those who traditionally underperform or face significant challenges as non-traditional students.

Background on Fayetteville State University

Fayetteville State University (FSU) is a comprehensive, regional constituent institution of the University of North Carolina. Founded in 1867 to prepare teachers for the children of recently freed slaves, the core aspect of FSU's mission is to ". . . promote the educational, social, cultural, and economic transformation of southeastern North Carolina and beyond." The institution continues to serve its original purpose and mission to provide quality education to underserved populations. The student population demographic is 66 percent

African American, 5 percent Hispanic, 75 percent Pell eligible, and 20 percent military-affiliated (the highest percentage of students (of total enrollment) in the UNC system). In addition, nearly half (49.2 percent) are adult learners and 95 percent of our students are in-State most of whom come from the region which is largely rural.

FSU has six *Strategic Priorities*, with "Retention and Graduation" expressed as its first priority. Given our emphasis on student access, success, and persistence to graduation, this year the Washington, DC-based "Institute for Higher Education Policy" named FSU as an "Exemplar Institution for Access and Success" for its commitment to high-impact access and success practices that are particularly targeted to improve underserved North Carolina populations. (FSU joins California State University-Northridge, Florida State University, and Miami Dade College in this distinction.)

Some of the University's "Points of Distinction" include the following:

1. The University of North Carolina General Administration's "Teacher Quality Impact Study" listed FSU's School of Education as producing highly effective teachers of science and English.
2. As of 2012, FSU enjoys the distinction of being the only UNC institution to house on its campus an International Early College High School.
3. FSU is one of 20 high performing institutions, with higher-than-predicted graduation rates according to the Indiana University-based National Survey of Student Engagement (NSSE) Institute. FSU joins other high performing schools such as Macalester College, Miami University of Ohio, University of Kansas, University of Texas El Paso, and University of Michigan.
4. The University actively supports the military by developing specialized online courses and offering classes on military installations in North Carolina and Fort Sam Houston in Texas.

The university has a longstanding commitment to student success with an institutional culture characterized by academic challenge and support. Student success and achievement initiatives include increasing admission standards, policy changes, strengthened academic support and advisement, and implementation of support programs for under-represented groups, consistent data analysis.

Best Practices and Innovation at Fayetteville State University

At FSU, African American males represent the lowest performing campus sub group. We are making strides in turning that around. On average, during the period of 2005 to 2010, male students have accounted for 36 percent of first-time, first-year students in contrast to females. The average rate at which males persisted to graduation during such periods and for which 4-year data were available was 10 percent, demonstrating FSU attracted a small proportion of men and, more troubling, graduated them at lower rates.

Because most academic performance measures showed that males were underperforming, FSU was intentional about initiating a set of student success interventions for male students, starting in spring 2012, with a unique "Assistant Vice Chancellor for Student Retention and Male Initiative" (AVC) position. A Coordinator for Academic Resources, Supplemental Instructor, Program Associate, and a cadre of peer tutors and mentors augment the senior-level Academic Affairs position.

FSU's male initiatives—the "Male Initiative on Leadership and Excellence" (MILE) and the "Boosting Bronco Brothers Transition to FSU Initiative" (B3)—take advantage of over $400,000 in title III funds to develop targeted student success initiatives and practices. Taken together, the MILE and B3 serve 205 males, which represents 18.4 percent of the target group of first-time male freshmen (1,114) or 12.3 percent of the total male student population at FSU (1,667).

In its initial year, the initiatives helped increase the fall-to-fall retention of males from 67 percent in 2010 to 74 percent in 2011, a 7-percentage point increase. As was stated earlier, males who participate in the BRONCO MILE program were retained at a significantly higher rate (84 percent) than non-participants (66 percent). In addition to its emphasis on academic success, the University's male initiatives now focuses on financial literacy—a desired institutional outcome—through a new summer course entitled 'Black Men Banking on Their Future," a hybrid-type course, which has a field study component on Wall Street in New York City, NY. FSU's male initiatives helped attract a College Access Challenge Grant from the University of North Carolina General Administration (system office)—only one of five institutions to receive the grant for the purpose of strengthening male mentoring.

FSU's strong relationship with Fayetteville Technical Community College (FTCC) has enabled both institutions to take their male initiatives to a more innovative level. Through The Links, Inc., FSU and FTCC have been collaborating over the past 2 years to better increase transfer rates from FTCC to FSU. FTCC's "Male Mentoring Program" and FSU's MILE now partner to create opportunities for men of color transferring to FSU to connect with a MILE peer mentor before entering FSU. While the initial grant did not require both male initiatives to partner together, Chancellor Anderson and FTCC President Larry Keen insisted on this innovative practice, which has been yielding positive results.

Accordingly, many HBCUs are improving African American male college completion rates through similar innovative programs, including the Morgan State University MILE and the North Carolina Central University Centennial Scholars.

Other Innovations That Undergird Student Success

In addition to the afore-mentioned initiatives, these additional programs have improved access and success for underserved populations at FSU: (1) Faculty Development; (2) Collegiate Learning Assessment; (3) CHEER Scholars Program; (4) Learning Communities; (5) Student Fairs for Selecting Majors; (6) Academic Support— Learning

Center, Supplemental Instruction; and (7) Pre-College Outreach. I will expound here on just a few of these.

- CHEER Scholars Program (Creating Higher Expectations for Educational Readiness), which began in 2002, is a residential summer bridge for incoming freshmen who do not fully meet FSU's admission standards. Serving 20 percent to 25 percent of FSU's first-year students each year, the program provides college access to students who perform poorly on standardized tests. Studies indicate that high school GPA is a strong predictor of college success, while standardized tests (SAT and ACT) are poor predictors, yet those tests continue to be the cause of denying college admission to good students. From 2008–12, over 99 percent of CHEER participants (549 out of 554), all of whom were denied full admission due to standardized test scores, earned a C or better in both summer courses, allowing full-time enrollment in the fall.
- Female Students find support through two unique programs: "Saving Our Sisters" (SOS) and "Strong Sisters Soaring" (S^3). These programs provide academic support for first-year females who were admitted on a provisional basis because of low GPA and/or test scores. The latter is an initiative designed to address health issues for women.
- Learning communities are sets of linked courses, usually exploring a common theme. Instructors in learning communities work together to develop the theme and coordinate the course content. Students enroll in all of the courses linked through the learning community. By linking together students, faculty, and courses, learning communities create more opportunities for enrichment, interaction, and exploration. For the last two decades the research on learning communities indicates that when they are structured effectively they almost always have a positive impact. Since 2009, nearly 80 percent of entering freshmen have participated in learning communities each year. Learning community participants at FSU have higher GPA's than students who are not in learning communities (2.5 to 2.04 in fall 2012) and return for the second year at a higher rate than students who are not in learning communities (75.4 percent to 60 percent).
- As it relates to pre-college outreach, the Office of College Access Programs provides a broad range of high-quality college preparatory services annually to an average of 3,000 youth low-income/first-generation students, their parents and professional development services for educators who teach at Title I Schools. The Office includes national youth programs Gaining Early Awareness for Undergraduate Programs (GEAR UP), Talent Search, Upward Bound, Upward Bound Math & Science and 21st Century Community Learning Centers. In addition, AmeriCorps VISTA (Volunteers In Service to America), an anti-poverty program, is housed in the Office of College Access Programs to provide capacity

building for mobilizing local resources to achieve sustainable solutions. Ninety percent (90 percent) of the students are of color with graduation rates of 91 percent and college placement rates of 75 percent.

- Financial aid education is also a major priority for this population of students. Financial aid education begins prior to enrollment with the FIRST STEPS program. FIRST STEPS is a program that helps prospective first-time students and their families take the first steps toward success at FSU, to include placement testing, advisement, registration, and financial aid counseling. During the financial aid counseling, students and families discuss decisionmaking related to financing their college education, including instruction on debt-burden, financial literacy, and true cost of education. Once enrolled the priority order of financial aid packaging is always free money (grants, scholarships); loans are packaged last as needed up to one's cost of attendance. Where loans are offered, students must go online to accept and if a new borrower (entrance counseling has to be completed) before funds will disburse. New initiatives in planning for academic year 2014–15 are: in person loan counseling sessions (schools did this before automation), and hiring of a Default Manager (many schools are going this route with the new default guidelines).

Conclusion

Fayetteville State University is working hard to ensure Federal investments are yielding high returns. Additionally, we are doing our part to leverage resources by partnering with majority institutions and others to provide greater academic support services to our students. I look forward to answering your questions.

Thank you.

Senator HAGAN. Thank you, Dr. DeSousa.

Dr. Bassett, president of Heritage University.

STATEMENT OF JOHN BASSETT, PhD, PRESIDENT OF HERITAGE UNIVERSITY, TOPPENISH, WA

Mr. BASSETT. Thank you, Senator Hagan and Senator Burr— great years in North Carolina, although I did have to tell Senator Warren this morning that immediately before Washington, I was in Massachusetts for 10 years—never could keep a job, you know, always moving around.

Senator Murray introduced Heritage University so well I wasn't quite sure I had anything left to say, except that when people say, "Well, what is Heritage?" I say, "Well, it's only had one president.

She's a Catholic nun, but it's not a Catholic school, and it is on tribal land, but it's not a tribal school." Well, what in the world is it?

It's a private university that was established about 32 years ago, not where Fort Wright was. That was in Spokane. But it did have a kind of branch in the Yakima Valley. Two Native American women, when Fort Wright folded, said, "There's no place to educate our teachers," and they started a new college.

Now, that's kind of hard to believe right now. How in the world do you start a new college that way? They raised money. They got land. They got some influential trustees, and they told Sister Kathleen Ross, who was the provost in Fort Wright then as it closed, that she had to be the first president.

So 28 years later, she handed off her baby to somebody coming in from Massachusetts. It's a remarkable place. The Yakima Valley is a great agricultural valley, where all your apples come from. We grow the hops and so forth. That's really what has led to the student population being about 55 percent Mexican American and about 10 percent to 15 percent Native American with the population on the Yakama Reservation.

The educational attainment in the valley is low, particularly the lower valley, which doesn't include the city of Yakima, as the upper valley. It includes a great deal of poverty. Only 6 percent of the adults in the lower valley have a bachelor's degree. Appalachia is 12 percent by comparison. The students grow up there with people telling them for one reason or another what they can't do. "Well, your people don't do that sort of thing? What is it that you think you're doing?"

Over and over again, we meet a person that's been told by counselors, you know, "You're very good with your hands, Juanita. You might think about beauty school." Now, I have nothing against beauty schools, but these Juanitas are capable of being brain surgeons, and they've been told all their life what they can't do, what the limitations are.

When I arrived at Heritage, I felt that as wonderful as it was, anecdotally, statistically, it wasn't performing the way it should. We've made a number of investments to improve performance in the last couple of years. One is to really increase the intentional tutoring and advising of all of our students. That individual attention, building on TRIO and CAMP programs too, is making a huge difference.

Second is attaching them to a major and a dream earlier. We find that almost all the students that drop out really don't have a clear image of themselves being an airline pilot or a doctor, lawyer, business person, or whatever it is.

Third is changing the financial aid formula to a more equitable formula so that more students can go. Fourth is raising expectations, creating a culture of higher expectations. The worst thing we can do is lower the bar for students. These students have amazing potential. Yes, they've been educationally disadvantaged, but they have wonderful potential.

Over and over again, I see students—a young woman named Brenda who dropped out of school, had a baby, and was working in the fields. Somebody said, "Why are you doing this? You're a smart young woman." And they got her to go back and get a GED, get a college degree. She graduates from Heritage, takes a couple of corporate jobs in the East, and is now managing a lot of the international marketing for St. Michelle Wineries.

I could tell the same story about people now with managerial positions at Costco, Walmart, and many other corporations like that, or holding excellent teaching positions. Our residency-based teacher training program is recognized maybe as the best in the State, and the teachers are culturally sensitive to the kinds of students in the classroom.

A couple of comments about the particular populations we have. The Hispanic population—very family-oriented. Students don't go to college. Families go to college. In fact, we know if we don't get out in the valley and reach the kids when they're this age, working with their families, we're always going to be fighting a rear guard action.

In order to improve statistically the performance in the valley, we need to get everybody up. The Native American population— much more reserved, harder to build up trust with that population, wonderful abilities there. We find cohorting that group, having them study in groups at least for the freshman year of students with like backgrounds and like interests, can make a huge difference in their long-term success. But raising the bar, providing a lot of support—these things make a huge difference for our populations. Thank you very much.

[The prepared statement of Mr. Bassett follows:]

Prepared Statement of John Bassett, PhD

Summary

Heritage University is a private commuter university on Reservation land deeded from the Yakama Nation. Only 32 years old, it has about 1,000 undergraduates of whom 55 percent are Hispanic, mostly children of Mexican farm workers, and 10– 15 percent Native, the others a mix. The mission is to provide high quality higher education to a population largely underserved, since there is no other 4-year college for miles. It has 400 graduate students, mostly in Education. The undergraduates are 90 percent Pell-eligible, 80 percent first gen; the average family ability to pay is $150. The average parent has a 6th grade education. Educational attainment in the Yakima Valley is low, but the intelligence and potential of the young people are great.

In my 4 years we have taken a number of steps to improve completion and success rates: (1) improved financial aid practices so through an equity-based formula more students can stay in school; (2) added professional support staff for tutoring and advising to build further on successful TRIO and CAMP programs; (3) built a culture of high expectations, for the worst thing is to let these talented students, through misplaced compassion, graduate by getting over a low bar; (4) hired more full-time (not less expensive adjuncts) faculty who are there all week for the students; (5) encouraged students to identify an area of study sooner, since students who drop out—usually because of competing pressures in their life—invariably have not identified a field of study or a dream to have as a goal; (6) changed admission practices to be more certain that students who matriculate are at a point of their life when they can do the hard work to succeed; (7) built faculty agreement that they must take attendance and report red flags quickly to allow intervention; and (8) started enrolling students in cohorts that take classes together so they can have a peer group with whom they are closely engaged.

Success stories are remarkable. Our teacher prep program, honored at Federal and State levels, is a national model and has a 90 percent+ placement rate. Our business program shows amazing transformational stories of inarticulate freshmen lacking confidence in themselves going out as eloquent, confident seniors with Fortune 500 companies seeking to hire them. Successes include students like Brenda, a dropout from a culture of poverty and gangs. She had a baby but no dreams until a mentor encouraged her through the GED and college. She went on to good jobs on the east coast and now manages a lot of the international marketing for St Michelle Winery. Similar students hold managerial jobs at Costco, Walmart, and elsewhere. Haydee received her diploma Saturday; 3 years ago you would have given her no chance to have so many companies trying to hire her. Haver Jim, a 43-year-old Yakama native who entered with a not uncommon distrust of western education, has become quite a success story and received his diploma Saturday. He is taking many skills back to his people. I have essays in my iPAD from graduating students—one Native, one Latina—who came out of cultures of drugs, gangs, and poverty and who because of TRIO and University support are headed to great careers.

The cultures are very different, although poverty and lack of personal dreams are common traits. Native students, like their elders, have a deep natural reserve; they are often not forthcoming. It can take a long time to buildup trust with them. These are a community-focused, less individualistic people, yet they can be good business people. Unlike the agriculture-centered Mexican immigrants, they are a fishing people (also hunters and gatherers). They are a people with a more rooted and organic sense of their relationship to the land, which they protect like a family member. They have amazing talents.

While family is important for Indians, I would say that family is the first issue to address with the Mexican population; students do not go to Heritage, families go. You need to have family support for Juanita or Jose to succeed at Heritage; and sometimes parents say, "If you were not in college but picking apples, we could have meat on the table." Heritage knows it must reach children and their families when the kids are little and give them a sense of dreams and opportunities; otherwise over half will be gone before 12th grade and enormous potential lost to America.

Heritage University was established in 1982 by two Native American (Yakama) women and Sister Kathleen Ross, a member of the Order of the Holy Names of Jesus and Mary who had been Provost of Fort Wright College. That institution had gone out of business, leaving the south central part of the State of Washington with no teacher-training program for the region. It is hard to imagine starting a private college the way Heritage started and also hard to imagine there was and is no other 4-year college within 70 miles of Toppenish in any direction. Heritage is located on tribal land (deeded to the University) of the Yakama Nation, the only college on reservation land that is not a tribal college.

Starting as a program in Education with 50–100 students on an impossibly tight budget, Heritage now has close to 1,000 undergraduates and 400 graduate students (mostly in Education), and a diverse set of majors. Its mission for almost its entire existence has been to provide higher education opportunities to an educationally disadvantaged and largely place-bound population. In its early years it had about the same number of Native and Hispanic students. Because of the large growth of Hispanic peoples, mostly Mexican-American farm workers, undergraduates are now about 55 percent Hispanic and 10–12 percent Native American. The rest are a mixture of everything else. There is currently capacity and planning to grow to 2,000 undergraduates and 1,000 graduate students.

About 90 percent of the undergraduates are Pell-grant eligible, a percentage matched at perhaps no other private college. About 75–80 percent of the students are first in their family to attend college and fewer than 10 percent have a college graduate as a parent. The average family ability to pay (on the FAFSA form) is only $150. So tuition is covered by Pell and State need-based grants, philanthropy, and loans. Heritage tries to manage student loan burdens through equity-packaging of aid; but most of the upper classmen are transfers from community colleges and often arrive with large burdens.

Heritage is a commuter campus without residence halls but with three regional sites on community college campuses elsewhere in the State. These take only transfer students. Many young people grow up in our Yakima Valley with no sense of a future, no ability to see themselves as an airline pilot, scientist, business owner, or doctor. Our Upper Valley includes the city of Yakima, which has poverty but also wealth. The Lower Valley is very poor and only 6 percent of the adults there have a bachelors degree (Appalachia is 12 percent). In the Lower Valley half the kids are gone from school before 12th grade to join a gang or have a baby or give up. The Reservation, moreover, like many reservations also includes a great deal of hopelessness. Our redefined mission at Heritage includes intentional strategies to reach children and their families at an early age, to help youth dream and to know the opportunities that are out there for anyone who is willing to work hard. Otherwise Heritage will always be treading water instead of effecting the major improvement in the region that is its goal.

I have been at Heritage 4 years. When I arrived, I realized Heritage scored badly on IPEDS graduation scores but also realized IPEDS covered only a teeny part of our population since many of our students were part-time students, most of our juniors were transfer students, and because our students' personal and economic conditions led to stop-out-and-return patterns that made 10-year graduation rates significantly better than 6-year rates.

To improve results, however, we have made several major changes. First a totally new admissions office is making sure that students who matriculate are ready to do the hard work needed to succeed. Second, a major investment in professional student support, advising and tutoring includes enhancement of the successful TRIO and CAMP programs. Students who get support in these programs, as well as those who get solid intentional tutoring elsewhere, have a much higher graduation rate than other students. Young people from the Yakima Valley can do anything a kid from Chevy Chase can do (I was a kid from Chevy Chase); they need more support because the Valley leaves them educationally behind. But the worst thing a teacher or adviser can do is let them graduate by getting over a low bar. If a Heritage graduate cannot compete effectively with a grad from Washington State or the University of Washington we are wasting our time.

Third we have developed a culture of high expectations, not always an easy transition for teacher or student. Fourth, we have invested in more full-time faculty who are there for the students all week, as part-time adjuncts cannot be. Fifth, we have deliberately tried to broaden our student base to include more students who enter college with a clearer sense of ambitions and opportunities to help build on campus a culture of completion and success, not just a culture of access. Sixth, having learned that students who drop out generally have not committed themselves to a major or program, we are trying to connect freshmen to an area of interest if not a major and to show them how that passion can lead to a productive career. Seventh, we are working more and more with cohorts, with groupings of students who take classes together and thereby become more engaged with their studies and programs because they bond with their shared group. Eighth, faculty members have agreed to take attendance regularly and to forward to the Dean of Students all red flags related to absence or poor performance. Ninth, we have improved our financial aid packaging to a more equitable formula that increases the number of students who can afford to stay in school.

The success stories at Heritage are what make almost everyone at the University love to come to work in the morning. Never have I seen a place where teachers are more dedicated to their students; and that is one reason I could forego retirement and have an encore career in the west. Our teacher prep program is a residency based (junior and senior years) program honored by the U.S. Department of Education and called by some in Olympia the best program in the State. Its placement rate is over 90 percent; and schools love the fact that the graduates are not only excellent teachers but have a culturally sensitive dimension for the region's diverse populations that no other program provides.

Some of the most amazing results are in our Business program. Professor Len Black provides a tough-love program for hard-working students and also has built a student team over the last decade that takes part every year in the SIFE (Students in Free Enterprise) Program that is now called Enactus. The team makes presentations in a regional, then a national competition about projects the group has done (for example, financial literacy for middle school kids; helping Mexican- American farmers start and market their new business; helping women in Belize use recycled products to make baskets). The presentations are judged by teams of corporate executives. What is unusual about the Heritage team, unlike others, is that the students are often second-language learners; they come from apple orchards and hop fields; as freshmen they were often inarticulate and totally lacked confidence. Now they are eloquent, educated, and confident. Fortune 500 companies are knocking at their door to hire them. Education there is transformative. The Heritage team, moreover, this year finished third in the entire nation against the likes of Syracuse and other national universities; four times in the last decade they have finished in the final four.

I think of so many examples of success. Brenda, a Mexican-American high school dropout from a culture of poverty but with a baby and no plans for a future, was encouraged by a mentor to go back and get her GED and then go on to college. After graduating from Heritage she went on to corporate positions in the east and now is back in Washington managing the marketing for St Michelle Wineries in that part of the world. I think of similar stories of young people who came from poverty and hold excellent positions at Costco or Walmart or another major company. Last weekend I gave a diploma to Haydee, one of the stars of the Enactus team with a great business career ahead of her. Three years ago I could hardly have imagined that with faculty guidance and her own determination she would be such a confident, capable, and eloquent future leader. I think of Crystal, a Native American with a similar story who completed Heritage, then finished a masters at Gonzaga, and later served as my chief of staff. Finally I lost her because she wanted to return to the Yakama Nation and help her people by taking a position managing its real estate purchases and sales. Now she is pursuing a doctoral degree as well. I think of Haver Jim, who just received his diploma. He is about 43 years old and entered several years ago with the not uncommon Indian suspicions of white man's education (they sent my daddy to boarding school, destroyed our culture, would not let us use our language) and became a very important part of the campus culture. He is bringing many skills back to his people as a leader. I have in my iPad essays by a Native American and a Mexican American student just graduating with the assistance of TRIO tutors. Both of them fought through youths in a culture of poverty, drugs, gangs, and low expectations. Both are graduating with honors and going on to a good job or graduate school.

The cultures are very different, and they have not always played nicely in the sandbox together. The Native American population at times has thought they were having a second colonial invasion—first the Anglos, now the Mexicans. The Yakama were traditionally a fishing population and hunters and gatherers. The Mexican population there has been largely agricultural. That leads to very different notions about water usage. Cultural practices differ. The Heritage campus is one of the few places in the region where the Mexican, Yakama, and white (the population with most of the wealth) can actually come together in civil discourse; and for many reasons the intercultural relations are better now than they used to be.

Our Native American students, like the Yakama adults, have a deep reserve that non-Indians may take a long time to appreciate. It can take a long time to buildup trust. More than any other group they can benefit in the first year from a cohort approach in which students take classes together and buildup mutual confidence and a mutual support group. The Native students often, moreover, believe they have to miss class, for example, for a family funeral that may last a week. Faculty members have a hard time figuring out how to balance academic and cultural values with these students. If a faculty and administration have patience, however, they can build strong partnerships over time with their Native populations.

I mentioned earlier the distrust many people in the older generation of Indians feel toward western education. There is a strong younger group, however, in their 30's or early 40's who want to retain many values of their elders but understand the need for a 21st century education to help the tribe be successful. They have a greater sense of oneness, wholeness, with their land and environment than other peoples do; but they insist on good science and relevant technology. They are very community-focused, interested in the common good more than individualistic goods, but they can be excellent businessmen and women.

Our Mexican-American students are very family-focused. This does not mean the Yakama people are not, although the term "family" may have a fuzzier definition in our minds as they use it than it does for Mexicans. "My younger brother" is a term that may be meant seriously by an Indian but not refer to a blood tie, although family is important for both populations. For Mexican-Americans, though, getting belief within the family in the importance of education for youth will triple the likelihood of a young person completing high school and college. While some families are supportive, others see college interfering with putting meat on the family table. I also have to add that I have not yet seen a person from these cultures of poverty who escaped, and by that I mean completed high school and at least a 2-year college degree, without a mentor urging him or her forward. It might be a family member or teacher or just another supportive adult able to bring young people back to the right path and give them confidence in their potential.

What one finds in our Valley are young people who have been told all their life what they cannot do: "Your people don't do that kind of thing" (become a doctor or scientist or engineer). We have students who were continually told "You are good with your hands, Juanita, so you might think about beauty school." I have nothing against beauty schools, but we are talking about someone who turns out to have the ability to be a brain surgeon.

How much of what I am discussing is grounded in poverty rather than ethnic identity? A lot of it, to be sure, but nonetheless there is still a great deal of correlation between economic and ethnic indicators in America. African American populations have, of course, a longer and more complex historical context that others here will cover more thoroughly than I. Native Americans have a different but also specific and complex historical context and a Reservation culture that very much needs an educational partnership between tribal education, including tribal colleges, and sympathetic mainstream education.

The Hispanic challenge differs because of the rapid and widespread recent growth of the Latino population in the United States. In our region immigration, itself a complicating factor for better or worse, has been largely of low-income and low-education workers and their families, yet smart and talented people with enormous potential—and unlike middle-class American students no sense of entitlement that the world owes them everything. Their potential, and the wasted potential, reminds us all that unless we face the crisis of low expectations and underachievement in our K–12 world, higher education is never going to do all the things in America we would like it to.

There are surely financial issues to consider as well. We worry a lot about the cost of tuition and affordability, although surely there is as great a range in the market between Ivy League tuitions (which research shows are well worth it given lifetime earnings of graduates) and community college and local 4-year-public-college tuitions as there is between an Aston Martin and a Chevrolet. Often the more expensive the school the more financial aid is available, although in truth it is the middle-income student who gets blocked out of the well-known private colleges: not wealthy enough to pay nor poor enough to get a big aid package.

Almost all students at Heritage who graduate do so without having a larger debt burden than the 25–30K range, manageable for most graduates to repay if not for those who have the burden but do not graduate.

I want to focus at the end, however, on one financial issue that hampers our Hispanic and Native students greatly but also HBCU students and poor white students. That results from the number of pre-college or remedial courses they must take to come up to the level of the Math 101 or English 101 college-level course. They use their Pell grant and State need-based grants to pay for these courses as well as others, but these courses do not count toward graduation because they are beneath college level. When these students become juniors and seniors they find they have run out of their financial aid, and their university may not have the resources to cover everything with institutional funds. Heritage may be unusual as a 4-year school in the large percentage of its students facing this crisis. Most such students may well be in 2-year colleges where they will not use up 4 years of funding; but they will face a crisis if they transfer later for a bachelors degree. Some national or State strategies will be needed to help students reach college-level coursework without a major risk to their future.

Senator HAGAN. Just listening to the opening testimony, I know we're going to have an incredible question and answer discussion period going on today. Thank you for all that you're doing on behalf of the minority serving institutions, because a mind is a terrible thing to waste, and we must be investing in it. I appreciate your testimony.

I did want to start with the questions, and we'll have 5-minute questions, and we'll go back and forth.

Dr. DeSousa, we know that we've got to provide better support service to help our African American males succeed and graduate. You opened with your MILE program. You were discussing it, and it obviously is a work in progress, but it's been successful.

Can you talk a little bit more about how you actually go into high schools, how you talk to families, how you work to be sure, and then the measurements that you're looking at to be sure that you are successful?

Mr. DESOUSA. Thank you, Senator Hagan. May I start my response by saying that one of the features of the MILE is getting young men from Fayetteville State University outside of North Carolina, making the United States of America the classroom, so moving beyond the traditional bricks and mortar of the campus.

I'll never forget when we took a group of students to Wall Street, a young man said to me, "Dr. DeSousa, I'm going to graduate from Fayetteville State University." I said, "William, why?" He said, "Because you see that young man across the street? He looks just like me. He's my height. He looks my age. He dresses like me, and I want to be a Wall Street banker one day."

Do you know that William's grade point average over the course of four semesters went from a 2.3 to a 3.7 by the mere fact of him being able to put in practice something that he can see himself in many years from now.

In Cumberland County, we have great relationships with many of the local high schools. The Bronco MILE has become known for its bow ties. We go into middle schools and high schools and do tutoring, and as a part of that, we teach them how to do bow ties. They are just absolutely thrilled about that.

We work with parents just about every day. We want to keep them abreast within the purview of FERPA. We want to see their young men, their sons, graduate from Fayetteville State University. We have some very targeted initiatives that work very closely with parents, middle schools, high schools, and, of course, with getting young men outside of the North Carolina area, which is a tremendous help to our program and to the success rates that we are realizing.

Senator HAGAN. Thank you, Dr. DeSousa.

Dr. Lomax, in your testimony, I think you also talked about the need for travel and different opportunities for students. Could you comment on that? And then I also wanted to ask about your financial literacy workshops and bank days for students. I'm a big believer in the fact that we don't teach financial literacy, and we need to be doing this.

I know that when I was in the State senate in North Carolina, I mandated that a course be taught, but we need to do more. It's not rocket science. We just don't teach it.

Mr. LOMAX. With respect to the travel programs, UNCF provided scholarships to over 12,000 students this year at 900 colleges and universities. About half of those will be students at HBCUs. The first and most important travel opportunity we provide to students is travel to and from college.

Our largest single scholarship program, the one funded by Bill and Melinda Gates—1,000 students a year, 17,000 students to date, and will be 20,000 when the program ends. So many of the young men and women who earn Gates scholarships—I can't tell you how competitive these scholarships are. For 1,000 scholarships, we have 14,000 completed applications. So these are the best of the best—35 percent African American, 35 percent Latino, 15 percent Native American, 15 percent Asian Pacific Islander. For so many of these young men and women, this is the first time they've had an opportunity to leave home.

They get the opportunity to attend the college of their choice. I think just as the president of Heritage has noted, and all of my colleagues, this opportunity to see a world beyond is what inspires them to work hard and to complete. And I might just note on the Gates program, we have a 90 percent completion rate for this program, and these are students attending the most competitive institutions in the world.

They've gotten an education at home, sometimes on the reservation, sometimes in the inner city, and worked hard. But now with this scholarship, they're able to leave home and go see a bigger world. The challenge is that that just doesn't happen for enough of our kids. So one of the things that we're trying to do is to find other ways. Bill and Melinda Gates aren't going to pay for everybody to go to college.

But one of our most exciting innovative programs has been one we've done with Citi, which is to teach financial literacy by doing.

It's a college savings program. We've done this with the KIPP Foundation, and we've initiated this at KIPP charter schools around the country. These young men and women are challenged— they learn about saving and planning for college, and they learn by doing. You can give them book learning on this, but when they actually have to raise the dollars and we match up to $250 a year, then if these students complete this program, they have the opportunity to get a scholarship as well.

What we've learned, Senator, is that low-income kids and their families know how important college is, and they will save. One of the things I'd say is that if we can look at other opportunities to learn about matching college savings, we can take the burden of all of this being scholarship or debt, and they can actually begin to save for college as well.

Senator HAGAN. Thank you.

Senator Paul.

Senator PAUL. Thank you to everyone on the panel for coming.

Dr. Lomax, one of the things that we've tried to get in Kentucky and are still fighting for is charter schools. I'm a big fan of them, because, to me, I just sort of see them as being equivalent to innovation and allowing people to make changes at a more local level. Senator Alexander and I have visited some of the KIPP schools in Nashville. I visited with some of the students here in DC and have been really amazed at the poise, the education, the articulation of their education.

I was just wondering what your thoughts are and whether or not you think that charter schools and school choice, in general, is part of getting our kids better prepared for college.

Mr. LOMAX. UNCF believes that we're not going to achieve our goals of significantly increasing the number of African Americans who graduate from college unless we ensure that the youngsters who graduate from high school are, in fact, college-ready. A big part of our message today is that to go to school is not just enough. You've really got to get the kind of rigorous academic preparation which is going to enable you to succeed in college.

According to the ACT, only 5 percent of African American high school graduates are college-ready in the major disciplines of math, science, English, and reading, which means that they've got a 75 percent chance of earning a C on a college level course or a 50 percent chance of earning a B. I believe that not all, but a number of the charter schools are demonstrating that we can introduce rigorous academic programs for kids who come from low-income communities.

At KIPP this year—and I serve on the KIPP Foundation board— we will have 160 charter schools across this country by the beginning of the new academic year. This fall, 2,000 KIPPsters have been admitted to colleges and universities across the country. Ten percent of those students have been admitted to UNCF member institutions. They are academically ready. Seventy-five of them have been admitted to Dillard University, where I was president.

The challenge these kids are going to have, Senator Paul, is that they can't finance the education that they have the academic opportunity to earn. I would say that what we've really got to focus on is both the academic readiness and the financial readiness.

Most of these young people are going to have to rely upon Federal financial aid. So the Pell grants have got to do a more effective job, and they're going to have to borrow. That's the truth. But if they're borrowing at interest rates that—I'll give you one example, the Parent-Plus loan. You combine the interest rate of 6.4 percent and the origination fee of 4 percent, it's 10 percent for that loan. The default rate is less than 5 percent. So they're paying an interest rate double the default rate.

Why is the interest rate so high? Because they're being told that the interest and the origination fee are high because the default rate is high. Well, we scrubbed that, and we found out that the default rate is not high. The Federal Government will earn $66 billion, according to the Government Accountability Office, on the Federal loans that are issued between 2007 and 2012—$66 billion on the backs of low- and moderate-income kids, including the graduates of public charter schools.

Senator PAUL. I agree with you that the financial burden is a real problem, but it is also, in some ways, a conundrum in the sense that when we stimulate the demand and subsidize the demand, we elevate the cost, and that has happened now decade after decade. Then we come back in on the back end and we have to say, "Well, how do we reduce the cost?"

Education gets more and more expensive, but we say we want everybody to go, so we subsidize people going to college. And I'm not saying we can stop doing that. I'm just saying that we have to realize that as we subsidize the demand, we put pressure on, and we raise cost.

Just one more thing, and I'll let you respond. We have to look at some way of reducing cost. The American Action Forum reports that Department of Education paperwork has doubled in recent times. It now costs us $2.7 billion in compliance costs.

We spoke in our office with Phillip Howard from Morehouse, who projects that just at Morehouse, it's a seven-digit range, in the million dollar range of compliance. We have to figure out something— and maybe part of it is excessive paperwork and regulation—but realize that it's the pressure pushing things up, and then people have to look for ways to clamp down on cost.

Mr. LOMAX. Streamlining is something which I think you, Senator Alexander, have spoken about with regard to these government regulations. And on the side of the institutions—and I was a college president for 7 years and a college professor for 20—I know how hard it was for my students at Morehouse and Spelman and at Dillard University to figure out the maze, m-a-z-e, of Federal financial aid.

I think that if you go back and look at the Higher Education Act, we could scrub it and remove some of these duplicative and oftentimes contradictory expectations. We're talking about kids who are oftentimes, like my colleagues have noted, the first in their families to attend college. Their parents have to have a Ph.D. to figure out how to get the Federal financial aid.

One of the things that needs to happen is that more of the folks who have loans today need to convert to income-based repayment. There are four different competing income-based repayment plans. It's so confusing that now only 25 percent of the eligible borrowers are, in fact, opting for something which they either don't know about or can't figure out how to manage their way through.

I think some of this could be improved, Senator, by, in fact, reviewing and streamlining all these actions that have been taken over the last 50 years which have made what was a great initiative in this Nation—to support students who are pursuing a college education—more effective and efficient.

Senator HAGAN. Thank you.

Senator Warren.

STATEMENT OF SENATOR WARREN

Senator WARREN. Thank you, Madam Chairman. Thank you for holding this hearing. Thank you, Ranking Member Paul.

And thank you all for being here today. I'd like to go back to this question about college loans. The rising cost of tuition is causing more and more students to have to take on more and more debt, and students of color are being hit the hardest. According to the Urban Institute, African Americans and Latinos are about twice as likely as other students to have loan debt.

Now, let's be really clear about this loan debt. This is not federally subsidized loan debt. In fact, what the numbers show is that the Federal Government is making a profit from the student loan program. I think you cited the GAO statistics that show that just one narrow slice, the loans from 2007 to 2012, are on track to produce $66 billion in profits for the U.S. Government.

In other words, young people whose parents can afford to write a check for college pay one price, and young people whose parents can't afford to pay up front for college and have to borrow that money pay a much higher tax in order to go to college. They pay more.

So we're starting to feel the effects of this throughout the economy. The Federal Reserve, the Consumer Financial Protection Bureau, the Treasury Department have all weighed in, talking about the fact that young people are not saving up to buy homes. They're not buying homes. They're not buying cars. They're not making the move, starting small businesses that we would otherwise expect.

But what I'd like you to do, if you could, for just a minute is— you work hard at your institutions—Dr. Lomax, at your organization—to give students opportunities so that they can realize from higher education an opportunity to build something in their own lives, in their communities, and in this country. What's the impact on these young students of having rising college student loan costs?

Maybe, Dr. Gasman, you could start.

Ms. GASMAN. Sure. One of the things that we know for sure— there's countless research that shows us that your income level correlates with your chances of graduating. I, personally, am a first- generation, low-income student and went to school on a Pell grant and took out student loans. So this hits home for me.

A couple of things happened, and I think the rest of the panelists can talk about this. If you are on a Pell grant, if you're a low- income student, you don't have a safety net. So when things happen, as they do in college, you have nothing to fall back on. It's sort of like a family that doesn't have a savings account, and they might only have a little bit of money left in their checking account. So the situation becomes more volatile.

There's quite a bit of research. One of my colleagues, Camille Charles, at the University of Pennsylvania has done research related to how African Americans and low-income students, in particular—and this correlates with what you said—tend to have more stress in their lives with regard to income as well. I think that I would back up what you're saying and say that all the research plays out and verifies it.

Senator WARREN. Good. Thank you.

Dr. DeSousa, did you want to add to this?

Mr. DESOUSA. Senator Warren, yes. Thank you. One of the things I'd like to say is that within North Carolina, Fayetteville State University is among the most affordable institutions to attend. The Fayetteville State University model is to give students grants and scholarships first, followed by loans if necessary. One of the things we've found, however, is that when students get the refund checks, they can—or I should say disbursement checks, more appropriately, they could use that money frivolously.

So what we are trying to do through the male initiative is if you're interested in a banking on your future course, or if you're interested in attending an educationally purposeful experience outside the State of North Carolina, you have to produce a disbursement plan or, slash, a refund check plan to tell us how you intend to use the moneys. Just don't go to the mall and spend it.

You are required to show evidence that you have created a savings account. We don't want to know how much is in there, but we just want proof that they've created that. I think through the male initiative, we're seeing men at Fayetteville State University create savings accounts for the first time.

Senator WARREN. That's wonderful to hear.

Madam Chairman, may I ask Mr. Oakley to respond as well?

Mr. OAKLEY. Yes. Thank you, Senator Warren. I think what I've heard missing thus far is that we need to begin to reward value. Value is the key to under-represented students. Our large access public institutions are the gateway to these individuals. The California State University system, for example, on my campus, in my back door—they are graduating over 8,000 students next week. There is great value there, and these are predominantly first-generation students receiving a great education.

California State University at Long Beach received over 83,000 applications for admission this last year, the fifth largest in the Nation. We need to reward that kind of value, and we need to encourage our young people to seek value so that they are not chasing a dream of a $50,000 education that may not return to them the value that an education such as our public universities offer. So I would say the more we can encourage those students and give them an opportunity to attend our large access public institutions, the better off they're going to be.

Senator WARREN. Thank you very much. And I see that I'm out of time. But I do want to thank Dr. Lomax publicly for your work on—talking about student loans and the importance of reducing student loan rates. I do not believe the Federal Government should be making a profit off the backs of our young people who are trying to get an education, and I worry about how this disproportionately falls hard on students of color.

Thank you, Madam Chairman.

Senator HAGAN. Thank you.

Senator Alexander.

Senator ALEXANDER. Thank you, Madam Chairman. I'm going to defer to Senator Burr.

Senator HAGAN. Senator Burr.

STATEMENT OF SENATOR BURR

Senator BURR. Thank you, Senator Alexander.

Let me again welcome all of our witnesses today. I'm reminded as we talk about the fact that the Federal Government had $66 billion worth of profits that we turned around, as Congress usually does, and we took $8.7 billion of it and we spent it on a healthcare plan, not on education.

We can talk the talk, but we don't always walk the walk, and I think you guys are on the front lines. I believe searching for every silver bullet that you can find, not to build an institution, but to graduate students that are marketable in the 21st century. That's what I'm impressed with and it's what I want to ask you about.

So I'll throw it out to all of you. What is an institution's responsibility, if any, to try to guide or influence a student's pathway to a degree that's marketable in the 21st century, in other words, their major? I'll open it up to you.

Mr. Oakley.

Mr. OAKLEY. Thank you for the question, Senator Burr. First of all, students come to college for a specific purpose. They want to improve their lives, and many first-generation students want to improve their families' lives. They want to obtain a good job. They want to improve their living wage.

It's incumbent upon us, particularly in the public institutions, to help guide students as best as possible, providing them access to the kinds of support services they need early in their first semester so that they not waste time getting to their degree. It's good for them if they get to their degree faster, and it's good for us as a State and as a Nation.

Senator BURR. How about if they've chosen a pathway that you, as educators and business people, look at and say, "You know, this is not a winner for the 21st century." Does an institution have an obligation to sit down and—like Dr. Bassett and Dr. DeSousa said, part of what you had as a challenge was to change people's expectations about what they could accomplish.

If their expectations are too low, you're trying to expand that. If their choice of academic path is not one of—let's use your analogy. If their earnings potential is less than the investment that they made in their education, does an institution have a responsibility to point that out to them and try to point them in a different direction?

Mr. OAKLEY. I think the first role of an institution is to ensure all of its degrees and certificates are quality degrees that lead to some sort of improved employment opportunity, and I think that's our first responsibility, to ensure that we are conferring degrees that matter.

Senator BURR. Dr. Bassett, you've got this puzzled look on your face.

Mr. BASSETT. I think you're always trying to balance two things. You're trying to balance the need to open them up to what is out there in terms of real careers, and our problem in the valley is so many of the young people have no sense of a future. That is, they don't imagine themselves doing any of these things that you would consider to be a successful career.

I picked up on Dr. DeSousa's comment about really giving them a sense of opportunity out there, and put it together with Dr. Lomax's comment on getting them over the wall to see that bigger world where there are people like them doing these things. But the balance I think I'd talk about in response to your question is explaining to them what those real options are and, clearly, what real careers are out there and what aren't. The balance is with their passion. That is, their passion is driving them in this direction, and you're inclined to say, "Well, that's going to be a pretty steep hill to go up there."

So we educate you, we prepare you, we advise you into what the career options are. But at some point, I also want to take advantage of that passion, because the student with ability and passion and the art major may be very successful. The person without much ability going into that field—whoops, I think we'd better get you over into the accounting major here.

I think it's always a balance between an education and what the real world is out there, but also take advantage of their passion and ability. And I think our responsibility is to provide intentional advising that helps them finally make the decision with as much of that information as we can give them.

Mr. DESOUSA. Senator Burr, may I comment?

Senator BURR. Yes, sir.

Mr. DESOUSA. Senator, one of the things about Fayetteville State University, I think, that is very unique is that during the first year, we demand that first year students take the Strong Interest Inventory, the SII, during freshman seminar. As a result of that, it helps to create opportunities for them to see where their strengths are and where they fall on this inventory, and they can connect with the proper major.

One of the things that we have found at Fayetteville State University is that for first-year students who select majors early, they are more likely to return the second year than students who do not select majors during their first year. To your point, what we have found is that some students are a little bit too ambitious about majors.

There was a young man who came in to see me and said, "I want to be a part of the nursing program at Fayetteville State University." I pulled up his academic profile, and I noticed that he wasn't strong in math and science. I said, "I want you to go over and talk to someone in nursing and ask whether or not you would be a candidate for that program in about 1 or 2 years." He has done that, and I believe that he has made some different choices about his major.

Senator BURR. Dr. Gasman.

Ms. GASMAN. Sure. One of the comments that I wanted to make kind of harkens to what the president of Heritage mentioned. That is, I think it's really important that institutions open up the possibilities to students and put those in front of them. I, personally, am a professor, but I do think that institutions have an obligation to make sure that students know what their earning potential is for particular majors. That information is available and I think can be given to students.

Part of the issue has to do with guidance counselors who are at the K through 12 level, however, in that they are not necessarily giving that information. I, in particular, am a case in point, in that like the Heritage students, I was told that I would make a lovely secretary because I could type 98 words a minute, but was never looked upon as someone who could be a professor. It was a teacher that told me that I could be something different, and also told me about the rewards of that profession.

I do think that institutions do have an obligation to make sure that students know what's out there ahead of them, and I think that that does happen among staff, among faculty, among career services offices. I think we could probably do a better job, but I do think it's essential.

Senator BURR. Once again, with a panel focused on higher education, all of you have referred it back to a reference to K through 12 at some point, and I think that's consistent with every time we've had a hearing on reauthorization. And it really doesn't matter whether it's charter schools or the KIPP academy or public schools. The one thing that you find in a successful K through 12 system is passionate teachers, exactly what Dr. Bassett was talking about. For KIPP, you find a large majority of those out of Teach for America, which is a fantastic program.

I want to thank all of you for being here. I want to thank Senator Alexander for yielding me his time. I'll just conclude with this, that this is important to North Carolina, and it's important to the country. But North Carolina produces the second largest pool of graduates of higher education annually of any State in the country other than California. That provides us the future workforce that business investment needs.

The challenging thing today is I don't think any of us look out, regardless of the State you come from, and say, "We'll build another university tomorrow." It's cost prohibitive. We've got to focus on how we take the infrastructure we have, grow it, make it better, utilize it in a fashion that everything that's coming out the door is intended for exactly the time we're in, which is the 21st century.

Thank you for the input—Dr. Lomax, thank you for all you do.

Thank you, Madam Chairman.

Senator HAGAN. Thank you, Senator Burr.

Senator Alexander.

Senator ALEXANDER. Thank you, Madam Chair. I know that the vote has started and that you and Senator Paul may have some additional questions. So I'll try to get right to the point.

First, thanks to every one of you for coming. We're in the middle of a reauthorization of the Higher Education Act, and I, for one, would like to start from scratch. It's been reauthorized eight times, and the stuff just piles up and piles up and piles up.

I'd like to deregulate higher education as much as we can and still be good stewards of the trillion dollars in loans and $33 billion in Pell grants of the taxpayers' money that we spend every year. Your specific suggestions to us about how to do that would be very helpful and very timely. We're working on that now.

For example, over-borrowing is a problem. Dr. DeSousa, you mentioned that you were working on helping a student make a plan. Under the current law, you can't require the student to do that as a condition for getting the loan. You have to offer the opportunity. Right?

Mr. DESOUSA. Yes, sir.

Senator ALEXANDER. Wouldn't it be helpful if the law made it clear that institutions that wanted to do a good job of counseling about that could? I mean, any 19-year-old can walk in and get $5,500 at 3.86 percent, I think, is what we cut it to. That's a pretty tempting offer. What to do with it is another thing and can lead to the over-borrowing problems we hear so much about.

Mr. DESOUSA. Senator Alexander, the best way I can respond to this question is to say that what Fayetteville State University does is entrance counseling. So when students visit the Office of Financial Aid, they sit down and talk with a financial aid advisor.

Senator ALEXANDER. Which, I guess, every single one does. Almost every single student must do that. Right?

Mr. DESOUSA. Yes, sir. They must do that. And, again, I just want to reiterate, Senator Alexander, that the model at Fayetteville State University is surely scholarships and grants first. That's what we must do at our institutions.

Senator ALEXANDER. Right. Do any of you—I mean, the average Pell grant is about $3,300. The average community college tuition is about the same. Do any of you work with community colleges to help low-income students have a chance to go there for 2 years and then reduce their expenses by coming on later to the 4-year institutions?

Mr. DESOUSA. Senator Alexander, one of the things that I'm proud to say is that Fayetteville State University, through a grant from The Links, Incorporated, is working very closely with Fayetteville Tech Community College. The purpose of The Links grant is to better create a pipeline for students from 2-year institutions to 4-year institutions. Fayetteville State University has sweetened the pot. While The Links has not required us to provide additional funds on top of what students are getting, the Office of the Provost has permitted us to provide an extra $1,000 to students who come in through The Links program initiative.

Senator ALEXANDER. Let me go on to other questions. I'm about out of time, and we're about to have a vote.

Dr. Lomax, you were president of a university twice—once?

Mr. LOMAX. Once. That's enough.

[Laughter.]

Senator ALEXANDER. I was going to say—I won't say it. But I respect that. Let me put it that way. When you were president of a university, did you have to hire extra people to help students fill out Federal application forms?

Mr. LOMAX. We really did. I was president of Dillard University in New Orleans, and, you know, so many of the—now, this was 10 years ago, and I think a lot has happened since then. People are more aware of Federal financial aid forms. I think we do a better job getting them to fill those out.

I think what they're not aware of is that loans aren't grants. I don't think we've really gotten them to fully understand that there's going to be a reckoning, and the reckoning is—even if you graduate, there's going to be a reckoning, and if you don't graduate, there'll be a reckoning as well. I think making students understand that this is—and their families—this is serious. This is an obligation. They will be required to repay it, and they should borrow only what they need, not what they want.

Senator ALEXANDER. Thank you. I'll make one observation, and then I'll go back to the chairman and thank her and Senator Paul for holding this hearing.

I've heard the comment that taxpayers are profiting off of students on loans. According to the law, that's true, but not according to the Congressional Budget Office, who has told us the reverse, that if we were to fairly account for the student loan program, it would be the students who are profiting off the taxpayers. They've told us that the accounting we use now is bad accounting, because it doesn't take in risk, and they've recommended instead that we use the accounting system that we use for the Troubled Relief Asset Program, which took into account risk.

There are two sides to that story, and I wouldn't want students around the country to believe that the taxpayers are profiting off the students when the Congressional Budget Office, who we pay to give us nonpartisan advice, tells us that it's the reverse.

Thank you, Madam Chairman.

Senator HAGAN. Thank you, Senator Alexander.

There's obviously more questions I want to ask. I want to talk quickly on one, and then we're going to recess while we go and vote, and then I will definitely come back and we can have another question or two and then some closing statements.

Dr. Gasman and Dr. Bassett, both of you have talked about the teacher education programs at our minority serving institutions and the impact that they make on other students, minority students, around the country.

Dr. Gasman, I think in your testimony, you said that 11 percent of teacher education degrees were awarded at minority serving institutions.

Could both of you talk just a minute or so about the impact that that means to our minority students and how we've got to be sure these education programs are of the highest caliber and quality?

Ms. GASMAN. Eleven percent is an interesting percentage because it's the percentage of teachers that MSIs award today. But if you were to look at the teachers who are out in the workforce, teachers of color, you would find that the majority of them were educated at minority serving institutions overall. That's also something really important.

I think that the most important reason why we need more teachers of color bears out in all of the research around the success of students of color, and that is—and I heard Jason say this—that it is really important to see people in the classroom who look like you. It is empowering, and there is a myriad of research that shows that that is true. That's incredibly important.

As our Nation is changing very rapidly, I think it is absolutely essential—not that it wasn't before—but absolutely essential that the teaching force look more like the students who they are going to serve.

Senator HAGAN. Dr. Bassett.

Mr. BASSETT. I think you've made the salient point. There's a huge disconnect between our current population of students in the classroom and the teachers that they have. I think the two most important points about the Heritage teaching program are, first, it is a residency-based program. Junior and senior year, they're actually in the school and learning early if they're not meant to be teachers.

Second, it builds cultural sensitivity into the teacher training program. One of the reasons the teachers graduating are so valued is that they bring that cultural sensitivity for the minority populations to their preparation, and the students coming out of the other colleges in the region do not.

Senator HAGAN. And I believe you said they tend to go back to their——

Mr. BASSETT. Our students do stay in the region, and they don't leave the teaching profession after 5 years. We lose so many people. So many young teachers we lose in the first 5 years.

Senator HAGAN. All right. We will take a very short recess, and then I'll be right back. Thank you.

[Recess.]

Senator HAGAN. We will resume the testimony, and thank you very much. Votes do cause us to interrupt a hearing every now and then. So I appreciate your time and the fact that you have stayed around.

I did want to ask Dr. DeSousa one question about our military bases. I know that probably other institutions also offer classes working with our active duty men and women on military bases. I know Fayetteville State offers classes on Fort Bragg, Camp Lejeune, and Seymour Johnson. And as we're talking about diversity in higher education, students on military bases are another distinct population with their own set of specific needs.

Dr. DeSousa, what lessons do you think the university has learned from offering these classes on military bases?

Mr. DESOUSA. Senator Hagan, thank you for the question, first of all. I think that given Fayetteville State University's location in Fayetteville, next door to Fort Bragg, we have had tremendous opportunities to work hand in hand with the soldiers there. And based on our presence at Fort Bragg, we can contribute growth in enrollment and increases in graduation rates.

One of the jewels, I think, that you'll be hearing more about over the course of the next year or so is this new certificate program in cyber security that we're now offering to returning veterans, a certificate program that allows them to be able to get jobs in homeland security and defense and related types of fields. But Fort Bragg has been a tremendous asset to Fayetteville State University, particularly our ability to grow enrollment.

Senator HAGAN. Especially with the African American males. I would presume that that would also be a number.

Do any of the other witnesses have any other comments on that issue?

I see Senator Scott here.

Senator Scott.

STATEMENT OF SENATOR SCOTT

Senator SCOTT. Thank you, Madam Chairwoman.

Thank you all, panelists, for being here today and participating in this process and for the enlightening information. I've had two committee hearings at the same time. I just wanted to ask a couple of questions on the public-private partnerships, and perhaps, Dr. DeSousa, you would have an opportunity to answer the question.

I think about the success in South Carolina with the partnerships with Claflin, Abney Foundation, AT&T, Bank of America, as well as other partnerships that exist around the State. Boeing has a partnership with my old high school, Stall High School, to promote instruction for aerodynamics and manufacturing.

The United Negro College Fund, of course, has a partnership with Merck to increase research at the undergraduate level and enhance career opportunities. We see success with Howard and GM, the foundation. We've had a longstanding partnership, and Lockheed Martin just partnered with Bowie State.

I have a piece of legislation called the SEA Jobs Act, which is looking at ways to create more seismic activity off the South Atlantic coast, giving an opportunity to some of the HBCUs to receive revenues from that stream of resources, realizing that over the next 20 years or so, we'll see another 1.3 million jobs in the oil, gas, and petrochemicals industry. Yet in 2010, about 8.2 percent of that workforce were black. So we're looking for ways to use the STEM opportunity to promote and to encourage more students to end up in the field that seems to be the highest or the largest growth opportunity in our economy.

My question to you, sir, is when you look at using existing resources, how can our schools replicate public-private partnerships on a larger scale to boost the number of STEM graduates and to help prepare our students for success in the job market?

Mr. DESOUSA. Senator Scott, that's a very good question. Thank you for asking it. As I mentioned to Senator Hagan in my comment about cyber security, this is an example of Fayetteville State University working directly in partnership with the University of Maryland Baltimore County, which, as you know, has a stellar record in the country in terms of producing African American STEM majors. So we're pleased about that partnership.

The cyber security program is funded through title III, so it's not a private resource. The university has a very strong partnership with North Carolina State University through a Two-Plus-Three program, where students start 2 years in the sciences, perhaps chemistry or biology, and then transfer to North Carolina State University where they will major in a STEM field, particularly in engineering. So those are two examples.

In terms of using private resources, Senator, earlier, you were not here when I mentioned the fact that through The Links Foundation with funding from Lumina and support from NAFIO, we are able to partner with Fayetteville Tech Community College. Throughout the country, there are only 14 schools nationally that have resources from The Links and Lumina with support from NAFIO that creates opportunities for 2-year students to transfer into 4-year institutions.

And, of course, our emphasis at Fayetteville State University is on many majors for these students transferring. But we highly encourage them to get involved in STEM fields. As a part of The Links program, students come in on Tuesdays—we call it transfer Tuesdays—and they meet with academic departments, and the sciences are among the most popular for Fayetteville Tech Community College students.

Senator SCOTT. Thank you.

Dr. Lomax, did you want to add something?

Mr. LOMAX. Thank you very much, Senator Scott. You referenced in passing the UNCF-Merck science initiative, which is now in its 18th year, and Merck has been a partner with UNCF to the tune of $44 million, providing undergraduate, graduate, and postgraduate funding for students to pursue degrees in research science.

We've produced to date, in partnership with Merck, 600 Ph.D.s in the research sciences. The big beneficiary has been the NIH. But that's been a demonstration that there is talent, and I would note for you that these are students who don't just attend HBCUs. They attend colleges and universities all across the country, but they are all African American, and many of them are the first in their families to graduate from college. So there's a big interest in STEM.

I would say there are two barriers. One is that to succeed in STEM, you've got to build a firm academic foundation. So math and science—I taught English, so communication doesn't hurt, either, but really grounding kids in the math. I have a 21-year-old daughter who is at Howard University. She will be an intern at Google this summer in computer science, a highly competitive opportunity. But she's a whiz in math, and she's been getting a strong math education.

So it's really to give them the foundation, and also give them the opportunity to see that there is a world out there. In 2013, UNCF launched the centerpiece of its new STEM initiative, a national HBCU Innovation Summit held in Silicon Valley. The purpose of the summit was to build bridges between HBCUs and the technology community and to develop and enhance the innovation and entrepreneurial capacity of HBCUs with the goal of establishing productive innovation, entrepreneurial ecosystems across the HBCU network.

I think it's also encouraging innovation, encouraging partnership. We did that with Stanford University, and we did it with a number of the major companies out there, Facebook, Google, and others. I think that innovation opportunity is there, Senator Hagan, if we'll just lift it up with some investment.

Senator SCOTT. Thank you. I'll wrap it up since my time has expired. I will say that I do concur that we need to find a way to not only focus on college level education but to focus perhaps more on the academic direction of our K through 12 education.

My nephew on Sunday graduated from Duke with his master's in engineering and management and spent 4 years at Georgia Tech getting his biomedical engineering major. And I will tell you that when you go onto those campuses and you see the diversity, the international diversity, and you see the workforce in the next 20 or 30 years as it continues to evolve, the global competition for the jobs in the STEM field will require us to have a greater focus on K through 12 to produce a competitive product in the upcoming workforce.

Thank you, ma'am.

Senator HAGAN. Senator Scott, thank you for your comments. I am one of the biggest proponents of STEM education in the Senate, because it is so important for the jobs today, the jobs of the 21st century, and the jobs that are going to move our country forward on a competitive basis worldwide.

With that in mind, Mr. Oakley, in your testimony and in your opening statement, you talked about how you are no longer using the standardized—or how you're looking at students' grades within the high school. I've been hearing a lot about the number of remedial classes that our students have to take at a community college after they've graduated from high school.

Of course, the problem here is that now they are paying for these remedial courses before they can ever really get toward their college 2-year associate's degree, college education, and it's expensive. And from what I've been reading, too, so many people actually then drop out because they don't see the payback, whether in the debt that they're already putting forward or how they're going to get through.

Can you talk about that? And do you think there's some feedback mechanism that we can set up with our high schools to know if a disproportionate number of their students are in need of remediation? We've got to have that strong background in our middle schools and in our high schools.

Mr. OAKLEY. Yes. Thank you for that question, Senator Hagan. First of all, as we all know, remedial education is really a burial ground for disadvantaged students, for under-represented students. We tend to oversubscribe our remedial classes with under-represented students, and that's where they wind up finishing, and they're not completing.

So because of our relationship with the Long Beach Unified School District, we've been working for several years, and the K–12 system has been doing tremendous work at better preparing students to be college- and career-ready. But when they were getting to our doors, we noticed that 90 percent, or virtually 90 percent, when we gave them the assessment test, were testing below college level. So we noticed that there was a clear disconnect. Something was wrong.

So we decided to look at 5 years of data, over 7,000 students, and what we found was that the best predictor of successful placement is past performance, and that makes sense to most normal people. Your experience tells you a lot about how you're going to succeed.

Senator HAGAN. I understand that. But what about those students who have not done well, or they haven't had the course offerings that would prepare them for a stricter academic study?

Mr. OAKLEY. If we can do a better job of placing students up front, we can do a better job of aligning the resources that we have to do a better job with remedial education and to work in the K–12 system to have a better communication structure with the K–12 system to understand early in their academic experience where those points are that we need to improve and to invest in those points, because those kids are all of our responsibilities. So we need to work more closely with the K–12 system.

Senator HAGAN. I agree.

Dr. Lomax.

Mr. LOMAX. I think there's one fix which is right there in front of us. A lot of these young people, for the time being, are going to require personalized education plans that will enable them to meet the standards for credit bearing courses at the college level. They shouldn't be paying full tuition to do that, and we ought to have opportunities to teach them using technology.

Right now, one of the barriers for HBCUs innovating in this area is that we can't use title III funds for online programs. I think if we could remove that barrier and really encourage investment in using technology as a low-cost way of personalizing the instruction for students who don't yet meet our standards and use blended learning and direct technology as a way of reaching those students, improving their skill levels, so that when they come to our campuses and they start paying full tuition, they're actually taking credit-bearing courses.

Senator HAGAN. And I think you also mentioned the need for Pell grants in the summertime, too.

Mr. LOMAX. Absolutely, because that's a time when many of our students, who need to get some direct improvement in some of their basic skills or want to try to finish within that 4-year period, could be on our campuses. Thank you.

Senator HAGAN. Dr. Gasman.

Ms. GASMAN. Sure. I wanted to comment just about developmental education overall. I think that there are organizations that have told us that developmental education doesn't work. But there are institutions where it does work.

Over the past 3 years, I conducted a large scale national study funded by Lumina Foundation, Kresge Foundation, and USA Funds with my colleague, Cliff Conrad. One of the things that we found is that at quite a few institutions—and I'll give you some examples—developmental education, when mainstreamed with other classes, works very well.

For example, at El Paso Community College, they track all of their students in developmental education at every stage along the way so that they know how—any student that you put in front of them, they can tell you how that student is doing. They're really a model for the whole nation. But developmental education works really well there.

Or at Chief Dull Knife College, which is a tribal college in Montana, they have a problem with math shame among Native Americans. And through developmental education, computer-assisted developmental education, they've actually made enormous strides. If you've ever been to Chief Dull Knife, they have no resources, but they've made enormous strides.

I think that matters, and I think it depends on where the developmental education takes place. It also depends on how it plays out. I don't think that we can forget students who are underprepared by the K through 12 system. What happens to them if we don't provide that kind of service, because we can't summarily fix the K through 12 system?

Senator HAGAN. Dr. Bassett.

Mr. BASSETT. Thank you, Senator Hagan. We have a tremendous under-utilized population with STEM potential, the minority population, whether African American, Hispanic American, Native American, that is never given an opportunity really to develop those skills in the K through 12 world in math and science. Picking up on Senator Scott's comment, I think one of the greatest potentials for a business philanthropy public sector partnership would be to have a major impact on STEM education for elementary age and middle school kids.

If you get them excited about real world problems, they then want to learn the math and the science. When it remains abstract, they're never quite sure why it's there, why they're learning it. I think there's a tremendous potential here with those populations for an initiative to change STEM education at the elementary and middle school level.

Senator HAGAN. I couldn't agree more. And with that, I really want to thank all of our witnesses today for being here, for traveling here, for your testimony, for staying through the recess, and certainly for what you do on the campuses—and Dr. Lomax—that you make such a difference to the minority serving institutions and the students, the faculty, and, obviously, the families.

These schools are richly diverse schools, and they're all working hard to meet the challenges and the changing needs of our students in America. I thank you for what you're doing. Hearing the testimony, it's clear in my mind that we need to support our minority serving institutions, our HBCUs, in their drive toward innovation on campuses and, in particular, in the STEM fields. We know we've got to work in partnership and buildup from elementary and middle school and our K–12 programs for STEM.

But there are great programs being implemented all over the country, like the MILE program, areas that we need to be sure that these schools have the support to create and expand these programs. The issue seems to be universal and reaffirms what I've heard from our chancellors at HBCUs in North Carolina.

That's why I am proud to announce that I'm going to be introducing the HBCU Innovation Fund as a mechanism to help HBCUs surmount the challenges that we've discussed today. This legislation is going to provide competitive grants to HBCUs to develop innovative initiatives to address specific outcomes that meet the needs of their students, their population base, the students that they serve in their communities.

This includes building partnerships between the HBCUs and their local high schools within those communities, increasing student enrollment in the STEM fields, developing partnerships to support entrepreneurship and research—we discussed the entrepreneurship demand—and increasing the number of African American males who attain postsecondary degrees. I look forward to sharing more information about this bill, encouraging my colleagues to support the HBCU Innovation Fund.

This hearing is going to remain open for 10 business days for other Senators to submit questions that they didn't get a chance to ask today and to obviously hear your response to those questions and those issues. So with that, once again, I thank you so much for your travel, your time, and being in this hearing. We have a great number of Senators that are very interested in these ideas and in the programs that you are carrying out.

With that, this hearing is now adjourned.

[Additional material follows.]

ADDITIONAL MATERIAL

U.S. Senate,
Washington, DC 20510–0609,
May 22, 2014.

Chairman Harkin and Ranking Member Alexander: I would like to submit a testimony for the record on Minority Serving Institutions from Dr. Dene Kay Thomas, president of Fort Lewis College in Colorado. Fort Lewis College serves over 4,000 students, including students from 146 American Indian Tribes. I believe her thoughts on this issue will provide necessary insight and helpful information as the HELP Committee continues the HEA reauthorization.

Thank you for your consideration of Dr. Thomas' testimony.
Sincerely,

Michael F. Bennet,
U.S. Senator.

Prepared Statement of Dene K. Thomas, PhD, President, Fort Lewis College, Durango, Co.

"I don't think anybody anywhere can talk about the future of their people without talking about education."—Wilma Mankiller, former principle chief, Cherokee Nation

Unique History and Mission of Native American-Serving Nontribal Institutions

Good morning Chairman Harkin, Ranking Member Alexander, Senator Hagen, Senator Paul and members of the committee. My name is Dr. Dene Thomas and I am the president of Fort Lewis College in Durango, CO. Fort Lewis College is named for Fort Lewis, a U.S. Army Post established in 1878 at Pagosa Springs, CO. Two years later, the military post was moved to Hesperus, CO, a location more central to American Indian settlements and pioneer communities in the early 1890s. On January 25, 1911, Governor John Shafroth of Colorado signed a contract with the Federal Government which transferred 6,279 acres in southwest Colorado to the State of Colorado "to be maintained as an institution of learning to which Indian students will be admitted free of tuition and on an equality with white students" in perpetuity (Act of 61st Congress, 1911). There were approximately 40 students in 1909. The school was an Indian boarding school and began to offer college-level courses in 1925.

Fort Lewis College moved to the Durango campus in 1956, and the first baccalaureate degrees were granted in 1964. The first graduate degree program, a Masters of Arts in

Teacher Leadership, began in fall 2013. Fort Lewis College continues to honor its historic commitment to Native Americans by offering tuition scholarships to Native Americans of all tribes who meet admission requirements. It is one of only two, public 4-year colleges in the Nation to grant tuition waivers to qualified Native American students from any federally recognized tribe and has done so for more than 100 years.

Fort Lewis College is proud of its dual mission as Colorado's only public liberal arts college and as a Native American-Serving, Nontribal College, a designation it received from the U.S. Department of Education in fall 2008 and still holds today. The college is 27 percent American Indian/Alaskan Native (AI/AN) and includes students from 146 tribes and 46 States. As of 2013, Fort Lewis College ranks fourth in the Nation in the percent of full-time Native American undergraduates enrolled in a baccalaureate institution.[34] Almost half of Fort Lewis College Native students are from the Navajo Nation (second largest tribe in the United States), closest border of this vast 25,000-square mile reservation is located 84 miles from campus, and 11 percent are from Native Alaskan tribes.

Fort Lewis College awards more degrees to Native American/Alaskan Native students than any other baccalaureate institution in the Nation (National Science Foundation, WebCASPAR, data retrieved September 2013). From 2006–10, Fort Lewis College awarded over 10 percent (556) of the total number of baccalaureate degrees earned by Native American students in the United States.[35] In 2010, Fort Lewis College was first in the Nation in baccalaureate STEM (science, technology, engineering and math) degrees earned by AI/AN students.[36]

At Fort Lewis College, programs and classes offer students the ability to learn or strengthen their collective Native culture through the Native American Center, the Native American Honor Society, American Indian Business Leaders, the American Indian Science and Engineering Society, and the Native American Indigenous Studies program. In our Elder-In-Residence program, Mrs. Lucille Echohawk, a member of the Pawnee Nation, encouraged students to stay strong in their Native traditions, as they move through College and beyond. We believe that it is this emphasis on academic and cultural support that has helped to make Fort Lewis College one of the top public institutions in the country where Native students excel and graduate.

Another public institution that qualifies as a Native American-Serving, Nontribal Institution to have the same mandate of free tuition is the University of Minnesota, Morris. The campus of the University of Minnesota, Morris (UMM) sits on land that was once home to people of the Anishinaabe (Ojibwe) and the Dakota and Lakota (Sioux) nations. In 1909, through Federal legislation and a Minnesota State statute, (in Laws 1909, chapter 184), about 290 acres and the buildings on the land in rural Minnesota were deeded to the

---

[34] EchoHawk, Sarah, ''Winds of Change, Expanding Opportunities for American Indians and Alaska Natives'', Spring 2013.
[35] Ibid.
[36] Ibid.

State of Minnesota for the purpose of establishing an agricultural boarding high school under the auspices of the University of Minnesota. The agreement stated "that said lands and buildings shall be held and maintained by the State of Minnesota as an agricultural school, and that Indian pupils shall at all times be admitted to such school free of charge for tuition and on terms of equality with white pupils" (Act of the 60th Congress, 1909). Today, 271 AI/AN students from 50 federally recognized tribes and Alaskan villages attend UMM, which comprise 15 percent of their total enrollment. More important, 61 percent of AI/AN students graduate within 6 years. Since 1960, over $20.0 million in tuition has been waived for AI/AN students.

The University of North Carolina, Pembroke is also a Native American-Serving, Nontribal College. The College was founded in 1887, as the State Normal School for Indians, in response to a petition from American Indians in the area to establish and train American Indian teachers. In 1909, it moved to its present day location in Pembroke, which was the center of the Indian community. In 1933, the College offered 2-year degrees, and by 1949 it began to offer 4-year degrees. American Indian/Alaskan Native students comprise 16 percent (863) of their fall 2013 student enrollment.

These institutions share a unique relationship to the land and the Native American people from which the origins of the higher education institutions were founded. These institutions are also connected to greater social movements and education initiatives in this country—from the American Indian boarding school movement to the agricultural boarding high school movement to the expansion of American higher education in the 1960s under the Johnson administration's Great Society. This expansion promised to prepare a workforce for a growing American economy, and to open public educational opportunities to a broader array of people—those under- represented in American higher education (Johnson, 2012).[37]

American Indian/Alaskan Native Education

Native American-Serving, Nontribal Colleges are comprised of mainly public institutions that are rural and centrally located to AI/AN populations in the southwestern, plains, and southeastern portions of the United States. According to the White House Initiative on American Indian/Alaskan Native Education, more than 90 percent of AI/AN postsecondary students attend institutions of higher education that are not tribally controlled. Many Native American-Serving, Nontribal Colleges have a strong relationship with TCUs. Often students complete their associate degree at a TCU and transfer to a Native American-serving, nontribal school to complete their baccalaureate degree, and have the chance to enroll in graduate and professional school.

---

[37] Johnson, Jackie, "Need for Assistance in Fulfilling Certain Federal Mandates to Provide Education Opportunities to American Indians"; Written Testimony, U.S. Senate Health Education, Labor, and Pensions Hearing, Denver, CO, August 2012.

According to 2010 U.S. Census Bureau, the AI/AN population increased twice as fast as the total U.S. population, growing by 18 percent, in comparison to the total U.S. population that grew by 9.7 percent from 2000–10.[38] However, the AI/AN population is under-represented in educational attainment rates. U.S. Census Bureau data show that 28 percent of the overall U.S. population has a bachelor's degree, while only 13 percent of the AI/AN population has a bachelor's degree.[39] Less than 1 percent (0.7 percent) of American Indians attain a Baccalaureate Degree annually, which is notably lower than all other minorities, (African American (8.9 percent), Hispanic (7.5 percent), and Asian American (6.6 percent). Yet, AI/AN students slightly outpace all other students in the percent of 2012 ACT-tested high school graduates that have educational aspirations beyond high school. Forty-eight percent reported an interest in obtaining a bachelor's degree, compared to 45 percent of all students. 28.4 percent of the AI/AN population lives in poverty, versus 15.3 percent of the overall population in the Nation as a whole.

The educational attainment rate gap for Native American students is widening as bachelor's degrees conferred by ethnicities has increased for every minority group, with Hispanics accelerating the highest from 5.6 percent in 1998 to 7.5 percent in 2008. Other ethnicities have also had positive percent changes in degree attainment rates, such as African Americans (2.8 percent) and Asian Americans (3.1 percent), while Native Americans remained flat over the 10-year period at 0.7 percent.[40]

While AI/AN students have stagnated at less than 1 percent of bachelor's degrees attained for decades. AI/AN populations have the highest suicide rates, unemployment rates, and poverty rates than any other population in the Nation. Education is the only way to address these systemic problems in AI/AN communities, as demonstrated in the success of Black and Hispanic student success. With additional support, it is anticipated that similar positive changes will occur in Indian country.

Recent U.S. population and demographic trends confirm that under-represented students, particularly undergraduate students are critical to fulfill 21st century workforce needs. More must be done to support AI/AN students achieve educationally and to help Native communities to thrive. At Fort Lewis College, the tuition waiver program provides important access and opportunity to the most underserved minority population, AI/AN students, but more support and robust policies and programs are needed to help increase the number of AI/AN students who enter and graduate college. AI/AN students need increased access to higher education, and also access to support systems that ensure greater completion rates once they enter the collegiate level.

---

[38] Norris, Vines, and Hoeffel, "The American Indian and Alaskan Native Population: 2010," U.S. Department of Commerce Economics and Statistics Administration, January 2012.

[39] Ibid.

[40] Ibid.

Federal Trust Responsibility for AI/AN Education

The Federal Government has a trust responsibility in improving postsecondary education attainment rates of AI/AN students, particularly as they face barriers to achieving and persisting in the higher education system. Financial aid programs provide assistance for Native students to succeed in higher education and prepare them to enter the workforce. Such need-based aid should be adequately funded and expanded to year-round assistance to help ensure Native students graduate in 4 years. Unfortunately, as the Federal Government tackles fiscal issues in Washington, budget cuts are decreasing the investment in education initiatives that could increase college attainment for Native students.

The tuition waiver programs at Fort Lewis College and UMM are a major factor in promoting the attendance and success of AI/AN students in postsecondary education, yet the Federal mandates have required two States to shoulder the responsibility that covers students from 231 congressional districts and 46 States. Today, the Colorado land where Fort Lewis College is situated is valued at $20 million; however, the cost of the Native American Tuition Waiver program has grown to over $12 million per year to the State of Colorado. In the past 12 years, Colorado has paid out nearly $120 million for what has become a very fast growing program that is national in scope. A more equitable distribution of costs to share the responsibility between the Federal and State government would restore the Federal trust responsibility. That is why I strongly encourage the Senate HELP Committee and Congress to pass The Native American Indian Education Act (S.765), introduced by Colorado Senator Michael Bennet.

Title III strengthening institutions grants have been a tremendous resource to minority serving schools that typically serve high number of low-income and first generation students.

Historically Black Colleges and Universities (HBCUs) and Hispanic-Serving Institutions (HSIs) have programs for capital financing, master's degree program development, STEM articulation and program development, post-baccalaureate program development, competitive grants, and formula grants. Investments in minority education for these groups have resulted in increased enrollment and graduation rates for Hispanic and African American students. It is important to expand programs and resources for all minority serving institutions, across Federal agencies and within them, so that funds are available for urgent needs in areas such as capital financing, master's degree development, and STEM articulation and programs, and minority science and engineering programs.

There is only a $5 million Federal allocation annually that was created in fiscal year 2008–09 to support Native American students outside of Tribal Colleges, through the Native American Serving, Nontribal College discretionary funds at the U.S. Department of Education. Currently, Fort Lewis is just 1 of 14 Native American-serving, Nontribal Colleges who focus on the attainment of the bachelor's degrees for Native American students. Bachelor's degrees offer an important educational experience for Native

American students so that they too can compete in the global market place and carry the hopes and dreams of their nation, and ours, into prosperity.

Institutional partnerships and programs need expanded resources, such as U.S. Department of Education, Indian Education Professional Development and other grant opportunities, to instruct Native educators to teach in higher education and schools that serve reservations and communities with high Native populations. At Fort Lewis College, through a partnership with the Navajo Nation, we have increased the percentage of certified Native (Navajo) teachers in reservations schools from 8 percent to 60 percent since 1990.

Further, education programs such as TRiO are invaluable resources for low-income Native students on college campuses, as many of whom are first generation and low-income students. They provide critical academic and student support services in higher education to help students stay in school and graduate at higher rates. However, with nearly 10 percent budget reductions in recent years, funding for TRiO programs such as Student Support Services, Upward Bound, and Talent Search have been greatly reduced. These services are critical for Native students who need remedial education services to succeed and close the collegiate preparation gap for Native students.

Executive Order 13592 established the White House Initiative on American Indian and Alaskan Native (AI/AN) Education, which has established goals for Fort Lewis College to fill 21st-century workforce needs by awarding 2,539 additional baccalaureate degrees or 46.2 per year by 2020. All Native American-Serving, Non-Tribal Institutions have similar goals and benchmarks, as noted here: http:// batchgeo.com/map/8b8fd7a96af2 aeb93211cead868d45c3. To reach this goal Native American-Serving, Non Tribal Institution representatives should participate in the national dialog on Indian education with the U.S. Department of Education, in such groups as the National Advisory Council on Indian Education, to collaborate and work with the Initiative and the Department on goals for these institutions in promoting American Indian/Alaskan Native education, as 90 percent of AI/AN postsecondary students attend institutions of higher education that are not tribally controlled.

Education Matters

The U.S. Census Bureau data show that the median household income of AI/AN households in 2012 was $35,310 in comparison to $51,371 for the Nation as a whole.[41] In 2011, the median earnings of bachelor's degree recipients with no advanced degree working full-time were $21,100 higher than those of high school graduates. The difference includes $5,000 in tax payments and $16,100 in after-tax income.[42] Education is a critical part of the American dream, particularly for the AI/AN population in this country where there is still the greatest educational and economic disparity.

---

[41] http://www.census.gov/newsroom/releases/pdf/cb13ff-26_aian.pdf.
[42] Baum, Ma, & Payea, "Education Pays 2013, The Benefits of Higher Education for Individuals and Society, The College Board, 2013.

Conclusion

Thank you, Mr. Chairman and committee members, for the opportunity to provide comments and suggestions about minority-serving institutions, in particular, the challenges faced by Native American-serving, Nontribal Institutions. I appreciate your time and would be happy to respond to any questions that you might have for me.

Prepared Statement Of Johnny C. Taylor, Jr., President & CEO, Thurgood Marshall College Fund (TMCF)

Introduction

Thank you Senator Hagan, Senator Paul, Chairman Harkin and Ranking Member Alexander and the entire committee for holding a hearing on best practices and innovations to promote student success on the campuses of minority serving institutions and Historically Black Colleges and Universities (HBCUs). My name is Johnny C. Taylor, Jr., and I serve as President & CEO of the Thurgood Marshall College Fund (TMCF). The Thurgood Marshall College Fund supports and represents 300,000 students attending the country's 47 publicly supported Historically Black Colleges and Universities, medical schools and law schools. More than eighty percent of all students enrolled in HBCUs attend TMCF member-schools. TMCF was established in 1987 under the leadership of Dr. N. Joyce Payne.

It is with great enthusiasm that I submit this written testimony in an effort to highlight some of the important work TMCF is doing to support our network of *publicly supported* HBCUs and the students they serve everyday. The contributions of HBCUs to the Nation's ability to be globally competitive are significant. Additionally, TMCF's role in ensuring our network of schools are graduating a pipeline of students who are ready to compete for and create jobs in the 21st Century is critical. Outlined below are a few suggestions the committee should implement in order to maximize use of precious Federal resources under critical programs that support institutional curriculum and student success. TMCF is creating success one student at a time. We are doing it with scholarship and leadership development support while creating a culture of entrepreneurship on our campuses. We also recognize that many students arrive on our campuses without adequate preparation from their K–12 academic period. In an effort to reach students sooner, TMCF is launching our first TMCF Collegiate Academy at Southern University in New Orleans, LA.

Background on the Thurgood Marshall College Fund

Last year TMCF expanded and acquired *The Opportunity Funding Corporation* (OFC). TMCF now owns the OFC not-for-profit and the OFC for-profit entities. OFC was created in 1970 to support minority and disadvantaged entrepreneurs with investment capital to support for-profit business ventures. The U.S. Office of Economic Opportunity, under President **Richard Nixon**'s administration, funded OFC in the amount of $7 million. Later, OFC, the not-for-profit was established. Today, TMCF uses OFC to support student innovation and entrepreneurship that will ultimately lead to job creation.

Our core values are focused on the following:

- *Scholarships:* TMCF provides merit and financial-based scholarships to students;
- *Capacity Building:* TMCF provides capacity building in the form of faculty research fellowships and internship opportunities as well as technical support and grants to our network of member schools.
- *Policy & Advocacy:* TMCF serves as the chief advocate for public HBCUs and remains engaged on Federal policy and programs that support our students and HBCUs nationwide.

Scholarships

To date, TMCF has provided more than $200 million in scholarships and programmatic and capacity building support to students and our member schools. Many TMCF member-school graduates have become leaders in the business, education, government and entertainment industries to name a few. Few of these achievements would be possible without TMCF.

Capacity Building & Programmatic Support

Each year TMCF convenes a capacity building conference entitled the Member-Universities Professional Institute (MUPI). This year's conference theme, 'Full STEAM Ahead: Improving Retention, Graduation & Career Readiness in Science, Technology, Engineering, Agriculture and Mathematics" (STEAM), proved to be extremely valuable. Through workshops, plenary sessions and forums TMCF-connected faculty, provosts and students with program officers from many Federal agencies including U.S. Department of Agriculture (USDA), Centers for Disease Control (CDC), and Department of Defense (DOD). MUPI conference attendees learned first-hand about how to successfully compete for resources at the Federal level and how to ensure students are prepared to compete for internships and full- time employment with Federal agencies.

Additionally, during the same week, TMCF hosted our member presidents and board chairs for a 2-day governance session. TMCF is committed to ensuring our HBCU member presidents have the opportunity to learn and share best practices around board engagement and governance generally.

Our programmatic support is very much focused on ensuring TMCF students have access to great internship and fellowship opportunities. Each year we host an Annual Leadership Institute. We know these internships do not always turn into a job after graduation but many do. All of these experiences help expose students to the possibilities of what can be achieved with their degree once they enter the job market.

This is critical for first generation college students who often do not have multiple role models to show them what opportunities exist across the public and private sectors. TMCF teams up with the top employers across the country and during the Annual Student Leadership Institute to create opportunity for high achieving students to interview with top employers nationwide. During this time students also receive leadership development training.

TMCF is also working to create a culture of entrepreneurship on our campuses. During April 2014, TMCF's new subsidiary, The Opportunity Funding Corporation (OFC) hosted our first Student Innovation & Entrepreneurship Venture Challenge. This competition brought HBCU and other MSI students to Atlanta, GA where they presented their business plans to a panel of real life CEO judges. The OFC venture challenge competition is designed to mimic the real world process of raising venture capital and helps student entrepreneurs showcase their business acumen. A total of 19 public and private HBCUs participated as well as the University of the West Indies. TMCF urges the committee to find ways to support student entrepreneurship on HBCU campuses. In today's job market when individuals more frequently change jobs, we know it is increasingly important for students to be able to develop skill sets and that will lead to job creation.

Recommendations for the Reauthorization of the Higher Education Act

While the average tuition at publicly supported HBCUs is about $6,300 per year, college costs are increasing and students and their families are continuing to accumulate record levels of college loan debt. TMCF would like the committee to consider finding ways to address and enhance existing loan programs in an effort to curb costs to families and reward students with great academic talent.

Enhance Title III B, Strengthening Historically Black Colleges & Universities

Title III, part B discretionary and mandatory funding accounts are critical formula-based aid that is effectively used to support undergraduate academic programs and activities. TMCF urges the committee to support continued and increased authorization levels for these accounts. Specifically, TMCF urges the committee to support a significant investment in title III part B that would restore pre-sequestration levels and account for inflation. Additionally, consider authorizing expanded permissible use of the funds to cover distance learning. Under current law, title III part B funds are not authorized to support distance learning for HBCUs. As HBCUs enhance their technology use on campus or work to find ways to attract more non- traditional students, providing long distance learning opportunities is critical.

Enhance and Grow the HBCU Capital Financing Program

The HBCU Capital Financing Program provides low-interest financing to eligible HBCUs to support infrastructure and facility building and improvements. Use of these funds results in restoration and creation of dormitories and academic buildings on HBCU campuses. The risk to the government in this loan program is extremely low.

Each approved borrower is required to contribute 5 percent of their loan funds to a pooled escrow account to cover any future defaults in the program. During the entire history of the program, there has only been one default and that was of a private HBCU that is no longer active.

During the last re-authorization of the Higher Education Act, TMCF worked with the HBCU Community to successfully secure several programmatic changes including an increase to the total authorized loan authority. In light of the ongoing economic challenges faced by institutions coupled with the well-documented use of dollars under this program, there is room for additional modifications. TMCF encourages the committee to authorize an increase from the current $1.1 billion loan authority to $3 billion to cover future construction and infrastructure projects over the course of the next re-authorization period.

Additionally, TMCF supports the recommendation of the President's Advisory Board on HBCUs that urges Congress to permit a lower interest rate to approved borrowers who are going to use the loan money to construct or expand STEM- related facilities on their campuses.

Modernize Pell Grants

For many students attending HBCUs and for the majority of first generation college students, the Pell Grant is extremely important. TMCF urges the committee to support the following:

1. Re-invest, authorize and support funding to cover summer Pell. The absence of summer Pell creates increased challenges for students to complete college within 4 to 6 years. This is especially true for the non-traditional students.
2. Restore the $32,000 income threshold for automatic Pell eligibility. Recent changes to Pell have reduced the number of students who are eligible for the award and result in fewer students securing the funding they need to complete their education.

As the Nation works to build long-term economic growth, we need to find ways to increase college completion rates. Increasing college completion rates will require Congress, the higher education sector and the private sector to find ways to create more support for first generation and low-income families to pay for college. TMCF feels strongly that the current Federal dollars allocated toward Pell can be maximized more effectively. Finally, TMCF urges the committee to continue to find ways to streamline the financial aid process for students and families.

Address Challenges with the Administration's Proposed College Rating System

TMCF opposes awarding Federal student aid assistance based on the college rating system proposed by the Administration. Any new college rating system should take into account the significant work HBCUs are doing to enroll often under-prepared low-income students and providing them with the resources needed to fill academic gaps and then complete college.

Allocation of aid under this new proposed rating system would result in harm to low-income students and inequities in the distribution of aid.

Delay Cohort Default Rate Sanctions

In 2008, new cohort default rate policies were instituted. Beginning this year, institutions are in jeopardy of losing their title IV eligibility if they exceed a 3-year cohort default rate of 30 percent for 3 consecutive years. TMCF supports a 2-year delay in instituting sanctions for HBCUs connected to cohort default rates.

Retain Original Credit Criteria for the Parent PLUS Loan Program

In October 2011, the Department of Education without notice or input from the education community decided to unilaterally change the credit criteria used to determine eligibility for Parent PLUS Loans. This impacted more than 400,000 students nationwide and at least 28,000 HBCU students on both public and private HBCU campuses. Our schools experienced significant drops in enrollment. Students who were persisting with strong academic records were suddenly forced to go home with debt and no chance of securing their degree. The impact of these changes is still felt today on our campuses.

TMCF urges the committee to support a return to the former credit criteria used to determine Parent PLUS Loan eligibility. According to the Department of Education data the Parent PLUS Loan program has the lowest default rate of any Federal education loan program, just over 3 percent for both public and private HBCUs.

[Whereupon, at 12 p.m., the hearing was adjourned.]

In: Higher Education
Editor: Lilian Wieck

ISBN: 978-1-53616-026-0
© 2019 Nova Science Publishers, Inc.

Chapter 6

PROGRAMS FOR MINORITY-SERVING INSTITUTIONS UNDER THE HIGHER EDUCATION ACT*

Alexandra Hegji

ABSTRACT

Minority-serving institutions (MSIs) are institutions of higher education that serve high concentrations of minority students who, historically, have been underrepresented in higher education. Many MSIs have faced challenges in securing adequate financial support, thus affecting their ability to develop and enhance their academic offerings and ultimately serve their students. Federal higher education policy recognizes the importance of such institutions and targets financial resources to them. Funding for MSIs is channeled through numerous federal agencies, and several of these funding sources are available to MSIs through grant programs authorized under the Higher Education Act of 1965, as amended (HEA; P.L. 89-329). Over the years, HEA programs that support MSIs have expanded and now include programs for institutions serving a wide variety of student populations. In FY2016, MSI programs under the HEA were appropriated approximately $817 million, which helped fund more than 929 grants to institutions.

Currently, the HEA authorizes several programs that benefit MSIs:

- Title III-A authorizes the Strengthening Institutions Program, which provides grants to institutions with financial limitations and a high percentage of needy students. Title III-A also authorizes separate similar programs for American Indian tribally controlled colleges and universities; Alaska Native and Native Hawaiian-serving institutions; predominantly Black institutions (PBIs); Native American-serving, nontribal institutions; and Asian American and Native American Pacific Islander-serving institutions. Grants awarded under these programs assist eligible institutions in strengthening their academic,

---

* This is an edited, reformatted and augmented version of Congressional Research Service, Publication No. R43237, dated September 12, 2017.

administrative, and fiscal capabilities. These programs are typically funded through annual discretionary appropriations, but additional annual mandatory appropriations are provided through FY2019 under Title III-F.

- Title III-B authorizes the Strengthening Historically Black Colleges and Universities (HBCUs) program and the Historically Black Graduate Institutions program, both of which award grants to eligible institutions to assist them in strengthening their academic, administrative, and fiscal capabilities. These programs are typically funded through annual discretionary appropriations; however, additional annual mandatory appropriations are provided for HBCUs through FY2019.
- Title III-C authorizes the Endowment Challenge Grant program, which has not been funded since FY1995.
- Title III-D authorizes the HBCU Capital Financing Program, which assists HBCUs in obtaining low-cost capital financing for campus maintenance and construction projects and is generally funded through annual discretionary appropriations.
- Title III-E authorizes the Minority Science and Engineering Improvement Program, which provides grants to MSIs and other entities to effect long-term improvements in science and engineering education and is funded through annual discretionary appropriations.
- Title III-F provides additional annual mandatory appropriations through FY2019 for many of the Title III-A and Title III-B MSI programs. It also provides mandatory appropriations through FY2019 for the Hispanic-serving institutions (HSIs) Science, Technology, Engineering, and Mathematics (STEM) Articulation Program, which provides grants to HSIs to increase the number of Hispanic students in STEM fields and to develop model transfer and articulation agreements.
- Title V authorizes the HSI program and the Promoting Postbaccalaureate Opportunities for Hispanic Americans (PPOHA), both of which award grants to eligible institutions to assist them in strengthening their academic, administrative, and fiscal capabilities. Typically, both programs are funded through annual discretionary appropriations, but additional annual mandatory appropriations were provided for the PPOHA program from FY2009 through FY2014.
- Title VII-A-4 authorizes Masters Degree Programs at HBCUs and PBIs, which provide grants to select HBCUs and PBIs to improve graduate educational opportunities. Typically, both programs are funded through annual discretionary appropriations, but additional annual mandatory appropriations were provided for both programs from FY2009 through FY2014.

INTRODUCTION

Minority-serving institutions (MSIs) are institutions of higher education[1] that serve high concentrations of minority students who, historically, have been underrepresented in higher education. MSIs tend to have relatively low educational and general expenditures and high enrollments of needy students.

---

[1] For purposes of this report, an "institution of higher education" is one that offers a postsecondary education and meets the HEA section 101 definition of institution of higher education.

Generally, many such institutions have faced challenges in obtaining access to financial support, thus affecting their ability to enhance their academic offerings and institutional capabilities and ultimately serve their students.[2] Federal higher education policy recognizes the importance of such institutions in improving access for and increasing completion of underrepresented minorities and targets financial resources to them. Funding for MSIs is channeled through numerous federal agencies, and several of these funding sources are available to MSIs through grant programs authorized under the Higher Education Act of 1965, as amended (HEA; P.L. 89-329). Over the years, HEA support of MSI programs has expanded to include a wider variety of underrepresented groups, and in FY2016, MSI programs under the HEA were appropriated approximately $817 million, which helped fund more than 929 grants.[3]

For purposes of this chapter, MSIs include, but are not limited to, American Indian Tribally Controlled Colleges and Universities (TCCUs); Alaska Native and Native Hawaiian-serving institutions (ANNHs); predominantly Black institutions (PBIs); Native American-serving, nontribal institutions (NASNTIs); Asian American and Native American Pacific Islander-serving institutions (ANNAPISIs), historically Black colleges and universities (HBCUs), and Hispanic-serving institutions (HSIs).

This chapter describes the several programs devoted to financially assisting MSIs under the HEA. This chapter does not attempt to describe all HEA programs for which an MSI may be eligible; rather, it aims to describe those programs that are directed specifically toward one or more types of MSIs. MSIs are eligible for other federal programs for which IHEs and nonprofit organizations are eligible if they meet the program eligibility criteria.

This chapter first discusses how the various HEA MSI programs are funded. It then provides a description of each program, organized by the type of MSI to which the program is available. Included in each program description is a discussion of eligibility criteria for program participation; a description of authorized uses of financial awards; and administrative procedures, including a description of how funds are allocated among multiple institutions either via a competitive award process or a formula-based grant.

Appendix A provides a list of acronyms used in this chapter. Appendix B details mandatory and discretionary appropriations for selected MSI programs authorized under the HEA.

All programs discussed in this chapter are administered by the U.S. Department of Education.

---

[2] See U.S. Congress, Senate Committee on Labor and Human Resources, *Higher Education Amendments of 1986*, report to accompany S. 1965, 99th Cong., 2nd sess., May 12, 1986, 99-296 (Washington: GPO, 1986), p. 24.

[3] Office of Management and Budget, http://www.usaspending.gov, downloaded July 13, 2017.

FUNDING FOR MINORITY-SERVING INSTITUTIONS UNDER THE HIGHER EDUCATION ACT

Typically, many of the MSI programs authorized under the HEA are funded through annual discretionary appropriations. However, in recent years, mandatory appropriations have been provided to many of the programs, which were in addition to discretionary appropriations, in some cases. In 2007, with the College Cost Reduction and Access Act (P.L. 110-84), Congress established the Strengthening Historically Black Colleges and Universities and Other Minority-Serving Institutions programs. The act created some new MSI programs[4] and provided mandatory appropriations for both the newly authorized and the preexisting Title III-A and III-B MSIs programs for FY2008 and FY2009. The programs receiving the mandatory appropriations were

- strengthening TCCUs;
- strengthening ANNHs;
- strengthening PBIs;
- strengthening NASNTIs;
- strengthening ANNAPISIs;
- strengthening HBCUs; and
- HSI STEM.

The Higher Education Opportunity Act (HEOA; P.L. 110-315) redesignated the Strengthening Historically Black Colleges and Universities and Other Minority-Serving Institutions programs under Title III, Part F of the HEA. The HEOA also authorized additional annual mandatory appropriations for Masters Degree Programs at HBCUs and PBIs and the Promoting Postbaccalaureate Opportunities for Hispanic American programs for each of fiscal years FY2009 through FY2014,[5] programs that typically receive discretionary appropriations.

Finally, the Student Aid and Fiscal Responsibility Act (SAFRA), as part of the Health Care and Education Reconciliation Act (P.L. 111-152) extended the Title III-F mandatory appropriations for Title III-A, III-B, and HSI STEM programs through FY2019.

Appendix B details mandatory and discretionary appropriations for each of these programs from FY2013 to FY2017.

---

[4] The Strengthening PBIs; Strengthening NASNTIs; Strengthening ANNAPISIs; and HSI Science, Technology, Engineering, and Mathematics and Articulation programs were newly authorized under the CCRAA.

[5] Authorization of mandatory appropriations for these programs, and an appropriation of mandatory funds, were provided through FY2014 (HEOA; P.L. 110-315). Mandatory funds have not been provided for these programs since the end of FY2014.

PROGRAMS TARGETING LOW-INCOME-SERVING INSTITUTIONS

The Strengthening Institutions Program (SIP) provides grants to institutions of higher education that serve a high percentage of low-income students and that have low educational and general expenditures. It is the foundational program upon which many other HEA programs designed to aid minority-serving institutions (MSIs) are based.

Background

Since the HEA's inception in 1965, Congress has authorized grant programs to strengthen and support postsecondary institutions that, because of financial limitations, were struggling to survive.[6] The original HEA Title III-A program was not specifically directed at MSIs, and in the 1986 reauthorization of the HEA, Congress found that the original program "did not always meet the specific development needs of historically Black colleges and universities and other institutions with large concentrations of minority, low-income students."[7] Congress then amended the program to make institutions with high minority and low-income student concentrations eligible. In subsequent reauthorizations, Congress established several additional Title III-A programs with separate appropriations, each targeting different institutions serving specific types of minority students.

Today, SIP grants are available to institutions that serve low-income students, regardless of minority enrollment, while separate Title III-A program grants are available to institutions that serve high concentrations of Native American, Alaska Native, Native Hawaiian, Black, Asian American and Native American Pacific Islander, and Hispanic students. This section of the report discusses the Strengthening Institutions Program. SIP's provisions and definitions also apply to several of the MSI-specific Title III-A programs.

Strengthening Institutions Program

The Strengthening Institutions Program (SIP) was authorized at the HEA's inception. Its purpose is to improve the academic quality and institutional management and increase the self-sufficiency of institutions with a high percentage of needy students and with low expenditures (financial limitations). The program provides competitive grants to eligible institutions of higher education (IHEs).[8] SIP is funded through discretionary appropriations and receives the largest appropriation of the Title III-A programs.

---

[6] P.L. 89-329, §301.

[7] P.L. 99-498, §301.

[8] In determining which grants to fund in a competitive competition, the Secretary evaluates an application based on an applicant's meeting statutory and regulatory requirements, and a review panel awards points based on

This section describes the basic eligibility criteria for institutions participating in SIP, authorized uses of grant monies, and SIP administration. Descriptions in this section are presented in greater detail than in each section for MSI-specific programs, as generally, unless otherwise noted in this chapter, other Title III-A and III-F program requirements and provisions mirror those of SIP.

Eligibility

The eligibility requirements for SIP are the basic eligibility criteria for several of the other Title III-A and III-F programs and are found in Section 312(b) of the HEA.[9] In general, an institution meets SIP eligibility criteria (hereinafter referred to as HEA Section 312(b) requirements) if it

- has low educational and general expenditures (E&G);
- has a requisite enrollment of needy students;
- is legally authorized within its respective state to award bachelor's degrees, is a junior or community college, or is specified in Section 312(b);[10]
- is accredited or pre-accredited by a Department of Education (ED)-recognized national or state accrediting agency;[11] and
- is located within one of the 50 states, the Commonwealth of Puerto Rico, the District of Columbia, or the outlying areas.[12]

An institution has low E&G if the total amount expended by the institution for instruction and operation per full-time equivalent (FTE) undergraduate student is low,[13] as compared to the average E&G per FTE at institutions that offer similar instruction.[14] The

---

selection criteria. If two grant applications receive the same amount of points and funding is available for only one grant, the Secretary may give special consideration (e.g., award a tie-breaking point) to an applicant IHE with endowment funds that, per full-time equivalent (FTE) student, have a market value less than the average current market value of endowments of similar institutions or an applicant IHE that has expenditures for library materials per FTE enrolled student that are less than the average expenditures for library materials per FTE enrolled students at similar institutions. Additionally, for development grants (grants to carry out activities that implement an IHE's strategy for achieving growth and self-sufficiency, rather than planning grants, which assist a grantee in formulating a strategy), the Secretary may give special consideration to strategies that propose to carry out one or more of several activities, including faculty development, development and improvement of academic programs, and student services. HEA §311(b)(2)(A) & (B) and 34 C.F.R. §607.23.

[9] An eligible institution may apply as an individual institution or as part of a cooperative arrangement with institutions that may or may not be eligible for SIP. HEA §394(a)(1).

[10] Currently, the College of the Marshall Islands, the College of Micronesia/Federated States of Micronesia, and Palau Community College are specified in Section 312(b).

[11] For additional information on state authorization and accreditation requirements, see CRS Report R43159, *Institutional Eligibility for Participation in Title IV Student Financial Aid Programs*, by Alexandra Hegji.

[12] The term "outlying areas" includes Guam, American Samoa, the U.S. Virgin Islands, the Commonwealth of the Northern Mariana Islands, the Freely Associated States of the Republic of the Marshall Islands, the Federated States of Micronesia, and the Republic of Palau.

[13] Included in the determination of amounts expended by an institution are amounts used for instruction, research, public service, academic support, student services, institutional support, scholarships and fellowships, operation and maintenance of physical facilities, and mandatory transfers that the institution is required to pay by law.

[14] Waivers are available (under all Title III-A programs) for institutions that do not meet the E&G requirement. The Secretary can waive the requirement if, based on persuasive evidence, it is determined that the institution's

Secretary has defined similar instruction as institutions within the same institutional sector (e.g., public four-year institutions).[15] An institution meets the enrollment of needy students criterion if (1) at least 50% of its degree-, certificate-, or credential-seeking students receive need-based assistance under Title IV of the HEA (e.g., Federal Supplemental Educational Opportunity Grant, Federal Work Study, and Federal Perkins Loan, but *not* Subsidized Stafford Loans) in the second fiscal year preceding the fiscal year for which the determination is being made or (2) the percentage of its undergraduate degree-, certificate-, or credential-seeking students who were enrolled at least half-time and received Federal Pell Grants exceeded the median percentage for similar institutions.[16]

Branch campuses of institutions of higher education are eligible for SIP if the institution as a whole meets the eligibility requirements, even if the branch campus does not meet the state authorization or accreditation requirements. Branch campuses must, however, individually meet the needy student enrollment and low E&G requirements.[17]

Authorized Uses

SIP grants are intended to assist institutions in improving "academic quality, institutional management, and fiscal stability ... in order to increase their self-sufficiency and strengthen their capacity to make a substantial contribution to the higher education resources of the Nation."[18] To that end, Section 311(c) of the HEA lists several authorized activities for which grants can be awarded.[19] Authorized activities include[20]

---

failure to meet the requirement is due to factors that distort the determination that it meets the E&G requirements and that the institution's designation as an eligible institution is otherwise consistent with the purposes of the program. HEA §392(b). The Secretary has determined that some factors to be considered that may distort an institution's E&G expenditures include low student enrollment, location of an institution in an area with an unusually high cost-of-living, high energy costs, an increase in state funding that was part of a desegregation plan for higher education, or the operation of high-cost professional schools (e.g., medical or dental schools). 34 C.F.R. 607.4(d).

[15] 34 C.F.R. §607.7(c).

[16] 34 C.F.R. §607.3(a)(2). The Secretary can waive the requirement for a number of reasons, including in the case of institutions that are extensively subsidized by the state in which they are located and that charge little or no tuition; that serve a "substantial number" of low-income students as a percentage of total student population; that are substantially increasing higher education opportunities for individuals in rural or isolated areas that are underserved by postsecondary institutions; that are located on or near an Indian reservation if the Secretary determines that the waiver will substantially increase higher education opportunities appropriate to the needs of American Indians; or, wherever located, if the Secretary determines that a waiver will substantially increase higher education opportunities appropriate to the needs of Black Americans, Hispanic Americans, Native Americans, Asian Americans, or Pacific Islanders (including Native Hawaiians). Additionally, tribally controlled colleges and universities, as defined in the Tribally Controlled Colleges and Universities Act of 1978 (but not as defined in HEA §317), are specifically exempt from this needy student criterion. HEA §392(a). The reasons for granting a waiver are further detailed in 34 C.F.R. §607.3(b).

[17] HEA §312(b)(2).

[18] HEA §311(a).

[19] The accompanying regulations also list those activities specifically prohibited, which include activities not included in a grantee's approved application; activities that relate to sectarian instruction or religious worship; the purchase of standard office equipment, such as filing cabinets and furniture; student recruitment activities, such as advertising; and the use of funds to cover the cost of health and fitness programs. 34 C.F.R. §607.10(c).

[20] The authorized uses listed in the HEA serve mainly as examples of potential uses. Generally, unless specifically required by the HEA or its accompanying regulations, grantees are given considerable discretion in how they use grant funds.

- the purchase, rental, or lease of scientific or laboratory equipment for educational purposes;
- the construction, maintenance, renovation, and improvement of instructional facilities;[21]
- the support of faculty exchanges, development, and fellowships to assist in attaining advanced degrees in the faculty's field of instruction;
- the development and improvement of academic programs;
- the purchase of library books, periodicals, and other educational materials;
- tutoring, counseling, and student services programs designed to improve academic success, retention, and completion, including innovative and customized courses that may include remedial education and English language instruction;
- financial literacy education or counseling;
- funds management, administrative management, and equipment acquisition for use in funds management;
- the joint use of facilities, such as laboratories and libraries;
- the establishment or improvement of a development office to strengthen or improve alumni and private sector contributions;
- the creation or improvement of facilities of Internet or other distance education technologies;
- other activities, approved by the Secretary of Education (Secretary), that contribute to the purposes of the program; and
- the establishment or enhancement of an endowment fund.[22]

Although institutions are allowed to establish or improve endowment funds with SIP grants, they may not use more than 20% of grant monies for such purposes. Additionally, if an institution does use SIP funds for endowment development, it must provide matching funds from nonfederal sources in an amount equal to or greater than the federal contribution.[23]

In awarding grants, statutory provisions direct the Secretary to give special consideration to institutions that propose to engage in faculty development, funds and administrative management, development and improvement of academic programs,

---

[21] Grantees cannot, however, use grants for the acquisition of real property. The Education Department General Administrative Regulations (EDGAR), which provide regulations that apply to all ED-administered grant programs, prohibit recipients of ED-administered grants from using grant monies for the acquisition of real property or for construction, unless specifically permitted by the authorizing statute or implementing regulations for a program. 34 C.F.R. §75.533.

[22] The Consolidated Appropriations Act, 2017 (CAA 2017; P.L. 115-31) authorizes IHEs that maintain endowment funds supported with funds appropriated for HEA Title III and Title V programs for FY2017 to use the income from the endowment fund to award student scholarships. This provision, enacted through Division H, Title III of the CAA 2017, will remain in effect until Title III and Title V are reauthorized. Previous appropriations acts have authorized the same use of endowment income in recent years.

[23] HEA §311(d).

equipment acquisition for the strengthening of funds management and academic programs, the joint use of facilities, and student services.[24]

Program Administration

There is a two-step application process for participation in SIP. In step one, an institution applies to be designated as eligible under the HEA Section 312(b) eligibility criteria.[25] If approved by the Secretary, the institution may then apply for a SIP grant. SIP grants are awarded through a competitive process. The SIP application must, among other requirements, detail the institution's comprehensive development plan, describe the policies it will use to ensure that the federal funds awarded will be used to supplement and not supplant funds that would have otherwise been made available for the authorized activities described in Section 311(b), provide for making at least one report annually to ED regarding the institution's progress towards achieving its objectives, and provide for fiscal control and fund accounting procedures necessary to ensure the proper disbursement and accounting for grant funds.[26] Applications are selected based on the score of a review panel; the applications with the highest score are selected for funding.

ED awards two types of SIP grants. Development grants, which are used to carry out activities to implement an institution's strategy for achieving growth and self-sufficiency, under this program are generally five years in length, unless otherwise requested. ED may also award one-year planning grants for the purpose of preparing plans and applications for SIP grants. Finally, each institution that receives a development grant under this part is subject to a two year wait-out period (i.e., they are ineligible for another SIP grant for two years after the date of the grant's termination).[27]

In awarding grants, the Secretary gives priority to applicants who are not already receiving development grants under another Title III-A program; however, grantees under other Title III-A programs (e.g., Strengthening PBIs) are prohibited from concurrently receiving funds under other Title III-A programs. Thus, in effect, SIP grantees cannot receive funds under other Title III-A programs.[28] Additionally, SIP grantees cannot receive funds under Title III-B (HBCU and HBGIs programs) or Title V-A (HSI program) in the

---

[24] HEA §311(b)(2)(3).

[25] Prior to the 2016 award cycle, an IHE wishing to be designated as eligible by ED submitted an application with relevant enrollment and E&G data. ED would verify the information, review any waiver applications, and then designate an institution as "eligible" or "ineligible." Beginning with the 2016 award cycle, ED annually develops an eligibility matrix (EM) that lists potentially eligible institutions using ED data. An IHE appearing on the EM as potentially eligible is not required to submit additional data to ED; rather, it must submit an eligibility certification, provided by ED. IHEs that do not appear on the EM may submit an application with institutional data showing they meet program eligibility requirements or may submit a waiver request for the relevant data element (e.g., low E&G, enrollment of needy students). See U.S. Department of Education, "Eligibility Designations and Applications for Waiver of Eligibility Requirements; Programs Under Parts A and F of Title III of the Higher Education Act of 1965, as Amended (HEA), and Programs Under Title V of the HEA," 80 *Federal Register* 72423, December 19, 2015.

[26] HEA §391.

[27] HEA §313.

[28] In practice, this typically results in all types of institutions receiving Title III-A, III-B, or V program grants being excluded from SIP eligibility.

same fiscal year in which it receives a SIP grant.[29] Institutions receiving SIP grants in a fiscal year, however, can receive a grant under any one type of the Title III-F programs in the same fiscal year.[30]

AMERICAN INDIAN TRIBALLY CONTROLLED COLLEGES AND UNIVERSITIES PROGRAMS

Section 316 establishes the Strengthening American Indian Tribally Controlled Colleges and Universities (TCCUs) program, which was first authorized under the Higher Education Amendments of 1998 (P.L. 105-244). It is the only HEA program specifically available to TCCUs and provides SIP-type grants to them. The program is intended to assist TCCUs in improving and expanding their capacity to serving American Indian students.

Typically, Strengthening TCCU program grants are funded through discretionary appropriations under Title III-A. Additional mandatory appropriations are provided annually through FY2019 in Title III-F and are treated "as part of the amount appropriated ... to carry out section [316]";[31] therefore, in this chapter, the Title III-A and III-F TCCU programs are collectively referred to as the Strengthening TCCU program and are discussed in conjunction with one another, unless otherwise noted.

Eligibility

To qualify for a Strengthening TCCU grant, an institution of higher education[32] must meet the HEA Section 312(b) requirements and qualify for funding under the Tribally Controlled Colleges and Universities Assistance Act of 1978 (TCCUAA)[33] or the Navajo Community College Act (P.L. 92-189, as amended), or be cited in Section 532 of the Equity in Educational Land-Grant Status Act of 1994 (EELGSA).[34]

Institutions that qualify under the TCCUAA are institutions of higher education that are formally controlled, or have been formally sanctioned or chartered, by the governing body of an Indian tribe or tribes. Additionally, such institutions must have a majority of students who are Indians and must be operated for the purpose of meeting the needs of

---

[29] HEA §312(h) and 34 C.F.R. §607.2(g).

[30] See, for example, Department of Education, Office of Postsecondary Education, "Native American-serving nontribal institutions program," Frequently Asked Questions," http://www2.ed.gov/programs/nasnti/faq.html, accessed July 12, 2017.

[31] HEA §371(b)(2)(D)(i).

[32] Generally, the HEA requires that grantees be IHEs as defined by HEA §101; however, TCCUs are not required to meet the Section 101(a)(2) requirement of being legally authorized to provide a postsecondary education within the state in which they are located, per HEA §316(b)(4).

[33] 25 U.S.C. §1801 et seq.

[34] 7 U.S.C. §301 note.

Indians.[35] For the purposes of Strengthening TCCUs, an Indian student is a member of an Indian tribe or a biological child of a member of an Indian tribe, living or deceased.[36] Institutions that qualify under the Navajo Higher Community College or EELGSA are specifically named in the relevant statute.

Authorized Uses

Strengthening TCCU grants must be used to carry out activities that improve an institution's ability to serve Indian students. The authorized uses for Strengthening TCCU grants include those authorized under SIP. Additionally, TCCUs are specifically authorized to use grant funds to acquire real property adjacent to their campuses on which they can construct facilities. Grant recipients are also permitted to establish or enhance programs designed to qualify students to teach in elementary and secondary schools, with a particular emphasis on teaching Indian youth, and to establish community outreach programs that encourage Indian elementary and secondary students to develop academic skills and interest in pursuing a postsecondary education. While TCCUs are allowed to use up to 20% of grant funds, like SIP grantees, to establish or increase endowments,[37] they must provide nonfederal[38] matching funds equal to federal funds.[39]

Allotments

Prior to the Higher Education Opportunity Act of 2008 (HEOA; P.L. 110-315), the Strengthening TCCU program was a competitive grant program. The HEOA, however, transformed the competitive program into a largely formula-based grant program.[40]

---

[35] 25 U.S.C. §§1801 & 1804.

[36] HEA §316(b)(1) & 25 U.S.C. §1801(a).

[37] The Consolidated Appropriations Act, 2017 (CAA 2017; P.L. 115-31 authorizes IHEs that maintain endowment funds supported with funds appropriated for HEA Title III and Title V programs for FY2017 to use the income from the endowment fund to award student scholarships. This provision, enacted through Division H, Title III of the CAA 2017, will remain in effect until Title III and Title V are reauthorized. Previous appropriations acts have authorized the same use of endowment income in recent years.

[38] For the purposes of Strengthening TCCU grants, funds provided to institutions under the Tribally Controlled Colleges or Universities Grant Program or specifically to Dine College under the Navajo Community College Act are treated as nonfederal, private funds of the institutions. 25 U.S.C. §1809(c) & 25 U.S.C. §640c-2(b).

[39] HEA §316(c).

[40] In FY2009-FY2012 Congress inserted language into ED's appropriations bills requiring that noncompeting continuation (NCC) grants, in amounts not less than the originally authorized amount, be made to grantees that had been selected for awards by the last competitive process in FY2008. NCC grants are awarded to current grantees for succeeding years of the life of a grant after the Secretary has determined that the grantee is making satisfactory progress in carrying out the grant. NCC funding for the older competitive grants under the Strengthening TCCU program was taken from the TCCU's new formula allotment; the institutions' funding, however, was allowed to exceed what the institutions were entitled to under the formula. See, for example, the Consolidated Appropriations Act of 2012, P.L. 112-74.

Under the program, the Secretary is given the option to reserve up to 30% of fiscal year appropriations for the purpose of awarding competitive one-year grants for construction, maintenance, and renovation needs; these grants may not be less than $1 million each.[41] After the Secretary awards such grants, 60% of the remaining appropriated funds are distributed among eligible TCCUs on a pro rata basis, based on the number of Indian student counts of the respective institutions.[42] The remaining 40% is then distributed in equal shares to all eligible TCCUs. The minimum grant amount a recipient can be awarded is $500,000.[43]

Program Administration

As with SIP, there is a two-step application process for participation in the Strengthening TCCU program. In step one, an institution applies to be designated as eligible under 312(b). In step two, institutions apply to the TCCU program and submit project plans. The application and project plan must contribute to the purposes of the program, not include unallowable activities, and meet any statutory provisions and regulations. If approved by the Secretary, the Secretary then makes an allotment to the institution based on the above-described formula. For formula-funded grants under this program, the performance period is five years.[44]

Institutions that receive grants under this section are not subject to the Section 313(d) two-year wait-out period.[45] Additionally, TCCUs that receive grants under the Title III-A, Section 316 program are prohibited from receiving funds from other Title III-A programs, Title III-B programs (Strengthening HBCU program and Historically Black Graduate Institutions (HBGIs) program), or Title V-A (the HSI program) during the same fiscal year; however, in general, they may receive a grant under any of the Title III-F programs in the same fiscal year. Generally, institutions receiving a Title III-F TCCU grant may simultaneously receive a grant under another Title III-F program.

---

[41] Although the Secretary has the discretion to award such grants, the option has not yet been exercised. Department of Education, Office of Postsecondary Education, "American Indian Tribally Controlled Colleges and University—Title III Part A Programs, Frequently Asked Questions," http://www2.ed.gov/programs/iduesaitcc/faq.html, accessed July 12, 2017.

[42] "Indian student counts" is defined in the TCCUAA as "a number equal to the total number of Indian students enrolled in each tribally controlled college or university ... on the basis of the quotient of the sum of the credit hours of all Indian students so enrolled, divided by twelve." 20 U.S.C. §180(a)(8).

[43] Generally, institutions are only allowed to receive one Title III-A grant; however, under the Strengthening TCCU program, an institution could receive both a one-year Strengthening TCCU construction grant and also a grant based on the Strengthening TCCU formula.

[44] HEA §313(a).

[45] HEA §316(d)(4)(B).

ALASKA NATIVE AND NATIVE HAWAIIAN-SERVING INSTITUTIONS PROGRAMS

Section 317 of the HEA establishes the Strengthening Alaska Native and Native Hawaiian-Serving Institutions (ANNHs) program, which was first authorized under the Higher Education Amendments of 1998 (P.L. 105-244). It is the only HEA program specifically available to ANNHs and provides SIP-type grants to them. The program is intended to enable such institutions to improve and expand their ability to serve Alaska Natives or Native Hawaiians.

Typically, Strengthening ANNH grants are funded through discretionary appropriations under Title III-A. Additional mandatory appropriations are provided annually through FY2019 in Title III-F and "shall be made available as grants under [Section 317ANNH program]."[46] Therefore, in this chapter, the Title III-A and III-F ANNH programs are collectively referred to as the Strengthening ANNH program and are discussed in conjunction with one another, unless otherwise noted.

Eligibility

To qualify for a Strengthening ANNH grant, an institution of higher education must meet the HEA Section 312(b) requirements and must also have an enrollment of undergraduate students that is at least 20% Alaska Native students or at least 10% Native Hawaiian students.[47] For purposes of the Strengthening ANNH program, a Native Alaskan is a citizen of the United States who is "of one fourth-degree or more Alaska Indian ... Eskimo, or Aleut blood, or a combination thereof."[48] A Native Hawaiian is a citizen of the United States who is a "descendent of the aboriginal people who, prior to 1778, occupied and exercised sovereignty in the area that now comprises the State of Hawaii...."[49]

Authorized Uses

Strengthening ANNH grants must be used to assist an institution in planning, developing, undertaking, and carrying out activities to improve an institution's capacity to

---

[46] HEA §371(b)(2)(D)(ii).

[47] Although different enrollment criteria apply depending on whether an institution wants to be designated as an Alaska Native-serving institution or a Native Hawaiian-serving institution, in its budget and its administration of the program, ED does not appear to otherwise differentiate between the two types of institutions, such that both types compete for funds from the same pool of money (i.e., ED does not allot a specified amount of grant funds to each type of institution).

[48] This term is defined in the Alaska Native Claims Settlement Act, 43 U.S.C. §1602(b).

[49] This term is defined in the Elementary and Secondary Education Act, 20 U.S.C. §7517(1).

serve Alaska Natives or Native Hawaiians. The authorized uses for grants under these provisions are similar to those authorized under Section 311(b) of the HEA. Unlike other Title III-A or III-F programs, neither the HEA nor the regulations specifically permit or prohibit ANNHs from using grant funds to create or improve institutional endowments; however, in ED's grant application for FY2015,[50] it appears that the use of up to 20% of grants awards was allowed for endowment investment.[51]

Program Administration

As with SIP, there is a two-step award process for participation in the Strengthening ANNH program. First, an institution applies for Section 312(b) designation. If approved by the Secretary, the institution may then apply for a Strengthening ANNH grant. Strengthening ANNH grants are awarded through a competitive process. Applications are selected based on the score of a review panel, and the applications with the highest score are selected for funding.

Strengthening ANNH grants are generally five years in length for general development grants and two years in length for grants used for facility renovation. ANNHs that receive grants under this program are not subject to the Section 313(d) two-year wait-out period.[52]

Institutions that receive Strengthening ANNH grants are prohibited from receiving funds under other Title III-A programs, Title III-B programs (Strengthening HBCU and HBGI), and Title V-A (HSI program) during the same fiscal year; however, in general, they may receive a grant under any of the Title III-F programs in the same fiscal year. Generally, institutions receiving a Title III-F ANNH grant may simultaneously receive a grant under another Title III-F program.

NATIVE AMERICAN-SERVING, NONTRIBAL INSTITUTIONS PROGRAMS

Section 319 establishes the Strengthening Native American-Serving, Nontribal Institutions (NASNTIs) program, which was first authorized in 2007 under the College

---

[50] The grant application reads, in relevant part, "if you propose to use up to 20% for endowment investing, do not write an activity narrative regarding this use of endowment investing, as we do not consider it an activity in the usual sense." Department of Education, Office of Postsecondary Education, *Fiscal Year 2015: Application for Grants Under the Title III, Part A Alaska Native and Native Hawaiian-Serving Institutions Program*, OMB No. 1840-0810, p. 73.

[51] The Consolidated Appropriations Act, 2017 (CAA 2017; P.L. 115-31) authorizes IHEs that maintain endowment funds supported with funds appropriated for HEA Title III and Title V programs for FY2017 to use the income from the endowment fund to award student scholarships. This provision, enacted through Division H, Title III of the CAA 2017 will remain in effect until Title III and Title V are reauthorized. Previous appropriations acts have authorized the same use of endowment income in recent years.

[52] HEA §317(d)(3)(B).

Cost Reduction and Access Act (CCRAA; P.L. 110-385). It is the only HEA program specifically available to NASNTIs and provides SIP-type grants to them. The program is intended to enable such institutions to improve and expand their ability to serve Native American and low-income students.

Since 2010, Strengthening NASNTI program grants have been funded through discretionary appropriations under Title III-A. Mandatory appropriations are provided annually through FY2019 in Title III-F.[53] In general, Title III-A and Title III-F NASNTI program grants are subject to the same eligibility criteria, authorized uses, and administrative procedures; therefore, in this chapter, the Title III-A and III-F NASTNTI programs are collectively referred to as the Strengthening NASNTIs program and are discussed in conjunction with one another, unless otherwise noted.

Eligibility

To qualify for a Strengthening NASNTIs program grant, institutions of higher education must meet the HEA Section 312(b)[54] eligibility requirements and must also have an enrollment of undergraduate students that is at least 10% Native American students. A Native American is defined as an individual who is of a tribe, people, or culture indigenous to the United States. Additionally, an eligible institution cannot be a TCCU.[55]

Authorized Activities

Title III-A and III-F NASNTI grants must be used to assist NASNTIs in planning, developing, and carrying out activities to improve their capacity to serve Native American and low-income individuals. The examples of authorized activities for NASNTI grants mirror the authorized uses under Section 311(b); however, NASNTIs cannot use grant monies to start or improve an endowment.[56]

---

[53] HEA §371(b)(2)(D)(iv).

[54] HEA §319 requires that IHEs meet HEA §312(b) eligibility requirements to receive Title III-A funds under the NASNTI program. HEA §371(c) does not require that IHEs meet HEA §312(b) requirements to receive Title III-F funds under the NASNTI program; however, in its Notice of Intent to Apply, ED requires that institutions applying for NASNTI III-F grants meet the §312(b) requirements. See U.S. Department of Education, "Eligibility Designations and Applications for Waiver of Eligibility Requirements; Programs Under Parts A and F of Title III of the Higher Education Act of 1965, as Amended (HEA), and Programs Under Title V of the HEA," 81 *Federal Register* 85212, November 25, 2016.

[55] HEA §319(b).

[56] Department of Education, Office of Postsecondary Education, "Native American-Serving Nontribal Institutions Program, Frequently Asked Questions," http://www2.ed.gov/programs/nasnti/faq.html, accessed July 13, 2017.

Program Administration

As with SIP, there is a two-step award process for institutions to receive grants under either the Title III-A or III-F NASNTI programs. In step one, an institution applies for eligibility by demonstrating it meets either the HEA Section 312(b) criteria for Title III-A NASNTI grants or the specific eligibility criteria set forth in Title III-F for those NASNTI grants. If approved by the Secretary, the institution may then apply for a NASNTI grant under the grant it wishes to receive. Both types of NASNTI grants are awarded through a competitive process. Applications are selected based on the score of a review panel, and the applications with the highest score are selected for funding.

Title III-A NASNTI grants were first awarded in FY2010, and Title III-F NASNTI grants were first awarded in FY2008. Both types of grants are five years in length. The minimum award for a Title III-A NASNTI grant is \$200,000;[57] there is no statutorily set minimum grant amount under the Title III-F NASNTI program.

Institutions that receive grants under the Title III-A or III-F NASNTI programs are not subject to the Section 313(d) two-year wait-out period. Institutions receiving a Title III-A NASNTI grant cannot receive funds under other Title III-A programs, Title III-B programs (Strengthening HBCU and HBGI), or Title V-A (HSI program) in the same fiscal year; however, in general, they may receive a grant under any one type of the Title III-F programs in the same fiscal year. Generally, institutions receiving a Title III-F NASNTI grant may simultaneously receive a grant under another Title III-F program.

ASIAN AMERICAN AND NATIVE AMERICAN PACIFIC ISLANDER-SERVING INSTITUTIONS PROGRAMS

Section 320 establishes the Strengthening Asian American and Native American Pacific Islander-Serving Institutions (AANAPISIs) program, which was first authorized in 2007 under the College Cost Reduction and Access Act (CCRAA; P.L. 110-85). It is the only HEA program specifically available to AANAPISIs and provides SIP-type grants to them. The purpose of the program is to enable such institutions to improve and expand their ability to serve Asian Americans and Native American Pacific Islanders and low-income individuals.

Section 320 Strengthening AANAPISI grants have been funded through discretionary appropriations since FY2009 under Title III-A. Additional mandatory appropriations are provided annually through FY2019 under Title III-F.[58] In general, eligibility requirements, authorized uses, and administrative processes for Title III-A and Title III-F AANAPISI

---

[57] HEA §319(d)(3)(D).
[58] HEA §371(b)(2)(D)(iii).

grants are the same; therefore, in this chapter, the Title III-A and Title III-F AANAPISI programs are referred to collectively as the Strengthening AANAPISI program and are discussed in conjunction with one another, unless otherwise stated.

Eligibility

To qualify for a Strengthening AANAPISI program grant under either Title III-A or III-F, institutions of higher education must meet the HEA Section 312(b) eligibility requirements. Additionally, at the time of application, an institution must have an enrollment of undergraduate students that is at least 10% Asian American students or Native American Pacific Islander students. For purposes of the Strengthening AANPISI program, an Asian American is an individual "having origins in any of the original peoples of the Far East, Southeast Asia, or the Indian subcontinent,"[59] and a Native American Pacific Islander is "any descendant of the aboriginal people of any island in the Pacific Ocean that is a territory or possession of the United States."[60]

Authorized Uses

Strengthening AANAPISI grants awarded under Title III-A and Title III-F must be used to assist an institution in planning, developing, and carrying out activities that improve and expand the institution's capacity to serve Asian American and Native American Pacific Islanders (AANAPIs) and low-income individuals.

Title III-A grants to AANAPISIs have authorized uses similar to the authorized uses under 311(b); however, AANAPISIs are also authorized to use grant funds to provide academic instruction in disciplines in which AANAPIs are underrepresented, to conduct research and data collection for AANAPI populations and subpopulations, and to establish partnerships with community-based organizations that serve AANAPIs.[61] Title III-F grants to AANAPISIs can be used only for activities authorized under Section 311(c).[62] Under both programs, grant recipients can use up to 20% of grant funds to establish or increase endowments, but they must provide matching nonfederal funds that are equal to the amount of federal funds.[63]

---

[59] Office of Management and Budget, "Revisions to the Standards for the Classification of Federal Data on Race and Ethnicity," HEA §320(b)(1) and 62 Federal Register 58787, October 30, 1997.

[60] HEA §320(b)(3).

[61] HEA §320(c)(2)(K)-(M).

[62] HEA §371(b)(2)(D)(iii).

[63] The Consolidated Appropriations Act, 2017 (CAA 2017; P.L. 115-31 authorizes IHEs that maintain endowment funds supported with funds appropriated for HEA Title III and Title V programs for FY2017 to use the income from the endowment fund to award student scholarships. This provision, enacted through Division H, Title III

Program Administration

As with SIP, there is a two-step award process for institutions to receive grants under either Title III-A or III-F Strengthening AANAPISI programs. First, an institution applies for designation as Section 312(b) eligible. If approved by the Secretary, the institution may then apply for either a Title III-A or III-F AANAPISI program grant. Grants under both programs are awarded through a competitive process. Applications are selected based on the score of a review panel, and the applications with the highest score are selected for funding.

Strengthening AANAPISI grants are generally five years in length. Additionally, AANAPISIs that receive grants under either the Title III-A or the Title III-F program are not subject to the Section 313(d) two-year wait-out period. Institutions that receive a Strengthening AANAPISI grant under Title III-A in a fiscal year are prohibited from receiving funds under other Title III-A programs, Title III-B (Strengthening HBCU and HBGI programs), or Title V (HSI program and Promoting Postbaccalaureate Opportunities for Hispanic Americans (PPOHA))[64] in the same fiscal year; however, in general, they may receive a grant under any of the Title III-F programs in the same fiscal year. Generally, institutions receiving a Title III-F ANNAPISI grant may simultaneously receive a grant under another Title III-F program.

HISTORICALLY BLACK COLLEGES
AND UNIVERSITIES PROGRAMS

Most historically Black colleges and universities (HBCUs) were established between 1867 and 1900 with the purpose of serving the educational needs of Black Americans.65 Before HBCUs were established, and to a certain extent afterwards, Black Americans were generally denied admission to traditionally white institutions.[66] As a result of these practices, HBCUs became a primary means for providing postsecondary education to Black Americans. As of 2015, there were 97 HBCUs located in 19 states, predominantly

---

of the CAA 2017 will remain in effect until Title III and Title V are reauthorized. Previous appropriations acts have authorized the same use of endowment income in recent years.

[64]. Generally, institutions receiving a Title III-A program grant are eligible to simultaneously receive a PPOHA grant; however, IHEs receiving Section 320 AANAPISI grants are specifically prohibited from concurrently receive PPOHA grants. HEA §320(d)(3)(A).

[65] Stephen Provasnik and Thomas D. Snyder, *Historically Black Colleges and Universities, 1976 to 2001*, National Center for Education Statistics, NCES 2004-062, Washington, DC, September 2004, p. 1.

[66] Department of Education, Office for Civil Rights, "Historically Black Colleges and Universities and Higher Education Desegregation," http://www2.ed.gov/about/offices/list/ocr/docs/hq9511.html, accessed July 13, 2017.

in the Southeast; the District of Columbia; and the U.S. Virgin Islands. They include private and public, two-year and four-year institutions.[67]

HBCUs are funded under Title III-B of the HEA. At various points in time, HBCUs were provided funding under HEA Title III, but it was not until the Higher Education Amendments of 1986 (P.L. 99-498) that a separate HBCU program was established under Title III-B. In establishing the Title III-B HBCU program, Congress found that many HBCUs were struggling to survive because of financial limitations and that "the current state of Black colleges and universities [was] partly attributable to the discriminatory actions of the States and the Federal Government."[68] The HBCU program was meant to address these issues and to ensure HBCUs' participation in providing equality in education.

HEA Title III-B authorizes programs for both undergraduate and graduate and professional programs at eligible HBCUs. Section 323, the Strengthening HBCUs program, authorizes the Secretary to award formula-based grants to eligible HBCUs for activities to strengthen academic, administrative, and fiscal capabilities; these grants are typically available through discretionary appropriations. The Historically Black Graduate Institutions (HBGIs) program, Section 326, provides funds for formula-based grants to specifically listed graduate and professional programs at HBCUs for authorized activities similar to those under Section 323, typically with discretionary funds. Title III-F authorizes additional appropriations for the Section 323 eligible institutions.

In addition to the Title III-B and Title III-F programs, Title VII, Part A, Subpart 4 of the HEA authorizes Masters Degree Programs at HBCUs, which provides grants to specifically listed institutions that make a substantial contribution to the graduate education of Black Americans at the master's degree level. Finally, the Historically Black College and University Capital Financing (HBCU Cap Fin) program assists HBCUs in obtaining low-cost capital financing for campus maintenance and construction projects.

This section of the report discusses both of the Strengthening HBCU Program, the HBGI, Masters Degree Programs at HBCUs, and the HBCU Cap Fin program, including eligibility criteria, authorized uses, and program administration.

Strengthening Historically Black Colleges and Universities

Section 323 authorizes the Strengthening Historically Black Colleges and Universities program, which provides institutional grants to HBCUs. The program is intended to enable HBCUs to participate in activities that strengthen their academic, administrative, and fiscal capabilities.

While the Strengthening HBCU program is similar in purpose and structure to the Title III-A programs in many ways, it is also markedly different from them. Unlike most of the

---

[67] HBCUs were identified using the Department of Education's FY2017 Eligibility Matrix.
[68] P.L. 99-489 §321(3).

Title III-A programs, which are competitive, the Title III-B Strengthening HBCU program is formula-funded. Additionally, HBCUs are not required to meet many of the Title III-A eligibility requirements related to educational and general expenditures or a requisite number of needy students.

Typically, the Strengthening HBCUs program is funded through discretionary appropriations under Title III-B. Additional mandatory appropriations are provided through FY2019 in Title III-F.[69] The Title III-F authorizing language states that the mandatory funds shall be made available to eligible HBCUs under Title III-B and shall be allotted in the same manner and for the same authorized purposes; therefore, in this chapter, the Title III-B Strengthening HBCU program and Title III-F Strengthening HBCU programs are collectively referred to as the Strengthening HBCUs program and are discussed in conjunction with one another.

Eligibility

HBCUs eligible for grants under HEA Title III programs are known as Part B institutions. In this chapter, the terms HBCU and Part B institution are used interchangeably. A Part B institution is defined as one

- established before 1964;
- with a primary mission that was, and is, the education of Black Americans; and
- that is accredited or preaccredited by an ED-recognized accrediting agency.[70]

Additionally, the accompanying regulations require that an eligible Part B institution be legally authorized by the state in which it is located to operate as a junior or community college or to award bachelor's degrees.

Institutions that were established after 1964 may also qualify as eligible Part B institutions. To do so, they must (1) have been a branch campus of a southern institution of higher education that, prior to September 30, 1986, received a grant as an institution with special needs under HEA Section 321;[71] and (2) have been an institution formally recognized by the National Center for Education Statistics as an HBCU but that, on or after

---

[69] HEA §371(b)(2)(C)(i).

[70] HEA §322(2).

[71] Prior to the HEA Amendments of 1986, the program authorized under HEA Title III, Part B was the Aid to Institutions with Special Needs program. This program provided short-term assistance for improving the management and fiscal capabilities of "special needs" institutions. Special needs institutions were determined based on eligibility criteria that included the number of Pell Grant recipients enrolled at the institution and the total amount of Pell Grant dollars awarded to students attending the institution and the total educational and general expenditures of the institution. Additionally, institutions were required to have no fewer than 100 FTE students enrolled. Finally, the Secretary was allowed to consider additional factors in awarding grants, such as little or no endowment, a high studentto-faculty ratio, and limited library resources. U.S. Congress, Senate Labor and Human Resources, *Reauthorization of the Higher Education Act: Program Descriptions, Issues, and Options*, committee print, prepared by the Congressional Research Service, 99th Cong., 1 sess., February 1985, S. Prt. 99-8 (Washington: GPO, 1985), pp. 227-228.

the date the enactment of the Strengthening HBCUs program (October 17, 1986), was determined not to meet the newly established Part B eligibility criteria. [72]

Authorized Activities

In general, many of the authorized activities listed in Section 323 mirror those authorized under the Strengthening Institutions Program. For example, Part B institutions may use grants for purchasing or renting laboratory equipment, constructing or renovating instructional facilities,[73] or tutoring or counseling students to improve academic success. However, several additional uses are specified in Section 323. These additional authorized uses include

- establishing or enhancing a program of teacher education designed to qualify students to teach in a public elementary or secondary school in the states and that includes preparation for teacher certification;
- establishing community outreach programs that will encourage elementary and secondary students to develop the academic skills and interest to pursue a postsecondary education; and
- acquiring real property in connection with the construction, renovation, or addition to or improvement of campus facilities.

Part B institutions are also authorized to use up to 20% of grant funds to establish or increase endowments.[74] If an institution chooses to do so, it must provide nonfederal matching funds that are equal to or greater than the federal funds.

Allotments

Strengthening HBCU grants are formula-based, such that each eligible Part B institution that meets the eligibility criteria and submits a qualifying application may receive a grant award. For amounts appropriated for these grants, the Secretary must allot to each institution a sum

---

[72] Additionally, the Secretary is authorized to make grants that encourage cooperative arrangements. With funds available to carry out Title III-B programs, cooperative arrangements can be entered into between institutions eligible under Title III-B and institutions that are not receiving assistance under Title III. The cooperative arrangements must support activities authorized by HEA Section 323. HEA §394(a)(2).

[73] No more than 50% of a Strengthening HBCU grant can be used for constructing or maintaining a classroom, library, laboratory, or other instructional facility. HEA §323(c)(2).

[74] The Consolidated Appropriations Act, 2017 (CAA 2017; P.L. 115-31) authorizes IHEs that maintain endowment funds supported with funds appropriated for HEA Title III and Title V programs for FY2017 to use the income from the endowment fund to award student scholarships. This provision, enacted through Division H, Title III of the CAA 2017 will remain in effect until Title III and Title V are reauthorized. Previous appropriations acts have authorized the same use of endowment income in recent years.

1. that bears a ratio equal to 50% of the number of Federal Pell Grant recipients in attendance at the institution at the end of the preceding academic year to the total number of Federal Pell Grant recipients at all Part B institutions;
2. that bears a ratio equal to 25% of the number of an institution's graduates for the academic year to the number of graduates for all Part B institutions;
3. that bears a ratio equal to 25% of the percentage of an institution's graduates who are admitted to and in attendance at, within five years of graduating with a bachelor's degree, a graduate or professional school in a degree program in disciplines in which Blacks are underrepresented to the percentage of such graduates per institution from all Part B institutions.[75]

If the amount of a grant to be awarded to an institution, based on the above formula, is greater than $250,000 and less than $500,000, then the Secretary must award the institution $500,000. If the amount of a grant to be awarded to an institution is less than or equal to $250,000, then the Secretary must award the institution $250,000. Additionally, if the amounts appropriated in any fiscal year are insufficient to make these minimum allotments to each eligible institution, then the minimum allotments are ratably reduced. Finally, if ED determines that an individual institution's allotment for any fiscal year is not needed by that institution, ED may redistribute the unneeded funds to other HBCUs as ED determines appropriate.[76]

Finally, Howard University and the University of the District of Columbia may not receive allotments if either institution's allotment under criteria 2 and 3 is less than the amounts they would receive under their permanent annual appropriations.[77]

Program Administration

The award process for Strengthening HBCU grants is a multi-step process. First, an institution must be designated by ED as a Part B institution. ED maintains a list of Part B institutions.[78] If an institution has been designated as a Part B institution, it must then

---

[75] If an otherwise eligible Part B institution did not have any enrolled Pell Grant recipients; did not graduate any students; did not have any students who, within five years of graduation, were admitted to and in attendance at a graduate or professional school in a degree program in disciplines in which Blacks are underrepresented; or failed to provide the Secretary with the data required for the formula, then it shall not receive an allotment (including the minimum allotment) for a fiscal year. HEA §324(h).

[76] HEA §324.

[77] HEA §324(g). Both Howard University and the University of the District of Columbia receive annual discretionary appropriations. See HEA. 20 U.S.C. §123 & 87 Stat. §774. Howard University has not received a Strengthening HBCU grant since at least FY2003.

[78] ED regulations, 34 C.F.R. §608.2, provide a list of institutions that the Secretary determined qualified as HBCUs under HEA Section 322 as of June 24, 1994. Those institutions listed in the regulations do not, however, reflect the current list of institutions that qualify as HBCUs, as some institutions have lost accreditation, gained accreditation, or have closed since the regulations were last updated. For instance, Mary Holmes College in West Point, MS, closed in 2005. See, for example, Garthia Elena Burnett, "Mary Holmes gets new lease on life," *Commercial Dispatch*, June 17, 2011. Unlike the Title III-A programs, this designation is generally granted outside of the grant-making process. Typically, a school wishing to be designated as an HBCU must contact ED's Office of Postsecondary Education and express its interest in being designated as an HBCU. The institution

submit to ED the data required to calculate the formula allotments. Finally, at a separate time, the institution submits a project plan to ED, which must describe the institution's proposed activities, not include unallowable activities, and meet any statutory provisions and regulations. If approved by the Secretary, the Secretary then makes an allotment to the institution based on the above-described formula.

Program grants are five years in length.[79] Any funds paid to an institution that are not used within the five-year time period can be carried over and expended during the succeeding five-year period, so long as those funds are obligated for the same purpose.[80]

Finally, institutions receiving a Title III-B Strengthening HBCU grant in a fiscal year cannot receive funds under any Title III-A, III-F, Title V (HSI program), or Title VII (Masters Degrees at PBIs) program not specifically established for HBCUs in the same fiscal year.

Historically Black Graduate Institutions

Section 326 of the HEA authorizes the Historically Black Graduate Institutions (HBGIs) program. As with the Strengthening HBCU program, the purpose of the HBGI program is to enable such institutions to participate in activities that strengthen their academic, administrative, and fiscal capabilities.

Like the Strengthening HBCU program, the HBGI program has been funded through discretionary appropriations. However, unlike institutions eligible under the Strengthening HBCU program or most of the Title III-A programs, Title III-F does not provide additional mandatory funding for the HBGI program.

Eligibility

All institutions or graduate programs eligible for HBGI grants are specifically listed in the HEA. HBGI grants are available to postgraduate institutions or institutions offering "qualified graduate programs" that have been determined by ED to be "making a substantial contribution to the legal, medical, dental, veterinary, or other graduate education opportunities in mathematics, engineering, or the physical or natural sciences for Black Americans."[81] Qualified graduate programs are graduate or professional programs that provide a program of instruction in law, physical or natural sciences, engineering, mathematics, psychometrics, or other scientific disciplines in which African Americans are

---

provides ED with evidence that it meets the HBCU criteria, and ED makes a determination of the institution's status.

[79] ED has not yet determined how to allocate funds if a school is newly designated as a Part B institution after a five-year grant cycle has started.

[80] HEA §327(b).

[81] HEA §326(a).

218   *Alexandra Hegji*

underrepresented and in which students are enrolled at the time of application for the grant.[82]

Originally, five institutions or schools were listed as eligible under Section 326,[83] and over the years, Congress has designated several other schools and programs as eligible to receive HBGI grants. Prior to passage of the Higher Education Opportunity Act of 2008 (HEOA; P.L. 110-315), 18 institutions, schools, and programs were specified in Section 326 and, therefore, were eligible for HBGI grants. Those institutions, schools, and programs were

- Morehouse School of Medicine,
- Meharry Medical School,
- Charles R. Drew Postgraduate Medical School,
- Clark-Atlanta University,
- Tuskegee University School of Veterinary Medicine and other qualified graduate programs,
- Xavier University School of Pharmacy and other qualified graduate programs,
- Southern University School of Law and other qualified graduate programs,
- Texas Southern University School of Law and School of Pharmacy and other qualified graduate programs,
- Florida Agricultural and Mechanical University School of Pharmaceutical Sciences and other qualified graduate programs,
- Morgan State University qualified graduate programs,
- Hampton University qualified graduate programs,
- Alabama Agricultural and Mechanical University qualified graduate programs,
- North Carolina Agricultural and Technical State University qualified graduate programs,
- University of Maryland Eastern Shore qualified graduate programs,
- Jackson State University qualified graduate programs,
- Norfolk State University qualified graduate programs, and
- Tennessee State University qualified graduate programs.

In 2008, the HEOA amended Section 326 of the HEA to include six additional postgraduate schools or programs that are now also eligible for HBGI grants. The distinction between the pre-and post-HEOA schools and program is important for award

---

[82] HEA §326(e)(2).

[83] The five original institutions and schools were Morehouse School of Medicine, Meharry Medical School, Charles R. Drew Postgraduate Medical School, Atlanta University (now Clark-Atlanta University), and Tuskegee Institute School of Veterinary Medicine (now Tuskegee University School of Veterinary Medicine). P.L. 99-498 §326(e).

allocation purposes, which are discussed later in this chapter. The six post-HEOA schools and programs are

- Alabama State University qualified graduate programs,
- Prairie View Agricultural and Mechanical University qualified graduate programs,
- Delaware State University qualified graduate programs,
- Langston University qualified graduate programs,
- Bowie State University qualified graduate programs, and
- University of the District of Columbia David A. Clarke School of Law.[84]

Authorized Activities

In general, many of the authorized uses of HBGI program grants are similar to those authorized under the Strengthening Institutions Program of Title III-A. For example, HBGI grants may be used for purchasing or renting laboratory equipment, constructing or renovating instructional facilities, or tutoring or counseling students to improve academic success. However, several other uses for HBGI grants are specified in Section 326. These additional authorized uses include

- scholarships, fellowships, or other financial assistance for needy graduate and professional students to permit them to enroll in and complete doctoral degrees in disciplines in which African Americans are underrepresented;[85]
- acquisition of real property that is adjacent to the campus and in connection with the construction or renovation of campus facilities; and
- development of a new qualified graduate program, so long as the institution does not use more than 10% of its HBGI grant for such a purpose.[86]

HBGI grant recipients are allowed to establish or maintain endowment funds with HBGI grants; however, in doing so, they must comply with the provisions for Endowment Challenge Grants (see subsequent entitled section) set forth in HEA Section 331.[87] Among other requirements in Section 331, HBGI grant recipients that wish to use grant monies for endowment funds must provide nonfederal matching funds equal to the federal funds provided.

---

[84] HEA §326(e)(1).

[85] Such disciplines include medicine, dentistry, pharmacy, veterinary medicine, law, physical or natural sciences, engineering, mathematics, and other scientific disciplines. HEA §326(c)(4).

[86] HEA §326(e)(2)(B). For purposes of this provision, new graduate programs are not subject to the eligibility requirement that qualified graduate programs have students enrolled in them.

[87] The Consolidated Appropriations Act, 2017 (CAA 2017; P.L. 115-31) authorizes IHEs that maintain endowment funds supported with funds appropriated for HEA Title III and Title V programs for FY2017 to use the income from the endowment fund to award student scholarships. This provision, enacted through Division H, Title III of the CAA 2017 will remain in effect until Title III and Title V are reauthorized. Previous appropriations acts have authorized the same use of endowment income in recent years.

Allotments

The HBGI program specifies how funds are to be allotted to institutions based on the amount of funds appropriated by Congress each year. Section 326 specifies that the first $56.9 million (or lesser amount appropriated) is available only to the 18 pre-HEOA eligible institutions, schools, and programs, and grant amounts must be at least as much as each institution's grant amount in FY2008. Any amount appropriated that is greater than $56.9 million and less than $62.9 million is available only to the six institutions or programs added to the statute by the HEOA.[88] Finally, any amount appropriated over $62.9 million is made available to any of the eligible institutions, schools, or programs pursuant to a formula to be developed by ED that uses the following elements:

- the ability of an institution, school, or program to match federal funds with nonfederal funds;
- the number of students enrolled in the program for which funding is being received;
- the average cost of education per student for all full-time graduate and professional students enrolled in the eligible professional or graduate school;
- the number of students in the previous year who received their first professional or doctoral degree from the programs for which funding was received in the previous year; and
- the contribution, on a percentage basis, of the programs for which the institution is eligible to receive funds to the total number of African Americans receiving graduate or professional degrees in the professions or disciplines related to the programs for the previous year.[89]

In FY2016, for the first time, program appropriations exceeded $62.9 million. Specifically, Congress appropriated approximately $63.2 million. ED has not yet developed an allocation formula for this additional amount.

Finally, grants in excess of $1 million cannot be made under the HBGI program unless the applicant provides assurances to ED that 50% of the cost of the purposes for which the grant is made will be paid from nonfederal sources. An award recipient is not required to match any portion of the first $1 million awarded.[90]

Program Administration

The HBGI program award process comprises a single step. Eligible institutions, schools, and programs need only submit an application to ED requesting funds and

---

[88] CRS had not identified any additional guidance regarding how aid is divided among these six institutions.
[89] HEA §326(f).
[90] HEA §326(a)(2).

detailing proposed project plans for those funds.[91] The application and project plans must contribute to the purposes of the program, not include unallowable activities, and meet any statutory provisions and regulations. If approved by the Secretary, the Secretary then makes an allotment to the institution based on the above-described formula.

HBGI program grants are five years in length. Funds awarded must be obligated during the five-year grant period and must be expended within 10 years of the start of the 5-year grant period.[92]

An HBGI grant recipient cannot receive more than one grant under this program in any fiscal year.[93] Institutions that are eligible for and receive awards under the Promoting Postbaccalaureate Opportunities for Hispanic Americans Program (PPOHA),[94] the Masters Degree Programs at HBCUs Program,[95] or the Masters Degree Programs at PBIs Program[96] are ineligible to receive grants under the HBGI program in the same fiscal year.[97] Finally, in general, institutions receiving an HBGI grant in a fiscal year cannot simultaneously receive funds under a Title III-A, Title III-F, or Title V (the HSI program) program not specifically established for HBCUs.

Masters Degree Programs at Historically Black Colleges and Universities

In 2008, the Higher Education Opportunity Act (HEOA; P.L. 110-315) established Masters Degree Programs at Historically Black Colleges and Universities under Title VII, Part A, Subpart 4. The program seems to have been established to address concerns that the Title III HBCU, PBI, and HBGI programs were limited in scope and did not extend eligibility to a variety of graduate opportunities for Black Americans.[98] The Title VII-A-4 program is intended to assist institutions in improving graduate education opportunities at the master's level for Black students in a variety of fields of study. The program is funded through discretionary appropriations under Title VII-A4, and was provided with mandatory

---

[91] Because grants are five years in length and the Secretary is prohibited from awarding more than one grant per institution in any fiscal year, the president or chancellor of a recipient institution that wishes to allot funds to multiple graduate or professional schools or programs at the institution may decide which graduate or professional school or qualified graduate program will receive funds under the grant for any one fiscal year, if the allocation of funds among such schools or programs is delineated in the grant application. HEA §326(e)(5).

[92] HEA §326(b).

[93] HEA §326(e)(4).

[94] HEA §512.

[95] HEA §723.

[96] HEA §724.

[97] HEA §326(h).

[98] For instance, in his testimony before Congress, Dr. Larry Earvin, president of Huston-Tillotson University, stated that the HBGI program "has always limited institutional and programmatic participation to those first, professional degree programs, such as law, medicine, and dentistry, and to those doctoral programs in physical and natural sciences.... The inclusion of master's degrees without restriction would dramatically expand institutional participation in the program." U.S. Congress, House Committee on Education and Labor, Subcommittee on Higher Education, Lifelong Learning, and Competitiveness, *Higher Education Act: Institutional Support for Colleges and Universities Under Title III and Title V*, field hearing held in Austin Texas, 110th Cong., 1st sess., June 4, 2007, 110-43 (Washington: GPO, 2008), pp. 23-24.

appropriations for FY2009-FY2014 under Title VIII.[99] Prior to FY2017, the program had not received discretionary appropriations. The program was provided mandatory appropriations annually for FY2009 through FY2014.[100] Authorization for mandatory appropriations lapsed at the end of FY2014, and for two years the program did not receive funds. In FY2017, discretionary appropriations for the programs were provided, totaling $7,500,000.[101]

HEA Section 723 specifically authorizes Masters Degree Programs at Historically Black Colleges and Universities (Masters Degrees at HBCUs). The program's purpose is to improve graduate education opportunities at the master's level in mathematics, engineering, physical or natural sciences, computer science, information technology, nursing, allied health, or other scientific disciplines for Black Americans.[102]

Eligibility

Masters Degrees at HBCUs program grants are available to those institutions specifically listed in the HEA that have been determined "to be making a substantial contribution to graduate education opportunities"[103] for Black Americans at the master's level in one of the several educational disciplines listed above. None of the institutions listed as eligible for the HBGI program (Title III-B, Section 326) are listed as eligible for the Masters Degrees at HBCUs program. Currently, 18 institutions are eligible for the Masters Degrees at HBCUs program; they are

- Albany State University,
- Alcorn State University,
- Claflin State University,
- Coppin State University,
- Elizabeth City University,
- Fayetteville State University,
- Fisk University,
- Fort Valley State University,
- Grambling State University,
- Kentucky State University,
- Mississippi Valley State University,
- Savannah State University,
- South Carolina State University,

---

[99] Authorization of mandatory appropriations for these programs, and an appropriation of mandatory funds, were provided through FY2014 (HEOA; P.L. 110-315). Mandatory funds have not been provided for these programs since the end of FY2014.

[100] HEA §897.

[101] U.S. Department of Education, FY2018 President's Budget Request.

[102] HEA §723(a).

[103] HEA §723(a).

- University of Arkansas at Pine Bluff,
- Virginia State University,
- West Virginia State University,
- Wilberforce University, and
- Winston-Salem State University.[104]

Although each of these institutions is eligible to receive funding, grants under this program must be used to support a graduate school or a qualified master's degree program at the institution. A qualified master's degree program is one that provides a program of instruction in mathematics, engineering, science, physical or natural sciences, computer science, information technology, nursing, allied health, or other scientific disciplines in which African Americans are underrepresented. Students must be enrolled in the program at the time of application for a grant, unless it is a new program, in which case, the institution cannot use more than 10% of the grant for the new program.[105]

Authorized Uses

Masters Degrees at HBCUs program grants are intended to enable eligible institutions to develop and enhance their capacity for graduate education and opportunities for Black Americans and low-income students. In general, the program activities authorized under the Masters Degrees at HBCUs program are the same as those authorized under the HBGI program. For instance, Masters Degrees at HBCUs program grants may be used for purchasing or renting lab equipment, constructing or improving classrooms and other instructional facilities, or tutoring students. As with the HBGI program, grants under this program can also be used for

- scholarships, fellowships, or other financial assistance for needy graduate students to permit the enrollment of the students in, and completion of, a master's degree in mathematics, engineering, the physical or natural sciences, computer science, information technology, nursing, allied health, or other scientific disciplines in which African Americans are underrepresented;
- the acquisition of real property that is adjacent to the campus and in connection with the construction or renovation of campus facilities;[106] and
- the development of a new qualified graduate program, so long as the institution does not use more than 10% of its grant for such a purpose.[107]

---

[104] HEA §723(b).
[105] HEA §723(b)(2).
[106] HEA §723(d).
[107] HEA §723(b)(2)(B).

Institutions may also use program grants to establish or maintain endowment funds.[108] However, in doing so, they must comply with the provisions for Endowment Challenge Grants set forth in HEA Section 331. Among other requirements, Masters Degrees at HBCUs grant recipients that wish to use grant monies for endowment funds must provide nonfederal matching funds equal to the federal funds provided.[109]

Allotments

Masters Degrees at HBCUs program grants are formula-based. Section 723 specifies that, subject to available appropriations, no grant awarded under the Masters Degrees at HBCUs program shall be less than $500,000. If an institution receives a grant that is greater than $1 million, however, it must provide assurances that 50% of the cost of a grant project will be paid with nonfederal funds.[110]

The first $9 million (or lesser amount) appropriated are available only to the 18 institutions currently listed in Section 723(b) for the purposes of making the $500,000 minimum grants. If the amount appropriated is insufficient to pay the minimum grant amount to each eligible institution, then each institution's award is ratably reduced. If other institutions are subsequently added to the list of eligible institutions, they are entitled to the minimum grant amount, unless such funds are not appropriated. In that case, the 18 institutions currently listed receive funding priority and subsequently added institutions' awards are ratably reduced.

Any appropriations greater than $9 million are available to each of the currently listed 18 institutions based on a formula, to be determined by ED. As of FY2017, the appropriation has not exceeded $9 million. The formula for appropriations greater than $9 million uses the following elements:

- the ability of an institution to match federal funds with nonfederal funds;
- the number of students enrolled in the qualified master's degree program in the previous academic year;
- the average cost of attendance per student for all full-time students enrolled in the qualified master's degree program;
- the number of students in the previous year who received a degree in the qualified master's degree program; and

---

[108] The Consolidated Appropriations Act, 2017 (CAA 2017; P.L. 115-31) authorizes IHEs that maintain endowment funds supported with funds appropriated for HEA Title III and Title V programs for FY2017 to use the income from the endowment fund to award student scholarships. This provision, enacted through Division H, Title III of the CAA 2017 will remain in effect until Title III and Title V are reauthorized. Previous appropriations acts have authorized the same use of endowment income in recent years.

[109] HEA §723(d)(6).

[110] HEA §723(a)(2) & (3). If an institution is unable to meet this matching requirement, the Secretary must distribute, on a pro rata basis, any amounts that the institution cannot use due to its failure to meet the matching requirements to those institutions that do comply with the matching requirements.

- the contribution, on a percent basis, of the master's level programs for which the institution is eligible to receive funds to the total number of African Americans receiving master's degrees in the disciplines related to the institution's programs for the previous year.

Notwithstanding the above formula to allocate funds, no eligible institution that received a grant under the program for FY2009 and that is eligible to receive a grant in subsequent years shall receive a grant that is less than the amount received in FY2009. However, this hold harmless rule does not apply if the amount appropriated for a fiscal year is insufficient to provide such grants to all such institutions or if an institution is unable to provide sufficient matching funds.[111]

Program Administration

Like the HBGI award process, the Masters Degrees at HBCUs award process is a single step. Eligible institutions need only submit an application to ED requesting funds and detailing proposed project plans for those funds. The application and project plans must contribute to the purposes of the program, not include unallowable activities, and meet any statutory provisions and regulations. If approved by the Secretary, the Secretary then makes an allotment to the institution based on the above-described formula.

Program grants are no longer than six years in length, but grants may be periodically renewed for a period determined by the Secretary. Additionally, an institution can only receive one grant per fiscal year under this program.[112] An institution that is eligible for and receives an award under the HBGI, PPOHA, or Masters Degree Programs at PBIs programs in a fiscal year is ineligible to receive grants under the Masters Degrees at HBCUs program in the same fiscal year.[113] An institution receiving a Masters Degree Programs at HBCUs grant may not concurrently receive a Title III-A or V-A grant but may concurrently receive a Title III-B (Strengthening HBCUs program) grant and generally may concurrently receive a Title III-F grant.

Historically Black College and University Capital Financing

The Historically Black College and University Capital Financing Program (HBCU Cap Fin) is a loan guarantee program that was established to provide federal assistance to

---

[111] HEA §723(g).

[112] Because program grants are six years in length and the Secretary is prohibited from awarding more than one grant per institution in any fiscal year, the president or chancellor of a recipient institution that wishes to allot funds to multiple graduate or professional schools or programs at the institution may decide which graduate or professional school or qualified graduate program will receive funds under the grant for any one fiscal year, if the allocation of funds among such schools or programs is delineated in the grant application. HEA §723(b)(3).

[113] HEA §723(e).

HBCUs in obtaining low-cost capital financing for campus maintenance, renovation, and construction projects. It was authorized by the Higher Education Amendments of 1992 (P.L. 102-325). The extension of such loans is intended to help HBCUs continue educating African Americans and low-income, educationally disadvantaged Americans.

When enacting the legislation, Congress found that the academic and residential facilities on many HBCU campuses suffered from neglect and deferred maintenance. Congress also found that HBCUs were often unable to obtain financing to perform needed maintenance and construction projects because of their small enrollments, limited endowments, and other financial risk factors.[114] To remedy this situation, Congress enacted HBCU Cap Fin to help provide HBCUs with access to low-cost capital financing. HBCU Cap Fin provides HBCUs with access to capital financing by issuing federal guarantees on the full principal and interest of qualified bonds, the proceeds of which are used for capital financing loans.

Eligibility

Institutions eligible for HBCU Cap Fin are those eligible as Part-B institutions under the Strengthening HBCU program, as defined in HEA Section 322(2).[115] Howard University is specifically excluded from program eligibility, while Lincoln University of Pennsylvania is specifically included in program eligibility.[116] An HBCU applicant wishing to receive a loan under the program must undergo a credit review to determine whether it is qualified to receive a loan under the program.[117]

Authorized Uses

HBCU Cap Fin loans provide low-cost financing for capital projects to HBCUs. Authorized capital projects include the repair, renovation, or, in exceptional circumstances the construction or acquisition of

- a classroom facility, library, dormitory, laboratory, or other facility customarily used by institutions of higher education for instructional or research purposes or the housing of students, faculty, and staff;
- an institutional administration facility or student center;[118]

---

[114] HEA §341.

[115] HEA §342(1).

[116] HEA §344(a).

[117] HEA §343(b)(4). Criteria that may be taken into account when determining credit worthiness include a school's accreditation status, eligibility to participate in HEA Title IV federal student aid programs, cohort default rates, enrollment, debt ratio, debt service coverage, and capital improvement plans. Department of Education, Office of Postsecondary Education, "Historically Black College and University Capital Financing Program: Frequently Asked Questions," http://www2.ed.gov/programs/hbcucapfinance/faq.html, accessed July 13, 2017.

[118] No more than 5% of the loan proceeds may be used for such purposes if the facility is owned, leased, managed, or operated by a private business that, in return for such use, makes a payment to the eligible institution. HEA §342(5)(B).

- instructional equipment and any capital equipment or fixture related to the facilities described above;
- a maintenance, storage, or utility facility that is essential to the operation of a facility;
- real property or any interest therein;
- a facility designed to provide primarily outpatient health care to students and faculty;
- physical infrastructure essential to support projects authorized under the HEA, including roads, sewer and drainage systems, and other utilities; and
- any other facility or equipment essential to maintaining accreditation.[119]

Program Administration

Rather than directly providing capital financing loans to HBCUs, ED contracts with a private, for-profit corporation to act as the Designated Bonding Authority (DBA) and to operate HBCU Cap Fin.[120] The DBA issues taxable bonds on behalf of HBCU borrowers, and ED guarantees full payment on the qualified bonds issued by the DBA. The DBA then sells the bonds to a third party,[121] and bond proceeds are then used by the DBA to provide loans to eligible HBCUs at interest rates that are slightly above the federal government's cost of borrowing.[122] The HEA limits the program to an outstanding balance of $1.1 billion in bonds and unpaid interest.[123] HEA Section 344(a) provides that no more than two-thirds of this limit may be held on behalf of private HBCUs, and no more than one-third may be held on behalf of public HBCUs; however, in recent years, appropriations acts have authorized ED to make programs loans to support both public and private HBCUs, without regard to these statutory limitations.[124]

Loan Terms

The HEA sets forth specific loan terms under HBCU Cap Fin, under which all parties must operate. These statutorily prescribed terms include the percentage of loan funds an HBCU may use for capital projects and the parties' recourses in the event of a delinquency or default.

---

[119] HEA §342(5).

[120] The current DBA is Rice Financial Products Company.

[121] The bonds have only ever been purchased by the Federal Financing Bank.

122 HEA §343.

[123] The Emergency Supplemental Appropriations Act for Defense, the Global War on Terror, and Hurricane Recovery, 2006 (P.L. 109-234) provided HBCU Cap Fin special terms for HBCUs located in areas affected by Hurricane Katrina or Rita that incurred physical damage resulting from one of the hurricanes. With these emergency appropriations, ED awarded approximately $400 million in loan guarantees to institutions affected by the hurricanes. Department of Education, *Historically Black College and University Capital Financing Program Account*, Fiscal Year 2018 Budget Request, p. U-8.

[124] See, for example, The Consolidated Appropriations Act, 2017 (P.L. 115-31), Division H, Title III.

HBCUs must use at least 95% of an HBCU Cap Fin loan to complete one or more of the statutorily authorized capital projects or to refinance a prior obligation, the proceeds of which were used to finance a capital project. The remaining 5% of the loan must be deposited into a pooled escrow account. The escrow account is used to cover any delinquencies or defaults by an institution in the program. If no institution defaults during the period in which the participating HBCU has an outstanding loan, the HBCU will receive the remainder of its escrow within 120 days of its final scheduled loan repayment.[125]

If an HBCU is delinquent on an HBCU Cap Fin loan, the DBA may assist the HBCU in making the payment within 45 days. If after that time, the HBCU is still delinquent or defaults on the loan, the DBA draws funds from the pooled escrow account to make payments on behalf of the HBCU. If the pooled escrow account is exhausted, ED will make payments according to the insurance agreement with the DBA. ED then collects remuneration directly from the delinquent or defaulted HBCU or disposes of the HBCU's collateral.[126]

While the statutory provisions of HBCU Cap Fin set forth several specific loan terms, many are left to the parties to negotiate. Such terms include interest rate, payment terms, frequency of payments, and the length of the loan.

HBCU Capital Financing Advisory Board

The HBCU Capital Financing Advisory Board (Advisory Board) provides advice and counsel to ED and the DBA on the most efficient means of implementing construction financing on HBCU campuses. It also advises Congress on the progress made in implementing HBCU Cap Fin.[127]

The Advisory Board is composed of 11 members who are appointed by the Secretary. The Advisory Board members are

- the Secretary or the Secretary's designee;
- three presidents of private HBCUs;
- three presidents of public HBCUs;
- the president of the United Negro College Fund, Inc.,[128] or the president's designee;

---

[125] HEA §343(b)(2) & (8).

[126] HEA §343(b) & (c).

[127] HEA §347(a).

[128] The United Negro College Fund, Inc. (UNCF) is a membership organization of 37 HBCUs. Its mission is to "build a robust and nationally-recognized pipeline of under-represented students who, because of UNCF support, become highly-qualified college graduates and to ensure that [its] network of member institutions is a respected model of best practices in moving students to and through college." United Negro College Fund, Inc., "Our Mission," https://www.uncf.org/our-mission, accessed July 13, 2017.

- the president of the National Association for Equal Opportunity in Higher Education,[129] or the designee of the Association;
- the executive director of the White House Initiative on HBCUs;[130] and
- the president of the Thurgood Marshall College Fund,[131] or the president's designee.[132]

The term of service for each president of an HBCU (public or private) that serves on the Advisory Board is three years. The term of service for all other Advisory Board members is the length of the tenure in their other professional capacities.[133]

PREDOMINANTLY BLACK INSTITUTIONS PROGRAMS

Predominantly Black Institutions (PBIs) are IHEs that enroll a high concentration of Black American students and that also enroll a high concentration of low-income or first-generation college students. Unlike HBCUs, PBIs were not necessarily established to serve the educational needs of Black Americans; additionally, their date of establishment need not fall within a certain timeframe. Two HEA programs are authorized specifically to assist PBIs; they are the Strengthening PBIs program and Masters Degree Programs at PBIs. This section discusses each of these programs, including their eligibility criteria, authorized uses of grant monies, and program administration.

Strengthening Predominantly Black Institutions

Title III-A, Section 318, of the HEA establishes the Strengthening Predominantly Black Institutions (PBIs) program, which was first authorized in 2007 by the College Cost

---

[129] The National Association for Equal Opportunity in Higher Education is a membership organization of HBCUs and PBIs. Its mission is to "champion interests of HBCUs and PBIs; provide membership services; build capacity of HBCUs; [and] serve as [an] international voice and advocate for preservation and enhancement of HBCUs and PBIs and for blacks in higher education." National Association for Equal Opportunity in Higher Education, "Our Mission," http://www.nafeonation.org/our-mission/, July 13, 2017.

[130] The White House Initiative on HBCUs was established in 1980 by Executive Order 12232 to overcome the effects of discriminatory treatment of HBCUs and to strengthen and expand their capacity.

[131] The Thurgood Marshall College Fund is a membership organization of public HBCUs and PBIs. Its mission is to "partner with [its] member-schools to increase access, retention and graduation rates of students; identify and prepare students attending member-schools who have significant leadership potential; [and] create a pipeline for employers to highly-qualified member-school students and alumni." Thurgood Marshall College Fund, "Our Mission & Vision," http://tmcf.org/about-us/who-we-are, accessed July 13, 2017.

[132] HEA §347(b).

[133] For additional information on the Advisory Board and its current members, see Department of Education, "Historically Black College and University Capital Financing Advisory Board," http://www2.ed. gov/about/bdscomm/ list/hbcu-finance.html, accessed July 14, 2017.

Reduction and Access Act (CCRAA; P.L. 110-84) and which provides SIP-type grants to PBIs. The program is intended to assist PBIs in expanding educational opportunities.[134]

Since FY2010, the Title III-A Strengthening PBI program grants have been funded through annual discretionary appropriations under Title III-A. Additional mandatory appropriations are provided annually through FY2019 under Title III-F. Grants awarded under the Title III-A program are formula-based; grants awarded under the Title III-F program are competitive.[135] Typically, eligibility requirements, authorized uses, and administrative processes for Title III-A formula PBI program and Title III-F competitive PBI program are the same. When discussed together, they are referred to as the Strengthening PBI programs.

Eligibility

Eligibility requirements for Strengthening PBI grants vary appreciably from eligibility requirements for the other Title III-A programs. To qualify for either Strengthening PBI program, institutions of higher education must meet the HEA Section 318(b)(1) requirements, rather than the Section 312(b) requirements that institutions participating in the other Title III-A programs are required to meet. Under Section 318(b)(1), institutions must have low educational and general expenditures (E&G) per full-time equivalent undergraduate as compared to institutions that offer similar instruction,[136] be accredited or preaccredited by an ED-recognized accrediting agency, and have authorization within their respective states to award a bachelor's degree or associate's degree.

In addition to the Section 318(b)(1) requirements, an institution's undergraduate student enrollment must be at least 40% Black American students and must have a requisite "enrollment of needy students."

The Section 318(b)(1) "enrollment of needy students" criterion means that at least 50% of an institution's undergraduate students enrolled in an academic program leading to a degree

- were Federal Pell Grant recipients in the second fiscal year preceding the fiscal year for which the determination is made;
- come from families that receive benefits under a means-tested federal benefit program; [137]
- attended a public or private nonprofit secondary school (a) that was in a school district of a local educational agency that was eligible for assistance under Title I, Part A of the Elementary and Secondary Education Act of 1965 (ESEA) for any

---

[134] HEA §318(a).

[135] HEA §371(b)(2)(C)(ii).

[136] The Secretary can apply the same waiver requirements as those for the other Part III-A programs.

[137] A "means-tested federal benefit program" is a federal program (other than those under HEA Title IV) in which eligibility is determined on the basis of an individual's or family's income or resources, for instance, Temporary Assistance for Needy Families (TANF) or Housing Assistance. HEA §318(b)(5).

year during which the student attended the school and (b) that was determined by the Secretary to be one in which the enrollment of children meeting a measure of poverty under Section 1113(a)(5) of the ESEA exceeded 30% of the total enrollment; or

- are first-generation college students and a majority of such first-generation college students are low-income individuals.[138]

Once an institution qualifies as an eligible institution under the Section 318(b)(1) criteria, it must then be designated as a PBI. A PBI is defined as an eligible institution with not less than 1,000 undergraduate students, at which not less than 50% of the enrolled undergraduates are low-income individuals or first-generation college students, and at which not less than 50% of the undergraduates are enrolled in programs that lead to a bachelor's or associate's degree.[139]

Authorized Uses

Authorized uses differ between the Title III-A formula PBI program and the Title III-F competitive PBI program. The Title III-A formula PBI program mandates required activities to be funded and authorizes additional uses for such grants. Title III-F competitive PBI grants have a different set of authorized uses from those authorized for Title III-A formula PBI grants.

Title III-A

PBIs that receive Title III-A formula PBI grants must use them for the following purposes:

- to plan, develop, undertake, and implement programs to enhance grantee's capacity to serve more low- and middle-income Black American students;
- to expand higher education opportunities for students eligible to participate in programs under Title IV of the HEA[140] by encouraging college preparation and student persistence in secondary education; and

---

[138] A "first-generation college student" is an individual both of whose parents did not complete a baccalaureate degree or, in the case of an individual who regularly resided with and received support from only one parent, an individual whose only such parent did not complete a baccalaureate degree. A "low-income individual" is an individual from a family whose taxable income for the preceding year did not exceed 150% of the federal poverty guidelines. HEA §402A(h)(3) & (4).

[139] HEA §318(b)(6). These two sets of criteria, in effect, ensure that institutions with a large enrollment (greater than 1,000) of undergraduate students and an above average proportion of Black American and needy students, but with only a small fraction of the total student population enrolled in a degree program, are ineligible for Strengthening PBI grants. For instance, an institution with an undergraduate population of 2,000 students and that otherwise meets the needy student criteria but that only has 100 undergraduate students enrolled in a degree program (with the other 1,900 students enrolled in certificate programs) would be ineligible to receive a Strengthening PBI grant, as only 5% of its total undergraduate population is enrolled in a degree program.

[140] HEA Title IV authorizes a variety of programs to help prepare students for a postsecondary education, including the Federal TRIO Programs, which authorizes grants to help prepare individuals from disadvantaged

- to strengthen the financial ability of the grantee institution to serve the academic needs of low- and middle-income Black American students and Title IV eligible students.

Additional grant activities that are authorized under Section 318 include most of the activities authorized under the Title III-A Strengthening Institutions Program (SIP), academic instruction in disciplines in which Black Americans are underrepresented, establishment or enhancement of a teacher education program designed to qualify students to teach in a public elementary or secondary school, and establishment of community outreach programs designed to encourage elementary and secondary school students to develop the academic skills and the interest to pursue postsecondary education. PBIs are also allowed to use Title III-A formula PBI grants to fund construction and maintenance projects; however, not more than 50% of a grant may be used for such purposes.

Finally, PBIs are allowed to use up to 20% of Title III-A grant funds to establish or increase endowments.[141] If a PBI chooses to do so, it must provide nonfederal matching funds that are equal to or greater than the federal funds.

Title III-F

Authorized uses of Title III-F competitive PBI grants differ from their Title III-A formula PBI counterparts. Title III-F competitive PBI grants must be used for programs in science, technology, engineering, or mathematics (STEM); health education; internationalization or globalization; teacher preparation; or improving educational outcomes of African American males.[142]

Title III-A Allotments

Unlike most other Title III-A programs, Title III-A PBI grants are formula-based, such that each institution that applies and meets the eligibility and application requirements receives a grant. After an institution has been designated a Section 318(b) eligible

---

backgrounds for a postsecondary education. For information on the TRIO programs, see CRS Report R42724, *The TRIO Programs: A Primer*, by Cassandria Dortch. Title IV also authorizes the majority of federal student aid programs, including the Pell Grant program, the William D. Ford Federal Direct Loan Program, and the Perkins Loan program. For information on the Pell Grant program, see CRS Report R42446, *Federal Pell Grant Program of the Higher Education Act: How the Program Works and Recent Legislative Changes*, by Cassandria Dortch. For information on the William D. Ford Federal Direct Loan Program, see CRS Report R40122, *Federal Student Loans Made Under the Federal Family Education Loan Program and the William D. Ford Federal Direct Loan Program: Terms and Conditions for Borrowers*, by David P. Smole. For information on the Perkins Loan program, see CRS Report RL 31618, *Campus-Based Student Financial Aid Programs Under the Higher Education Act*, by Joselynn Fountain.

[141] The Consolidated Appropriations Act, 2017 (CAA 2017; P.L. 115-31) authorizes IHEs that maintain endowment funds supported with funds appropriated for HEA Title III and Title V programs for FY2017 to use the income from the endowment fund to award student scholarships. This provision, enacted through Division H, Title III of the CAA 2017 will remain in effect until Title III and Title V are reauthorized. Previous appropriations acts have authorized the same use of endowment income in recent years.

[142] HEA §371(b)(2)(C)(ii).

institution, it must submit data relevant to the Title III-A PBI grant formula. The Secretary then reviews these data and allots funds accordingly among all such institutions. For amounts appropriated for these grants, the Secretary must allot to each eligible institution submitting formula data a sum

- that bears a ratio equal to 50% of the number of Federal Pell Grant recipients in attendance at the institution at the end of the preceding academic year to the total number of Federal Pell Grant recipients "at all such institutions"[143] at the end of the preceding year;
- that bears a ratio equal to 25% of the number of an institution's graduates for the academic year to the number of graduates of all such institutions for the academic year; and
- that bears a ratio equal to 25% of the percentage of graduates from the institution who are admitted to and in attendance at, not later than two years after graduation with an associate's or bachelor's degree, a bachelor's degree-granting institution or a graduate or professional degree program, respectively, in disciplines in which Black American students are underrepresented to the percentage of all graduates for all such institutions.[144]

Notwithstanding the above formula, grants to each eligible PBI must be at least $250,000. If the amounts appropriated in any fiscal year are insufficient to make these minimum grants, then the minimum amount is ratably reduced.[145] If ED determines that an individual institution's allotment for any fiscal year is not needed by that institution, ED may redistribute the unneeded funds to other PBIs as ED determines appropriate.[146]

Program Administration

Like other Title III-A programs, there is a two-step award process for the Title III-A formula PBI program. First, an institution wishing to receive assistance must be designated by ED as an eligible institution that meets the Section 318(b)(1) eligibility criteria.[147] If an institution is designated as an eligible institution,[148] during the second step of the award process, the institution must demonstrate that it meets the additional criteria of the statutory

---

[143] For purposes of the Strengthening PBI formula-based grants under Title III-A, "all such institutions" means all Strengthening PBIs formula-based grant applicants whose application has been accepted by the Secretary.

[144] HEA §318(e).

[145] If additional sums become available later in a fiscal year, reduced allotments must be increased on the same basis as when the allotment was reduced, until the $250,000 minimum grant amount is met.

[146] HEA §318(e)(5).

[147] ED allows institutions to demonstrate meeting the Section 312(b) and/or the Section 318(b) basis eligibility requirements in a single application package.

[148] In awarding grants under the Title III-A formula PBI program, the Secretary is required to give priority to PBIs with larger numbers or percentages of needy undergraduate students or Black American students. PBIs with large numbers or percentages of needy undergraduate students are given twice the level of priority as PBIs with large numbers or percentages of Black American students. HEA §318(c)(2).

definition of a PBI and submit a proposed project plan to ED. The project plan must contribute to the purposes of the program, not include unallowable activities, and meet any statutory provisions and regulations. If approved by the Secretary, the Secretary then makes an allotment to the institution based on the above-described formula.[149] Unlike other Title III-A program participants, PBIs receiving grants under this section are subject to a two-year wait-out period.[150] A grantee must return any grant funds not expended within 10 years of an award.[151]

Grants awarded to PBIs under Title III-F are competitive. Of the amounts made available each year, 25 competitive grants in the amount of $600,000 each are awarded.[152] Applicants for the Title III-F competitive PBI grant must also go through the two-step award process described above, which includes being designated as an eligible PBI per Section 318(b)(1). Applicants must then submit a project plan to ED and prove that it meets the additional criteria of the statutory definition of PBI. However, because Title III-F PBI grants are competitive, project plans are selected based on the score of a review panel, and the project plans with the highest score are selected for funding.[153]

Institutions receiving Title III-A formula PBI grants may not receive grants under other Title III-A programs, Title III-B (Strengthening HBCU and HBGI programs), Title V-A (HSI program) or the Howard University program during the same fiscal year;[154] however, in general, they may receive a grant under any of the Title III-F programs in the same fiscal year. Generally, institutions receiving a Title III-F PBI grant may simultaneously receive a grant under another Title III-F program.

Unlike other Title III-F programs, institutions receiving a Title III-F competitive PBI grant are specifically prohibited from also receiving a Title III-B or Title V-A grant in the same fiscal year.[155]

Masters Degree Programs at Predominantly Black Institutions

In 2008, the Higher Education Opportunity Act (HEOA; P.L. 110-315) established Masters Degree Programs at Predominantly Black Institutions (Masters Degrees at PBIs)

---

[149] Department of Education, Black Institutions Program—Formula Grants: Applicant Information," http://www2.ed.gov/programs/pbihea/applicant.html, accessed July 14, 2017.

[150] The authorizing language for all other MSI-specific Title III-A programs specifically waives the section 313(d) two-year wait-out period. The authorizing language for Strengthening PBIs does not waive this wait-out period.

[151] HEA §318(h).

[152] HEA §371(b)(2)(C)(ii).

[153] Department of Education, Office of Postsecondary Education, *Application for Grants Under the Predominantly Black Institutions Program: Fiscal Year 2015*, OMB No. 1840-0797, http://www.reginfo.gov/public/do/DownloadDocument?objectID=54275101.

[154] HEA §§318(b)(1)(F)((iii), 318(i), & 371(c)(9)(F)(iii). Howard University receives annual appropriations to provide for partial support of construction, development, and maintenance. For additional information on the program, see Department of Education, Office of Postsecondary Education, "Howard University," http://www2.ed.gov/programs/ howard/index.html, accessed January 20, 2016.

[155] HEA §371(c)(9).

under Title VII, Part A, Subpart 4 (Section 724).[156] The program's purpose is to improve graduate education opportunities at the master's level in mathematics, engineering, physical or natural sciences, computer science, information technology, nursing, allied health, or other scientific disciplines for Black Americans.[157] The program is provided authorization for discretionary appropriations under Title VII-A-4 but has never received funds under this authority. Authorization for mandatory appropriations, and mandatory appropriations, were provided for the program under Title VIII for FY2009-FY2014. Authorization for mandatory appropriations lapsed at the end of FY2014.

In general, the Masters Degrees at PBIs program operates in the same way as the Masters Degrees at HBCUs program. This section will discuss elements of the Masters Degrees at PBIs program and will highlight which provisions of the program differ from the Masters Degrees at HBCUs program, for all other provisions, see the section of this chapter titled "Masters Degree Programs at Historically Black Colleges and Universities."

Eligibility

Masters Degrees at PBIs program grants, like Masters Degree at HBCUs program grants, are available to those institutions that have been determined "to be making a substantial contribution to graduate education opportunities at the master's level in mathematics, engineering, the physical or natural sciences, computer science, information technology, nursing, allied health, or other scientific disciplines for Black Americans."[158] All eligible institutions for this program are specifically listed in the HEA. Currently, five institutions are eligible for the Masters Degrees at PBIs program; they are

- Chicago State University;
- Washington Adventist University; [159]
- Long Island University, Brooklyn campus;
- Robert Morris University, Illinois;[160] and
- York College, The City University of New York.[161]

Also like the Masters Degrees at HBCUs program, grants awarded under this program must be used to support a graduate school or a qualified master's degree program.

---

[156] See the section of this report titled "Master's Degree Programs at Historically Black Colleges and Universities" for a brief background of both Masters Degrees at PBIs and Masters Degrees at HBCUs.

[157] HEA §723(a).

[158] HEA §724(a).

[159] Formerly Columbia Union College.

[160] Formerly Robert Morris College.

[161] HEA §724(b)(1).

Authorized Uses

The authorized uses of grants awarded under the Masters Degrees at PBIs program are the same as the authorized uses of grants awarded under the Masters Degrees at HBCUs program.[162]

Allotments

Masters Degrees at PBIs grants are formula-based and awarded in a manner similar to grants awarded under the Masters Degrees at HBCUs program. Subject to appropriations, no grant awarded under the Masters Degrees at PBIs program shall be less than $500,000. If an institution receives a grant that is greater than $1 million, however, it must provide assurances that 50% of the cost of a grant project will be paid with nonfederal funds.[163]

The first $2.5 million (or lesser amount) appropriated is available only to the five institutions currently listed in Section 724 for the purposes of making the $500,000 minimum grants. If the amount appropriated is insufficient to pay the minimum grant amount to each institution, then each institution's award is ratably reduced. If other institutions are subsequently added to the list of eligible institutions, they are entitled to the minimum grant amount, unless such funds are not appropriated. In that case, the five institutions currently listed receive funding priority and subsequently added institutions' awards are ratably reduced.[164]

Any appropriations greater than $2.5 million are available to each of the currently listed five institutions based on a formula, determined by ED, that uses the same elements as the formula for the Masters Degrees at HBCUs program. Masters Degrees at PBIs also has the same hold harmless rule as Masters Degrees at HBCUs: notwithstanding the above method to allocate funds, no eligible institution that received a grant under the program for FY2009 and that is eligible to receive a grant in a subsequent year shall receive a grant that is less than the amount received in FY2009. However, this hold harmless rule does not apply if the amount appropriated for a fiscal year is insufficient to provide such grants to all such institutions or if an institution is unable to provide sufficient matching funds.[165]

Program Administration

Administration of the Masters Degrees at PBIs program also mirrors the administration of the Masters Degrees at HBCUs program. The award application process, grant duration, and limit of one grant per institution per fiscal year are the same. Additionally, an institution that is eligible for and receives an award under the HBGI, PPOHA, or Masters Degree Programs at HBCUs programs in a fiscal year is ineligible to receive grants under

---

[162] HEA §724(d).

[163] HEA §724(a)(2) & (3). If an institution is unable to meet this matching requirement, the Secretary must distribute, on a pro rata basis, any amounts that the institution cannot use due to its failure to meet the matching requirements to those institutions that do comply with the matching requirements.

[164] HEA §724(f).

[165] HEA §724(g).

the Masters Degrees at PBIs program in the same fiscal year. An institution receiving a Masters Degree Programs at PBIs grant may not concurrently receive a Title III-A grant, a Title III-B (Strengthening HBCUs program) grant, or a Title V-A (HSI program) grant, but may generally receive a Title III-F grant.

HISPANIC-SERVING INSTITUTIONS PROGRAMS

Under the Higher Education Amendments of 1992 (P.L. 102-325), Congress created the Developing Hispanic-Serving Institutions (HSIs) Program under HEA Title III-A. Under the Higher Education Amendments of 1998 (P.L. 105-244), the Developing HSI program was moved to its own title, HEA Title V.[166] In moving the HSI program to Title V, Congress stated, "[I]n recognition of the importance of finding new ways of serving our Nation's rapidly growing Hispanic community, [Congress] has created a new part within Title V dedicated solely to supporting the needs of Hispanic-Serving Institutions." The purpose of the program was and is to expand educational opportunities for and improve the academic attainment of Hispanic students and to enhance the institutional stability of institutions that are educating the majority of Hispanic college students.

Currently, Title V is divided into two parts. Part A contains the HSI program, which provides grants to HSIs to support and expand educational opportunities for Hispanic students and is similar to the various HEA Title III-A and III-B MSI programs. Part B contains the Promoting Postbaccalaureate Opportunities for Hispanic Americans program, which assists in expanding postbaccalaureate education opportunities for Hispanic students.

Title III-F contains the HSI Science, Technology, Engineering, and Mathematics and Articulation Program (HSI STEM), which assists in increasing the number of Hispanic and low-income students attaining degrees in STEM fields and in the development of transfer and articulation agreements between two-year and four-year institutions in STEM fields. Although HSI STEM is not part of Title V, grants made under HSI STEM are generally subject to the same requirements as grants made under the Title V-A HSI program; therefore, Title V-A and Title III-F HSI STEM will be addressed in the same section of this chapter. This section of the report will discuss each of the three HSI programs; for each program, this chapter will discuss eligibility criteria, authorized uses, and program administration.

---

[166] U.S. Congress, Senate Committee on Labor and Human Resources, *Higher education Act Amendments of 1998*, report to accompany S. 1882, 105th Cong., 2nd sess., May 4, 1998, S.Rept. 105-181 (Washington: GPO, 1998), p. 79.

Title V-A: Hispanic Serving Institutions

Section 501 of the HEA establishes the Hispanic Serving Institutions (HSI) program. The purpose of the program is to expand educational opportunities for Hispanic students and to enhance academic offerings and institutional stability at HSIs.[167] The HSI program is funded through annual discretionary appropriations.

Eligibility

To qualify for an HSI program grant, institutions of higher education must meet the HEA Section 312(b) criteria.[168] Additionally, an institution must have an enrollment of undergraduate full-time equivalent (FTE) students that is at least 25% Hispanic students at the end of the award year immediately preceding the date of application for a grant.[169] A Hispanic student is one of Mexican, Puerto Rican, Cuban, Central or South American, or other Spanish culture or origin.[170]

Branch campuses of institutions of higher education are eligible for the HSI program if the institution as a whole meets the eligibility requirements, even if the branch campus does not meet the state authorization or accreditation requirements. Branch campuses must, however, individually meet the needy student enrollment and low E&G requirements.[171]

Authorized Uses

HSI program grants are intended to assist institutions in planning, developing, undertaking, and carrying out programs to improve institutions' ability to serve Hispanic and low-income students.

Authorized uses of HSI program grants largely mirror the authorized uses of Title III-A SIP grants. However, HSI program grants are authorized for several additional activities, including

---

[167] HEA §501(b).

[168] Although HEA §502(2) does not specifically reference HEA §312(b), the eligibility criteria are the same. However, Section 502 does not specifically include the College of the Marshall Islands, the College of Micronesia/Federated States of Micronesia, and Palau Community College, which are included in §312(b). Waiver requirements for low E&G expenditures and needy student enrollment are substantially similar as those of the Title III-A programs; however, the Secretary cannot waive the needy student requirement for HSIs located on or near an Indian reservation or a substantial population of Indians. The Secretary can grant waivers if it is determined that doing so would substantially increase the higher education opportunities appropriate to the needs of Hispanic Americans. Finally, waiver requirements for the low E&G criterion are the same as for Title III-A programs. HEA §522(b).

[169] HEA §502(a)(5). Eligible institutions may apply as an individual institution or as part of a cooperative arrangement with institutions that may or may not be eligible for the HSI program. HEA §524(a).

[170] 34 C.F.R. §606.7(b).

[171] HEA §502(a)(2).

- articulation agreements and student support programs designed to facilitate the transfer of students from two-year to four-year institutions;
- establishing or enhancing teacher education programs designed to qualify students to teach in public elementary and secondary schools;
- establishing community outreach programs that encourage elementary and secondary school students to develop academic skills and the interest to pursue postsecondary education; and
- expanding the number of Hispanic and other underrepresented graduate and professional students that can be served by an institution through expanding institutional resources and courses offered.[172]

The Title III-A programs, HSIs are permitted to use up to 20% of grant funds to establish or improve an endowment, but they must provide nonfederal matching funds equal to or greater than the amount of federal funds used.[173]

Program Administration

As with many of the Title III-A programs, there is a two-step award process for institutions to receive HSI program grants. First, an institution applies for designation as a Section 312(b)/Section 502 eligible institution. If approved by the Secretary, the institution may then apply for an HSI program grant. Grants under this program are awarded through a competitive process. Applications are selected based on the score of a review panel, and the applications with the highest score are selected for funding.

HSI program grants are five years in length. HSIs that receive grants under this program are not subject to a wait-out period. Unlike many of the other MSI programs, institutions may simultaneously receive multiple HSI program grants. Additionally, institutions that receive grants under this program are prohibited from receiving grants under any Title III-A or Title III-B program for the duration of its HSI program grant;[174] however, in general, they may receive a grant under any of the Title III-F programs in the same fiscal year. Generally, institutions receiving an HSI STEM Title III-F grant may simultaneously receive a grant under another Title III-F program.

---

[172] HEA §503(b).

[173] The Consolidated Appropriations Act, 2017 (CAA 2017; P.L. 115-31) authorizes IHEs that maintain endowment funds supported with funds appropriated for HEA Title III and Title V programs for FY2017 to use the income from the endowment fund to award student scholarships. This provision, enacted through Division H, Title III of the CAA 2017 will remain in effect until Title III and Title V are reauthorized. Previous appropriations acts have authorized the same use of endowment income in recent years.

[174] HEA §505.

Title III-F: HSI STEM and Articulation Programs

HEA Title III-F authorizes the HSI Science, Technology, Engineering, and Mathematics and Articulation Program (HSI STEM). This is a competitive grant program funded with annual mandatory appropriations through FY2019.[175]

HSIs eligible under the Title V-A HSI program are also eligible for HSI STEM grants. Although grants can be used for any authorized purpose listed under Title V-A, priority is given to applicants that propose to (1) increase the number of Hispanic and low-income students attaining degrees in STEM fields and (2) develop model transfer and articulation agreements between two-year HSIs and four-year institutions in STEM fields. The administration of the HSI STEM program generally mirrors that of the Title V-A HSI program.

Title V-B: Promoting Postbaccalaureate Opportunities for Hispanic Americans

HEA Section 511 establishes the Promoting Postbaccalaureate Opportunities for Hispanic Americans (PPOHA) program, which was first authorized in 2008 under the Higher Education Opportunity Act (HEOA; P.L. 110-315). The purpose of the program is to enable HSIs to expand postbaccalaureate educational opportunities for Hispanic students.[176]

Since FY2009, PPOHA program grants have been funded through discretionary appropriations under Title V-B. In FY2009, Congress provided $10 million for PPOHA within the Fund for the Improvement of Postsecondary Education (FIPSE) appropriation account. Mandatory appropriations were provided annually for FY2009 through FY2014 under Title VIII-AA, Section 898. Authorization for mandatory appropriations lapsed at the end of FY2014.

Eligibility

To qualify for a PPOHA grant, an institution of higher education must meet the same criteria as for the HSI program, and it must offer a postbaccalaureate certificate or degree-granting program. [177]

---

[175] HEA §371(b)(2)(B).

[176] HEA §511.

[177] HEA §513. Eligible institutions may apply as an individual institution or as part of a cooperative arrangement with institutions that may or may not be eligible for the PPOHA program.

Authorized Uses

The PPOHA program is intended to expand postbaccalaureate opportunities and academic offerings for, and improve the academic attainment of, Hispanic and low-income students. Authorized uses of PPOHA grants include one or more of the following activities:

- the purchase, rental, or lease of scientific or laboratory equipment for educational purposes;
- the construction, maintenance, renovation, or improvement of classrooms, libraries, laboratories, and other instructional facilities, including the purchase and rental of telecommunications equipment or services;
- the purchase of library books, periodicals, technical and scientific journals, and other educational materials;
- support for faculty exchanges, development, and research;
- curriculum development and academic instruction;
- the creation or improvement of facilities for distance education;
- collaboration with other IHEs to expand postbaccalaureate educational offerings;
- and other activities that serve the purposes of the program and that are approved by the Secretary.[178]

Additionally, a PPOHA grant can be used to provide direct financial assistance to Hispanic and low-income postbaccalaureate students. Types of assistance offered can include scholarships, assistantships, fellowships, travel expenses for graduate students at professional conferences, funds for students to conduct research, and other forms of financial assistance. Institutions may use up to 20% of their PPOHA grant for direct student financial assistance.[179]

Program Administration

Like the HSI program, there is a two-step award process for institutions to receive PPOHA grants. First, an institution applies for designation as an eligible institution. If approved by the Secretary, the institution may then apply for PPOHA program assistance. Grants under the program are awarded through a competitive process. Applications are selected based on the score of a review panel, and the applications with the highest score are selected for funding.

Grant awards provided under this program may not exceed five years in length. Institutions are prohibited from receiving more than one grant under this program in a fiscal

---

[178] HEA §513.
[179] Department of Education, Office of Postsecondary Education, "Promoting Postbaccalaureate Opportunities for Hispanic Americans Program, Frequently Asked Questions," http://www2.ed.gov/programs/ppoha/faq.html, accessed July 14, 2017.

year, [180] and an institution receiving a PPOHA grant in a fiscal year cannot also receive an HBGI, Masters Degrees at HBCUs, or Masters Degrees at PBIs program grant in the same fiscal year. An institution receiving a PPOHA grant may not concurrently receive a Title III-A or III-B grant but may concurrently receive a Title V-A Strengthening HSIs grant. In addition, an institution receiving a PPOHA grant generally may receive a Title III-F grant.

ADDITIONAL PROGRAMS

Additional programs are available specifically to MSIs under the HEA.[181] These programs are not targeted to a specific type of MSI but, rather, are available to most IHEs with a high concentration of minority students. Two such programs are the Endowment Challenge Grant and the Minority Science and Engineering Improvement Program.[182]

Endowment Challenge Grants

The Endowment Challenge Grant program under HEA Title III-C provides matching grants to eligible institutions to either establish or increase endowments and to increase self-sufficiency at such institutions. Eligible institutions are those that are eligible under HEA Title III-A and Title III-B and institutions of higher education that make substantial contributions to postgraduate medical educational opportunities for minority and economically disadvantaged students. Grants under this program may not exceed $1 million, and recipients must provide nonfederal matching funds equal to the amount of federal funds provided.[183] This program has not been funded since FY1995.

---

[180] HEA §514.
[181] HEA Title III-E authorizes two additional programs: the Yes Partnerships Grant Program and Promotion of Entry into STEM Fields. The Yes Partnerships Grant Program authorizes the Secretary to make grants to support the engagement of underrepresented minority youth in STEM outreach. Promotion of Entry into STEM Fields authorizes the Secretary to contract with a firm to implement an advertising campaign to encourage youths to enter STEM fields. Neither program has been implemented; therefore, they are not discussed in detail in this report.
[182] HEA Title VI-C authorizes the Institute for International Public Policy (IIPP), which is a program that provides a single grant to assist a consortium of colleges and universities to establish an institute designated to increase the representation of minorities in international services. This report does not attempt to describe all HEA programs for which an MSI may be eligible; rather, it aims to describe those programs that are directed specifically toward one or more types of MSIs. Thus, because IHEs that are not MSIs may receive IIPP grants, this report does not detail the IIPP. For more information on IIPP, see U.S. Department of Education, Office of Postsecondary Education, "Institute for International Public Policy," http://www2.ed.gov/programs/iegpsiipp/index.html, accessed July 14, 2017.
[183] HEA §331.

Minority Science and Engineering Improvement Program

The Minority Science and Engineering Improvement Program (MSEIP) was first authorized in the National Science Foundation Act of 1950 (P.L. 81-507),[184] and its administration was transferred to the Department of Education under HEA Title III-E by the Department of Education Organization Act of 1979 (P.L. 96-88). In creating the program, Congress had found that minority-serving institutions provide important educational opportunities for minority students, particularly in science and engineering fields, but that such institutions often face significant limitations in resources and, therefore, lag behind in program offerings and student enrollment. To counter this, MSEIP was established to provide grant-based assistance to predominantly minority institutions to effect long-term improvements in science and engineering education. Additionally, MSEIP is intended to increase the number of underrepresented ethnic minorities, particularly minority women, in science and engineering careers.[185]

This section of the report first discusses general MSEIP eligibility criteria and then details the four types of MSEIP grants. Included in the discussion of each grant type are specific eligibility criteria, and authorized uses. Finally, this section of the report then discusses how MSEIP as a whole is administered.

Eligibility

MSEIP grants, generally, are available to a variety of entities, not just institutions of higher education. However, MSEIP is divided into four categories of grants, each of which is used to address specific issues in science and engineering educational opportunities for minority students. Only certain entities that are eligible for MSEIP grants generally are eligible for each specific type of MSEIP grant, as determined by ED, through regulations.

In general, Section 361 lists the following entities as eligible for MSEIP grants:

- *Public and private nonprofit minority-serving institutions of higher education* that either (1) award bachelor's degrees or (2) award associate's degrees and have a curriculum that includes science or engineering subjects and that enter into partnerships with public or private nonprofit IHEs that award bachelor's degrees in science and engineering.

---

[184] While under the authority of the National Science Foundation, MSEIP was operated as the Minority Institutions Science Improvement Program.
[185] HEA §§350 & 351.

- *Nonprofit science-oriented organizations, professional scientific societies, and bachelor's degree awarding IHEs,* all of which must provide a needed service to a group of minority-serving institutions or provide in-service training for project directors, scientists, and engineers from minority-serving institutions.

- *Consortia of organizations* that provide needed services to one or more minority-serving institution. Consortia membership may include (1) public and private nonprofit IHEs that have a science or engineering curriculum; (2) IHEs that have a graduate or professional program in science or engineering; (3) research laboratories of or under contract with the Department of Energy, the Department of Defense, or the National Institutes of Health; (4) relevant offices of the National Aeronautics and Space Administration, National Oceanic and Atmospheric Administration, National Science Foundation, and National Institute of Standards and Technology; (5) quasi-governmental entities that have a significant scientific or engineering mission; or (6) IHEs with state-sponsored centers of research in science, technology, engineering, and mathematics fields.[186]

For purposes of MSEIP grants, HEA Section 365 defines a minority-serving institution as an IHE with an enrollment of a single minority, or a combination of minorities, that exceeds 50% of the total enrollment. The definition of minority includes American Indian, Alaskan Native, Black (not of Hispanic origin), Hispanic (including persons of Mexican, Puerto Rican, Cuban, and Central or South American origin), Pacific Islander, or another ethnic group that is underrepresented in science and engineering.[187]

Although each of the above types of entities is eligible for MSEIP grants generally, ED has set regulations that direct which entities are eligible for specific types of MSEIP grants.

Grant Types

MSEIP is broken into four different grant types, each of which is intended to serve specific objectives. The four grant types are institutional grants, cooperative grants, design project grants, and special project grants.

Institutional Grants

Institutional grants are awarded for projects that support the implementation of a comprehensive science improvement plan. Such plans may include any combination of activities for improving the preparation of minority students for careers in sciences.[188]

---

[186] HEA §361.

[187] HEA §354(2) & (3). "Underrepresented in science and engineering" is defined as a minority group "whose number of scientists and engineers per 10,000 population of that group is substantially below the comparable figure for scientists and engineers who are white and not of Hispanic origin." HEA §365(5).

[188] HEA §365(6).

Specifically authorized uses for institutional grants include, but are not limited to, faculty development programs and the development of curriculum materials.[189]

ED has determined that eligibility for institutional grants is limited to public and private nonprofit minority-serving institutions of higher education and consortia of such institutions.[190]

Cooperative Grants

Cooperative grants are awarded for projects that assist groups of public and private nonprofit accredited IHEs to work together to conduct a science improvement project[191] Specifically authorized uses for cooperative grants include, but are not limited to

- assisting institutions in sharing facilities and personnel;
- disseminating information about established programs in science and engineering;
- supporting cooperative efforts to strengthen the institution's science and engineering programs; and
- carrying out a combination of the above listed activities.[192]

ED regulations limit cooperative grant eligibility to groups of nonprofit accredited colleges and universities. The primary fiscal agent of each group must be an eligible minority-serving institution, as defined in Section 365.[193]

Design Project Grants

Design project grants are awarded for projects that "assist minority institutions that do not have their own appropriate resources or personnel to plan and develop long-range science improvement programs."[194] Specifically authorized uses for design project grants include, but are not limited to, developing planning, management, and evaluation systems or developing plans for initiating scientific research and for improving an institution's capacity for scientific research. Funds for design project grants may be used to pay the salaries of faculty involved in a project; however, not more than 50% of the funds can be used during any academic year for such purposes.[195]

---

[189] HEA §353(b)(1).
[190] Department of Education, "Applications for New Awards; Minority Science and Engineering Improvement Program," 81 *Federal Register* 72791, October 21, 2017.
[191] HEA §365(7).
[192] HEA §353(b)(2).
[193] Not all members of the group must be eligible minority institutions. 34 C.F.R. §637.15(c).
[194] HEA §365(8).
[195] HEA §353(b)(3).

ED regulations do not limit eligibility for design project grants beyond statute; therefore, unless otherwise determined by ED, design project grants are available to all MSEIP-eligible entities listed under HEA Section 361.

Special Project Grants

There are two types of special project grants. The first is available only to minority-serving institutions. Grants must support activities that either improve the quality of training in science and engineering or enhance research capabilities at minority-serving institutions.

The second type of special project grant is available to any MSEIP-eligible entity. These grants must either provide a needed service to a group of minority-serving institutions or provide training for project directors, scientists, and engineers from minority-serving institutions.[196]

Authorized uses for either type of special project grant include, but are not limited to

- advanced science seminars;
- science faculty workshops and conferences;
- faculty training to develop science research or education skills;
- science education research;
- programs for visiting scientists;
- preparation of films or audio-visual materials in science;
- development of learning experiences in science beyond those normally available to minority institutions;
- development of pre-college enrichment activities in sciences; or
- other activities that address barriers to the entry of minorities into science.[197]

Program Administration

Like many of the HEA Title III-A and III-B grant programs, all types of MSEIP grants are competitively awarded. MSEIP funding is provided through annual discretionary appropriations.

Unlike many other HEA Title III grant programs, the MSEIP award process consists of a single step. To apply, applicants must submit a proposed project plan for the relevant MSEIP grant.[198] Applications are selected based on the score of a review panel, and the applications with the highest score are selected for funding.

---

[196] HEA §365(9).
[197] HEA §353(b)(4).
[198] Although MSEIP has a one-step application process, IHEs applying for funds must provide documentation of minority enrollment as part of their application package.

In awarding grants, ED is required to give priority to applicants who have not previously received funding under MSEIP and to previous grantees with a proven record of success. ED can also give priority to applicants that contribute to achieving balance across geographic regions, academic disciplines, and project types among all projects that are funded.[199]

APPENDIX A. LIST OF ACRONYMS

The following is a list of acronyms that have been used throughout this chapter.

AANAPISI Asian American and Native American Pacific Islander-Serving Institution
ANNH   Alaska Native and Native Hawaiian-Serving Institution
HBCU   Historically Black Colleges and Universities
HBGI   Historically Black Graduate Institution
HSI   Hispanic-Serving Institution
MSEIP   Minority Science and Engineering Improvement Program
NASNTI   Native American-Serving, Nontribal Institution
PBI   Predominantly Black Institution
PPOHA   Promoting Postbaccalaureate Opportunities for Hispanic Americans
SIP   Strengthening Institutions Program
STEM   Science, Technology, Engineering, and Mathematics
TCCU   American Indian Tribally Controlled Colleges and Universities

APPENDIX B. APPROPRIATIONS FOR SELECTED HEA-AUTHORIZED MSI PROGRAMS

Table B-1 of this appendix lists the authorizations and discretionary and mandatory appropriations for selected HEA-authorized MSI programs, from FY2013 to FY2017.

---

[199] HEA §352(b).

Table B-1.

Program	Auth. Section	Disc./Mand.[a] (D/M)	Fiscal Year				
			2013	2014	2015	2016	2017
SIP	§399	D[b]	76,406	79,139	80,462	86,534	86,534
	—	M	—	—	—	—	—
Strengthening TCCUs	§399	D[b]	24,368	25,239	25,662	27,599	27,599
	§371	M[c]	28,470	27,840	27,810	27,960	27,930
Strengthening ANNHs	§399	D[b]	12,186	12,622	12,833	13,802	13,802
	§371	M[c]	14,235	13,920	13,905	13,980	13,965
Strengthening PBIs	§399	D[b]	8,778	9,092	9,244	9,942	9,942
	§371	M[c]	14,235	13,920	13,905	13,980	13,965
Strengthening NASNTIs	§399	Db	2,956	3,062	3,113	3,348	3,348
	§371	M[c]	4,745	4,640	4,635	4,660	4,655
Strengthening AANAPISIs	§399	Db	2,956	3,062	3,113	3,348	3,348
	§371	M[c]	4,745	4,640	4,635	4,660	4,655
Strengthening HBCUs	§399	D[b]	216,056	223,783	227,524	244,694	244,694
	§371	M	80,665	78,880	78,795	79,220	79,135
Strengthening HBGIs	§399	D[b]	55,874	57,872	58,840	63,281	63,281
	—	M	—	—	—	—	—
MSEIP	§399	D[b]	8,971	8,971	8,971	9,648	9,648
	—	M	—	—	—	—	—
Developing HSIs	§528	D[b]	95,179	98,583	100,231	107,795	107,795
	—	M	—	—	—	—	—

Program	Auth. Section	Disc./Mand.[a] (D/M)	Fiscal Year				
			2013	2014	2015	2016	2017
HSI STEM and	—	D	—	—	—	—	—
Articulation	§371	M[c]	94,900	92,800	92,700	93,200	93.100
PPOHAs	§528	D[b]	8,540	8,845	8,992	9,671	9.671
	§898	M	10,914	10,672	0d	0	0
Masters Degrees	§725	Db	0	0	0	0	7,500
at HBCUs[e]	§897	M	10,914	10,672	0d	0	0
Masters Degrees at PBIs[e]	§725	Db	[combined with §725 above]	[combined with §725 above]	[combined with §725 above]	[combined with §725 above]	0
	§897	M	[combined with §897 above]	[combined with §897 above]	[combined with §897 above]	[combined with §897 above]	[combined with §897 above]

Source: Compiled by CRS from U.S. Department of Education, Budget Tables for various years, http://www2.ed.gov/about/overview/budget/tables.html?src=ct.

[a]"D" indicates discretionary funding; "M" indicates mandatory funding. All amounts presented reflect the final amount appropriated, including any spending reduction authorized by the Budget Control Act of 2011 (BCA; P.L. 112-25), commonly referred to as "sequestration."

[b]Authorization for appropriations expired at the end of FY2014. Section 422 of the General Education Provisions Act extended authorization of appropriations through FY2015.

[c]Authorized through FY2019.

[d]Authorization of mandatory appropriations for these programs, and an appropriation of mandatory funds, were provided through FY2014 (HEOA; P.L. 110-315). Mandatory funds have not been provided for these programs since the end of FY2014.

[e]Although Masters Degrees at HBCUs and Masters Degrees at PBIs are administered by ED as separate programs, prior to FY2017, they were grouped together within the Department of Education's budget for budgetary purposes; and therefore, no separate appropriations for the individual programs are listed for FY2013-FY2016. However, for the first time in FY2017, Congress provided discretionary appropriations for the Masters Degrees at HBCUs program, but not the Masters Degrees at PBIs program.

In: Higher Education
Editor: Lilian Wieck

ISBN: 978-1-53616-026-0
© 2019 Nova Science Publishers, Inc.

Chapter 7

PRELIMINARY OBSERVATIONS ON EFFORTS TO FOSTER ENTREPRENEURSHIP WITH HISTORICALLY BLACK COLLEGES AND UNIVERSITIES*

Anna Maria Ortiz

WHY GAO DID THIS STUDY

Historically Black Colleges and Universities play an important and unique role in the higher education system and in their local and regional economies. SBA works with many colleges and universities to provide entrepreneurial training and counseling on campuses. SBA is also part of a long-standing White House Initiative to expand the capacity of HBCUs, including their ability to participate in federal programs. However, little is known about the extent to which SBA has worked with the 101 HBCUs to foster entrepreneurship among students and others.

This statement is based on (1) GAO's March 2019 report (GAO-19-328R) on SBA's plans and programs for working with HBCUs and (2) preliminary observations from GAO's ongoing review of any HBCU-specific information SBA collects and reports and collaboration of selected HBCUs and SBA.

GAO reviewed recent executive orders related to enhancing HBCU capacities; agency documents, including SBA's 2018 agency plan for supporting HBCUs; and statutes and regulations for key programs and activities. GAO also interviewed SBA headquarters and selected district officials based on criteria including (1) the number of HBCUs in the state,

---

* This is an edited, reformatted and augmented version of the United States Government Accountability Office Testimony Before the Subcommittee on Investigations, Oversight, and Regulations, Committee on Small Business, House of Representatives, Publication No. GAO-19-515T, dated April 30, 2019.

and (2) agreements, if any, between HBCUs and SBA. GAO also interviewed six HBCUs based on their relationship with SBA.

WHAT GAO RECOMMENDS

GAO is not making recommendations in this testimony, but will consider them, as appropriate, as it finalizes its work.

WHAT GAO FOUND

Small Business Administration (SBA) programs and activities that foster entrepreneurship have included, but do not specifically target, Historically Black Colleges and Universities (HBCU). SBA funds 63 Small Business Development Centers (SBDC) that are generally hosted by colleges or universities. Two of the 63 SBDCs are hosted by HBCUs—Howard University and the University of the Virgin Islands—and at least 16 of the more than 900 SBDC satellite locations have been at HBCUs. SBA's district offices also can initiate and oversee outreach activities to foster entrepreneurship. While these activities are not targeted to HBCUs, some district offices have worked with HBCUs. For example, district offices co-sponsored 10 counseling and training activities in 2013–2018 with six HBCUs and signed memorandums with at least 27 HBCUs to strengthen local small business development in 2008–2018.

Source: GAO. | GAO-19-515T.

Business Workshop at the Small Business Development Center at the University of the Virgin Islands.

GAO's preliminary observations indicate SBA has limited data on entrepreneurship-related efforts at HBCUs. In 2018, SBA established two goals for working with HBCUs: (1) to raise awareness and provide information to help raise the capacity of HBCUs to participate in federally funded programs, and (2) to promote collaboration among HBCUs, SBA resource partners, and SBA district offices. GAO's ongoing work identified that HBCU-specific data (such as the number of outreach events involving HBCUs or the number of HBCU students or alumni who participated) are incomplete at an agency-wide level. Moreover, SBA does not systematically collect written feedback from event participants, including for events involving HBCUs. GAO's preliminary observations also indicate that SBA resource partners, such as SBDCs, have established relationships with some HBCUs. GAO will continue to examine the extent of SBA efforts to foster entrepreneurship with HBCUs.

Chairwoman Chu, Ranking Member Spano, and Members of the Subcommittee:

Thank you for the opportunity to discuss the Small Business Administration's (SBA) efforts for fostering entrepreneurship with Historically Black Colleges and Universities (HBCU). HBCUs play an important and unique role in the higher education system as well as in their local and regional economies.[1] SBA is part of a long-standing White House Initiative to expand the capacity of HBCUs to provide quality education, including by increasing HBCU access to and participation in federal programs. SBA also works with many colleges and universities to provide entrepreneurial training and counseling on campuses. But little is known about the extent to which SBA has worked with HBCUs to help students and others start, build, and expand businesses.

Today, I will discuss SBA's plans and programs for working with HBCUs and preliminary observations about our ongoing work on SBA's efforts to foster entrepreneurship with HBCUs. Specifically, I will discuss (1) SBA goals for working with HBCUs and the extent to which its activities targeted HBCUs, and (2) our preliminary observations on what information SBA collects and reports specific to HBCUs and collaboration of selected HBCUs and SBA. My statement is based on findings from our March 2019 report and ongoing work examining SBA efforts related to the White House Initiative on HBCUs, including to what extent SBA met its goals for working with HBCUs to foster entrepreneurship.[2]

For our March 2019 report, we reviewed executive orders relating to the White House Initiative and SBA's plan for addressing the initiative (a requirement of recent executive orders) for 2018 and identified SBA's goals for working with HBCUs. We reviewed SBA's congressional budget justifications (fiscal years 2008–2017), strategic plans, and standard operating procedures to identify key programs and counseling or training activities related to fostering entrepreneurship. We also reviewed statutes and regulations associated with the

---

[1] Jeffrey M. Humphreys, *HBCUs Make America Strong: The Positive Economic Impact of Historically Black Colleges and Universities*, technical report (Washington, D.C.: 2017). Study commissioned by the United Negro College Fund, Frederick D. Patterson Research Institute.

[2] GAO, Small Business Administration: Key Entrepreneurship Programs and Activities Do Not Specifically Target Historically Black Colleges and Universities, but Collaboration Exists with Some Schools, GAO-19-328R (Washington, D.C.: Mar. 7, 2019).

key programs and activities to determine the extent to which any target HBCUs. This chapter includes a detailed description of our scope and methodology.

To develop our preliminary observations, we interviewed SBA officials in the Office of Entrepreneurial Development and in eight district offices to better understand the information SBA has collected and the extent of collaboration with HBCUs. We selected the district offices based on (1) a high number of HBCUs in the state, and (2) a mixture of types of agreements SBA signed with the HBCUs (cooperative agreement, strategic alliance memorandums, and co-sponsored agreements). We also interviewed six HBCUs about those efforts. We selected HBCUs that had formal agreements with SBA or proximity to any SBA district office. We also reviewed additional documents that SBA provided related to its plans and reports for the White House Initiative and that we identified related to strategic alliance memorandums and SBA resource partners.

The work on which this statement is based was performed in accordance with generally accepted government auditing standards. Those standards require that we plan and perform the audit to obtain sufficient, appropriate evidence to provide a reasonable basis for our findings and conclusions based on our audit objectives. We believe that the evidence obtained provides a reasonable basis for our findings and conclusions based on our audit objectives.

BACKGROUND

Executive Orders on White House Initiative

Executive Order 12232 (1980) established the White House Initiative on Historically Black Colleges and Universities to expand the capacity of HBCUs to provide quality education. Subsequent administrations issued executive orders to continue the initiative.[3] Most recently, as expressed in Executive Order 13779 (2017), federal priorities for working with HBCUs encompass two missions: (1) increasing the role of private-sector entities in helping to improve capacity at HBCUs, and (2) enhancing HBCUs' capabilities for helping young adults.[4] The initiative used to be located in the Department of Education, and has been housed in the Executive Office of the President since 2017 (although maintaining operational presence within the Department of Education), according to representatives from the initiative.

---

[3] For example, see Exec. Order No. 12320 (Sept. 15, 1981), Exec. Order No. 12766 (April 28, 1989), Exec. Order No. 12876 (Nov. 1, 1993), Exec. Order No. 13256 (Feb. 12, 2002), Exec. Order No. 13532 (Mar. 3, 2010), and Exec. Order No. 13779 (Feb. 28, 2017). The current Executive Order (13779) supersedes the previous Executive Orders.

[4] Areas of focus noted for the second mission of Executive Order 13779 include strengthening HBCU participation in federal programs, developing public-private partnerships to promote research and programmatic excellence at HBCUs, and sharing administrative and programmatic best practices within the HBCU community.

The more recent executive orders (from 2002, 2010, and 2017) require that each department and agency designated by the Secretary of Education prepare an annual plan on efforts to strengthen HBCU capacity.[5] SBA is among the agencies designated to prepare a plan. The plans are to describe how the department or agency intends to increase the capacity of HBCUs, including by identifying federal programs and initiatives in which HBCUs are underserved or that HBCUs may underutilize.[6]

The more recent executive orders also state that a Board of Advisors on HBCUs (in the Department of Education) shall report annually to the President on the Board's progress in carrying out its duties, which include advising the President on matters pertaining to strengthening the educational capacity of HBCUs.[7] To prepare the report, the designated agencies were asked to provide data on funds awarded to HBCUs in the previous fiscal year. The annual reports generally were published on the website of the White House Initiative on HBCUs.[8] We discuss the reports in more detail later in this statement.

SBA Offices and Partners with Business Development and Counseling Responsibilities

SBA's Office of Entrepreneurial Development oversees several programs, primarily through a nationwide network of public and private resource partners that offer small business counseling and technical assistance. Key resource partners include Small Business Development Centers (SBDC), Women's Business Centers, and SCORE chapters.

- SBDCs provide technical assistance to small businesses and aspiring entrepreneurs. The SBDC network has 63 lead centers (which generally must be hosted by institutions of higher education) and more than 900 service centers (subcenters and satellite locations).[9]

---

[5] For our ongoing work, we focused on SBA's partnerships with HBCUs during the last 10 years and therefore primarily reviewed Exec. Order No. 13256 (2002), Exec. Order No. 13532 (2010), and Exec. Order No. 13779 (2017).

[6] Exec. Order No. 13779, § 2(c) (2017). Agency plans are to describe, where appropriate, (1) how the agency intends to increase the capacity of HBCUs to compete effectively for grants, contracts, or cooperative agreements; (2) identify federal programs and initiatives in which HBCUs are not well represented, and improve HBCUs' participation; and (3) encourage public-sector, private-sector, and community involvement in improving the overall capacity of HBCUs. See also, Exec. Order No. 13256, § 7 (2002); Exec. Order No. 13523, § 2(d) (2010).

[7] Exec. Order No. 13779, § 3 (2017). The President's Board of Advisors on HBCUs was established in the Department of Education. The Board consists of not more than 25 members appointed by the President and includes the Secretary of Education, the Executive Director of the Initiative, representatives of multiple sectors (such as philanthropy, business, and finance), and sitting HBCU presidents. See also, Exec. Order No. 13256, § 1 (2002); Exec. Order No. 13523, § 3(a) (2010).

[8] See https://sites.ed.gov/whhbcu/policy/reports-studies/.

[9] More specifically, 63 organizations receive SBA funding to help operate SBDCs (in each state, the District of Columbia, Puerto Rico, the U.S. Virgin Islands, Guam, and American Samoa). The recipient is responsible for establishing a lead center and a network of service centers for a designated area. According to SBA officials,

- More than 100 private nonprofit Women's Business Centers provide counseling and training to assist women in starting and growing small businesses.
- SCORE is a nonprofit organization that fosters the development of small businesses through mentoring and education. SCORE mentors (volunteers with prior business or entrepreneurial experience) provide free or low-cost mentoring and training to entrepreneurs through more than 300 chapters in the United States and its territories.

SBA also provides services through a network of 10 regional offices and 68 district offices. SBA district offices serve as the point of delivery for most SBA programs and services. Some district office staff (including business opportunity, lender relations, and economic development specialists) work directly with SBA clients.[10]

SBA's district offices can initiate and oversee outreach activities to foster entrepreneurship. For example, SBA district offices can plan and conduct events (including training and informational sessions), participate in third-party activities, or co-sponsor activities such as counseling and training.[11] Moreover, district offices can enter into a 2-year strategic alliance memorandum with a nonprofit, institution of higher education, or government party to foster a working relationship designed to strengthen small business development in a local area.

SBA'S 2018 PLAN PRIORITIZES COLLABORATION WITH HBCUS BUT KEY PROGRAMS AND ACTIVITIES THAT FOSTER ENTREPRENEURSHIP DO NOT SPECIFICALLY TARGET HBCUS

SBA's Goals for Working with HBCUs Include Raising Awareness of Its Programs and Promoting Collaboration

SBA's agency plan (2018) for the White House Initiative includes two goals.[12] The first goal is to raise awareness and provide information to help raise the capacity of HBCUs to participate in federally funded programs. More specifically, the plan states that SBA will

---

service centers do not have a relationship with SBA; rather, they have a contractual agreement with the SBDC lead center. The institution hosting a lead center is to promote an inclusive vision of entrepreneurship, expand the scope of activities, and coordinate with SBA district offices, federal and local agencies, and nongovernmental entities.

[10] Business opportunity specialists recruit, train, educate, and develop small businesses interested in SBA's contracting programs. Economic development specialists market SBA programs and conduct outreach, training, and education. Lender relations specialists interact with lenders to deliver SBA loan programs and services in the district.

[11] SBA enters into co-sponsorship agreements with nonprofit and governmental entities (federal, state, or local) to provide training, education, and information to small businesses.

[12] https://www.sba.gov/document/report--white-house-initiative-historically-black-collegesuniver sities.

engage with HBCUs and provide them with information needed to access and compete for federal grants and contracts.[13] The second goal is to promote collaboration among HBCUs, SBA resource partners, and SBA district offices. For instance, the plan states that SBA will encourage the formation of strategic alliance memorandums between SBA district offices and HBCUs to promote and support entrepreneurship in underserved markets.

While the three most recent executive orders (which covered the period of our review, 2008–2018) require designated agencies, including SBA, to prepare annual plans, SBA was unable to provide us with agency plans for 7 of the 10 years we reviewed. We discuss SBA's limited information on activities at HBCUs that fostered entrepreneurship later in this statement.

SBA's Key Programs and Activities for Fostering Entrepreneurship Are Not Targeted to HBCUs

SBA's key programs and activities that foster entrepreneurship have included, but do not specifically target, HBCUs.[14] For instance, the SBDC program is a key program for fostering entrepreneurship but does not target HBCUs.[15] However, some HBCUs host SBDCs or have service centers. More specifically, 2 of the 63 lead SBDCs are hosted by HBCUs—Howard University in Washington, D.C. and the University of the Virgin Islands in St. Thomas, U.S. Virgin Islands—and at least 16 HBCUs have hosted SBDC service centers.[16] Since 1979, Howard University has hosted the lead SBDC for the District of

---

[13] For instance, the plan identifies the Small Business Innovation Research and Small Business Technology Transfer programs, which SBA oversees, as available resources that are underutilized by HBCUs. The Small Business Innovation Research program began in 1982 and has four main purposes: (1) use small businesses to meet federal research and development needs, (2) stimulate technological innovation, (3) increase private-sector commercialization of innovations derived from federal research and development efforts, and (4) foster and encourage participation in technological innovation by small businesses owned by women and disadvantaged individuals. The Small Business Technology Transfer program began in 1992 and has three main purposes: (1) stimulate technological innovation, (2) foster technology transfer through cooperative research and development between small businesses and research institutions, and (3) increase private-sector commercialization of innovations derived from federal research and development.

[14] As of December 2018, there were 101 HBCUs recognized by the Department of Education as accredited institutions eligible for participation in federal student financial aid programs. Of these HBCUs, 50 are public and 51 are private nonprofit (private).

[15] In fiscal year 2018, SBA allocated more than $131 million for the SBDC program. SBDC regulations permit SBA to conduct "special emphasis initiatives" to identify portions of the general population to target for assistance. 13 C.F.R. § 130.340(c). SBA has identified certain populations of business owners as special emphasis groups (thus, they do not include HBCUs). According to SBA officials, SBDCs target underrepresented groups in the population of business owners near HBCUs.

[16] As of September 2018, the 16 SBDC service centers that SBA identified were at Alabama State University, Bluefield State College, Delaware State University, Elizabeth City State University, Fayetteville State University, Florida A&M University, Jackson State University, Lincoln University of Missouri, North Carolina A&T State University, North Carolina Central University, Prairie View A&M University, South Carolina State University, Southern University and A&M College, Tennessee State University, Winston-Salem State University, and Xavier University of Louisiana. While SBA considers Hinds Community College-Utica as an HBCU with an SBDC subcenter, we did not count Hinds as an HBCU because the Department of Education had

Columbia, which offers workshops and counseling on marketing, business financing, social media, and other topics. The District of Columbia SBDC has two subcenters in its network—at the Anacostia Economic Development Center and the Greater Washington Urban League. The University of the Virgin Islands has been a host institution since 1985 and the Virgin Islands SBDC provides one-on-one counseling, training, and other resources at locations on St. Croix, St. Thomas, and St. John.[17] According to the Virgin Island SBDC representatives, they have two physical offices—St. Croix and St. Thomas (which also serves St. John).

Co-sponsored activities represent another key SBA effort to foster entrepreneurship. While co-sponsorship activities are not targeted to HBCUs, SBA has implemented them with HBCUs. SBA documented cosponsored activities with six HBCUs to foster entrepreneurship in 2013– 2018, mostly through collaborations with SBA district offices (see table 1).[18] For instance, SBA's West Virginia district office and West Virginia State University in Institute, West Virginia coordinated workshops devised to help individuals over the age of 50 start and expand small businesses, while SBA's North Florida district office and Edward Waters College in Jacksonville, Florida designed a series of entrepreneurial training sessions for students and the community.

SBA's strategic alliance memorandums are key for fostering entrepreneurship in local communities, including HBCU communities. Strategic alliance memorandums are 2-year agreements that state the parties involved will develop and foster working relationships with the intent of strengthening small business development in a local area. SBA identified 24 HBCUs with which it had signed strategic alliance memorandums during 2008–2018; we determined that at least another three HBCUs signed strategic alliance memorandums during this period (see table 2)[19] As of April 2019, SBA officials were able to provide us with documentation of nine memorandums signed during 2008–2018. Each of the nine memorandums said SBA district office staff were to invite participating HBCUs to attend SBA events, workshops, and training. SBA staff told us that because a strategic alliance memorandum does not sanction, authorize, or fund an event or activity, by design it is largely symbolic. Additionally, SBA officials from five of the eight district offices with

---

not defined it as such at the time of our review. We did not independently verify whether all SBDC service centers at HBCUs were open as of September 2018.

[17] Lead SBDCs hosted by colleges or universities that are not HBCUs also can establish relationships with HBCUs. For example, the SBDC at the University of Maryland in College Park, Maryland has an agreement with Morgan State University in Baltimore, Maryland to assist businesses in the region.

[18] SBA provided us with documentation for 14 co-sponsorship agreements with HBCUs made during 2013–2018. However, 4 of the 14 agreements did not cover counseling and training activities related to fostering entrepreneurship, which is the focus of our review. In the same period, SBA officials said they co-sponsored about 880 activities with other (non-HBCU) entities. It is possible that district offices co-sponsored additional activities with HBCUs that were not reported to SBA headquarters.

[19] During the same time period, SBA officials said that they signed 206 strategic alliance memorandums with other (non-HBCU) entities. Nonprofit organizations and governmental agencies are eligible to enter into strategic alliance memorandums. We will continue to review SBA's policies and procedures for retaining records related to the White House Initiative as a part of our ongoing work.

which we met with told us that strategic alliance memorandums are not necessary if the district office already has established a good working relationship with an HBCU.

Table 1. Documented Counseling and Training Activities to Foster Entrepreneurship That the Small Business Administration (SBA) Co-Sponsored with Historically Black Colleges and Universities, 2013–2018

SBA office	Historically Black College or University	Activity
North Florida District Office	Edward Waters College	SBA/Edward Waters College Entrepreneurial Workshop Series
	Bethune Cookman University	SBA/HBCU Entrepreneurial Workshop Series
Louisiana District Office	Southern University and A&M College	"Connecting Businesses with Contracts"Procurement Conference
Baltimore District Office	Morgan State University	EmergingLeaders
Mississippi District Office	Jackson State University	Emerging Leaders
West Virginia District Office	West Virginia State University	Finding New International Customers Workshop
	West Virginia State University	Encore Entrepreneur (2014)
	West Virginia State University	Encore Entrepreneur (2015)
	West Virginia State University	How to Open a Rural Lodging Business (webinar series)
Office of Entrepreneurship Education	West Virginia State University	Encore Entrepreneur

Source: GAO analysis of SBA documents. | GAO-19-515T.

Other SBA resource partners that foster entrepreneurship, including Women's Business Centers and SCORE chapters, do not specifically target HBCUs. As of February 2019, there was one Women's Business Center at an HBCU and no SCORE chapters at HBCUs, according to SBA officials.[20] But HBCUs can form relationships with these resource partners.[21] For instance, representatives from Morgan State University in Baltimore, Maryland told us that a SCORE mentor from the area chapter has office hours on campus to provide mentoring.

---

[20] According to SBA officials, the Maryland Women's Business Center has a service center at Bowie State University in Bowie, Maryland.

[21] Statutory provisions for Women's Business Centers and SCORE, which are not generally affiliated with colleges and universities, do not mention HBCUs. However, when SBA evaluates applicants for Women's Business Centers, SBA must consider the ability of the applicant to "provide training and services to a representative number of women who are both socially and economically disadvantaged." 15 U.S.C. § 656(f)(3). Provisions for SCORE do not specify any socioeconomic, gender, or ethic/racial groups to be targeted. 15 U.S.C. § 637(b)(1)(B). According to SBA officials, Women's Business Centers and SCORE do not specifically target HBCUs as institutional organizations but each specifically targets under-represented groups in the population of business owners served by HBCUs.

Table 2. Historically Black Colleges and Universities That Signed Strategic Alliance Memorandums with the Small Business Administration (SBA), by State, 2008–2018

State	Historically Black College or University[a]
Alabama	Alabama A&M University[b]
	J.F. Drake State Technical College
	Lawson State Community College
	Miles College
	Stillman College
	Concordia College Alabama[c]
	Shelton State Community College
	Tuskegee University
Delaware	Delaware State University
Florida	Edward Waters College
	Florida A & M University
	Bethune-Cookman University
	Florida Memorial University
Georgia	Morehouse College
	Savannah State University
Louisiana	Dillard University
Mississippi	Rust College
	Alcorn State University
	Mississippi Valley State University
	Tougaloo College
	Coahoma Community College
North Carolina	Johnson C. Smith[b]
	Shaw University
	St. Augustine University
South Carolina	Benedict College[b]
Tennessee	LeMoyne-Owen College
	American Baptist College

Source: GAO analysis of SBA documents. | GAO-19-515T

[a] Schools listed signed one or more strategic alliance memorandums with SBA between 2008 and 2018.

[b] These schools were not previously identified in GAO-19-328R, which was based on information provided by SBA. We identified these schools through subsequent research on strategic alliance memorandums with HBCUs.

[c] Concordia College Alabama in Selma, Alabama closed at the end of spring semester 2018.

PRELIMINARY OBSERVATIONS ON SBA'S EFFORTS RELATED TO HBCUS

As part of our ongoing work, we have been reviewing SBA agency plans for the White House Initiative on HBCUs and assessing the extent to which SBA met the goals in its annual plans. Our preliminary observations indicate that information about the SBA office in charge of the agency's efforts related to HBCUs has been unclear; information about pre-2018 SBA plans, recent year efforts, and activities at HBCUs is limited; and relationships among SBA, its resource partners, and selected HBCUs varied. For example:

- *Changing information about agency office responsible for Initiative on HBCUs.* Until recently, SBA officials told us that no one office was responsible for the White House Initiative on HBCUs. In August 2018 officials told us that the agency's Office of Entrepreneurial Development and Office of Strategic Alliance, a suboffice within the Office of Communications and Public Liaison, had responsibilities for programs or efforts that may involve HBCUs, but that neither office had primary responsibility for the initiative. SBA later determined that the SBA Administrator had designated the Office of Entrepreneurial Development as the program lead in 2018, and prior SBA leadership also designated this office as the lead in 2012.

- *Limited information on agency plans.* SBA appears to not have documentation of the agency plans it prepared for the White House Initiative for 7 of the 10 years in the period we reviewed (2008–2018). SBA prepared an annual plan in 2018 on its efforts to strengthen HBCUs capacity and according to SBA officials, has been finalizing its 2019 agency plan. SBA also prepared plans for 2010 and 2011 which describe the total amount of funding the agency planned to provide to HBCUs for SBDCs and other activities. SBA is not aware of records for other plans developed in 2008–2018, according to Office of Entrepreneurial Development officials.[22] According to officials from the White House Initiative, they are unable to comment on SBA agency plans prior to 2018.

- *White House Initiative annual reports not available after 2013.* Annual reports on the results of agencies' efforts related to the White House Initiative, including data on SBA's funding for SBDCs hosted by HBCUs, are available for only 2008–2013. For example, the 2013 annual report noted that about 2 percent of SBA funding for SBDCs at institutions of higher education was distributed to HBCUs.[23] White House Initiative officials told us they are unable to explain why no reports were issued during 2014–2016. The officials also told us that the 2017 and 2018 reports had not yet been prepared because, as of April 2019, the President's Board under Executive Order 13779 had not yet been chartered, and is therefore prohibited from convening under the Federal Advisory Committee Act.[24]

- *Minimal HBCU-specific data on entrepreneurship-related efforts.* HBCU-specific data—at an agency-wide level—on entrepreneurship-related efforts, such as the number of outreach events involving HBCUs or the number of attendees who are

---

[22] We will continue to follow up as part of our ongoing work.

[23] The reports issued for 2008–2013 were entitled *Annual Report to the President on the Results of the Participation of Historically Black Colleges and Universities in Federal Programs.*

[24] White House Initiative officials also told us that the Executive Director of the Initiative (established under Executive Order 13779) was appointed on or about October 2017, and that the Chairman of the President's Board of Advisors was appointed on or about February 2018. We will continue to examine the gaps in the annual report as part of our ongoing work.

HBCU students or alumni, is incomplete. SBA officials told us that they track co-sponsored activities, but do not track such information by specific institution or category of institution (such as an HBCU), and that their systems are not set up to collect data on an event or activity in that manner.[25]

SBA officials told us that because district offices directly connect with HBCUs, district offices would have more information about efforts with HBCUs than offices at headquarters. As we previously reported, district offices are considered by officials as SBA's "boots on the ground," delivering most SBA programs and services.[26] While each of the eight district offices with which we spoke said that they conduct outreach activities, there is not a systematic approach for these offices to use to collect data on their outreach with HBCUs.[27] For example, Maryland district office officials told us they are required to report the total number of annual outreach events to SBA headquarters but have no reporting requirements specific to HBCUs. Similarly, West Virginia district office officials said that they do not report any information to SBA headquarters on specific entities, which would include HBCUs. However, the West Virginia district office tracks its activities with the two HBCUs in its region—West Virginia State University in Institute, West Virginia and Bluefield State College in Bluefield, West Virginia. Of the eight district offices, two also told us they had never heard of the White House Initiative on HBCUs and six told us they could not comment on whether they were familiar with the initiative.

- *Feedback from event participants not collected systematically.* SBA does not systematically collect written feedback from event participants, including for events involving HBCUs. All eight districts offices with which we spoke said they have not collected feedback using a survey designed by SBA headquarters for co-sponsored events.[28] Some of the district offices with whom we met collect feedback using their own methods. For example, North Florida district office officials told us that they have their own satisfaction survey, which is not reported to SBA headquarters. Officials from the West Virginia district office told us that they collect oral feedback.

- *SBA resource partners have established relationships with some HBCUs.* Three SBDCs with whom we spoke have relationships (some long-standing) with HBCUs and engaged in a variety of entrepreneurship-related activities, particularly

---

[25] We will continue to examine the information SBA collects as part of our ongoing work.

[26] GAO, Small Business Administration: Leadership Attention Needed to Overcome Management Challenges, GAO-15-347 (Washington, D.C.: Sept. 22, 2015).

[27] One district office added that it does not track participation by HBCU students or alumni.

[28] SBA's Outreach Event Survey (Form 20) includes questions on the quality of the presenter, usefulness of the event, and areas for improvement. According to SBA's standard operating procedures for outreach activities, Form 20 should be distributed to participants at the conclusion of co-sponsored activities, provided that there are staff available and it is not burdensome to distribute. The standard operating procedures also state that distribution of the form is optional for SBA-sponsored activities.

in cases in which HBCUs are host institutions. More specifically, the Washington D.C. SBDC, Virgin Islands SBDC, and one of the Alabama SBDC subcenters work with the students, faculty, and alumni of Howard University, the University of the Virgin Islands, and Alabama State University in Montgomery, Alabama, respectively. For example, Washington D.C. SBDC representatives told us they currently work with 10–15 Howard University student clients and provide research support to Howard University.[29] Similarly, Virgin Islands SBDC representatives told us they make presentations to upper-level business classes and freshmen development seminars at the University of the Virgin Islands. They also counsel students who participate in an annual entrepreneurial competition. The Alabama SBDC subcenter (housed in Alabama State University's College of Business Administration) works with several faculty members who have provided training at SBDC workshops, and assisted the subcenter on specialized topics, such as marketing, according to Alabama SBDC representatives. Through its relationship with faculty members, the Alabama SBDC subcenter also conducts outreach to students.

Although Maryland's resource partners—the state's lead SBDC and a SCORE chapter—are not hosted by HBCUs, they have relationships with Morgan State University. For example, the Maryland SBDC has a formal partnership with Morgan State University's College of Business and Management. As a result of this partnership, the school has provided office space for SBDC staff in the School of Business in exchange for counseling and business development assistance for Morgan State students, at no cost. Additionally, a SCORE mentor from an area chapter keeps office hours at Morgan State University to provide mentoring, according to university representatives.

- *Two HBCUs said they had little or no involvement with SBA or its resource partners.* Two HBCUs with which we spoke had little or no involvement with SBA or its resource partners. For example, a representative from Morehouse College in Atlanta, Georgia told us the school had little involvement with the Georgia SBA district office since signing a strategic alliance memorandum in April 2013. Officials from the Georgia district office agreed that little collaboration existed with the school because Morehouse College had not asked them to participate in any events.

Representatives from Coppin State University in Baltimore, Maryland (which is located near an SBA district office and a SCORE chapter) told us they have not interacted with any of SBA's offices or resource partners. The representatives said the school has an entrepreneurship program that began a few years ago, and would

---

[29] From time to time, the Washington D.C. SBDC provides research support to Howard University on national and districtwide small business trends. Recent research includes characteristics of minority-owned businesses and data on access to capital for minority-owned enterprises.

be interested in learning more about SBA, but were not aware of any outreach from SBA. Coppin State University representatives recognized that their School of Business is small and has not had the capacity to manage a formal relationship with SBA. SBA officials at the Maryland district office (which includes Coppin State University and Morgan State University in its network of HBCUs in its service area) said that their relationship with Coppin State University has not been as robust as their relationship with Morgan State University because the district office does not have a physical presence on Coppin State University campus.

As part of our ongoing work, we will continue to examine the extent to which SBA has met its goals for fostering entrepreneurship with HBCUs and make recommendations, as appropriate.

Chairwoman Chu, Ranking Member Spano, and Members of the Subcommittee, this concludes my prepared statement. I would be pleased to respond to any questions that you may have at this time.

INDEX

A

academic performance, 152, 155
academic progress, 73, 150
academic success, 152, 155, 202, 215, 219
access, 8, 10, 13, 17, 26, 28, 34, 52, 53, 54, 55, 56,
    57, 60, 62, 63, 65, 67, 68, 69, 70, 73, 75, 82, 89,
    91, 112, 116, 118, 120, 122, 127, 135, 136, 138,
    139, 140, 143, 149, 150, 154, 155, 156, 162, 171,
    172, 187, 191, 197, 226, 229, 253, 257, 263
accountability, vii, 1, 3, 12, 13, 21, 52, 54, 87, 94
accounting, viii, 2, 9, 10, 11, 16, 17, 19, 29, 33, 34,
    41, 119, 173, 176, 203
accounting standards, viii, 11, 16, 33, 34, 41
accreditation, 4, 5, 7, 26, 32, 63, 65, 83, 88, 133,
    134, 200, 201, 216, 226, 227, 238
accrediting agencies, vii, 1, 3, 4
administrators, viii, 10, 16, 17, 33, 35, 40, 133
adult learning, 52, 54
adults, 131, 147, 158, 161, 164
African Americans, 113, 114, 119, 124, 127, 131,
    132, 133, 135, 168, 170, 187, 217, 219, 220, 223,
    225, 226
agencies, vii, viii, 1, 2, 3, 4, 8, 10, 19, 34, 35, 41, 51,
    52, 53, 54, 59, 61, 85, 87, 95, 188, 191, 195, 197,
    255, 256, 257, 258, 261
Alaska, ix, 112, 128, 185, 195, 197, 199, 207, 208,
    247
Alaska Natives, 185, 207, 208
American Samoa, 200, 255
appropriations, ix, x, 196, 197, 198, 199, 202, 204,
    205, 206, 207, 208, 209, 210, 212, 213, 214, 215,
    216, 217, 219, 220, 221, 222, 224, 227, 230, 232,
    234, 235, 236, 238, 239, 240, 246, 247, 249
armed forces, 74
articulation, ix, 167, 188, 196, 237, 239, 240
assessment, 3, 9, 23, 32, 34, 35, 39, 58, 84, 134, 135,
    141, 145, 146, 147, 148, 149, 181

B

bank failure, 35
banking, 35, 171
bankruptcy, 36
barriers, 52, 53, 54, 63, 66, 67, 68, 70, 134, 141, 143,
    144, 147, 149, 180, 181, 188, 246
basic education, 89
benefits, 53, 54, 55, 61, 62, 63, 65, 68, 69, 72, 77,
    78, 79, 80, 82, 84, 85, 86, 89, 91, 94, 122, 125,
    150, 230
borrowers, 2, 6, 7, 11, 12, 13, 86, 94, 97, 98, 99, 100,
    101, 102, 103, 104, 105, 106, 107, 108, 109, 169,
    193, 227
budget cuts, 188
businesses, 253, 257, 258, 263

C

campus climate, 75
capacity building, 135, 157, 191
career counseling, 48
career development, 135
certificate, 59, 78, 92, 150, 178, 201, 231, 240

266 *Index*

certification, 4, 5, 76, 77, 134, 203, 215

challenges, vii, viii, 7, 9, 28, 31, 32, 49, 64, 71, 75, 98, 112, 113, 115, 127, 130, 133, 136, 138, 147, 151, 153, 183, 190, 193, 195, 197

children, 72, 76, 113, 115, 153, 159, 160, 161, 231

citizens, 61, 92, 130, 147

civil rights, 114, 121

civilian life, vii, 48

classes, 71, 72, 131, 154, 160, 162, 164, 177, 178, 180, 181, 182, 185, 263

classroom, 56, 57, 58, 62, 63, 64, 71, 72, 138, 159, 166, 177, 215, 226

closure, vii, viii, 9, 11, 16, 17, 18, 21, 26, 27, 29, 30, 31, 32, 36, 39

college campuses, 48, 123, 161, 189

College Cost Reduction and Access Act, 198, 209, 210, 230

college students, 116, 140, 142, 144, 149, 150, 192, 193, 229, 231, 237

colleges, vii, ix, x, 9, 32, 48, 50, 51, 60, 62, 63, 65, 81, 83, 85, 112, 113, 114, 116, 117, 119, 121, 124, 125, 127, 128, 129, 130, 137, 140, 141, 142, 144, 146, 147, 148, 150, 161, 165, 166, 168, 175, 177, 179, 185, 195, 197, 199, 201, 212, 213, 242, 245, 251, 252, 253, 258, 259

competition, 162, 192, 199, 263

competitive grant program, 205, 240

competitive process, 203, 205, 208, 210, 212, 239, 241

compliance, 16, 23, 26, 27, 31, 32, 37, 49, 61, 93, 133, 151, 169

computer, 98, 126, 180, 182, 222, 223, 235

Congress, iv, viii, 3, 13, 65, 75, 79, 95, 111, 128, 137, 150, 172, 184, 186, 188, 193, 197, 198, 199, 205, 213, 214, 218, 220, 221, 226, 228, 237, 240, 243, 249

congressional budget, 253

consolidation, 62, 65, 99, 103

construction, ix, 33, 38, 193, 196, 202, 206, 213, 215, 219, 223, 226, 228, 232, 234, 241

cost, ix, 38, 40, 55, 65, 83, 87, 98, 102, 127, 136, 149, 157, 165, 168, 169, 170, 174, 181, 188, 196, 201, 213, 220, 224, 226, 227, 236, 256, 263

counseling, vii, x, 48, 52, 54, 56, 57, 89, 91, 127, 137, 149, 157, 175, 202, 215, 219, 251, 252, 253, 255, 256, 258, 263

credentials, 59, 63, 65, 142

credit rating, 10, 19, 34, 41

criminal justice system, 124

culture, 53, 55, 75, 135, 154, 158, 159, 160, 162, 163, 165, 185, 190, 192, 209, 238

curricula, 4, 121, 144

curriculum, 60, 134, 149, 190, 241, 243, 244, 245

curriculum development, 241

D

data analysis, 104, 154

data collection, 73, 126, 211

data set, 99, 103

database, 98, 103, 147

debt service, 226

debts, 10, 22, 26, 35

demographic change, 118, 120

Department of Defense, 48, 55, 57, 59, 62, 82, 85, 87, 92, 191, 244

Department of Education, vii, 2, 3, 5, 6, 7, 15, 16, 18, 21, 24, 25, 31, 36, 38, 39, 43, 51, 52, 53, 59, 61, 79, 83, 85, 86, 87, 93, 94, 97, 101, 102, 106, 124, 136, 137, 142, 148, 162, 169, 185, 188, 189, 194, 197, 200, 203, 204, 206, 208, 209, 212, 213, 222, 226, 227, 229, 234, 241, 242, 243, 245, 249, 254, 255, 257

Department of Energy, 244

Department of Justice, 49, 94, 95

Department of Labor, 114

Department of the Interior, 35

disadvantaged students, 181, 242

disbursement, 171, 203

discharges, 11, 31, 32, 36

disclosure, 19

displacement, 2

distance education, 138, 202, 241

distance learning, 192

diversity, 19, 75, 112, 119, 123, 126, 150, 177, 180

documentary evidence, 60

E

earnings, 35, 148, 165, 172, 189

economic development, 256

economic disparity, 189

economic downturn, 10, 34

economic growth, 193

economic status, 142

economic transformation, 153

education, vii, viii, ix, 1, 2, 3, 4, 8, 13, 18, 19, 22, 29, 31, 37, 38, 40, 48, 49, 50, 52, 53, 54, 55, 56, 57, 58, 59, 60, 61, 62, 63, 65, 66, 67, 68, 69, 70, 71, 72, 74, 75, 76, 77, 78, 80, 82, 83, 85, 86, 89, 90, 92, 93, 98, 99, 103, 114, 115, 116, 118, 119, 120, 122, 123, 125, 126, 127, 131, 132, 135, 136, 137, 138, 140, 142, 143, 144, 145, 149, 151, 153, 157, 159, 163, 164, 165, 167, 168, 169, 171, 172, 173, 176, 177, 180, 181, 182, 183, 184, 186, 188, 189, 191, 193, 194, 195, 196, 201, 202, 204, 205, 212, 213, 214, 215, 220, 231, 232, 237, 239, 243, 246, 253, 254, 256

educational attainment, 64, 65, 158, 187

educational experience, 151, 153, 188

educational institutions, 52, 53, 54, 60, 61

educational materials, 202, 241

educational opportunities, 52, 54, 62, 112, 121, 230, 237, 238, 240, 242, 243

educational programs, 59, 62

educational quality, 1, 2, 3, 13

educationally disadvantaged, 158, 161, 226

educators, 156, 172, 189

elementary school, 143

eligibility criteria, 197, 200, 203, 209, 210, 213, 214, 215, 229, 233, 237, 238, 243

employees, 48

employers, 66, 129, 192, 229

employment, 57, 62, 64, 74, 122, 126, 137, 172, 191

encouragement, 68, 69

endowments, 33, 38, 125, 133, 200, 205, 208, 211, 215, 226, 232, 242

engineering, ix, 76, 115, 124, 129, 179, 180, 185, 188, 196, 217, 219, 222, 223, 232, 235, 243, 244, 245, 246

enrollment, viii, 7, 16, 20, 30, 32, 41, 68, 69, 73, 75, 98, 116, 122, 124, 130, 142, 148, 149, 151, 154, 156, 157, 178, 186, 188, 194, 199, 200, 201, 203, 207, 209, 211, 223, 226, 230, 231, 238, 244, 246

entrepreneurial training, vii, x, 251, 253, 258

entrepreneurs, 190, 192, 255, 256

entrepreneurship, x, 183, 190, 191, 192, 251, 252, 253, 256, 257, 258, 259, 261, 262, 263, 264

environment(s), 50, 53, 55, 66, 67, 73, 86, 118, 120, 129, 133, 151, 153, 164

equality, 184, 186, 213

equipment, 201, 202, 203, 215, 219, 223, 227, 241

equity, 20, 27, 28, 149, 159, 161

ethnic background, 118, 120, 126

ethnic groups, 140, 142

ethnic minority, 142

evidence, 3, 20, 100, 104, 146, 147, 150, 171, 200, 217, 254

executive order, x, 52, 54, 56, 58, 59, 61, 83, 189, 229, 251, 253, 254, 255, 257, 261

expertise, 19, 52, 54, 68, 70

F

faculty development, 200, 202, 245

faith, 5, 20, 21, 22, 137

false belief, 123

families, vii, 1, 3, 18, 48, 51, 52, 53, 54, 59, 61, 62, 64, 71, 73, 87, 97, 115, 124, 127, 130, 131, 132, 140, 143, 157, 159, 160, 161, 164, 165, 166, 167, 169, 172, 176, 179, 183, 192, 193, 230

family members, 73

family support, 131, 160

federal assistance, vii, 1, 3, 225

federal banking regulators, 35

federal funds, 8, 9, 203, 205, 211, 215, 219, 220, 224, 232, 239, 242

federal government, 3, 8, 9, 12, 13, 18, 31, 32, 36, 48, 57, 61, 62, 75, 85, 86, 88, 92, 95, 120, 126, 128, 136, 137, 138, 147, 149, 150, 168, 170, 171, 172, 184, 188, 213, 227

federal law, viii, 2, 5, 11, 13, 16, 19, 20, 29

Federal Register, 59, 203, 209, 211, 245

federal regulations, 22

Federal Reserve, 170

Federal Student Aid, 6, 21, 22, 24, 36, 37, 38, 40, 42, 91, 149

federal student loans, vii, 2, 7, 12, 16, 18, 21, 31, 97, 98, 100, 102, 104, 105, 107, 232

financial, vii, viii, 1, 2, 3, 5, 6, 9, 10, 11, 13, 15, 16, 17, 18, 19, 20, 21, 22, 23, 24, 25, 26, 27, 28, 29, 31, 32, 33, 34, 35, 36, 37, 39, 40, 41, 42, 49, 51, 52, 54, 58, 59, 64, 65, 68, 69, 77, 78, 82, 83, 87, 91, 92, 98, 102, 127, 130, 132, 133, 136, 137, 138, 139, 140, 142, 143, 144, 149, 150, 152, 155, 157, 158, 159, 162, 165, 166, 167, 168, 169, 175, 176, 191, 193, 195, 197, 199, 202, 213, 219, 223, 226, 232, 241, 257

financial condition, vii, viii, 1, 3, 5, 6, 9, 10, 11, 15, 16, 18, 21, 22, 23, 24, 27, 35, 36, 39, 40, 42

financial crisis, 35, 127, 130

financial data, 65

financial development, 28

financial incentives, 150

financial institutions, 87

financial oversight, vii, viii, 5, 9, 16, 17, 18, 19, 21, 22, 32, 40, 41

financial reports, 28

financial resources, viii, 195, 197

financial stability, 1

financial support, viii, 58, 78, 138, 195, 197

first generation, 76, 142, 188, 189, 192, 193

fiscal year, vii, viii, 1, 3, 7, 12, 15, 18, 23, 25, 26, 34, 36, 61, 64, 188, 198, 201, 204, 206, 208, 210, 212, 216, 217, 221, 225, 230, 233, 234, 236, 239, 242, 253, 255, 257

formula, 6, 7, 9, 10, 11, 19, 24, 32, 33, 34, 35, 36, 37, 40, 41, 42, 138, 158, 159, 162, 188, 192, 197, 205, 206, 213, 214, 215, 216, 217, 220, 221, 224, 225, 230, 231, 232, 233, 234, 236

funding, viii, 27, 56, 58, 100, 122, 123, 125, 126, 133, 136, 148, 149, 165, 179, 189, 192, 193, 195, 197, 200, 201, 203, 204, 205, 208, 210, 212, 213, 217, 220, 223, 224, 234, 236, 239, 241, 246, 247, 249, 255, 261

fundraising, 119, 125, 128

funds, 8, 10, 13, 22, 23, 25, 26, 35, 100, 105, 108, 132, 134, 138, 139, 152, 155, 157, 165, 175, 181, 188, 192, 193, 197, 198, 200, 201, 202, 203, 205, 206, 207, 208, 209, 210, 211, 212, 213, 214, 215, 216, 217, 219, 220, 221, 222, 224, 225, 227, 228, 232, 233, 234, 235, 236, 239, 241, 242, 245, 246, 249, 252, 255

G

global competition, 180

global economy, 64

global scale, 119

globalization, 232

graduate and professional students, 219, 220, 239

graduate education, x, 196, 213, 217, 221, 222, 223, 235

graduate program, 217, 218, 219, 221, 223, 225

graduate students, 98, 159, 161, 172, 223, 241

grant programs, viii, 195, 197, 199, 202, 246

grants, viii, ix, x, 20, 56, 58, 118, 127, 133, 138, 140, 142, 148, 157, 161, 165, 168, 171, 175, 176, 182, 183, 188, 191, 195, 196, 197, 199, 201, 202, 203, 204, 205, 206, 207, 208, 209, 210, 211, 212, 213, 214, 215, 216, 217, 218, 219, 220, 221, 222, 223,

224, 225, 230, 231, 232, 233, 234, 235, 236, 237, 238, 239, 240, 241, 242, 243, 244, 245, 246, 247, 255, 257

growth, 99, 104, 116, 123, 161, 165, 178, 179, 200, 203

guidance, viii, 10, 16, 17, 19, 23, 35, 37, 38, 39, 40, 41, 42, 60, 94, 95, 163, 174, 220

guidance counselors, 174

guidelines, 99, 104, 157, 231

H

health, 2, 10, 16, 17, 18, 22, 33, 34, 37, 41, 43, 48, 101, 104, 156, 201, 222, 223, 227, 232, 235

health care, 227

health education, 232

health services, 48

high school, 130, 131, 132, 136, 141, 144, 147, 149, 153, 156, 163, 164, 166, 168, 178, 180, 181, 183, 186, 187, 189

high school diploma, 131

high school grades, 141, 144, 147

higher education, 1, iii, vii, viii, x, 1, 3, 4, 5, 8, 9, 11, 13, 15, 18, 19, 20, 21, 22, 23, 28, 30, 31, 34, 36, 37, 38, 39, 47, 48, 49, 50, 51, 52, 54, 56, 60, 62, 63, 64, 65, 67, 68, 69, 70, 71, 73, 76, 77, 78, 81, 84, 86, 88, 91, 92, 93, 94, 95, 97, 98, 112, 115, 116, 118, 120, 121, 122, 123, 127, 128, 131, 133, 136, 138, 139, 140, 142, 143, 144, 148, 149, 150, 151, 153, 154, 159, 161, 165, 169, 170, 174, 175, 177, 186, 187, 188, 189, 192, 193, 195, 196, 197, 198, 199, 201, 203, 204, 205, 207, 209, 211, 212, 213, 214, 218, 221, 226, 229, 230, 231, 232, 234, 237, 238, 240, 242, 243, 245, 251, 253, 255, 256, 261

Higher Education Act, vii, viii, 1, 3, 4, 18, 19, 20, 21, 22, 48, 49, 77, 78, 94, 95, 97, 112, 122, 127, 136, 140, 142, 169, 175, 192, 193, 195, 197, 198, 203, 209, 214, 221, 232

Historically Black Colleges and Universities, vii, ix, x, 120, 121, 122, 123, 125, 128, 188, 190, 196, 198, 212, 213, 221, 222, 235, 247, 251, 252, 253, 254, 259, 260, 261

history, 112, 113, 114, 118, 120, 130, 193

household income, 189

Index

I

improvements, vii, viii, ix, 10, 35, 48, 137, 138, 142, 192, 196, 243

income, 12, 78, 98, 99, 102, 103, 104, 107, 113, 115, 118, 120, 122, 123, 127, 128, 129, 130, 131, 132, 133, 135, 136, 137, 138, 139, 156, 165, 167, 168, 169, 170, 175, 188, 189, 193, 194, 199, 201, 202, 205, 208, 209, 210, 211, 215, 219, 223, 224, 226, 229, 230, 231, 232, 237, 238, 239, 240, 241

increased access, 187

information sharing, 41, 73, 83, 90

information technology, 222, 223, 235

infrastructure, 119, 125, 126, 138, 174, 192, 193, 227

institutions, vii, viii, ix, 28, 50, 52, 53, 54, 55, 56, 57, 59, 60, 63, 65, 66, 68, 69, 70, 73, 75, 82, 83, 87, 88, 91, 93, 112, 113, 115, 116, 117, 118, 119, 120, 121, 122, 123, 124, 125, 127, 128, 129, 130, 131, 132, 133, 134, 135, 136, 137, 138, 139, 142, 143, 148, 150, 151, 152, 154, 155, 157, 165, 167, 168, 169, 170, 171, 172, 174, 175, 176, 177, 179, 182, 183, 185, 186, 188, 189, 190, 193, 194, 195, 196, 197, 199, 200, 201, 202, 203, 204, 205, 206, 207, 208, 209, 210, 211, 212, 213, 214, 215, 216, 217, 218, 220, 221, 222, 223, 224, 225, 226, 227, 228, 230, 231, 233, 234, 235, 236, 237, 238, 239, 240, 241, 242, 243, 244, 245, 246, 255, 257, 261, 263

interest rates, 99, 102, 104, 127, 137, 139, 168, 227

internal controls, 19

international relations, 62

investment(s), vii, 1, 3, 10, 13, 28, 34, 35, 40, 63, 67, 118, 119, 120, 125, 133, 138, 148, 149, 152, 157, 158, 162, 172, 174, 180, 181, 188, 190, 192, 208

investment capital, 190

issues, 4, 8, 11, 18, 26, 27, 32, 37, 38, 49, 50, 51, 82, 86, 88, 98, 115, 133, 156, 165, 183, 188, 213, 227, 243

L

law enforcement, 61

leadership, 67, 69, 72, 114, 117, 118, 120, 133, 190, 192, 229, 261

learning, 52, 54, 57, 58, 60, 68, 69, 74, 80, 90, 116, 118, 120, 126, 134, 138, 142, 156, 167, 177, 181, 183, 184, 192, 246, 264

legislation, 13, 48, 60, 70, 78, 89, 95, 120, 125, 178, 183, 185, 226

loans, vii, 2, 3, 7, 9, 10, 12, 16, 17, 18, 20, 21, 31, 35, 36, 40, 42, 56, 58, 59, 62, 65, 87, 93, 97, 98, 99, 100, 102, 103, 104, 105, 106, 107, 109, 127, 136, 137, 138, 139, 157, 161, 168, 169, 170, 171, 175, 176, 226, 227

M

marketing, 61, 82, 84, 106, 159, 160, 163, 258, 263

mathematics, 129, 217, 219, 222, 223, 232, 235, 244

matter, iv, viii, 1, 13, 80, 83, 94, 173, 174

median, 92, 100, 104, 189, 201

medical, 48, 81, 190, 201, 217, 242

membership, 228, 229, 244

mentor, 155, 160, 163, 164, 259, 263

mentoring, 126, 151, 152, 153, 155, 256, 259, 263

mentorship, 68, 69

military, 48, 49, 52, 53, 54, 56, 57, 58, 59, 60, 61, 62, 66, 67, 68, 70, 71, 72, 73, 74, 75, 78, 79, 80, 81, 82, 85, 86, 87, 88, 90, 91, 92, 94, 140, 142, 151, 154, 177, 178, 184

minorities, 115, 116, 120, 125, 129, 187, 197, 242, 243, 244, 246

minority students, viii, 120, 125, 127, 128, 129, 139, 148, 150, 176, 177, 195, 196, 199, 242, 243, 244

minority-serving institutions (MSIs), vii, viii, ix, 1, 112, 113, 118, 119, 120, 121, 123, 124, 125, 126, 133, 134, 140, 141, 142, 148, 177, 190, 195, 196, 197, 198, 199, 242, 243, 244, 245, 246

mission, 72, 74, 112, 122, 126, 129, 153, 159, 161, 185, 214, 228, 229, 244, 254

models, 89, 91, 99, 103, 104, 118, 119, 120, 125, 150, 192

N

national community, 149

Native Americans, 121, 124, 164, 182, 185, 187, 201

natural science, 217, 219, 221, 222, 223, 235

needy, viii, 136, 195, 196, 199, 200, 201, 203, 214, 219, 223, 230, 231, 233, 238

nonprofit organizations, 19, 34, 197

nursing, 173, 222, 223, 235

O

Office of Management and Budget, 197, 211
Office of the Inspector General, 36
officials, viii, x, 2, 4, 8, 9, 11, 12, 16, 19, 20, 23, 26, 27, 28, 32, 33, 34, 36, 37, 38, 99, 251, 254, 255, 257, 258, 259, 261, 262, 264
operations, 22, 29, 31, 34, 39, 77, 132
opportunities, x, 1, 56, 57, 58, 59, 60, 88, 114, 115, 121, 133, 136, 138, 148, 155, 156, 160, 161, 162, 166, 167, 170, 173, 178, 179, 181, 186, 189, 191, 192, 196, 201, 217, 221, 222, 223, 231, 235, 237, 238, 241
outreach, 49, 66, 70, 91, 156, 205, 215, 232, 239, 242, 252, 253, 256, 261, 262, 263, 264
outreach programs, 205, 215, 232, 239
oversight, vii, viii, 2, 6, 7, 8, 16, 18, 19, 20, 21, 23, 25, 26, 27, 28, 31, 32, 38, 40, 41, 42, 52, 54, 56, 57

P

parental involvement, 135
parents, 113, 136, 137, 143, 156, 160, 166, 169, 170, 231
peer relationship, 62, 63
peer review, 117
peer support, 68, 69
permit, 193, 208, 219, 223, 257
personal development, 62
policy, viii, 19, 22, 59, 70, 85, 88, 89, 94, 116, 122, 136, 140, 141, 142, 149, 154, 191, 195, 197, 255
policymakers, 84, 92, 93
population, 20, 56, 58, 61, 99, 113, 116, 120, 123, 125, 129, 130, 131, 138, 140, 142, 153, 155, 157, 158, 159, 160, 161, 163, 165, 177, 182, 183, 187, 189, 201, 231, 238, 244, 257, 259
poverty, 99, 104, 123, 156, 158, 160, 161, 163, 164, 187, 231
poverty line, 123
preparation, iv, 120, 124, 130, 139, 142, 143, 144, 149, 151, 168, 177, 189, 190, 215, 231, 244, 246
president, 50, 52, 53, 59, 62, 77, 82,114, 115, 116, 117, 119, 126, 128, 139, 140, 141, 146, 155, 157, 158, 167, 168, 169, 174, 176, 184, 190, 191, 193, 221, 222, 225, 228, 229, 254, 255, 261
profit, 5, 6, 19, 20, 21, 23, 24, 25, 26, 27, 28, 29, 30, 31, 36, 38, 82, 170, 171, 190, 227

program administration, 213, 229, 237
project, 92, 125, 206, 217, 221, 224, 225, 228, 234, 236, 244, 245, 246, 247
public markets, 28
public schools, 5, 6, 20, 21, 23, 24, 29, 174
public sector, 182
public service, 98, 102, 200
public-private partnerships, 178, 179, 254

R

real property, 202, 205, 215, 219, 223, 227
reality, 48, 50, 82, 116, 123, 127
regulations, viii, x, 3, 4, 5, 8, 11, 16, 19, 20, 29, 33, 37, 135, 136, 137, 151, 169, 201, 202, 206, 208, 214, 216, 217, 221, 225, 234, 243, 244, 245, 246, 251, 253, 257
requirement(s), 6, 10, 16, 17, 18, 20, 21, 22, 23, 25, 26, 28, 37, 41, 56, 59, 60, 83, 98, 99, 103, 123, 133, 136, 137, 151, 185, 200, 201, 203, 204, 207, 209, 210, 211, 214, 219, 224, 230, 232, 233, 236, 237, 238, 253, 262
resources, 10, 35, 39, 52, 54, 63, 67, 73, 91, 121, 122, 130, 137, 138, 139, 147, 150, 152, 153, 157, 165, 178, 179, 181, 182, 188, 189, 190, 191, 194, 201, 214, 230, 239, 243, 245, 257, 258
risk(s), vii, viii, 2, 8, 9, 11, 13, 16, 17, 18, 19, 28, 29, 32, 34, 35, 36, 38, 39, 40, 41, 42, 65, 119, 124, 132, 137, 138, 165, 176, 193, 226
risk assessment, 19, 32
risk factors, 226
risk of closure, vii, viii, 9, 16, 17, 18, 32, 39

S

savings, 13, 75, 132, 147, 167, 170, 171
savings account, 132, 170, 171
SBA, vii, x, 92, 251, 252, 253, 254, 255, 256, 257, 258, 259, 260, 261, 262, 263, 264
scholarship, 113, 127, 128, 132, 167, 190
school, vii, viii, 1, 2, 3, 4, 5, 6, 7, 8, 9, 10, 11, 12, 13, 15, 16, 17, 18, 19, 20, 21, 22, 23, 24, 25, 26, 27, 28, 29, 30, 31, 32, 33, 34, 35, 36, 37, 38, 39, 40, 41, 42, 49, 50, 56, 57, 59, 61, 64, 65, 68, 69, 76, 77, 78, 81, 82, 83, 84, 85, 86, 89, 90, 92, 93, 102, 109, 112, 113, 115, 117, 120, 122, 123, 130, 131, 132, 134, 137, 139, 140, 142, 143, 146, 147, 153, 154, 157, 158, 159, 161, 162, 163, 164, 165, 166,

Index 271

167, 168, 170, 174, 177, 179, 180, 181, 182, 183, 184, 186, 187, 188, 189, 190, 191, 194, 201, 215, 216, 217, 218, 220, 221, 223, 225, 226, 229, 230, 232, 235, 260, 263

science, ix, 76, 117, 123, 124, 126, 129, 131, 134, 154, 164, 166, 168, 173, 179, 180, 182, 183, 185, 188, 196, 222, 223, 232, 235, 243, 244, 245, 246

secondary education, 72, 231

secondary school students, 232, 239

secondary schools, 148, 205, 239

secondary students, 205, 215

service members, vii, 47, 48, 49, 51, 52, 53, 54, 55, 56, 57, 58, 62, 73, 74, 77, 82, 83, 87, 91, 92, 94

small business(es), 170, 252, 255, 256, 257, 258, 263

social capital, 121, 123

social movements, 186

socioeconomic status, 123

student achievement, 4

student enrollment, 28, 30, 59, 68, 69, 122, 133, 183, 186, 201, 230, 238, 243

student loan default rates, vii, viii, 1, 3

student populations, viii, 123, 130, 139, 195

student success, vii, 55, 68, 111, 112, 117, 118, 127, 138, 140, 141, 142, 150, 151, 152, 153, 154, 155, 187, 190

success rate, 159, 166

suicide rate, 187

support services, 52, 54, 125, 130, 139, 152, 157, 172, 189

T

taxpayers, 2, 3, 9, 13, 31, 37, 40, 42, 138, 147, 175, 176

teacher preparation, 232

teacher training, 159, 177

technical assistance, 127, 133, 134, 255

technical support, 68, 69, 191

technology, 73, 76, 122, 123, 129, 135, 138, 164, 180, 181, 185, 192, 202, 232, 244, 257

test scores, 141, 144, 147, 153, 156

Title I, vii, viii, ix, 1, 3, 18, 20, 36, 59, 78, 97, 138, 148, 156, 188, 192, 195, 196, 198, 199, 200, 201, 202, 203, 204, 205, 206, 207, 208, 209, 210, 211, 212, 213, 214, 215, 216, 217, 219, 221, 222, 224, 225, 226, 227, 229, 230, 231, 232, 233, 234, 237, 238,239, 240, 242, 243, 246

Title II, viii, ix, 138, 148, 188, 192, 195, 196, 198, 199, 200, 202, 203, 204, 205, 206, 207, 208, 209, 210, 211, 212, 213, 214, 215, 216, 217, 219, 221, 222, 224, 225, 227, 229, 230, 231, 232, 233, 234, 237, 238, 239, 240, 242, 243, 246

Title IV, vii, 1, 3, 18, 20, 36, 59, 78, 97, 200, 201, 226, 230, 231, 232

Title V, ix, x, 196, 202, 203, 205, 206, 208, 209, 210, 211, 212, 213, 215, 217, 219, 221, 224, 232, 234, 235, 237, 238, 239, 240, 242

training, vii, x, 4, 22, 52, 54, 58, 60, 78, 79, 80, 91, 115, 120, 133, 160, 192, 244, 246, 251, 252, 253, 256, 258, 259, 263

tuition, 48, 56, 57, 60, 66, 70, 72, 74, 75, 76, 82, 83, 87, 89, 90, 98, 102, 119, 132, 161, 165, 170, 175, 181, 182, 184, 185, 187, 188, 192, 201

tutoring, 158, 159, 162, 166, 202, 215, 219, 223

U

U.S. Bureau of Labor Statistics, 65

U.S. Department of Agriculture, 191

U.S. Department of Agriculture (USDA), 191

U.S. Department of Commerce, 187

U.S. Department of Labor, 65

U.S. economy, 149

underrepresented minority youth, 242

unemployment rate, 48, 64, 65, 115, 187

United States, viii, 1, 15, 18, 67, 97, 111, 112, 116, 118, 119, 122, 123, 125, 146, 165, 166, 185, 186, 207, 209, 211, 251, 256

universities, vii, ix, x, 48, 50, 56, 58, 60, 62, 63, 80, 82, 83, 85, 93, 112, 114, 117, 119, 121, 124, 125, 128, 129, 134, 148, 150, 163, 166, 168, 171, 179, 195, 197, 199, 201, 212, 213, 242, 245, 251, 252, 253, 258, 259

V

venture capital, 127, 138, 192

veteran benefits, 66

W

White House, x, 186, 189, 229, 251, 253, 254, 255, 256, 258, 260, 261, 262

witnesses, 50, 51, 81, 111, 115, 117, 172, 178, 183

workers, 119, 159, 161, 165

workforce, 57, 62, 67, 69, 116, 120, 129, 142, 151, 174, 177, 178, 180, 186, 187, 188, 189

young adults, 254

young people, 128, 136, 159, 161, 163, 164, 168, 170, 171, 173, 181

young teachers, 177

Related Nova Publications

ONLINE LEARNING IN HIGHER EDUCATION

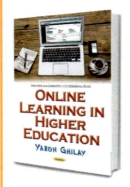

AUTHOR: Yaron Ghilay (Senior Lecturer, The Neri Bloomfield School of Design and Education, Haifa, Israel)

SERIES: Education in a Competitive and Globalizing World

BOOK DESCRIPTION: The aim of this book is to enrich the knowledge of educators, specifically academics in higher education with regard to online learning. The text deals with the creation, development, management and updating of online courses.

HARDCOVER ISBN: 978-1-53610-565-0
RETAIL PRICE: $82

HIGHER EDUCATION: BENEFITS, FUNDING CHALLENGES AND THE STATE OF STUDENT DEBT

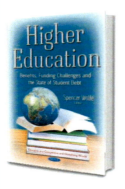

EDITOR: Spencer Wolfe

SERIES: Education in a Competitive and Globalizing World

BOOK DESCRIPTION: This book presents benefits, funding challenges and the state of student debt in higher education.

EBOOK ISBN: 978-1-53610-192-8
RETAIL PRICE: $95

To see a complete list of Nova publications, please visit our website at www.novapublishers.com

Related Nova Publications

HIGHER EDUCATION: GOALS AND CONSIDERATIONS

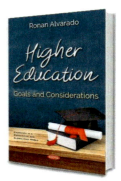

AUTHOR: Ronan Alvarado

SERIES: Education in a Competitive and Globalizing World

BOOK DESCRIPTION: The first chapter of this book is an introduction to the TRIO programs. The TRIO programs are the primary federal programs providing support services to the disadvantaged students to promote achievement in postsecondary education.

SOFTCOVER ISBN: 978-1-53614-157-3
RETAIL PRICE: $82

INNOVATIVE TEACHING STRATEGIES AND METHODS PROMOTING LIFELONG LEARNING IN HIGHER EDUCATION: FROM THEORY TO PRACTICE

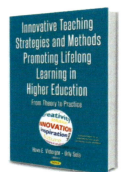

EDITORS: Hava E. Vidergor and Orly Sela (Gordon Academic College of Education, Israel)

SERIES: Education in a Competitive and Globalizing World

BOOK DESCRIPTION: This book is a comprehensive study of innovative strategies and methods in higher education, and may serve as a guide for college and university lecturers wishing to expand their teaching repertoire. The book offers theoretical constructs and their practical applications in a wide variety of fields demonstrating the implementation of field-tested methods and techniques.

HARDCOVER ISBN: 978-1-53612-083-7
RETAIL PRICE: $195

To see a complete list of Nova publications, please visit our website at www.novapublishers.com